THE REPUBLIC OF ROCK

The Republic of Rock

MUSIC AND CITIZENSHIP IN THE SIXTIES COUNTERCULTURE

Michael J. Kramer

OXFORD
UNIVERSITY PRESS

OXFORD
UNIVERSITY PRESS

Oxford University Press is a department of the University of Oxford.
It furthers the University's objective of excellence in research,
scholarship, and education by publishing worldwide.

Oxford   New York

Auckland   Cape Town   Dar es Salaam   Hong Kong   Karachi
Kuala Lumpur   Madrid   Melbourne   Mexico City   Nairobi
New Delhi   Shanghai   Taipei   Toronto

With offices in

Argentina   Austria   Brazil   Chile   Czech Republic   France   Greece
Guatemala   Hungary   Italy   Japan   Poland   Portugal   Singapore
South Korea   Switzerland   Thailand   Turkey   Ukraine   Vietnam

Oxford is a registered trade mark of Oxford University Press
in the UK and certain other countries.

Published in the United States of America by
Oxford University Press
198 Madison Avenue, New York, NY 10016

Library of Congress Cataloging-in-Publication Data
Kramer, Michael J.
The Republic of rock : music and citizenship in the sixties counterculture / Michael J. Kramer.
p.   cm.
Includes bibliographical references and index.
ISBN 978-0-19-538486-4 (alk. paper)
1. Rock music—Social aspects—United States—History—20th century.
2. Rock music—Social aspects—Vietnam—History—20th century.
3. Rock music—United States—1961–1970—History and criticsm.
4. Rock music—Vietnam—1961–1970—History and criticsm. I. Title.
ML3918.R63K73   2013
306.4′8426097309046—dc23   2012038480

3 5 7 9 8 6 4 2

Printed in the United States of America
on acid-free paper

To all my teachers,
starting with my mother,
Judith M. Kramer, 1946–2005

Contents

Acknowledgments

I QUITE LITERALLY owe my life to the music of the 1960s: my parents met on the way to the 1968 Newport Folk Festival. They were not particularly countercultural, but their sensibilities were forged in the era I examine in this study. I dedicate the project to them, especially to my mother, who did not live to see the book's completion but who taught me to appreciate history deeply.

The research for this study began at the University of North Carolina at Chapel Hill, where John Kasson taught me to take culture, especially popular culture, seriously. Larry Grossberg will not agree with everything in this book, but his ideas about musical context, apparatuses, and affect deeply shaped it. Jerma Jackson always answered the knocks on her office door to talk about music and history. Robert Cantwell shared far too many cups of coffee with me; his approach to music, to the life of the mind, and to thinking about the world as a whole will forever inform mine. Charles Capper, John Chasteen, Peter Filene, Leon Fink, Jacquelyn Hall, Gerald Horne, Michael Hunt, Richard Kohn, Lloyd Kramer, Jocelyn Neal, Sarah Weiss, and others were model scholars and master teachers of graduate education. Gail Radford and Steven Hart provided important insights early on and Joshua Shannon and Rona Marech have been sources of provocative conversation throughout. I also sing the praises of my graduate school colleagues, among them Matthew Brown, Spencer Downing, Josh Guthman, Ethan Kytle, Joel Revill, Kerry Taylor, Adam Tuchinsky, Montgomery Wolf, and my writing group comrades Blain Roberts, Matt Andrews, and Leah Potter. Michael Flamm helped me get started way back in my high school US history class before going on to complete his own magnificent scholarship on the 1960s.

I have benefitted from a strong network of supportive scholars interested in discussing culture, music, citizenship, and the sixties counterculture: Paul Anderson, Casey Blake, Howard Brick, Nick Bromell, Richard Butsch, Richard Cándida Smith, Daphne Carr, Alice Echols, Lydia Fish, Devorah Heitner, Hugo Keesing, *Michigan Historical Review* editor David Macleod, Charles McGovern, John McMillian, Louise Meintjes, Jim O'Laughlin, Devon Powers, Lisa Rubens, the late great Dave Sanjek, Zach Schiller, Barry Shank, David Suisman, Jeremy Varon, Steve Waksman, and many others. Meredith Lair deserves special thanks for making key suggestions late in the game. I have also benefitted from conversations with many rock music critics, especially "Ice" Alexander a.k.a. Tony Reay, Roberta "Robbie" Cruger, Greil Marcus, Dave Marsh, Jann Uhelszki, and Paul Williams.

Barry Olivier helped me better understand the Wild West Festival, documentary filmmaker Eric Christensen and labor historian Harvey Schwartz helped me contextualize the KMPX strike, Chuck Kenney sent me a batch of invaluable AFVN recordings, Lydia Fish welcomed me to her archive of Vietnam War recordings, Bob Morecook helped me with AFVN materials, filmmaker Rick Holen told me a bit more about the CMTS shows of the Entertainment Branch in Vietnam, and Frank Ford deserves extra-special thanks for his help locating and teaching me about the CBC Band. Historian and literary scholar Dennis McNally was extraordinarily generous with his time and contacts. Corry Arnold and Ross Hannan's work on the Chicken on a Unicycle website and their weblogs demonstrates that there are important links to forge between academic and nonacademic historians of popular music and culture. Other interviewees and correspondents included Ami Magill, Sue Kagan, Larry Miller, Jacob Powell, Reg. E. Williams, Dusty Street, Ron Polte, Norman Davis, Ed Bear, Bonnie Simmons, Johnny Sundstrom, Cliff Woolley, Jan Wiatt, Giang Cao Nyugen, the Vietnam veterans who attended the 2011 CBC Band Reunion, and the Phan family.

A yearlong postdoctoral fellowship at George Mason University was helpful in continuing to develop the book. I deeply appreciated getting to talk with a very special intellectual beacon, the late Roy Rosenzweig. The History Department and Weinberg College of Arts and Sciences at Northwestern University have been supportive environments to complete the book. The Northwestern University Research Committee provided a timely subvention grant. I owe special thanks to Dan Lewis for his wise thinking about the twin "ships" of scholarship and citizenship. I have too many conference copanelists and commentators to thank, but they all helped to shape and improve the book. The staffs at Brothers K and Other Brother coffeeshops always played the right tunes and kept my cup full. Heartfelt appreciation to the numerous librarians and archivists who helped me with research: at Northwestern University's

Charles Deering McCormick Library of Special Collections, I thank Scott Krafft, Sigrid Perry, Susan Lewis, and Nick Munagian; at the Library of Congress Sound Division, Bryan Cornell; at the San Francisco State University Bay Area Television Archive, Alex Cherian; at the San Francisco State University Labor Archives and Research Center, Catherine Powell; and at Wolfgang's Vault, Katherine York. I also extend my appreciation to the librarians and archivists at the National Archives, the Popular Culture and Music Libraries at Bowling Green State University, the Vietnam Veterans Oral History and Folklore Project, the Bancroft Library at the University of California–Berkeley, the California Historical Society, the San Francisco History Center at the San Francisco Public Library, the Hoover Institution Archives, the Ronald Reagan Presidential Library, the Center for Oral History at Columbia University, the New York Public Library of the Performing Arts, the Southern Folklife Collection at the University of North Carolina, and the Texas Tech Vietnam Center and Archive. I would also like to thank the various photographers, artists, estates, and companies that allowed me to reproduce images: Gene Anthony, Wolfgang's Vault, Baron Wolman, Zane Kesey, the estate of Jim Marshall, Wes Wilson, Larry Miller, Sue Kagan, Barry Olivier, Nicky Hall of George Hall Photography, Tim Page and Corbis, AP Photos, Josh Bempechat of Postertrip, Joe Armstrong of Vintage Concert Posters, Greg Burchard of the estate of Jerry Burchard, Craig Sams of the estate of Kenneth Sams, Scott Roberts, Dallas Delay, Chandler Delay, and the estate of C. David Delay, Jr., Allen Quinn, and the Phan family. There are a number of images whose creators have been extremely difficult to locate; I hope they will contact me.

The anonymous (and sometimes self-identified) readers of the manuscript and related articles made it enormously better. I also thank the staff at Oxford University Press, particularly production editor Natalie Johnson and copy editor Katherine E. Ulrich, as well as indexer J. Naomi Linzer. I cannot praise Susan Ferber, my editor at Oxford, enough. Her encouragement, keen insights, and sense of deep intellectual engagement and encouragement are unparalleled. I am surely forgetting other important people to acknowledge, but I will not forget to mention that any errors in this book are mine alone.

I thank my family for their steadfast support: Kenneth Kramer and Caren and Eric Kramer Elias for always being there; Matthew Pearson and Marjorie Jolles for our commune adventure; James Kramer for faithful phone calls and huge heart; Amy and Mark Feingold for good cheer and Boston housing; and P. David and Mary Alyce Pearson for Berkeley housing, generosity, and love. Dog Kyrie is still wagging her tail and, while dog Lucas and cats Pip and Emma did not make it to see the completion of the book, their fur is still on my computer keyboard. Finally, this book on the republic of rock is for the rock of my republic: my own band of conspirators, Susan, Toby, and Jane. You are the true rock stars of my life.

THE REPUBLIC OF ROCK

Introduction

IN THE SPRING of 1967, a young rock music critic named Paul Williams visited San Francisco from the East Coast. Writing a few months later in *Crawdaddy!* magazine, Williams excitedly described the city's new venues for rock music as "induction centers." The metaphor was a powerful one given the escalating war in Vietnam and mandatory military conscription in the United States. In Williams's opinion, instead of processing young men into the Armed Forces, venues such as San Francisco's Fillmore Auditorium (figure 0.1) drafted a wide range of people into a new social configuration: the counterculture. "The teenyboppers," he wrote, "the college students, the curious adults come down to the Fillmore to see what's going on, and they do see, and pretty soon they're part of it."[1] Audiences went in to listen to music, but Williams believed they exited into an enlivened sense of community and possibility that was increasingly taking over San Francisco's streets, parks, and public spaces.

Comparing the Fillmore to an induction center implied that rock offered a very different experience of citizenship than the US military. Williams suggested that the Armed Forces turned male citizens into dehumanized soldiers while the Fillmore and other rock halls transformed all sorts of people into more fully realized democratic participants.[2] "If you examine San Francisco closely," he noted, "you'll find major changes taking place in almost every aspect of city life. New attitudes towards jobs, towards education, towards entertainment and the arts. Basic shifts in the relationships between man and his environment, shifts that have affected every facet of that environment." Rock was at the center of these developments,

FIGURE 0.1. "Induction center": The Jefferson Airplane at the Fillmore Auditorium, 1966.
Photographer: George Hall.

which, according to Williams, were "changes that best can be communicated not in words but in music."[3]

Like Williams, other commentators thought of Vietnam when they analyzed the emerging counterculture in San Francisco. Taking stock of the Haight-Ashbury neighborhood that was fast becoming ground zero for countercultural life, one underground-newspaper letter writer argued, "There probably would be no Haight-Ashbury without the war."[4] Some thought that the counterculture in San Francisco might even stop America's ill-fated military intervention in Southeast Asia. Anticipating the 1967 Human Be-In in Golden Gate Park, Haight-Ashbury poet Allen Cohen and store owner Ron Thelin hoped that "[u]ltimately the energy generated in gatherings like this could shift the balances enough to end the war in Vietnam and revitalize many dead hearts."[5] For these and other participants in the San Francisco counterculture, it was diametrically opposed to the Vietnam conflict. But not all who experienced the scene up close agreed. The novelist and broadsheet publisher Chester Anderson, a friend and colleague of Williams, went so far as to contend that there were troubling similarities between the San Francisco counterculture and the war. According to Anderson, the cynical marketing of the 1967 Summer of Love turned the Haight into "a scale model of Vietnam." It had become a place where "minds & bodies are being maimed as we watch," "kids are starving to death," and "rape is as common as bullshit." This was because "Hip Merchants" such as Cohen and Thelin were too busy "polishing the Hippy Image &

persuading The System that hippies are solid, hard-spending consumers."[6] In Anderson's view, "Hip Merchants" should have devoted their time and resources to solving serious civic problems of housing, public health, and mental well-being for the millions of people—especially young people—flocking to San Francisco. Focused on marketing San Francisco to the world, countercultural leaders lost sight of the quality of public life at the local level. In doing so, Anderson believed, they wound up replicating the dehumanizing violence of "The System" of American consumer and military empire as epitomized by the war in Vietnam.

Anderson's critique manifested the ways in which the American military intervention informed understandings of San Francisco rock music and the counterculture; but moving in the other direction, San Francisco rock music and its countercultural associations also suffused the war effort. The very thing that Anderson protested—the commodification of phenomena such as hippies—allowed the US military and its personnel to transport the energies of the Fillmore and the Haight-Ashbury to Southeast Asia: troops brought rock on records and cassettes; family and friends sent countercultural materials such as posters, magazines, books, clothes, instruments, and hippie bric-a-brac to GIs; and the Armed Forces imported rock to Vietnam in hopes of raising morale among young troops. A poster for a touring soldier rock band in Vietnam, approved by the military for official use, featured a Haight-Ashbury-like neighborhood of head shops, music stores, and street art transposed to the confusing space of military struggle as if to suggest that American GI's could become hippies in their downtime even if they were still warriors at work (figure 0.2).[7] The poster seemed to come to life in an image by photojournalist Tim Page that captured an American GI sitting beneath a pink umbrella during the mini-Tet Offensive of May 1968; on his helmet in large letters, he had ostentatiously labeled himself a hippie (figure 0.3).[8] Another GI scrawled "San Francisco City of Love" across his helmet (figure 0.4).[9] Peace signs, symbols of the counterculture as it connected to the domestic antiwar movement, also turned up all over Vietnam on helmets, zippo lighters, and in graffiti. They were often accompanied by snippets from famous rock lyrics.[10] Tim Page photographed one American soldier wearing a large gold peace medallion; but in a paradox indicative of the war's dizzying swirl of countercultural fantasies of peace and military realities of violence, it dangled from his neck between a bullet-filled bandoleer (figure 0.5).[11]

Peace signs and bandoleers, helmets and hippies; guns and guitars, the induction center of the Fillmore Auditorium and an imagined Haight-Ashbury in Vietnam: moving between the "City of the Summer of Love" and the country in which the United States waged war, rock music became a crucial cultural form. It sustained a hyper-charged interplay of identity and community, personal experience

FIGURE 0.2. Visions of the Haight-Asbury transposed to Vietnam: A poster for The Local Board, A Cav Touring Show, South Vietnam, date unknown. NARA.

FIGURE 0.3. The paradoxes of the Vietnam GI: A hippie at war, 1968. CORBIS. Photographer: Tim Page.

FIGURE 0.4. "San Francisco City of Love": GI helmet graffiti in Vietnam, 1970. Photographer: Gunbunny.

FIGURE 0.5. A GI's bandoleer and peace sign together: War and counterculture in DMZ, South Vietnam, 1968. CORBIS. Photographer: Tim Page.

and public participation, self-expression and collective scrutiny, cultural exploration and political engagement. Revisiting how the music resonated with listeners in San Francisco and Vietnam reveals how rock heightened the stakes of democratic life during wartime.[12] To be sure, other locations mattered—London, New York, Detroit, Los Angeles, Paris, Chicago, and clubs, bedrooms, cars, and street corners all around the world—but none at the level of these two places in relation to each other. The circulation of rock music between the city of peace, love, and flowers and the country of war, turmoil, and Napalm created a counterculture that pulsated with life-or-death questions of belonging, dissent, hope, and fear. As if to prove this point, a few years after Paul Williams described the Fillmore Auditorium as San Francisco's countercultural induction center, a popular Vietnamese rock group, the CBC Band, performed nightly in Saigon. The CBC played the latest rock hits to both American GIs and local youth. One might not expect to discover such a mingling of Americans and Vietnamese in civil association in the midst of war, but the concerts became key spaces for the infusion of San Francisco's counterculture into Vietnam.

The name of the venue where the band played? The Fillmore Far East.[13]

HOW DO WE more deeply understand the role of rock in shaping the sixties counterculture? As historian Howard Brick points out, despite many studies we still only have a "sketchy formula" of the counterculture's significance.[14] This book looks at (and listens to) the responses that rock generated in San Francisco and Vietnam to fill in the picture more fully. Examining new archival and oral sources, I argue that rock most of all inspired a counterculture defined by issues of citizenship.[15] As the music moved between San Francisco and Vietnam—from the Fillmore West to the Fillmore Far East and back again—it gave rise to a strange new federation of participants.[16] I call this polity of sound the republic of rock. Appearing most vividly in San Francisco and Vietnam, the republic of rock circulated within the mass-mediated channels of American empire during the 1960s and into the early 1970s. It was a stateless entity, more accurately thought of as a state of being or a state of becoming than a state in the conventional political sense. It was constituted by voluntary participation rather than by mandated policies. Like the Enlightenment republic of letters, it was more a mindset than a set of sovereign governmental institutions.[17] The republic of rock had no borders, no formal administration, no official laws, and no army. Nonetheless, for those who took refuge in it simply by listening and responding to music, this country of sonic experience mattered immensely.[18] Along with hallucinogenic drugs and new mores about sex, rock became a means of addressing, through culture, two of the core mysteries of democratic citizenship: how do disparate *persons* legitimately assemble into a *people*? And when they do, how does this affect them as individuals and a community?[19]

The term counterculture itself originally appeared in academia, in the abstract theorizing of Talcott Parsons's functionalist sociology. Following Parsons, J. Milton Yinger used the term "contra culture" in a famous 1960 article in the *American Sociological Review* about juvenile delinquency.[20] The concept moved into common usage after historian and social critic Theodore Roszak borrowed, and slightly altered, it for the title of his best-selling 1969 book, *The Making of a Counter Culture: Reflections on the Technocratic Society and Its Youthful Opposition.*[21] Only by the end of the decade did the two words collapse into one and become shorthand for the effort, usually by young people, to reimagine and change the world through cultural means. From its origins in the academy to its entrance into popular usage to its continued presence in popular memory (whether vilified by the right or nostalgized by sectors of the left), the counterculture has remained a vexed label.[22] Even the dates of it remain uncertain, which is why I use "sixties" rather than "1960s" in the title of this book.

Not only the periodization, but also the ideological coherence of the countercultural concept is debatable. Two competing narratives dominate the historical interpretation of the phenomenon. The first imagines the counterculture as an authentic underground social movement ultimately co-opted by mainstream mass culture. The second frames the counterculture from the opposite perspective: it was a marketed, commodified "lifestyle" that substituted fashion for substance, harmless cultural expression for radical political resistance. But to reduce the counterculture to a unitary definition of any sort is problematic. This is because, as historians Peter Braunstein and William Michael Doyle contend, "The term 'counterculture' falsely reifies what should never properly be construed as a social movement. It was an inherently unstable collection of attitudes, tendencies, postures, gestures, 'lifestyles,' ideals, visions, hedonistic pleasures, moralisms, negations, and affirmations."[23] They rightly suggest that the counterculture was hybrid and syncretic, always an uneasy aggregation of tendencies and developments.

Howard Brick similarly emphasizes the contradictions of the counterculture. It improbably brought together an older "romantic-bohemian critique of modern life" which "aimed to free libidinal energy and expand consciousness" and "a large constituency shaped by mass culture" and "built around a market-mediated form of popular expression (rock music) inflected with the rebellious sentiments of the working class and oppressed peoples, particularly African Americans."[24] Many historians, like Brick, rightfully notice how counterculturalists, many though not all of them middle-class and white, appropriated older working-class and African-American modes of leisure and culture to open up their own spaces of freedom. But they also note the ways in which counterculturalists took these inspirations in surprising directions.[25] Rock music most of all provided access to an associational life that transcended older familial ties: friendship increasingly replaced kinship and sometimes even substituted for it.[26] As Braunstein and Doyle remind us, counterculturalists were most interested in rethinking the "essential ground of identity."[27] They did not seek to stabilize their senses of self or community, but to uproot and challenge assumptions about individuals and their social relationships. Using rock to do so, they called the very nature of citizenship into question.

Citizenship—which we might understand as the relationship between individuals and the larger political and social modes of organization in which they are enmeshed—became intensively opened up to scrutiny in the countercultural milieu. When historians, political theorists, and other analysts examine phenomena such as the counterculture, they typically distinguish between culture and citizenship. Culture, for them, involves beliefs, values, worldviews, practices, and aesthetics. Citizenship, by contrast, refers to formal, governmental, political, and legalistic definitions of membership, rights, and duties. Yet sociologist Nick Stevenson calls our attention to how "notions of cultural citizenship offer an opportunity to link the way changes in the economic and political sphere have had impacts upon the ways in which citizenship is commonly experienced."[28] For

Stevenson, culture is the medium through which abstract, institutionalized categories of citizenship affect people's immediate lives. Many participants in the counterculture shared this reasoning. They added to it the notion that everyday experiences in the cultural arena could also influence economic and political citizenship.[29] For them, the culture-citizenship dynamic flowed in both directions.

Rock music became important to the claim that citizenship was both political and cultural because as it offered spaces of aesthetic interaction in the realm of leisure and entertainment, it also connected individuals to larger structures of power.[30] To enjoy commercial recordings and concerts, to "rock out" while listening to roaring electric guitars, thundering drums, and intense amplification was, at some level, to join larger forces of technological control even if one opposed them or felt ambivalent about them. Some participants in the counterculture grew suspicious of rock's uses of the technologies of mass mediation. They felt that these made the music complicit with the exploitations and horrors of Cold War American consumer and military empire. But others in the counterculture were struck by how rock's "incorporated" qualities were precisely what allowed for reflection on the kinds of citizenship available in the historical moment of the sixties: the music's complicity was what made it useful for civic engagement.[31] As it generated varied responses, rock defied typical definitions of outside and inside, rebellion and incorporation, escape and engagement. It raised questions and challenged listeners, enlivening a counterculture that did not supplant larger norms of citizenship so much as charge them intellectually, emotionally, and physically with all the dilemmas of modern democratic belonging and autonomy.[32]

Because San Francisco and Vietnam were both actual places and potent symbols during the sixties, they provide good vantage points for glimpsing how rock did this—how it mattered to the formation of the counterculture as a civic phenomenon. In these two places, rock offered great fun and a chance to escape into the pleasures of sound, light shows, psychotropic substances, spirituality, erotic encounters, and communal fellowship. At the same time, escaping into the music also led back to engagement.[33] Rock allowed listeners to probe the nature of human individuality, liberty, freedom, community, commitment, and coercion. It did so not by presenting a stable ideological position for listeners to adopt, but rather by mediating uncertain questions of citizenship through what ethnomusicologist Steven Feld calls "feelingful activity."[34]

ROCK RAISED ISSUES of citizenship up for scrutiny just as the ideology of Cold War liberalism was losing authority in the 1960s. As the pressures of war abroad and conflicts over civil rights, equality, and justice at home tore apart the consensus politics that arose out of the New Deal and World War II, rock provided one resource for grappling with the dissolution of liberalism.[35] Because rock was so ambiguously embedded within consumerism and militarism, so strangely connected to the technological means of producing American power both domestically and internationally, the music provided immediate access, in cultural form, to urgent political questions about the nature of rights and obligations, freedom and its limits. What has made the counterculture so difficult to understand is that while its participants largely rejected liberalism in its Cold War form, they did not consistently advocate or adopt one alternative ideology. They neither definitively embraced a libertarian emphasis on rights, nor endorsed a communitarian emphasis on obligations. The counterculture, instead, remained poised between these opposing tendencies. In the libertarian vein, counterculturalists longed to wrest individual liberty away from the tyranny of larger systems of control they discovered in the military-industrial complex. In the communitarian tradition, they found themselves asking what obligations ensued once they did. As the liberalism of the Cold War consensus gave way, the counterculture that emerged in responses to rock became a way to grapple with the fraught question of what might replace it.[36]

The political stresses of war abroad and dissent at home were not the only factors undermining Cold War consensus liberalism and contributing to the rise of the counterculture; economic transformations were also at work. The 1960s were a time of unprecedented abundance. As President Lyndon Johnson tried to maintain a "guns and butter" economy by escalating the war in Vietnam and expanding the social safety net at home, he created a monetary policy that overheated the economy.[37] The counterculture arose, paradoxically, on this cresting wave of prosperity even as it seemed to oppose it. The 1960s also saw the United States begin to shift from a Fordist economic order to a post-Fordist one as the mid-twentieth-century system of large-scale industrial production coupled with mass consumption gave way increasingly to a "symbolic economy" of postindustrial, information-driven "flexible accumulation." A new kind of consumerism appeared as part of post-Fordism's fragmentation of production: in place of one mass market, niche markets appeared as corporations, advertisers, and marketers began to segment consumers into taste groups.[38]

Rock and the counterculture were at the cutting edge of these changes. By the middle of the 1960s, mass consumerism in the United States was rapidly transitioning from what historian Lizabeth Cohen describes as a national "consumers' republic" to a far more fractured polity.[39] Differences among consumers, and by extension citizens, came to replace similarities. Numerous taste groups came to be defined not by commonalities, but by the contrasting goods and services they aspired to own and use. But the demise of the homogenous consumers' republic, contrary to Cohen's arguments, did not mean the end of political engagement with civic life. While the republic of rock was in some sense merely a niche market that emerged from the breakup of the mass consumers' republic, it also provided new kinds of spaces for civic investigation.[40] Cohen celebrates the mid-twentieth-century consumers' republic and bemoans its decline; others, such as sociologist Daniel Bell, thought it contained built-in tensions that could not be sustained in the first place. But Bell too did not notice the civic dimensions of rock.

To Bell, the mass consumer system was illustrative of the "contradictions of capitalism": it functioned through a combination of disciplined labor and hedonistic leisure, the Puritan work ethic on the one hand and the urge for immediate self-gratification on the other.[41] By the 1960s, these were increasingly in tension, unleashing instability into the system without replacing it with something better. Within this framework, Bell thought rock was merely noise, sound and fury signifying nothing other than the "repeating in more raucous form" of "the youthful japes of Greenwich Village bohemia a half century before."[42] Worse yet, he argued that, "[b]eginning with the 'new sound' of the Beatles in 1964, rock reached such soaring crescendos that it was impossible to hear one think, and that may have indeed been its intention."[43] But responses to rock in San Francisco and Vietnam belie Bell's analysis. Many listeners did use rock to think. They were not mindless hedonists. And they did not merely replicate the ideology of a previous generation's youthful rebels. Instead, they used rock to confront the confusing transformations in consumer capitalism that Bell himself had noticed.[44]

In San Francisco, rock provided a way to grapple with what has been called *hip capitalism*, a tactic by which, as Tom Frank and others have argued, rebelliousness against mass consumerism turned out merely to establish a new consumer niche market.[45] From its emergence in the 1950s, the genre of rock 'n' roll had always been an oddly commodified expression of revolt; at the same time, as a music of cross-racial, gender-bending, class-defying dimensions, it never lost noncommercial energies of civic confrontation and experimentation. San Francisco's counterculture witnessed a particularly volatile mix of commerce and civics with the result that it featured intensive struggles over the contradictions of capitalism. In Vietnam, rock was part of a strategy that paralleled domestic *hip capitalism*: what I call *hip militarism*. Faced with declining morale among young draftees, the managers of the US military tried to use the "new mod" sounds of domestic entertainment to help personnel make it through a year of duty in Vietnam. They modeled warfare on a mass consumer model: put in your hours in the war effort and enjoy your time off however you wished. This meant that rock music arrived as a component of a more tolerant military culture. Hip, rebellious styles could be bent toward the war effort. As far as the Armed Forces were concerned, countercultural modes of leisure were fine in Vietnam; access to them might even improve morale. Accommodating the urge for nonconformity among a segment of GIs became, the military hoped, a way, paradoxically, to get these troops to conform. Rock also marked the growing realization in 1968 that as the Armed Forces began a slow shift toward an all-volunteer military, they would need to attract troops to enlist rather than coercively drafting them.[46] The acceptance, even cultivation, of rock music in the military was one way to do so. But just as rock marked both an example of hip capitalism and a response to it in San Francisco, so too in Vietnam, it was indicative of the Armed Forces' new tactic of hip militarism and it was also a source of critical engagement with a terrifying and confusing war.

THE EMERGENCE OF hip militarism in Vietnam could only have occurred after the countercultural dynamic of rock music, citizenship, and hip capitalism coalesced in San Francisco. In the Bay Area, many participants in the counterculture were well aware of hip capitalism. They grappled with the new kinds of commerce they were surrounded by and, at times, helping to invent. As the political street theater group known as the Diggers wrote in October of 1967, "Media created the hippie with your hungry consent." The Diggers went so far as to organize a parade called "Death of Hippie" at which they urged fellow counterculturalists to move beyond the hippie identity. The group was especially concerned about rock music's corruption of a purer countercultural movement. As early as 1966, they had published a broadsheet that asked, "When will the JEFFERSON AIRPLANE and all ROCK-GROUPS quit trying to make it and LOVE?"[47]

Yet even associates of the Diggers, such as Chester Anderson, the very same person who had critiqued the troubling turn to commercialism in the Haight, wondered if rock music might also offer insights into contemporary problems. Despite his complaints of exploitation by so-called Hip Merchants, Anderson held out high hopes that rock was "evolving Sturgeonesque homo gestalt configurations," "superfamilies," and "pre-initiate tribal groups" through its "intensely participational & nonlinear art form." The music was "far from being degenerate or decadent." Instead, by responding to "technological & population pressures," rock became a "regenerative . . . art, offering us our first real hope for the future." Despite its "apparent domestication by record companies & top-40 DJs," no one could "counteract its political effects," Anderson claimed.[48] For Anderson, the Diggers, and others in San Francisco, rock provided a useful perspective on consumer processes of co-optation precisely because it was part of them.[49]

Participants in the San Francisco rock scene drew upon their experiences of rock music to address their own historical moment—to think, feel, and dance their way more deeply into the conditions behind the contradictions of capitalism. Rock fostered heightened feelings of community among strangers who, both alone and together, confronted the very issue of what a public was and how it might function both within and against the new forces of hip commerce. As critic Sandy Darlington put it, the community that rock engendered was "complete with all the contradictions of people who advertise Peace & Freedom, Record City, Pepsi Cola, and the Highway Patrol." This was, for Darlington, precisely why the music was so crucial to sustaining encounters with contemporary dilemmas. "Week after week we go inside the music," Darlington reported of attending rock shows at the Fillmore and other psychedelic ballrooms, "and as [the bands] play and we listen and dance, the questions and ideas slowly germinate in our minds like seeds." Darlington insisted that even though the music was commercial, it was also "more than entertainment"; it "helps us to define a way of life we believe in." Rock was, he argued, "our school, our summit conference."[50] In doing so, it did not offer solutions, but rather what the Bay Area rock critic Greil Marcus described, in a 1968 essay, as a "feeling for the political spaces."[51] Even as the music incorporated fans within larger, contradictory structures of control, it also became an arena for negotiating one's way through them.

As a medium for inquiry, rock also offered a powerful perspective on the war in Vietnam. Reg E. Williams, a San Francisco State College student who later helped to run the Straight Theater, a psychedelic ballroom in the Haight-Ashbury, remembered how while living in San Francisco, he and his friends continually drew sketches and doodles that combined images from the war with the burgeoning counterculture around them. "It was like I was over in Vietnam and still here all at the same time," one of Williams's friends remarked.[52] Glimpsing Navy ships headed out to the South Pacific in the fog below the Golden Gate Bridge one moment and dancing to the Grateful Dead and other groups the next, Williams and others found themselves struggling to make sense of the collapse of vast distances between war overseas and the fervent pursuit of peace all around them in San Francisco. Rock helped them to do so.

The connections between Vietnam and the Bay Area were further solidified whenever antiwar activists featured bands as the main attraction at benefit concerts.[53] These events brought together the bohemian and artistic milieu of the counterculture with the more explicitly political antiwar movement. A "Rock and Roll Dance Benefit" for the Vietnam Day Committee at the University of California–Berkeley on March 25, 1966, was indicative of the overlap. The show, which featured the Jefferson Airplane, became infamous when California gubernatorial candidate Ronald Reagan portrayed the dance's details as "so contrary to our standards of human behavior that I couldn't possibly recite them to you." Then he did just that, reading a report that described "three rock and roll bands . . . playing simultaneously all during the dance" while psychedelic films projected gyrating nude bodies and the smell of marijuana permeated Cal's Harmon Gymnasium.[54] Reagan went on to win the 1966 California governorship in part by associating the hedonism of rock music with unruly student protest against the war.[55] As a leading figure in the rising New Right conservative movement, Reagan skillfully effaced the boundaries between cultural experimentation and overt political engagement. While his comparisons were distorted, designed to stir controversy, he was not entirely wrong to make the connection. The March 1966 benefit was just one among many that featured rock bands. Others included "Peace Rock 3" at Cal, with the Grateful Dead; the Loading Zone at the Steppenwolf club on San Pablo Avenue to benefit the Vietnam Day Committee; and a "Folk Rock Festival" at San Francisco State College in April of 1967 for "Angry Arts Week West," a series of cultural events protesting the war.[56]

The antiwar movement was but one way in which the military conflict in Vietnam affected life in San Francisco. The Bay Area as a whole was diverse. As a university town, Berkeley attracted political activists.[57] Working-class cities in the East Bay were more conservative. Oakland was a center of African-American life on the West Coast. The Peninsula to the south contained the affluent suburbs around Stanford University. San Francisco itself possessed a colorful history of artistic bohemianism, radical labor unions, and a tolerance for outlandish behavior.[58] But Vietnam's presence transcended these particularities, in part because the Bay Area served as a center for military operations across the Pacific. Much of the war was managed and administered from the Army's enormous base in San Francisco's Presidio, and many troops left for Vietnam from the Oakland Army Base.[59] This meant that while the burgeoning counterculture in the Bay Area and the war in Southeast Asia were geographically distant from each other, they were also fundamentally linked. For instance, when the Oakland-based airline World Airways won a large government contract to fly GIs to Vietnam, flight attendant Cherri Olson traveled constantly between the two places. Rock music helped her make sense of her journeys. She remembered spending "weekends listening to rock groups like the Jefferson Airplane in Golden Gate Park and Crosby, Stills and Nash at the Fillmore Auditorium," "'Then Monday,'" Olson told historian Charles Wollenberg, "'we left for Vietnam, putting people off on the tarmac at Tan Son Nhut air base.'" For Olson, rock contributed to a sense of surreal contrasts and connections occurring all at once. "'It was instant,'" she remarked to Wollenberg, "'We were there, we were back . . . San Francisco-Berkeley-Vietnam.'"[60]

If Olson had lingered in Vietnam, she might have noticed how the circuit of rock was not unidirectional.[61] While the Jefferson Airplane performed the music for antiwar benefits in the Bay Area, soldier bands in Vietnam played Jefferson Airplane songs to raise morale within the war effort itself. Rock was far from the only genre of popular music in the Vietnam War, but it was the one that best exemplified the logic of hip militarism. In response to growing resistance, dissent, and even outright mutiny by lower-level GIs, Richard Nixon's secretary of defense, Melvin Laird, even went so far as to encourage decentralization and "participatory management" in the command structure itself, echoing a central political idea of the early New Left student movement.[62] In this context, rock became part of the war machine. But as it did so, the music also connected GIs to the domestic counterculture and its civic energy of questioning the war. As Charles Perry wrote in *Rolling Stone* magazine after conducting a mail-in survey of GIs, "There is a flowering of rock and roll and dope among the unwilling soldiers of today."[63]

By the later years of the war, the managers of the American Armed Forces grew increasingly concerned that they could not maintain order among troops. "By every conceivable indicator," retired officer and military analyst Robert Heinl wrote after touring Vietnam in 1971, "our army that now remains in Vietnam is in a state of approaching collapse, with individual units avoiding or having refused combat, murdering their officers and noncommissioned officers, drug-ridden and dispirited where not near-mutinous."[64] Hip militarism seemed to be one way to channel dissent, paradoxically, into morale building. By allowing for the appearance of antiauthoritarian anger and disenchantment in the sounds of rock, the military hoped to keep troops fighting. Rock indeed kept the war effort going at times by providing emotional release for the bitter alienation felt by younger, lower-level GIs, but in doing so, the music also allowed for the awakening of civic identity among soldiers caught within a conflict whose surreal confusions and frustrations resonated powerfully with rock's psychedelic style. Brought in to Vietnam as a taste of the latest domestic consumer culture, rock provided a framework for making sense of old-fashioned military imperialism even though it was also a striking example of the new tactic of hip militarism.[65]

WITHIN THE TWIN dynamics of hip capitalism and hip militarism, listeners to rock became what the hit song "San Francisco (Be Sure to Wear Flowers in Your Hair)" called "people in motion." They were physically moved to dance to the music. They were also moved by rock emotionally. Many joined explicit political movements against racism, sexism, and the war. But many more were "people in motion" because it was through rock that they faced, in ways both large and small, the possibilities of creating a sense of democratic citizenship in the ungrounded, instant flow of electricity, mass communications, militarized leisure, and tactics of control that made the line between rebellion and acquiescence more elastic, more flexible, more confounding than ever before.[66]

The story of the song "San Francisco (Be Sure to Wear Flowers in Your Hair)" itself demonstrates how rock raised questions about citizenship by increasingly occupying the main currents of American popular culture yet also seeming to oppose them. Musically, the song was an odd fit for the countercultural rock scene it was supposed to celebrate. It was far more melodic—and melodramatic—than much of the dissonant, experimental, blues-based music actually emanating from San Francisco's rockers such as the Jefferson Airplane, Grateful Dead, Big Brother and the Holding Company, and Quicksilver Messenger Service. Yet it became a theme song for the 1967 Summer of Love in the Bay Area. Written by John Phillips, leader of the group the Mamas and the Papas, "San Francisco" was a smash hit for his friend Scott McKenzie.[67] Though Phillips and McKenzie resembled a good number of San Francisco rock performers in that they had roots in the folk music revival of the late 1950s and early 1960s, they were not part of the loose consortium of musicians, bands, promoters, and artists in the Bay Area.[68] They were from the East Coast and, by 1967, they had moved to Los Angeles to seek success within the mainstream recording industry.[69] "San Francisco" had not even been written for the city. Phillips wrote the song for the Monterey International Pop Festival, which he and his manager Lou Adler helped to organize just south of San Francisco in June of 1967. The festival featured many Bay Area bands, but behind the scenes it was as much a Los Angeles recording industry affair as anything else.[70]

The growing popularity of the so-called "San Francisco Sound" at the Monterey festival and its integration into the mainstream recording industry revealed the increasingly permeable boundaries between rock and pop.[71] By 1967, rock retained a vague association with youthful energy, electric-guitar raucousness, rebelliousness, and a new spirit of avant-garde experimentation, but the music was moving to the center of popular music. The Beatles, already occupying the rock-pop intersection, released the groundbreaking *Sgt. Pepper's Lonely Hearts Club Band* album just a few weeks before Monterey Pop, and rumors were rampant that they would make a surprise appearance at the festival. At Monterey itself, the British band The Who famously smashed their instruments, while the American guitarist Jimi Hendrix, who had gained fame in London, one-upped them by lighting his guitar on fire. Janis Joplin, lead singer of the San Francisco group Big Brother and the Holding Company, was also a big hit at the festival with her mix of blues anguish and ecstatic calls for audience participation. These were examples of rebellious rock attitudes breaching the mainstream of mass culture. Monterey included plenty of other sounds too: the rootsy soul of Stax artists such as Otis Redding and Booker T. and the MGs, the more melodious pop of the Mamas and the Papas and the Association, the folk harmonies of Simon and Garfunkel, the folk-rock jangle of the Byrds and Buffalo Springfield, white versions of the blues by Canned Heat and the Butterfield Blues Band, and the proto–world music sounds of Indian sitar player Ravi Shankar and South African jazz trumpeter Hugh Masekela. If Monterey was a pop festival, then pop music seemed to be cracking open, with rock as the blunt instrument doing the breaking up of old norms and boundaries.

For many at the time, rock was a term reserved especially to describe a "psychedelic" sound. Many associated it with hallucinogenic drugs and "taking a trip." As musicologist Sheila Whiteley points out, a set of sonic codings signified the genre: manipulation of timbres to make them blurred, bright, and overlapping; a sense of upward movement connoting psychedelic flight; oscillating and lurching harmonies; a mix of regular and irregular rhythms; a movement between foregrounded and background sounds; and a focus on juxtaposition and collage.[72] But sound alone did not suffice to define rock. As music critic Ellen Willis wrote in a 1967 essay on Bob Dylan, "psychedelic music . . . was a catch-all label."[73] It represented the merging of 1950s rock 'n' roll with other genres, such as folk, blues, soul, classical, British music hall sounds, and various kinds of music from around the world.[74] Many began to use the term as a veritable synonym for pop music as a whole. This was not inaccurate, at least in a commercial sense. By the end of 1967, sales of music marketed as rock had overtaken the pop category. By the end of the 1970s, rock would account for 80 percent of all recorded music.[75]

However one defined rock, the music became big business by the end of the 1960s even as it was marketed as anti-authoritarian, anti-commercial, rebellious, or even revolutionary.[76] By 1968, people under twenty-five—the much-heralded Baby Boom Generation—were spending over one billion dollars per year on music recordings.[77] Yet in the republic of rock, listeners were not merely passive consumers, but rather an active citizenry within a shifting economic and political order. When mainstream Columbia Records incongruously advertised "The man can't bust our music" in the pages of San Francisco's hip new *Rolling Stone* magazine, many in the counterculture knew that something odd was occurring. "Guess who 'busts' more music than anyone else, often for periods of time longer than the usual grass or draft sentence?" Richard Mangelsdorff playfully asked in another rock magazine, *Creem*. "Sure, it's the record companies."[78] Rock sparked engagement with its own pop qualities, helping to form the counterculture as a sphere of inquiry embedded within the very mass culture from which it ostensibly diverged.

All of this is not to claim that rock was a miraculous panacea. It could foster civic engagement, but just as often it asserted existing stereotypes, reinscribed inequities without redressing them, and justified overly simplistic and inadequate answers to larger structural and cultural problems. For instance, critic Robert Christgau noticed how Jimi Hendrix seemed to be celebrated as "a psychedelic Uncle Tom" at

Monterey Pop as he performed a limiting kind of hyper-masculinized blackness for white audiences. Janis Joplin, who rocketed to fame after Monterey, became a star, the ultimate "hippie chick," but she was also restricted in her options as a counter-cultural woman.[79] Yet for all of rock's inadequacies, fans also used the music to unravel, unpack, and at times even undo existing assumptions about race, gender, class, ethnicity, region, nation, and the world. Coded as white, rock drew participation and attention from Americans of color, who used the genre to ponder larger issues of culture, commerce, and politics.[80] Coded as hyper-masculinized and misogynist, rock also made available spaces for public expressions of nonnormative female, gay, and queer desire, sexuality, and power.[81] Coded as middle-class, rock combined middle-class and working-class cultural styles, so that even as it drew middle-class youth toward a romanticized vision of "realness" associated with working-class life, the music also provided passage to middle-class formations of art, bohemianism, and creativity for working-class youth.[82]

None of this was pure or perfect, but for those who adopted rock as their own, the music sparked powerful encounters with pressing cultural and political dilemmas of both self and society. When listeners used the music to grapple with questions of justice, happiness, and collective participation, what political theorists call a *counterpublic sphere* emerged.[83] But that term suggests something too coherent and precise for the messiness of rock. It is better pictured as a tessellated social body, a psychedelically mutating set of spaces and moments in motion, proliferating to millions through the mechanisms of American mass culture. Difficult to glimpse because it was always in motion, rock inspired what the art critic Dave Hickey evocatively called a "motley republic . . . of freakdom."[84] It generated a radically pluralistic spirit of democratic belonging that merged a kaleidoscopic sense of individuality with a polyglot ideal of togetherness.[85]

It did so in large part by connecting everyday life to grand-historical transformations.[86] This is why participants and observers alike have often emphasized the spiritual dimensions of rock: in a secular setting, the music evoked religious feelings. "The Grateful Dead, the Airplane, the Anonymous Artists of America, Big Brother and the Holding Company played the music that was our hymnal," Elizabeth Gips wrote of her favorite San Francisco bands in her memoir, *Scrapbook of a Haight-Ashbury Pilgrim*. These groups and others "lifted both spirit and body into a timeless space." Rock pulled listeners out of their day-to-day worlds, and even out of history itself, bringing them toward visceral experiences of the sacred. But paradoxically, it did so by heightening the immediacy of the moment. At rock shows, Gips remembered feeling like a vessel for God as she and others strove to "get into our bodies so intensely that we could be granted out-of-body experience." The music's power for Gips was that it created an environment in which to discover the mysterious sources of identity and community, of self and world. The relationship between interiority and exteriority, me and we, the close at hand and the far away, the here and now and the then and there, became up for grabs in the rock dance.[87]

The liminality that Gips and many others discovered in the rock experience—the ways in which the music evoked the feeling that the immediate, the grand-historical, and even the eternal were at stake in the dance—linked the music to spirituality and religion.[88] For many, the rock concert was a path to American popularizations (and often exoticized distortions) of the mysticism found in Eastern religions such as Hinduism and Buddhism. As Gips wrote, "Moving to the rhythms and light shows at The Fillmore, Avalon or Family Dog, or, more likely, at the free concerts in the park or even on Haight Street itself, we felt as though we had been dancing forever, drums beating in Africa, China, India."[89] But rock also transposed Judeo-Christian traditions to a secular milieu. Particularly in the Protestant prophetic tradition, the music sparked demands for action against complacency. It did so directly, in its lyrics and sound, but also as a resource for mounting arguments about the proper path to a revolution in human spirit. "We feel that a rock dance should change your life," wrote Chester Anderson as he outlined his philosophy for organizing an upcoming concert in San Francisco. Anderson believed his event had to draw upon the power of religion to achieve its aim of social transformation: "Any rock dance that isn't a religious event is a stone drag," he decided.[90]

As a secular musical form infused with religious energies, rock was not just part of the unholy trinity of sex, drugs, and rock 'n' roll; it also inspired calls for moral inquiry and activity. Many historians have thus argued that rock's spiritual dimensions were part of a larger countercultural turn toward "prefigurative politics."[91] Like many religious movements, the music seemed to offer the sensation—and even the preliminary structures—of a better future. Attending a free concert in the Golden Gate Park Panhandle or listening to a psychedelic rock record imported from stateside to an American barracks in South Vietnam seemed like a gateway to a new utopia—all you had to do was join in; if everyone did, then global social transformation would surely follow. This was a powerful quality of rock, but far less acknowledged by historians is how the music also became a means of critically confronting the present. Rock was *figurative* as well as prefigurative. As much as it served as the setting for starting to live as if the revolution had already arrived, rock also provided a medium in which to work through the conundrums of the moment. It did so especially when it came to questions of economic and military power.

In San Francisco and Vietnam, rock bent but never broke the emerging apparatus of hip capitalism and hip militarism. The music streaked through the wires, lines, and channels of mass-mediated society with what Walter Benjamin famously called "profane illuminations," but it never blasted away the dominant system.[92] Rock was too much a part of the new strategies of control to do so. But this was precisely what made it important for generating a counterculture that was not so much a glimpse of post-revolutionary society as a corrupted setting in which to examine contemporary dilemmas.[93] By countering existing systems of communication without overthrowing them, the music became part of what cultural studies scholar Stuart Hall described, in 1969, as a "modern 'bush-telegraph'" among countercultural participants around the world.[94] All along this communications mechanism, which connected the imagination to deliberation, rock developed into a form—and a forum—for addressing what was wrong in both American and global society.[95] As participant-historian Nick Bromell has written, "Rock was fun, but it was also a vital and spontaneous public philosophizing, a medium through which important questions were raised and rehearsed, and sometimes focused, and sometimes (rarely) answered."[96] The music became a means for registering wrongs; and it served as a medium for trying to envision solutions.

Taking experiences of rock in San Francisco and Vietnam more carefully into account suggests that the flowering of flower power in the counterculture was never just the naïve blossoming of a simplistic ideology of peace and love, nor only the torrid pursuit of ecstasy in a hothouse of sex, drugs, and rock 'n' roll, nor solely the deceptive growth of American consumer capitalism and military might through their seeming opposites. It was all these things, but it was also something more: the music fostered an efflorescence of civic engagement that continues to matter because the need remains to invent modes of citizenship suitable for the difficult conditions of more recent times. Rock, the counterculture, and the whole sixties mythos are important not because they come from some lost magical era, some garden to which we must get back, some time when "you had to be there, man," but rather because they offer a history of how struggles over citizenship often take place in surprising ways: within dominant systems as well as against them; simultaneously at levels of deep philosophical and intellectual questioning and through intensely sensorial bodily experiences; both in immediate contexts and across vast distances; and most of all through commodified forms of leisure, pleasure, and culture that intersected with the conventional sphere of politics.

THIS BOOK INTERPRETS the history of rock music's connections to citizenship within the new economic and political dynamics of hip capitalism and hip militarism. My focus on San Francisco and Vietnam is not meant to downplay other centers of rock music.[97] Nor is it to render invisible nonmusical participants in the counterculture: rural communards, techno-utopian idealists, environmentalists, cultural feminists, and political activists.[98] It is to illuminate how these places—San Francisco and Vietnam—were dialectically related as no two other locations were, and to argue that rock brought them together to render citizenship a defining countercultural issue. To document this entanglement, I draw upon new archival and oral sources to probe what "actually happened" during the late 1960s and early 1970s. But what actually happened was fundamentally tied to the countercultural imaginary—the visions, desires, and wishes that people used rock to express about their lives.[99] As much as concrete realities, what film critic J. Hoberman calls the "dream life" of the 1960s also produced struggles over citizenship. For participants in the counterculture, representation as an aesthetic *act* corresponded to representation as a political *fact*, and it did so in ways that ask us to take culture seriously in the making of history.[100]

Starting in San Francisco during the mid-1960s, this book documents rock's relationship to citizenship within the new context of hip capitalism. Chapter 1 recovers a forgotten aspect of a familiar story. Many know the adventures of Ken Kesey and the Merry Pranksters from Tom Wolfe's best-selling book, *The Electric Kool-Aid Acid Test*, which positioned the novelist and his high-flying friends as important founders of the counterculture. What has not been recognized is the way in which they invoked citizenship, particularly American citizenship. At the Acid Tests, the seminal happenings of LSD ingestion, rock music, and festive technological experimentation that Kesey and his acquaintances organized in 1965 and 1966, issues of citizenship arose repeatedly. The deeply imperfect but powerful responses that emerged at the Acid Tests provided the blueprint for rock music in the Bay Area and beyond for years to come.

Chapter 2 turns from Kesey and the Pranksters' Acid Tests to the unlikely story of a labor strike at a hippie radio station. This work stoppage was not your typical industrial union affair. In 1968, disc jockeys at KMPX-FM, one of the first "underground" rock radio stations in the country, walked off the job. In the postindustrial factory of hip capitalism, they struck as much for the right to a more creative and fulfilling civic life as they did for better wages and working conditions. Their strike, in fact, revealed the links between citizenship and labor in the context of hip capitalism.

These links continue in chapter 3, which turns to another important but forgotten story: the effort by various rock music promoters and bands to put on a large arts and music festival in Golden Gate Park during the summer of 1969. There is a good reason why few remember the Wild West Festival—the event never occurred. Planned for the weekend after Woodstock, the epic gathering of rock stars was canceled at the last moment due to a strike and boycott against the festival by none other than participants themselves, who protested that Wild West violated the principles of countercultural citizenship. Chapter 3 assesses the ambitious effort by various Bay Area rock impresarios to put on Wild West as a free, cooperatively organized, cross-arts gathering. And it chronicles the ensuing struggle over who, exactly, "the people" were in the counterculture, and how they, exactly, would benefit from a gathering such as the festival. The ill-fated Wild West Festival brings to light much about the civic ideals—and the uncivil conflicts—that rock music unleashed in San Francisco during the late 1960s.

The second half of the book follows rock across the Pacific Ocean to Vietnam. I investigate rock's place in the quotidian spaces of the war. For American GIs, this was largely, though not entirely, a zone of men, which meant that issues of citizenship were entangled with questions of masculinity.[101] On the front lines, music was sometimes available during the downtime from active fighting, but it was in the rear echelon—in offices, barracks, clubs, and other venues—where rock could be heard more often. GIs took many genres of music with them to war, from country to soul to pop. Rock was just a part of this commercial mix of sounds imported by the military apparatus itself. But rock also delivered the style, and some of the substance, of the domestic counterculture to Southeast Asia. The music was loaded with the sense that an alternative to normal American life was emerging on the home front. Glimpsing this alternative life, GIs used the music to begin to renegotiate, in nascent but powerful ways, their relationship to the military. In the moments when they listened to rock, GIs returned to a civilian identity that now assumed countercultural dimensions. In doing so, they confronted issues of what it meant to serve as a citizen-soldier in a confusing war far from home. The stakes of being a civilian and being a citizen intermingled. Particularly after 1968, as the war effort went increasingly awry, rock blared forth in Vietnam with contradictory forces, at once incorporating dissent into the war machine through the Armed Forces' tactic of hip militarism and unleashing intense civic questioning.

Chapter 4 examines how the dynamic of hip militarism and countercultural citizenship played out over the airwaves in a war fought through highly mediated and technological means that were part of the new logic of military "corporatization" in Vietnam.[102] Many know the story of disc jockey Adrian Cronauer as acted by Robin Williams in the film *Good Morning, Vietnam*.[103] The film suggested that rock was censored on the radio in Vietnam, and it was in certain instances. But after 1968, for the most part the music blared out on the Armed Forces Vietnam Network's officially sanctioned broadcasts. Rock also appeared on what became known as the "bullshit band," the unused radio channels that GIs used to socialize and converse. Pirate and "underground" rock radio stations even came to exist in Vietnam. As it was absorbed into the continued waging of the war, the music also established zones of heightened civic consciousness. These ranged from spaces in which GIs registered their own personal feelings to moments when they articulated a sense of the incomprehensible tragedy of the American intervention to instances in which they expressed outright dissent and resistance.

Chapter 5 moves from the airwaves to the live performance of rock music in Vietnam. It documents a little-known United States Army Entertainment Branch program, the Command Military Touring Shows. The CMTS organized soldiers into rock bands to entertain fellow troops. These groups created odd moments of civic dissonance when with official sponsorship they performed counterculturally tinged songs such as "War (What Is It Good For? Absolutely Nothing!)."[104] Here hip militarism rendered Vietnam into a surreal and hedonistic leisure playland in which the effort at morale building may have indeed improved spirits, but also inspired unexpected engagements with issues of citizenship among America's citizen-soldiers.[105]

Americans were not the only ones to use rock to grapple with questions of citizenship. Chapter 6 tells the story of the CBC Band, a Vietnamese rock group. After 1968, CBC became one of the top ensembles in the Republic of Vietnam (South Vietnam). Comprised primarily of siblings, the group sang for a mix of Vietnamese youth, American troops, and the international community stationed in Saigon. They used rock to explore the politics of the US intervention. Wearing American flag t-shirts, they performed cover songs such as Grand Funk Railroad's "People, Let's Stop the War," delivering what they called a "little peace message, like straight from Saigon."[106] As they appropriated music from the very country that was waging war in their homeland, the members of CBC were not flunkeys of colonialism, but rather aspiring citizens in what many called, by 1970, Woodstock Nation.[107] They used rock to access the cosmopolitan modernity that the Western counterculture offered. But as a family band, CBC also connected countercultural ideals of fellowship and community to the traditional Vietnamese focus on the family. In the process, they were among those who hybridized new and old in the republic of rock.

The epilogue of the book takes up the nature of Woodstock Nation, which might more accurately be called the Woodstock Transnational.[108] Out of the San Francisco–Vietnam dialectic, a circuit of civic participation emerged worldwide, especially among young people in disparate locales who used rock music to navigate questions of identity and social belonging. Whether in the so-called Third World or even behind the Iron Curtain, rock music brought individuals and groups within the wavelengths of American consumerism. But it did not merely win them over to American hegemony.[109] Instead, rock connected what Czechoslovakian playwright and future president Václav Havel called the "hidden sphere" of "prepolitical" life to larger public and political concerns. The music inspired an effort to confront the existential challenge of "living within the truth" in a global "post-totalitarian society" that was not exclusive to the communist bloc, but rather was a "consumer and industrial (or post-industrial) society" spanning both the obviously undemocratic East and the supposedly democratic West.[110]

A conveyer of fleeting experiences of hybridized, cosmopolitan freedom, rock allowed participants in the Woodstock Transnational to seek out what Havel calls the true "aims of life": happiness, dignity, freedom, togetherness, solidarity, conviviality, community. It did so within the complexities of a consumer system that operated around the world not by dictatorial domination but rather through more subtle and calibrated (and often hip) mechanisms of ideological manipulation. Offering passage to a global countercultural imaginary within this context, the Woodstock Transnational provided a fantastical, stormy space of music, masses, electricity, and mud in which all had to confront the deepest, most basic dilemmas of civic participation. Though it appeared at first as an escape, a way out of the problems of contemporary society, the Woodstock Transnational produced a counterculture that was most of all a startling *encounter*: a reaching toward what it might mean to become citizens of the world.

In San Francisco, Vietnam, and beyond, rock music inspired a counterculture marked by a robust engagement with citizenship: its norms, possibilities, dreams, and problems. As rock musician Joe McDonald muttered to a young radical political activist who pestered him before a concert in 1969, "You're no revolutionary, you're just a young American citizen in the twentieth century."[111] This was a surprising comment coming from a Bay Area red-diaper baby who took his moniker from Joseph Stalin's nickname and led a band named after a Chairman Mao slogan.[112] But despite his political background, McDonald decided that rock did not offer easy categories of analysis. It did not place its listeners within the domains of politics or culture in any definitive way, and it neither fostered opposition nor achieved co-optation. Instead, rock rang out in the murkier realms of civic life.

McDonald pointed out that his band's music was "nothing to believe in. I mean . . . it's just sound." At the same time, he argued that all the music his group produced was dissent; it was "all noise . . . protest noise."[113] As the singer's inconsistent position indicated, rock was contradictory. It immersed listeners in its paradoxes, circulating a social energy of uncertainty, of doubt. The music could, at times, become a pointed and sharp political weapon for a mass social movement, but just as often, it was only the soundtrack for a pseudo-rebellion that undercut its very own radical potential. Rock was part of the problem, but in being so, it became a means of searching for the solution. It cleared out temporary spaces and moments for involvement with the issues of how to seize—or reject—American commercial and military power from within its expansive networks, institutions, and cultural conundrums. The music did not provide any answers or clear guidelines, but it did awaken engagement. At its best, rock encouraged people to become citizens in the fullest cultural and political way possible: by determining themselves, through widespread individual and collective exploration, what their citizenship might entail.

Decades after the 1960s, we still struggle to understand the nature of democratic citizenship within the context of American consumerism and militarism. While future generations may not wear flowers in their hair and may not even want to rock out at all, they still might draw upon the fraught civic legacy of rock and the counterculture. If they do so, let us hope they discover a freedom far more powerful than the one Janis Joplin sang about in her famous version of Kris Kristofferson and Fred Foster's countercultural anthem, "Me and Bobby McGee"—a freedom that is more than just another word for nothing left to lose.[114]

San Francisco

1

UNCLE SAM WANTS YOU TO PASS THE ACID TESTS

AT THE CLOSE of *The Electric Kool-Aid Acid Test*, Tom Wolfe's famous portrait of the Bay Area bohemians the Merry Pranksters, "non-leader" Ken Kesey and fellow Prankster Ken Babbs found themselves in a barn-turned-psychedelic-rock-nightclub on the unincorporated outskirts of Santa Cruz, California. Performing to an empty room, they sang, "We blew it! . . . We blew it! . . . WE BLEW IT!" as they made up lines of rueful doggerel between their refrain.[1] But what exactly had the best-selling novelist and his right-hand man, a former Marine helicopter pilot who had served in the Vietnam War, failed to achieve? What had come to naught by the wee hours of this November 1966 morning?

The Pranksters had many shortcomings to answer for by the end of Wolfe's narrative. However, taking Kesey and his band of psychedelic adventurers to task is of less of concern here than grasping a submerged but crucial framework in which they imperfectly pursued their artistic and social mission: Kesey and the Pranksters attempted to remake the meaning and practice of American citizenship. In his best-selling book, Wolfe emphasized the religious dimensions of the group. He positioned Kesey as a charismatic leader, Christ among his early disciples. The Pranksters were his core group of followers. They sought, according to Wolfe, to spread the gospel, in this case of the transformational possibilities of LSD.[2] Yet it was the Pranksters' encounter with hyper-technological, Cold War America that mattered as much as their mystical qualities. From their appropriations of national symbols to their explorations of associational life, they sought to transform what social belonging, individual identity, and collective interaction meant in the United States during the 1960s. Theirs was a religious mission, to be sure, but it was also a secular one. It would leave an indelible mark on rock music and the developing counterculture of San Francisco.

What is most striking about Kesey and the Merry Pranksters is that they wanted to achieve authentic American civic ideals within the framework of Cold War American abundance and empire.[3] Often using absurdist humor, they *put on* the flag in both senses of the term. They literally donned the stars and stripes: Tom Wolfe called them the "Flag People" when he glimpsed "ten or fifteen American flags walking around" a warehouse in San Francisco.[4] But like a number of artists in the 1960s, they also probed the meaning of the flag as a national symbol. Mark Christensen, one of Kesey's biographers, has noted that the novelist was "one of the first to take the American flag off its staff and really fuck with it."[5] Kesey and the Merry Pranksters went about "stirring up consternation and vague befuddling resentment among the citizens," deploying patriotic iconography in much of their publicity materials and artwork.[6] Their activities culminated in the wild, chaotic parties they called Acid Tests. The Acid Tests became unconventional conventions, gatherings that sparked intensive investigations of selfhood, democratic interaction, patriotism, and national identity not outside but within mass-mediated and militarized Cold War American culture. In doing so, the events fundamentally influenced the countercultural framework in which rock music and citizenship intersected during the late 1960s.

Joining the "Neon Renaissance": The Origins of the Acid Tests

Ken Kesey's own background reveals the sources of engagement with—even celebration of—American bounty and power. Born in 1935, he grew up in Springfield, Oregon, an agricultural center that was suburbanizing during the novelist's teenage years in the late 1940s and early 1950s. Kesey (figure 1.1) was the son of a successful businessman who ran the region's major dairy cooperative. Absorbing his family's traditions of rugged, outdoorsy individualism while also participating in the new comforts and pleasures of American mass consumerism, Kesey went on to become an actor and Olympic-level wrestler as an undergraduate at the University of Oregon. He then enrolled in Stanford University's Creative Writing graduate program, after which he published the best-selling novel *One Flew Over the Cuckoo's Nest* (1962) and the experimental *Sometimes A Great Notion* (1964).[7] By the mid-1960s, Kesey embraced a more performative and collaborative mode of art than novel writing. Fascinated by the mingling of high and low art forms in Pop Art, jazz, dance, comic books, and film, he wanted to join what he called America's postwar "neon renaissance."[8]

FIGURE 1.1. Ken Kesey, 1966. Wolfgang's Vault. Photographer: Gene Anthony.

Kesey's novels manifested an anti-institutional critique of postwar liberalism's administered society. He reshaped and reworked this position as he increasingly abandoned conventional fiction writing.[9] Encounters with hallucinogenic drugs, particularly LSD, inspired Kesey's turn away from the novel. He first took the drug as a volunteer subject at a Menlo Park laboratory near Stanford. Though Kesey did not know it at the time, the lab was covertly funded by the Central Intelligence Agency, bespeaking the militarized world in which the Pranksters forged their sense of civics.[10] When suburban tract development uprooted Kesey from the bohemian Perry Lane neighborhood near Stanford, he relocated to a cabin among the redwood trees in La Honda, just south of San Francisco. But Kesey was no back-to-nature mountain man. The woods, as Tom Wolfe describes, became a kind of theatrical stage for investigating collective social life. Believing that psychedelic drugs could be used as a tool for enlightenment, Kesey and his friends began to explore interpersonal group communications in both their art and their partying, which increasingly became one and the same. Participants included Kesey's wife and brothers, writers and visual artists from around the Bay Area. Among the visitors to La Honda were journalist Hunter S. Thompson, the

Hells Angels, avant-garde filmmaker Kenneth Anger, Beat poet Allen Ginsberg, and the real-life hero of Jack Kerouac's novel *On The Road*, Neal Cassady. Cassady would become the driver for the Pranksters on their famous 1964 bus trip across the United States as they went about "messing up the minds of the citizenry" with outlandish costumes and strange behavior.[11]

Returning to the Bay Area at the end of 1964, they turned from travels and private experiments at Kesey's La Honda cabin to increasingly public events.[12] Ken Babbs complained of the increasingly "motley collection" of participants showing up at Prankster events, but Kesey insisted, "When you've got something like we've got . . . you've got to move off of it and give it to other people. It only works if you bring other people into it."[13] The Pranksters started to host parties not just at their houses, but also at rented lodges, nightclubs, and eventually at the old ballrooms and vaudeville theaters of San Francisco that would soon be palaces of psychedelic rock.[14] The Acid Tests were, according to Tom Wolfe, "the *epoch* of the psychedelic style and practically everything that has gone into it."[15] Guitarist Jerry Garcia, whose performed at the wild events with his band, the Warlocks—soon to be the Grateful Dead—echoed Wolfe's analysis: "the Acid Test is the prototype for our whole basic trip."[16]

The events presaged the style of much of the psychedelic rock to follow in San Francisco: loud music, light shows, psychedelic poster art, and intense communion between performers and audiences. They also fused music to issues of citizenship and civic organization. Of course, the Acid Tests were not typical examples of civil society, for they were not particularly civil. They were not the equivalent of a peaceable town commons or a weekly bowling league or a PTA meeting. Face-to-face fellowship took place, but it did so within environments of electronic and hallucinogenic overstimulation and at times even trauma. The critique of civility by the Pranksters was part of their civic point. Coming of age in 1950s America, they believed that civility often masked oppressive conformity and an unwillingness to probe modern life in all its scary complexity. Connecting the avant-garde traditions of modernist artists and bohemians to contemporary crises, the Pranksters wanted to assess the true nature of human association and shared public life stripped of the restraints of so-called American civilization, which by the 1960s seemed increasingly barbaric as the civil rights movement's simple call for human equality met with enormous resistance and the Cold War gave way to a military intervention in Vietnam that was so coldly rational as to be mad.

The Pranksters created gatherings that became funhouse microcosms of the ideals of Cold War culture in the United States. Participants experimented with what kinds of civic interactions were possible in an inhospitable yet alluring world of the technological sublime.[17] Amplifiers, tape loops, film projectors, strobe lights, black lights, and other modes of sound and image manipulation combined with LSD and a collective spirit of adventure to create what Tom Wolfe called a "chemical refinery."[18] At one level, the Acid Tests were merely parties, but partying wound up meaning more than simply having a good time. It also became a way for strangers to establish bonds of affiliation and connection through risk-taking, particularly through drug use and electronically generated chaos. These were festive assemblies, convened among an overwhelming buzz of energy. Performers and audiences blurred into a vital space of interaction and association. Normative roles fell away and the boundaries between self and group as well as between humans and technology grew ambiguous, fluid, and open to change and transformation.

Attendees at the Acid Tests wanted to have fun, but their pleasures were linked to trying to understand the American ideals of life, liberty, and the pursuit of happiness within the setting of Cold War American power, abundance, and, more ominously, the ever-growing shadow of the escalating war in Vietnam. They often reproduced problematic ideologies of American exceptionalism, racism, and sexism, but the proceedings were too volatile to keep these ideologies stable. To attend an Acid Test was most of all, in a phrase of the time, to "make the scene." But making the scene was about far more than just feeling cool or hip. The Pranksters invited attendees to contribute to the Acid Tests in order to move from passive reception to the *poesis* and politics of active scene-making.[19] The events became collective attempts to reshape the meaning and boundaries of collectivity itself. Questions of citizenship hung in the balance—or, better said, the imbalance. Stirred up by Kesey and the Pranksters, the Acid Tests awaited answers that only participants could provide.

"The Merry Pranksters Welcome the Beatles": Rock Music and the Origins of the Acid Tests, 1964–1965

The Acid Tests made a dramatic impact on the rock music scene that subsequently developed in San Francisco, but rock music inspired Kesey and the Pranksters to organize the events in the first place. Late in the summer of 1964, a number of the Pranksters attended a performance by the Beatles at San Francisco's Cow Palace. According to Tom Wolfe, the Beatles concert both frightened the Pranksters and intrigued them. For Kesey, flying high on LSD, what the concert most of all looked like was a monstrous social formation that exploded with a dangerous but tantalizing new mode of civic participation. Kesey observed that the Beatles wielded enormous power, but they were unable to grasp the opportunity to organize the group's amorphous mass of screaming fans. Though rock's electrified sounds brought to life a "single colonial animal with a thousand waving pink tentacles" whenever one of the Beatles tilted "his long electric guitar handle," the concert ultimately left participants—both the band and their fans—at a loss for how to harness this new sense of collectivity. "It is perfectly obvious," Kesey realized, that the Beatles "have brought this whole mass of human beings to the point where they are one, out of their skulls, one psyche." The group had "utter control," yet to Kesey, "they don't know what in the hell to do with it, they haven't the first idea, and they will lose it."[20] Attempting to wield the very energy he witnessed at the concert, Kesey pictured the Acid Tests as something quite different from the Beatles show. The Acid Tests would be gatherings among equals, in which the audience members were empowered to create, investigate, and perhaps even seize the energy that he glimpsed shooting out from the guitar necks of John Lennon, Paul McCartney, and George Harrison. The Acid Tests would use LSD and electronic stimulation to do so.

Calling the events Acid Tests was a clever double entendre: these were gathering not only dedicated to acid, the nickname for LSD, but also to the medieval experiments conducted by alchemists to see if they could transmute common metals to gold. Kesey and the Pranksters proposed that like these metals, participants at the Acid Tests might find themselves miraculously transformed. Certain participants would succeed while others failed (these were tests after all). Certain people would find a sense of belonging while others might end up excluded. But all were welcome to explore the possibilities for togetherness within the chaotic setting of the events.

Kesey hoped to recast his experience of the Beatles concert into a form that might provide a better format for grappling with the tensions of belonging and exclusion endemic to democratic and civic assembly in a mass society. He and the Pranksters would welcome the public at large into these events, but from there they were on their own, free to make their way through what Kesey called the "the Dome fantasy":

This was going to be a great geodesic dome on top of a cylindrical shaft. It would look like a great mushroom. Many levels. People would climb a stairway up the cylinder . . . and the dome would have a great foam-rubber floor they could lie down on. Sunk down in the foam rubber, below floor level, would be movie projectors, video-tape projectors, light projectors. All over the place, up in the dome, everywhere, would be speakers, microphones, tape machines, live, replay, variable lag. . . . Lights, movies, video tapes, video tapes of themselves, flashing and swirling over the dome from the beams of searchlights rising from the floor from between their bodies. The sounds roiling around in the globe like a typhoon. Movies and tapes of the past, tapes and video tapes, broadcasts and pictures of the present, tapes and humanoid sounds of the future. . . .

The dome, which the Pranksters subsequently attempted to create at the Acid Tests in 1965 and 1966, would be "an incredible concentration of energy." And it would provide a space where, eventually, "not only the Pranksters, but people from all over, heads, non-heads, intellectuals, curiosity-seekers, even cops, had turned up and gotten swept up in the incredible energy of the thing." Though they were a small group, the Pranksters emphasized that the Acid Tests were meant to be wide-open gatherings: events not for the already-initiated, but also for a diverse group of strangers. "People from all over" could enter "the Dome fantasy" (figure 1.2) to see for themselves what was possible.[21]

Even after their initial encounter with the Beatles at the 1964 Cow Palace concert, Kesey and the Pranksters continued to return to rock music for inspiration. As they sought public venues beyond Kesey's cabin in La Honda, they began to collaborate with the members of a rock band, The Warlocks. When he had lived on Perry Lane in Palo Alto, Kesey had thrown the members of the Warlocks out of parties because they seemed like a bunch of rough-mannered kids. But now, pushing toward a more confrontational aesthetic, Kesey and the Pranksters embraced the Warlocks, who by the end of 1965 would be known by their more familiar name: the Grateful Dead.

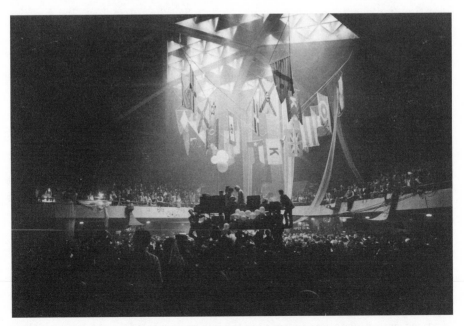

FIGURE 1.2. "The Dome fantasy": The Prankster tower of control at the Trips Festival, January 1966. Wolfgang's Vault. Photographer: Gene Anthony.

The two groups became coconspirators in generating an electronic racket at the Acid Tests. Rock music from beyond the Bay Area also continued to influence the Acid Tests. After the Beatles concert, dozens of intrigued bohemians had turned up at Kesey's La Honda cabin, where the Pranksters unveiled a banner that read, "The Merry Pranksters welcome the Beatles." When the Rolling Stones came to town a few months later, on December 4, 1965, at the Cow Palace, Kesey and the Pranksters held an Acid Test at a house in San Jose, unfurling a similar banner. This event, while still at a private location, marked the first time that the Pranksters organized an Acid Test outside one of their own homes.[22] The Pranksters hoped to "reach out into the world" with their fantasy of a new kind of shared experience.

As Kesey related to Tom Wolfe, the Pranksters wanted to direct the energies of rock toward a reconfiguration of society. Thinking about the Beatles and Rolling Stones concerts, Kesey remarked that, "All the wound-up wired-up teeny freaks and assorted multitudes pouring out of the Cow Palace" had come "still aquiver with ecstasy" but "aimless with no flow to go off in." Perhaps they could find each other—and themselves—at the Acid Tests. Through these hallucinogenic, electronic events, they might figure out how to convene a new kind of community not by warding off the technologies of the contemporary world, but by diving directly into their intensified energies.[23] The party in San Jose was a raucous affair that marked an effort to do this. Kesey and the Pranksters sought to create a setting to harness what they heard and saw at mid-60s rock concerts. It was telling, however, that the Pranksters kept blowing fuses at the San Jose Acid Test. The energies unleashed by music, drugs, electronics, and "all the wound-up wired-up teeny freaks and assorted multitudes" were potent and would not necessarily resolve into civic order even as they brought issues of civics and citizenship to the fore.

"Can You Pass the Acid Test?": The Pranksters Go Public, December 1965

At the next Acid Test, which occurred on December 11, 1965, Kesey and the Merry Pranksters went fully public, holding an Acid Test at a lodge on Muir Beach, just north of San Francisco in Marin County.[24] Expanding upon earlier efforts to publicize their events, the Pranksters created and circulated handbills and posters around the Bay Area. These publicity materials suggested in visual form how the group was imagining the purpose of the Acid Tests. Conceived and drawn by Prankster artist Paul Foster (or possibly by writer and fellow Prankster Norman Hartweg, according to some accounts), the imagery revealed the group's ambitions to rearrange both the self and the collective through "the Dome fantasy."

Rudimentary handbills had been made for earlier, private Acid Tests and put up in local bohemian bookstores and coffee shops as well as handed out to friends as gifts, but as the events grew more public, these simple fliers gave way to more ornate efforts. According to the Muir Beach handbill (figure 1.3), the "happeners" at the event would include "Roy's Audioptics," a light show developed by Prankster

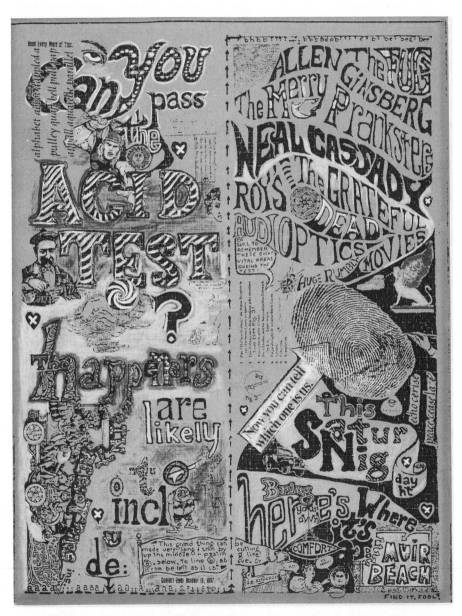

FIGURE 1.3. "Now you can tell which one is us": The Muir Beach Acid Test Handbill, December 1965. Key-Z Productions/Postertrip Archives. Artist: Paul Foster.

Roy Seburn, along with what the handbill called "huge rumbly movies." The New York rock band the Fugs were "likely" participants, as were the Grateful Dead. Additionally, the handbill claimed, Beat poet Allen Ginsberg and *On The Road* legend Neal Cassady were to attend the Muir Beach Acid Test. On the handbill, as if to presage the maelstrom to come, names of participants swirled around a clutter of information and imagery. There were instructions for turning the handbill into a scroll, perhaps referencing Jack Kerouac's famous *On The Road* manuscript, written on a continuous roll of paper, and alluding to the quasi-Buddhist enlightenment that the Acid Test might inspire. Cartoon panels appeared in parts of the handbill, à la Roy Lichtenstein's Pop Art paintings. Superheroes held strange conversations in bubbles over their heads. The Merry Pranksters' famous psychedelic bus drove up the side of the handbill. A gargoyle poked out from letters. An artist in a beret appeared. A sun gave off rays. Eyeballs blinked with flirty eyelashes. As if a viewer had opened a door on a party raging inside, the handbill evoked the sensorial immersion and pandemonium that the event promised attendees.

The Muir Beach handbill also stressed the daring nature of the party in a tone that mingled humor and seriousness. Included on the handbill was the question "Can You Pass the Acid Test?" This phrase would become a kind of mantra among the Pranksters. In its prominent positioning on the publicity handbill, "Can You Pass the Acid Test?" took on the tone of the rural American medicine show hawker or carnival barker. Yet these events were not escapes into nostalgia; they were startling in their embrace—indeed, their intensification—of futuristic technological stimulation. The Acid Tests were to be a search for the new, but only for those brave enough to take the entrance exam. As if to reinforce this point, the handbill hid coded messages within its dense iconography. At its bottom, two phrases merge to reveal a third. "Bring your own" flowed into "Here's where it's at . . . Muir Beach" to create a new instruction: "Bring Heroes." "Bring your own" was already a sly signal to attendees that they were free to arrive with hallucinogenic drugs in hand. But the lurking phrase "Bring Heroes" went a step further to suggest that profound insights were to be had at the gathering, but only for those who looked closely and dared to believe what they thought they saw.

The concealment of hidden messages within the handbill also represented another Prankster ideal: to bridge the divide between intimate experience and public communion. If you "got" the clues, your innermost feelings of significance might connect to a larger group of people, including friends, acquaintances, and even strangers. The ambiguity of the handbill also signaled that doubt—does it really say that?—was crucial to the project of remaking citizenship and civic life at the Acid Tests. Uncertainty formed an affective mood for potential social bonding. "Bring your own" and "Here's where it's at" were the straightforward directions, but the deeper question of passing the Acid Test involved the willingness to entertain the endless array of potential social transmutations that might occur at the event, even the impossible alchemical trick of turning the dross of everyday life, including the onslaught of American mass culture, into a golden freedom for both individuals and the collective. Expanding upon the question "Can you pass the Acid Test?" a giant thumbprint blot appeared on the bottom of the Muir Beach handbill. An arrow pointed to the thumbprint and, reasserting the event's goal of exploring the relationship between individuality and collectivity, playfully announced: "Now you can tell which one is us." There was the possibility of discovery here: an attendee at the Acid Test might finally be able to perceive the mysteries of selfhood and social belonging in an ecstatic communion of shared affiliation ("Now you can tell . . ."). But in the grammatical incongruity of the singular and the plural (". . . which one is us"), there was also a sense that individual identity and group formation intersected in ways that would never resolve into an authoritative and stable whole. The handbill proposed no guarantees of success, no program for social improvement, no carefully orchestrated plan; instead, it positioned the Acid Tests as something more unruly. These events were a philosophical hoax, a seriously funny joke, a prank that might snap people—presto!—into a new spirit of civic rebirth . . . or perhaps not. "Can you pass the Acid Test?" the Pranksters dared attendees at their events. But could they themselves pass the acid test? The Pranksters were not sure where they were going, but they invited participants to ride the curve of the question mark at the end of their signature phrase wherever it might lead.[25]

The question mark turned up repeatedly on publicity for the Acid Tests. Questioning was at the heart of the events. Kesey's goal was for the events was to discover "all of the conditioned responses of men and then to prank them. This is the surest way to get them to ask questions, and until they ask questions they are going to remain conditioned robots."[26] Almost all the handbills and posters enlarged the grammatical symbol or featured it multiple times (figure 1.4). The Pranksters hoped to foster public spaces bedecked with question marks, as one early handbill literally visualized.[27] They also wanted to bring time itself into a state of uncertain aliveness. The use of strobe lights at the Muir Beach Acid Test inspired Tom Wolfe to picture "history . . . pinned up on a butterfly board":

> To people standing under the mighty strobe, everything seemed to fragment. Ecstatic dancers—their hands flew off their arms frozen in the air—their glistening faces came apart—a gleaming ellipse of teeth here, a pair of buffered highlit cheekbones there—all flacking and fragmenting into

images as in an old flicker movie—a man in slices!—All of history pinned up on a butterfly board; the experience, of course. The strobe, the projectors, the mikes, the tapes, the amplifiers, the variable lag Ampex—it was all set up in a coiling gleaming clump in the Lincoln Log lodge, the communal clump. . . .[28]

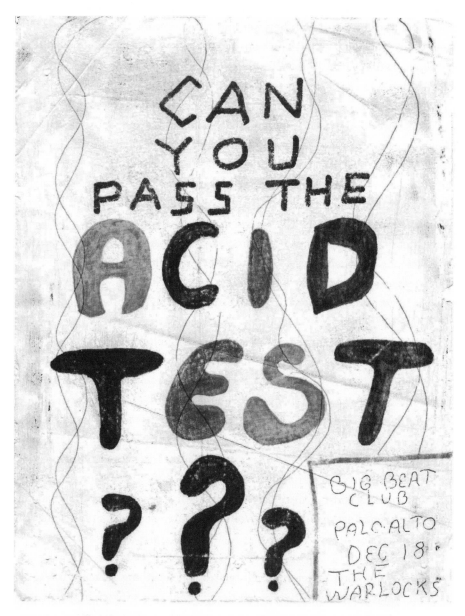

FIGURE 1.4. Bedecked with question marks: An early Acid Test at the Big Beat Club in Palo Alto, December 1965. Key-Z Productions/Postertrip Archives. Artist unknown.

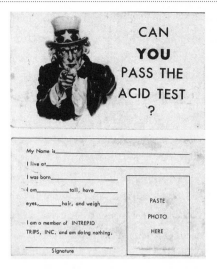

FIGURE 1.5. "Can You Pass the Acid Tests?": Merry Pranksters membership card, 1966. Key-Z Productions/Postertrip Archives. Artist unknown.

Space and time opened up at the Acid Tests, with participants feeling a heightened sense of seizing history itself through the psychedelic warping of consciousness.[29]

All of this was a touch absurd, of course, but then again the group organizing the Acid Tests called themselves the Pranksters. Core to their self-perceived psychedelic mission was to oscillate between joy and fear in the name of discovery. They were not political theorists, of course, and they were not even political activists, but their use of question marks and questioning led them to engagements with Cold War American state power. This appeared most vividly on their playful use of ID cards that featured Uncle Sam, but substituted the phrase "I want you for the U.S. Army" with "Can you pass the acid test?" (figure 1.5). By appropriating this symbolic figure, first used on World War I military recruitment posters, the Pranksters implicitly referred to the draft and the growing American involvement in Vietnam. Their repurposing of Uncle Sam, however, pointed to a very different sense of civic duty. Instead of hailing citizens to enlist in the Armed Forces, this Uncle Sam asked viewers to rise to the challenge of remaking the self—and by extension American citizenship—at the intense communal gatherings of the Acid Tests.[30]

The Prankster's reference to Uncle Sam connected their technologically and aesthetically experimental gatherings to the American state, but those who experienced the events also linked the Acid Tests to the very future of democratic practice itself. Jerry Garcia decided that the events were "meant to do away with old forms, with old ideas" and "try something *new*." This new thing, crucially, was profoundly collective, even as it was about individuals exploring their own self-identities. "Nobody was doing *something*," Garcia declared, "It was everybody doing bits and pieces of something, the result of which was something else." Out of these cooperative moments, Garcia thought that "the Kesey thing" became "open, a tapestry, a mandala—it was whatever you made it."[31] At the Acid Tests, participants asked questions about whether greater freedom might result from embracing rather than fighting the feeling that the world lacked unified and timeless foundations. Drawing from Romantic notions of art's revolutionary potential, they wondered whether falling apart in a cutting-edge onslaught of technological and hallucinogenic stimuli might paradoxically lead to a new kind of coming together.[32]

The Acid Tests became events at which participants were to worry less about boundaries and definitive end points than to delve into what light-show artist and Acid Test participant Ben Van Meter called the "point of no point." For Van Meter, this was the sense that self and group were porous and that out of an awareness of the mutable relationships between interior and exterior a new civic ethos could arise. To delve into the pluralistic experience of the world without worrying about answers was key to the Acid Tests. "The job," Kesey reflected years later, was "to seek mystery, evoke mystery. . . . The need for mystery is greater than the need for an answer."[33] This fervent pursuit of mystery, enigmas, and anti-foundationalist liberation made the Acid Tests radically democratic, but also scary and dangerous.[34] Richard Alpert (soon to be known as Ram Dass) described the Acid Tests as events that seemed to pull the rug out from under participants. "They had an incredibly strong sensual immediacy," Alpert remembered. "They turned people inside out into the moment, in a way that they felt extremely alive. These events were crowded, wild, and confusing. . . . For some, the surrender was great; but others didn't like that feeling of having no safe ground." Alpert's memories of the Acid Tests resemble what historian-memoirist Nick Bromell has described as the realization of "radical pluralism" he and others experienced through intense engagement with rock music and hallucinogenic drugs during the 1960s. The world suddenly seemed a "buzzing, blooming confusion," as American philosopher William James famously wrote, and this led both to a glimpse of emancipation from old limits and, disconcertingly, a feeling of dismay at overpowering uncertainties.[35]

Carolyn Adams Garcia, better known at the time by her Prankster name of Mountain Girl, remembered the Muir Beach Acid Test in December of 1965 because it raised troubling—if perversely pleasurable—questions about how identity took shape within the intensifications of electronic communication that were becoming so much a part of the world of American power during the 1960s. "The delay machine was . . . one of the most important things there, because there was this short lag on your voice," she remembered, "it was just long enough to be really uncomfortable. . . . It was exactly the length of time it would take you to form a thought, so just as your next thought was formed, you heard your voice speaking the previous thought. It was really hard to make progress through that." The Grateful Dead had trouble too. The band found it difficult to connect with each other musically in the electronic and hallucinogenic mayhem of the Muir Beach Acid Test. "That was a strange night," Mountain Girl recalled. "The poor band couldn't get anything going. . . . The lighting was bad in there and the band would go up and play for about five minutes and then they'd sit down; that was all they could do." So too, the famous LSD-manufacturer Owsley "Bear" Stanley, who would become the financial backer and electronic wizard of the Grateful Dead, freaked out on his own product, dragging a chair across the floor for hours before leaving and crashing his car on the winding roads of Marin County.[36]

Despite the problems they encountered at the Muir Beach Acid Test, the Pranksters and their fellow travelers were excited to extend their avant-garde experimentations to a broader public. Years later, in a rumination on the death of Jerry Garcia, Ken Kesey wrote, "I remember standing out in the pearly early dawn after the Muir Beach Acid Test, leaning on the top rail of a driftwood fence with [Garcia] and [Grateful Dead bassist Phil] Lesh and [Ken] Babbs, watching the world light up, talking about our glorious futures." For Kesey, "the gig had been semi-successful and the air was full of exulted fantasies." Yet the event also raised the very problem that Kesey had glimpsed when watching the Beatles perform a few years earlier: how to harness positive social energies without losing them either to the entropy of not knowing what to do with them or the usurpation by larger, more ominous systems of control. When the others imagined releasing a successful pop music recording of the event, Garcia quipped that "Yeah, right . . . and a year from tomorrow be recording a Things Go Better With Coke commercial."[37] It was a telling scene, registering the eagerness among Acid Test participants to crack open the existing structures of postwar consumer culture in order to reach more people but also, as Garcia sardonically articulated, the awareness that even their extreme, psychedelic, avant-garde techniques could be absorbed by mass culture without necessarily transforming the society around them.

"A New Configuration": Pirate Democracy at the Fillmore Auditorium Acid Test and the Trips Festival, January–September 1966

Ken Kesey may have recalled his sense of hope in the aftermath of the Muir Beach Acid Test, but others remembered him vacillating between wanting to spread the spirit of exploration at the events and worrying about whether such widening gyres of publicity were wise. "A good time was had by all except Kesey," Paul Perry wrote. The Prankster non-leader "told the other Pranksters that the Acid Tests were over. Too many people, too much weird energy, too many bad vibes."[38] But the Acid Tests continued and they did so in far more public ways than even at Muir Beach. On January 8, 1966, over two thousand participants turned up for an Acid Test at the Fillmore Auditorium, the very venue rock critic Paul Williams would later label a countercultural "induction center." At the Fillmore Acid Test, the San Francisco scene truly began to emerge as an assembly of strangers gathered together not just for a party, but for a festive inquiry into the nature of their lives.

If LSD was still the semisecret magic potion at this event, electronics defined the more open and widely available experiences of the Acid Tests as they began to encompass associations beyond just a small cohort of friends or even a wider network of acquaintances.[39] The Fillmore was an old San Francisco auditorium in the largely African-American, working-class district of the Western Addition. Built in 1911 as the Majestic Theater and long an entertainment venue for dances and balls, it would, by the end of 1966, become the first primary venue for promoter Bill Graham's psychedelic rock concerts. But in January of that year, it was simply a hall available to rent for quite affordable rates from Charles Sullivan, an African-American businessman.[40] Despite the venue's location in a primarily African-American part of San Francisco, the Pranksters were less interested in referencing jazz or blues or other signifiers of what Norman Mailer called the "white Negro" than in using the old, vaudeville-era space to create a microcosm of mediated life in postwar consumer culture, a kind of mini-version of Marshall McLuhan's concept of a "global village."[41]

At the Acid Test, the Fillmore became a wildly disorienting and decontextualizing setting in which the new networks of global mass communications and mediation were manipulated, compacted, and intensified. As journalist Charles Perry described the event, "The Pranksters were able to wire the place up with microphones and speakers in unexpected places, so you might be downstairs watching somebody make a fool of himself on the closed-circuit TV and suddenly hear something you'd said upstairs a few minutes ago broadcast all over the hall." The Fillmore event hinged on how electronic mediation might reknit individuals together into new community formations, particularly through sound. "There were microphones distributed all over the place," Jerry Garcia remembered, echoing Charles Perry's recollections, "and all different people with mixers and tape recorders, and speakers all over the place. And so somebody might say something in the corner and it would go through a delay and you might hear it up in some other room completely unrelated, but there would be this incredible timing thing that would be happening so that everything that happened would sort of fit right in perfectly."[42]

This was a strange new public space, for it defied unitary spatial or temporal constraints. As a carnivalesque setting, it both borrowed from and reconfigured the electronic nexus of postwar American life, pulling participants into new associations and connections. Berkeley political activist Michael Rossman noticed how within the festive electronic stimulation of strobe lights, TVs, and other devices at the Fillmore Acid Test, a kind of porousness emerged between performers and audience members. "There was a lot of electronic equipment which sent out a low reverberation that resonated throughout the hall. And the whole place was full of streamers and balloons. There were TV cameras and a TV screen, and you could see yourself on it," Rossman recalled. "On stage there was a rock group; anybody could play with them. It was a kind of social jam session."[43]

Within the exaggerated recontextualization of mass-mediated culture, the Pranksters did not ask attendees to enjoy a show or passively watch a performance, but rather to experiment with new kinds of democratic assembly within an enigmatic swirl of extreme sonic and visual stimulation. "A guy in a white mechanic's suit with a black cross on the front, and on the back a sign saying 'Please Don't Believe in Magic' ran up and down all night," Rossman remembered. "Periodically the lights went out and everybody cheered." There were "giant Frisbees, balloons like basketballs, acrobats, girls in felt eyelashes four inches long, fluorescent painting on jeans, glasses low on the nose with eyes painted on them, people with eyes painted on their foreheads, men with foxes on their shoulders!"[44] Tony Martin, a light-show artist, echoed Rossman's observations of an event that fostered a wide-open sense of involvement. "Within the high energy" of the Acid Tests, Martin thought "a communal resonance of partaking and joining together occurred between individuals of many kinds: merchants, artists, bikers, office workers, and students." A fellow traveler of the Pranksters, Martin shared the vision of the Acid Tests: he hoped that within the intensification of electronic media, new associations might emerge among people of very different backgrounds.[45]

As strangers gathered together in venues such as the Fillmore, the Acid Tests posed the question: when explicit systems of control were lifted away but the technologies (from electronics to drugs) of military-industrial America remained, what new sorts of social formations might emerge? Reflecting optimistically on what he called the "mindless chaos" at the Acid Tests, Jerry Garcia decided that, "Formlessness and chaos lead to new forms. And new order. Closer to, probably, what the real order is." The hope at the Acid Tests was that spaces of identity in flux and social relations without rigid rules might provide the setting for a more liberating social body than the terrifying beast Kesey and his friends glimpsed at the Beatles concert in 1964.[46] But the Pranksters were not afraid of dissonance and risk. As Garcia's memories suggested, they were willing to enter into chaos in the name of discovering freedom. Social unity might result, but it might not: the important task was to investigate the unknown. Prankster Ken Babbs (figure 1.6)

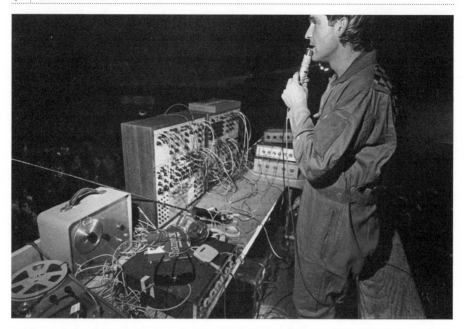

FIGURE 1.6. Ken Babbs at the controls, Trips Festival, January 1966. Wolfgang's Vault. Photographer: Gene Anthony.

went so far as to perceive the gathered crowd at the Fillmore Auditorium as a group of astronauts who rivaled the Cold War heroes of NASA. Ranting over the microphone system at the event, he imagined the attendees hurtling toward undiscovered realms of self and society as they fearlessly embarked on quest to discover the "furthur" reaches of inner space. Aboard a kind of imaginary rocket ship, the assembled crowd soared on flashing lights, roaring sounds, and copious ingestions of LSD. "There's the engine room coming in loud and clear," Babbs announced over the Pranksters' time-warped amplification system. Referring playfully to the ingestion of LSD at the event, he remarked, "The captain has just informed me that we are on the verge of going into the operation crystallization." Eventually, Babbs quipped, they would reach a "new configuration."

But a new configuration of what? In place of the Beatles as the head of the electronic teen beast at the Cow Palace in 1964, the science-fiction fantasy of the Acid Test rocket ship featured a Prankster crew at the helm, navigating the vessel toward impossible destinations. There was a contradiction playing out in this LSD-fueled vision since astronaut teams were among the most hierarchical and undemocratic, as were the ranks of engineers helping them in command centers back on earth. It would seem that as the Acid Tests became larger and more public affairs, order and control became as important to Kesey and the Pranksters as chaos and the search for freedom. Kesey himself became known as "the chief engineer." Neal

Cassady was "co-pilot" of the Prankster vessel. At one point, Babbs alerted him to "remain at his post in the projection booth in order to keep driving this ship through whatever electrical and meteor shower we encounter." The ex-Vietnam helicopter pilot bantered on, playing the role of "old pointy head," the interlocutor-navigator for the voyage.[47]

But for all the hierarchical order and ranking emerging among the Pranksters, Ken Babbs's metaphor of the spaceship suggested more than just a reassertion of larger systems of control. He also evoked a setting of imaginative plenitude in which the earthly commingled momentarily with inconceivable otherworlds. The spaceship of the Fillmore Acid Test was a kind of pirate vessel. The event became what Michel Foucault famously called, in a 1967 lecture, a heterotopic space. Writing one year after the Acid Tests, Foucault described "the ship" as "the heterotopia par excellence." For the French philosopher, who in the 1970s moved to the Bay Area and taught at the University of California in Berkeley, the ship best symbolized the radical possibilities of heterotopia. "In civilizations without boats," Foucault wrote, "dreams dry up, espionage takes the place of adventure, and the police take the place of pirates."[48] At the Fillmore, the Pranksters seemed to presage Foucault's pessimistic theory of threatened heterotopia in a far more vernacular form. Babbs identified the assembled strangers at the Fillmore as renegade mutineers aboard a spaceship on which they had absconded with the booty of both private identity and public life in postwar American mass culture. Swashbuckling impersonators of the astronauts and engineers of the Cold War space race, the Pranksters pretended to be heroic experts of scientific modernity, technocrats of psychedelic consciousness. But their ultimate goal was not technocratic; it was to discover an unprecedented democratic equality through collective inquiry.[49]

In place of order and hierarchy, the Pranksters wanted to create a kind of pirate democracy. Kesey modeled himself as an exemplary new citizen for this temporary political order (or disorder, as the case may have been). At the next Acid Test, which took place at the Trips Festival on January 21, 22, and 23 at Longshoreman's Hall, he literally donned a space helmet. He did so to hide his identity, since he was not supposed to consort with the Pranksters due to a court injunction from an arrest for possession of marijuana at his house in La Honda and another arrest the night before the Trips Festival. But for Kesey, the space helmet was not just a disguise; it was a way to extend the Prankster metaphor of technocratic American society turned upside down.

The Pranksters wanted to understand better what the connections were between chaos and order in modern America. They were curious to know if a kind of social harmony lurked beyond entropic experiences. Garcia's fellow band member in the Grateful Dead, bassist Phil Lesh, went so far as to believe that he glimpsed the workings of "mysterious laws" at the Acid Tests. Participants seemed to be suddenly "ordered only by those same mysterious laws that govern the evolution of weather patterns, or the turbulence in a rising column of smoke."[50] Unlike the Pranksters, who at times seemed hell-bent on exploration even if it led to destruction, Lesh pictured the social interactions at the Acid Tests resolving from chaotic anarchy into a surprising harmony. "See how the entire wildly dancing audience behaves like waves in the ocean," he wrote in his memoir, "whole groups of dancers rising and falling, lifting their arms or spinning rapidly in synchronized movement, darting swiftly through the crowd or languidly undulating in place—manifesting the same sort of spontaneous consensus seen in flocks of birds, schools of fish, or clusters of galaxies." This was a vision of the "beast" that Kesey had perceived among the Beatles and their fans, but now transformed into a new, more beautiful creature.

While Ken Babbs had envisioned the Acid Test as a space-age pirate democracy, with a roughhewn equality born of the tenuousness and brutality of the event, Lesh pictured something more hopeful, spiritual, and cosmic. The Acid Test was not only an intergalactic pirate ship, but also the ocean itself, as well as the sky and galaxies, all assembled with instantaneous organized grace. Music played a central role, but to Lesh "it wasn't that the music was making everything move a certain way, and it wasn't the dancers or the lights or the drugs even." For him, "There was a very strong sense of connection to another order of reality which was filtering down into our everyday world. It was absolutely magic. That was one of the moments that made me realize that everything isn't as it seems, on heaven and earth." Like his bandmate Garcia, Lesh wondered if something "closer to . . . the real order" might arise out of the "formlessness and chaos" at the Acid Test events. In science-fiction terms quite similar to Ken Babbs's space-travel hallucinations, Lesh believed that a new kind of communal harmony, a "group mind," began to appear among strangers as the Acid Tests grew into "larger-scale" events.[51]

Though the Tests were navigated by the Pranksters, the Grateful Dead, or by other temporary leaders, the gatherings were never carefully coordinated. They were not meant to be guided entertainment or even art "happenings," the kind of orchestrated event that visual artist Allan Kaprow pioneered on the East Coast during the 1960s.[52] The Acid Tests were meant, at their best, to be created and controlled from the bottom up. Participants themselves engaged together in configuring the social body formed the event. The goal was to repurpose the tools of electronic technology that seemed to be dominating and deadening postwar life. If the wavelengths of mass-mediation were beamed down to the people by the mainstream forces of Cold War America, if the spaces of associational life in the country were dominated by unidirectional messages from centralized powers, then at the

Acid Tests the ambition was to realize a culture of participatory democracy by putting the multi in multimedia. From the oppression of one-way messages, the Pranksters sought to move to a cacophonous but potentially liberating—and perhaps even miraculously harmonious—symphony of bodies and machines in associational motion.[53] The ultimate end of this new dynamic system was in fact no end at all, but rather continual movement, flow, and "spontaneous consensus."[54] Moreover, shape-shifting mutations of engagement brimming with intense pleasures but also rife with frightening traumas might lead, Phil Lesh hoped, to a sense that participants had become "co-responsible for the dance of the cosmos."[55] Ideally, the right to be free and the duty to care for others came together.

The printed program for the Trips Festival explicitly linked this vision to rock music. It featured a black-and-white swirl at its center, emanating from a radar-like circular screen (figure 1.7). Designed by Wes Wilson, who would go on to create many rock concert posters, the image suggested a technological console gone psychedelic. "Maybe this is the ROCK REVOLUTION," the writers of the program wondered. "The general tone of things has moved on from the self-conscious happening to a more JUBILANT occasion where the audience PARTICIPATES." The

FIGURE 1.7. Wes Wilson's handbill for the Trips Festival, January 1966. Artist: Wes Wilson.

Trips Festival organizers even encouraged the audience "to bring their own GADG-ETS" and plug in to become performers themselves. "A.C. outlets will be provided," the program noted.[56] From active creativity using mass communications technologies, the organizers hoped a truly democratic culture suitable for the hyper-mediated postmodern world might arise.

A number of Pranksters, such as part-time member Stuart Brand, were quite optimistic about this possibility. Brand went on from the Acid Tests to form the *Whole Earth Catalog*, which sought to organize and collate the wild associations and energies of events such as the Trips Festival into useable information for constructing a new sense of American and global community. He also played a formative role in shaping the environmental movement and the development of the personal computer and the Internet.[57] But if the Acid Tests beckoned with joyous liberation—just plug in, drop acid, and join the pirate democracy!—they also called forth new demands for participants. Most obviously, one could get metaphorically (or even literally) electrocuted, or electrocute others, when the sockets were opened up for all. More subtly, people might think they were free when they were in fact only more firmly tethered to the sockets.

At the conclusion of the Fillmore Acid Test, the problem of diagnosing responsibility and authority in the liberated zones of Prankster democracy became particularly acute. When San Francisco policemen entered the building to shut down the event, it was as if they were literally acting out Foucault's essay on heterotopia, in which "the police take the place of pirates."[58] Lesh recalled that, "after eternities of ecstatic ego loss, a voice was heard, asking, 'who's in charge here?'" The voice belonged to a policeman who tried, fruitlessly, to stop various Pranksters from continuing with the event. "The depth of existential thought revealed in that question dropped us all right into the theater of the absurd," Lesh remarked. The transformation of an offhand comment by a baffled law enforcement official into an "existential" dilemma was typical of the heightened zone of inquiry at the Acid Tests. Small details took on allegorical casts. Who really was in charge here? Was it the police, the astronaut-pirates of Ken Babbs's Acid Test rocket ship, or, as Lesh would have it, some other cosmic force? The question suggested to Lesh that participants all had to become deeply "responsible for keeping it going in some harmonious manner." The freedom of the Acid Tests demanded a new kind of individual and collective responsibility that moved beyond the abilities of the police. The electrifying combination of music and dance at the Acid Tests offered freedom, but also implied obligation. Everyone was charged up, but this demanded that everyone now had to be in charge. Trying to do their part in "holding the line against the depredations of entropy and ignorance," as Lesh put it, they would not only discover a space of liberation, but in doing so also to improve the society around them. "The fervent belief we shared then," he wrote, was "that the energy liberated by this combination of music and ecstatic dancing [was] somehow making the world better."[59]

Participants at the Acid Tests constituted a public life that was intensely dialectical: it drew on the technologies and ideologies of Cold War America and even exaggerated them, but it also sought to turn them toward a new sense of citizenship. The dance floor itself became a public space of reshaped personal politics. Whereas previous musical genres inspired tightly structured couple dancing, as if partners were pistons locked in the gendered roles of the industrial age, the Acid Tests was more amorphous and open. This was the dance floor as a nuclear reaction, with the dancers as subatomic particles colliding and reassembling into new, unstable entities. The dangerous social conditions that resulted could often be radioactive in terms of gender and power: rock did not provide the answer to gender inequality or misogyny, and it sometimes created even more retrograde attitudes and actions. But for many women, the psychedelic dance floor in the aftermath of the Acid Tests also became a surprising space for bold new experiences of self, intimacy, and larger social relationships that included, but were not limited to, coupling.

Women could participate in new ways at these events, floating among partners without any implied commitment. Or they could simply move to their own ecstatic experiences of the music (figure 1.8). "It was an emotional entangled group spirit calling to the potent human energy welling up," Carolyn Adams Garcia wrote of the dancing that emerged at rock shows in the aftermath of the Acid Tests.[60] "I stood close to the band and let the vibrations engulf me," Clair Brush remembered of taking LSD and listening to the Grateful Dead at the Watts Acid Test in Los Angeles. "They started in my toes and every inch of me was quivering with them . . . they made a journey through my nervous system . . ., traveling each tiny path, finally reaching the top of my head, where they exploded in glorious patterns of color and line. . . ." For Brush, the experience was scary, but ultimately enlightening as she moved between connecting with individuals at the event and exploring her own sensations alone.[61] Florence Nathan (later Rosie McGee) also experienced dancing to the Grateful Dead as liberating. Attending the Muir Beach Acid Test, she remembered having "a wonderful night, twirling and dancing to the music."[62] In later years, she would join the Dead on stage (figure 1.9). "I wasn't all that great a dancer, but that wasn't the point," she recalled. The point was to lose herself in the sounds. "I was barely aware of my body as I merged with the music and danced away the hours." For her, these were "the most un-self-conscious and transcendent moments I have had in my life."[63] Eventually, rock concerts—even the Dead's—would become star-focused presentations. Audiences increasingly turned into passive spectators and women were put in the constricted role of "groupies."[64] But the Acid

FIGURE 1.8. The new gender politics of the psychedelic dance floor: Woman dancing at the Trips Festival, January 1966. Wolfgang's Vault. Photographer: Gene Anthony.

Tests proposed a different blueprint, one that prevailed for a time in the psyche-delic palaces of San Francisco and still lingered afterward in the growing shadows of the rock show spectacle: individuals danced in concert with the musicians and each other, assembling into formations that turned the dominant technologies of mass-mediation toward new democratic possibilities.

FIGURE 1.9. Florence Nathan, later Rosie McGee, dancing in the strobe lights at the Fillmore Auditorium, 1966. Jim Marshall Photography LLC. Photographer: Jim Marshall.

That the Acid Tests could be severely limiting for women but also, at times, enthrallingly liberating was indicative of the Pranksters' emphasis on immersive anarchy. Kesey and his group hoped to inspire a new spirit that combined individual emancipation and social commitment in response to the chaos they unleashed. In the confusing, heterotopic swirl of the events, attendees would, ideally, widen the range of accepted behavior, probe the possibilities of limitlessness, and grasp the need for certain kinds of collective dependence and obligation. The Acid Tests mirrored and even intensified the technologies of mass-mediation in the hopes that they might reveal a way to understand them and turn them toward more enlightened cultural and political ends. This was a vision of modern radical pluralism that sought to avoid becoming either a simplistic libertarianism or a constraining communitarianism.[65]

One way to navigate between an anything-goes attitude of rebellion and a spirit of comradeship that became inhibiting in its pressures to conform was through irreverence. These were parties after all, and the Pranksters pictured them as playful revelries filled with madcap antics. But the gags often doubled as engagements with serious questions of authority and freedom. At the end of the Fillmore Acid Test, for example, with the San Francisco police bearing down on the delirious party, Ken Babbs offered a crazed monologue over the Pranksters' amplifier system in which he used humor to bring out the paradoxes of civic belonging in America's controlled society. "The cops seem to be turning everything off," Babbs wryly noted as the police took the stage, "and they have asked everybody to be turned off." Continuing his frantic narration, Babbs responded to himself, "That's impossible. You know as well as I do that nobody is going to be turned off. We're not machines after all. We're human beings! He can try to turn me off, but all my switches have been short-circuited."[66] Babbs's maniacal rant was comical in part because of its multiple meanings. Getting "turned off" evoked the idea of being "turned on" to LSD, a popular expression of the time. Timothy Leary would famously call for Americans to "turn on, tune in, and drop out" later that year.[67] But more than the reference to drugs, Babbs's improvised rant also emphasized the uncanny subjectivity he and others felt they achieved through the Acid Test's media overstimulation. At the hyper-electrified event—charged not only by LSD, but also by the chaos of amplified sound, strobe lights, and more—participants became "human beings" and "not machines" because, paradoxically, their "switches have been short-circuited." It was as if by "short-circuiting" not only themselves but also the very logic of differentiating between humanness and machinery, the Acid Test attendees had achieved a new kind of cyborgian identity beyond the categories that the police officers on the scene could comprehend. They confronted the mechanisms of state power by pranking them through humorous paradox.[68]

The Pranksters irreverently reached down to the constitutive elements of public life to do so. Using humor to reimagine individual identity and group solidarity among the intensifications of LSD and electricity, they "short-circuited" established norms and fostered new circuits of meaning as they madly pursued what Babbs himself called "new configurations." Immediately following Babbs's speech at the Fillmore Auditorium, the civic dimensions of the Acid Test erupted in full and quite funny fashion. Responding to the presence of the police on stage, Grateful Dead guitarist Bob Weir led attendees in the singing of the "Star-Spangled Banner."[69] The appropriation of the national anthem was farcical, ironic, and not a little bratty, but it also pointed to the incorporation of the symbols of American citizenship at the Acid Tests.[70] For the Pranksters, patriotism was to be approached through a mix of irreverence and seriousness. At a Unitarian conference a few months after the Fillmore Acid Test, Kesey stepped on an American flag and then, at the urging of Carolyn Adams Garcia, led the audience in "America, the Beautiful."[71] Weir and company, while simply having a good time razzing the puzzled police at the Fillmore, redirected the national anthem toward a new country, perhaps the strange landless land of "inner space" about which Ken Babbs so furiously and comically babbled. The Grateful Dead guitarist also presaged Jimi Hendrix's more famous appropriation of the "Star-Spangled Banner" a few years later in the waning hours of the Woodstock Festival.[72] Once again, the Acid Tests set the stage for the later, larger civic meanings of rock music and the counterculture.

"A Nirvana Army": The Shadow of Vietnam at the Acid Tests, October 1966

The Pranksters were patriotic in many respects, but they were certainly not pro-war. While they avoided conventional politics and recommended that others simply ignore the escalating American military intervention in Vietnam, the group's interest in the symbols and meaning of American nationhood inevitably cast the shadow of the war across the Acid Tests. When Kesey tootled on a harmonica and told anti–Vietnam War protesters at a 1965 rally on the University of California–Berkeley campus to "look at the war, and turn your backs and say . . . Fuck it," he alienated many antiwar activists with his purposely silly antics, but he was also deadly serious.[73] He called upon Americans to reject the hierarchical authority of the government and its ability to wage war and asked them instead to assert their autonomy as democratic citizens. Turning away from the war was, in Kesey's judgment, a kind of confrontation.

Kesey's famous speech at the Vietnam Day Committee protests seemed to advocate a kind of quietism, but the way in which Kesey and the Pranksters arrived at the VDC event communicated something far different. Kesey's idea for a "prank" at the antiwar protest was to stage a kind of mock "military invasion," with the Pranksters dressed in uniforms, their bus covered in fake gun turrets, and the Hell's Angels leading them in formation to the antiwar rally. They would loudly display the absurdities of militarism. But ironically, even as they mocked the Armed Forces, Kesey and the Pranksters sometimes seemed to embrace a kind of militaristic organization in their own collective organization. Others may have referred to Kesey as the "non-leader" or the "non-navigator," but he dominated the group. "That's the hilarious thing about it," Carolyn Adams Garcia reflected many years later, "We had this system which was truly democratic a lot of the time, but occasionally veered into a dictatorship."[74] As concert promoter Chet Helms remarked, "There was a very military tone to Kesey's trips." Helms summed up their efforts as "a kind of militancy in collective action."[75]

At the "Whatever It Is" Festival on the weekend of September 30, 1966, better known as the San Francisco State College Acid Test, Kesey imagined the participants at the San Francisco State College Acid Test in precisely these tangled terms of militarized hierarchy and civic empowerment. Returned from Mexico, where he had fled after his arrest for marijuana possession in April 1966, Kesey broadcast commentary from a concealed room into the cafeteria where the event was held. On a recording of the event, Kesey pictured the event in military terms, calling the assembled dancers a "nirvana army." But ultimately he tilted toward a civic vision of democratic participation rather than a militarized one of control. The attendees at the Acid Test no longer "hupped to the olden tunes," Kesey remarked. But they did "know they're an army. . . . And we know it," Kesey continued, as if he and the other Pranksters were commanders of this military unit. Then he suddenly shifted direction from a top-down perspective to a more democratic orientation: "we don't know exactly what direction we're marching."[76] This was a funny kind of army: its soldiers were not following orders, and no one knew where they were headed, or why for that matter. Nonetheless, an army they were, part of the emerging counterculture.

In other locales, a more explicitly militarized vision of the counterculture took shape. In Detroit, the "White Panther" activist John Sinclair called on hippies to form a "guitar army." In New York, the "Motherfuckers," an anarchistic "street gang with analysis," urged hippies to practice a paradoxical "armed love."[77] But Kesey made a point to describe the "nirvana army" of the counterculture as possessing neither a clear chain of command, nor a precise end toward which they were "marching." Moreover, he did not want to be their general, even though many pushed him into the role of "chief." Perhaps with the Vietnam War in mind, Kesey refused to issue clear directives; instead, he invited participants at the San Francisco State College Acid Test to dance their own ways toward the future. "We don't know it all," he remarked to the assembled crowd, "but some of you sittin' out there do. And the ones that do mooooovvveee."[78] This call to participation, caught up in the tension between a command and an invitation, was indicative of the kind of civic intervention that Kesey and the Pranksters provoked at the Acid Tests. Theirs was a vision of festive participatory democracy—of *communitas* under the spell of LSD and intense electronic mediation.[79] It registered Cold War American militarism, but it did so to show how civic alternatives still possessed traces of the very hierarchical destructiveness they seemed to reject. By bringing war and peace into relationship through his narrations at the Whatever It Is Festival, Kesey heightened the importance of choices that audience members might make between the two. Rock music added to the dramatization of the contrast. As one attendee, artist Dan Wilson, recalled after listening to the Pranksters and the Grateful Dead perform at the San Francisco State College Acid Test, "The music they played was so full of fun—*life*! And I was worried already about the Army and the Vietnam War, and that was so dreary—it's death. And here was the Grateful Dead, just the opposite."[80]

Wilson found refuge and escape in the sounds of rock at the Whatever It Is Festival, but the shadows of the war keep creeping back. Seeking to undertake "great public put-ons" and inspire the "citizens" around them into a new social configuration, Kesey and the Pranksters became a kind of shock troop, a guerrilla unit spreading the civics of rock music, a paramilitary force for psychedelic change. In one sense, the novelist and his group imagined themselves as ex-citizens of the United States, an invading force from another, more psychedelic dimension. But at the same time, American citizenship remained an essential concern. At the final Acid Test held in San Francisco by the Pranksters, the October 1966 Acid Test Graduation, this tension erupted fully.[81]

"The Acid Test Graduation": From Pirate Democracy to Panopticon, Halloween 1966

On October 6, 1966, LSD was made illegal by California state law. Despite being a fugitive, Ken Kesey turned up at the Love Pageant Rally, a concert and party in the Golden Gate Park Panhandle to commemorate the criminalization of acid. Finally, on October 20, 1966, Kesey was arrested while driving on the Bayshore Freeway section of Highway 101 in San Francisco. His lawyers arranged for his release on bail on the agreement that he would warn young people about the dangers of LSD. To do so, Kesey and the Pranksters arranged to rent out the Winterland Ballroom on Halloween for what they called the Acid Test Graduation (figure 1.10).

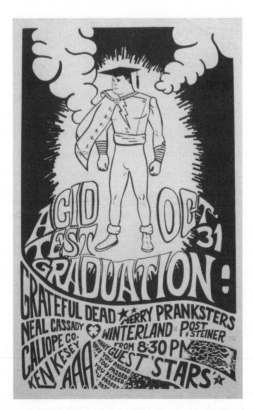

FIGURE 1.10. Acid Test Graduation Poster, October 31, 1966. Key-Z Productions/Vintage Concert Posters. Artist unknown.

In the two weeks leading up to the event, Kesey spoke of the need to go "beyond acid," but he also hinted in media interviews that this was not at all what he intended. To Chet Helms, it seemed as if this might be an example of Kesey's militaristic "tactical deceit and façade game": the Acid Test Graduation feigned reform and acquiescence but was to be one last epic prank.[82] Rumors circulated that the Pranksters planned to cover the walls of Winterland in soluble LSD so that the participants at the following night's Democratic Party rally for Governor Pat Brown would experience the drug's psychedelic effects. Continuing to play the elite paratrooper of the counterculture's growing "nirvana army," Kesey would appear in a superhero costume at the height of the graduation's festivities, proceed to climb a rope to the roof, and then ride away on a helicopter flown by Ken Babbs.[83] These unverified plans marked a direct attack on the political establishment, a daring Prankster effort to subvert the existing order and offer new openings for American civic life.

Whatever the actual vision for the event was, it ultimately demonstrated the great challenges of forging a more broadly available democratic civics. Kesey and the Pranksters exacerbated divisions within the growing counterculture in San Francisco. A number of participants were eager to follow Kesey and the Pranksters wherever they led, whether it be away from LSD toward a new kind of communal spirituality or further toward pranks that exploited the drug's possibilities for social transformation, now made all the more alluring by LSD's illegality. Others, however, worried that the novelist and his friends knew no boundaries and would hurt people in their quest for personal and shared breakthrough. Worse yet, for increasingly powerful members of the Bay Area counterculture, Kesey and the Pranksters might ruin the increasingly commercially viable rock music scene in the Bay Area. Promoter Bill Graham, who had secured the contract to hold the Acid Test Graduation at the Winterland Ballroom, pulled out of the event at the last minute. The Grateful Dead, already booked for another event on Halloween, also turned down an offer to participate. Firmly on their way to rock stardom, they were hesitant to turn back to serving as the Prankster house band.

As they learned about the cancellation of the Winterland contract, the Pranksters seemed to abandon their militarized appropriation of and assault on American identity. Tom Wolfe notes that the Pranksters had taken off their US flag costumes when they convened at a grungy warehouse in downtown San Francisco: "they're not Flag People any more, the costumes are off like the war is over." But what war? Wolfe implies that the Pranksters began to turn away from their infiltration of American civic identity. "One reason it didn't come off," Wolfe reported Kesey telling his compatriots about the Acid Graduation, "was that it was too big and too hot and they all got frightened." Kesey's former allies within the emerging San Francisco counterculture shied away from their mission to transform

FIGURE 1.11. Pranksters as the "flag people" at the Benefit for Mime Troupe—Appeal 1, November 6, 1965. Wolfgang's Vault. Photographer: Gene Anthony.

American society and turned instead to commodifying the radical social forces unleashed at the Acid Tests. In response to the compromising of their initial goals, Kesey also rejected the objective of fostering open, anarchistic encounters with the technoworld of the Cold War United States. In their place, Kesey called for contraction, focus, and a program.[84] The radical pluralism of the Acid Tests grew more constricted.

Kesey decided that the Pranksters should hold the Acid Test Graduation in the gritty warehouse where they were encamped. They could then control their message more effectively. "We're going to keep it down to those people who are going to make it as tight a scene as we can get," Kesey remarked. "They are the kind of people who, if they've got anything to say, it will spread out from them, and they can say it straight, and there will be no stopping it." At the event, the Pranksters once again donned their costumes and resumed their civic mission. "The Pranksters have turned into the Flag People again," Wolfe noticed in the days leading up to the Acid Test Graduation (figure 1.11). Kesey still believed his group could reach people far and wide with their vision of a transformed American civic life, but now they had to start smaller, in more manageable ways; instead of creating "mindless chaos," they would concentrate on "as tight a scene as we can get." There was a sense of growing limitation. As Wolfe evocatively wrote, with more press coverage from the mainstream and growing suspicion from within the counterculture, the Acid Test Graduation became not only "a hell of a circus" but also a "panopticon."[85]

Wolfe's use of the word "panopticon" is striking because it presages none other than Michel Foucault's adoption of the term in his 1975 book *Discipline and Punish*.[86] Foucault took the concept of the panopticon from Jeremy Bentham's utilitarian prison design of 1791, which had a tower with a screened window overlooking cells arranged in a semicircle. Bentham theorized that inmates would believe they were being watched even if no guard was actually present: no longer was the spectacle of punishment necessary; instead, people would police themselves, internalizing a paralyzing feeling of surveillance and control that came from the mere suspicion that they were being monitored. Foucault turned Bentham's architectural design into a symbol of how power operated after the Enlightenment. What seemed liberating in liberalism—the turn from horrific external displays of torture to the education of citizens in disciplining themselves—was in fact a cunning mode of social control.

Foucault's analysis of the modern liberal state as panopticon was not far from Kesey's position. Both were concerned with the problematic ways in which modern bureaucratic rationalism defined certain behaviors and people as nonnormative in order to exert social control. *One Flew Over the Cuckoo's Nest* suggested that contemporary American society resembled a mental hospital—"The Combine," as Kesey called it—whose medical staff had convinced its inhabitants they could be healed of their illnesses by remaining docile and controllable. Foucault's *History of Madness*, published one year before *Cuckoo's Nest*, articulated a similar critique.[87] While neither Foucault nor Kesey thought that madness was a good thing, both believed that people must daringly push themselves beyond existing regimes of order. Foucault argued for the pursuit of "limit-experiences," where people might find liberation through sensations felt at the edge of mortality itself. Kesey encouraged American citizens to journey toward what he called "Edge City," a place where the frontiers of human possibility might be discovered in a technologically enhanced outpost of individual and collective inquiry.[88]

It was Tom Wolfe, however, who used the word panopticon, not Ken Kesey. Wolfe grasped the wickedly oscillating dialectic of freedom and control that haunted the efforts by Kesey and the Pranksters to become the founding citizens of "Edge City." A few months earlier, the Acid Tests had been a wild and radically democratic, adventurous spacecraft journeying toward unknown "new configurations." By the Acid Test Graduation, they turned into creepy spaces of manipulation that echoed the very institutions of incarceration Kesey derided in *One Flew Over the Cuckoo's Nest*. But then again, at the center of the "the Dome fantasy," Kesey and the Pranksters had imagined a tower upon which they could orchestrate the events below without being seen. At the Acid Test Graduation, Kesey kneeled below a solitary spotlight, surrounded by a circle of Prankster disciplines. The specter of control emerged in all its bleakness. Looking down, he muttered inscrutably into a microphone, holding forth without so much as looking out over the crowd. The audience hung on his every word instead of speaking their own. This centralization of power was exactly what the Acid Tests had sought to dislodge. The ideal had been to discover a winning formula of individual freedom and collective communion that might transform society into a more radically democratic place. The Acid Tests had been about pursuing this goal by offering a stage—a theatrical commons—for strangers to contribute multiple voices to a shared experience that was dominated, perhaps even enriched, by technological manipulation and overstimulation. The events were efforts to transform centralized power into a proliferation of uncertain social interactions that might constitute a new, more organic order—a pirate democracy. But they concluded with Kesey and the Pranksters in a panoptic circle, processing new arrivals into a counterculture that neither Kesey, nor his friends had any interest in ruling or even governing.

To his credit, Kesey ultimately abandoned the fantasy of panoptic control at the Acid Tests. As described by Tom Wolfe, the Acid Test Graduation did not become a panopticon; instead, it took on the qualities of a very different civic ritual when Kesey and the Pranksters staged a school graduation ceremony. Humor once again emerged as a way of navigating between control and freedom, panopticon and pirate democracy. Participants arrived, danced, took LSD, and moved among the cameras of the local news media. Neal Cassady took the stage to hand out diplomas as the perfectly named band The Anonymous Artists of America performed a psychedelic-rock version of *Pomp and Circumstance*.[89] Kesey and the Pranksters graduated and they encouraged participants in the counterculture to do the same. If they were not going to be able to keep their pirate democracy afloat, they were not going to build what amounted to a prison house of routinized, disciplined psychedelic utopianism. Their choice to do so meant that Kesey and the Pranksters were no longer at the center of the developing Bay Area rock scene, but their antics haunted it nonetheless. As the Winterland Ballroom and other psychedelic dance halls became palaces of a commodified counterculture, the Pranksters' fixation on citizenship still rattled in the eaves.

"Prophecy of a Declaration of Independence": The Aftermath of the Acid Tests

In the aftermath of the Acid Test Graduation, rock music did not lose the quality of civic questioning that had been so central to the Acid Tests. Even as rock brought the most radical dimensions of the counterculture closer to the emerging logic of hip capitalism, the music also sustained a widening gyre of investigation into many facets of citizenship. Social questions about communal connection, economic conflicts over the nature of work, and political debates about who, exactly, counted as a citizen in the new and amorphous counterculture of the late 1960s continued to reverberate in the memories of the technologically manipulated echo chambers of the Acid Tests. By magnifying rather than rejecting the electronic mass-mediation of Cold War America in order to probe what their implications were for social interaction, the Acid Tests left a lasting legacy for rock music. As Carolyn Adams Garcia remarked in 2007, "It's really a mistake to qualify all this as sex, drugs, and rock and roll. Because that was not what was going on. What was going on was experimental communications of a whole, new kind using these new technological tools."[90]

Even as concert promoters began to commodify the "experimental communications" of the Acid Tests into more standardized entertainment, even as corporate record labels scoured the San Francisco music scene for bands, and even as the mainstream media turned the city's nascent counterculture into a distorted Summer of Love spectacle, rock music would continue to pull participants toward deep inquiries into civic life and citizenship. One of the central goals of the famous Human Be-In/Gathering of the Tribes held in Golden Gate Park in January of 1967 was precisely this. Organized by a group of Haight-Ashbury merchants and activists, the Be-In generated publicity far beyond what the Acid Tests did. Some 20,000 to 30,000 participants attended an afternoon of rock music, speeches, and festive engagement. They did so to have fun, but also in a collective effort to reimagine the boundaries between the personal and the civic by occupying public space together. To gather in the park and engage in ecstatic communion—all to the sound of rock—was to bring isolated experiences of cultural ferment into common view in order to try to glimpse new vistas of social organization.

As if speaking directly to matters of American citizenship, the Human Be-In was accompanied by the publication of a leaflet, a "Prophecy of a Declaration of Independence." The manifesto had originally been written by Allen Cohen and Michael Bowen for the Love Pageant Rally in October 1966, the gathering in the Gold Gate Park Panhandle to commerorate the illegalization of LSD. As its title suggested, the "Prophecy of a Declaration of Independence" drew upon the foundational document of the United States to call for individual, collective, and even planetary liberation. "We hold these experiences to be self-evident," Cohen and Bowen wrote, "that all is equal, that the creation endows us with certain inalienable rights, that among these are: the freedom of the body, the pursuit of joy, and the expansion of consciousness, and that to secure these rights, we the citizens of the earth declare our love and compassion for all conflicting hate-carrying men and women of the world."[91] In classic Prankster fashion, the "Prophecy" expressed hopes and desires playfully, but also sought to make a serious intervention in the way people experienced and conceptualized a sense of individual identity and collective belonging in the name of freedom and justice for each and for all.

The Be-In generated much of the same friction within the San Francisco Bay Area counterculture that the Acid Test Graduation had.[92] A number of participants, such as the members of the radical theater troupe the Diggers, saw the event as a commercialization and co-optation of the counterculture.[93] Others saw it as an announcement of the coming utopia. While it was less radical in spirit than the Acid Tests, the Be-In did preserve the civic quest at the heart of Kesey and the Pranksters's mission. Borrowing from a romanticized vision of Native Americans, the Be-In promoters pictured participants in the counterculture as "tribes" attending a "Pow-Wow." The term "tribes" was a problematic appropriation of indigenous culture, but it also represented the countercultural effort to re-envision the relationship between individuals, small groups, and a mass movement in contemporary America. For one Saturday afternoon, the Polo Fields in Golden Gate Park became a kind of civic forum, a public space for considering citizenship as both an everyday practice and a dramatic alteration of normality.

The morning after the Acid Test Graduation, the Pranksters abandoned their American flag costumes in a neat trash pile outside the dank warehouse in the San Francisco Tenderloin where the event took place. But at the Human Be-In/Gathering of the Tribes, the flagship sound of the Acid Tests—psychedelic rock—retained its civic qualities and only grew more popular and commercially viable.[94] At the event, none other but the Grateful Dead, now recording for Warner Brothers Records, performed. Joining the marketing of the San Francisco Sound, they also remained committed to the larger civic vision of the Human Be-In. On a film of the event, a boy triumphantly held aloft a tie-dyed marijuana-leaf banner from the front of the stage as the band began to play. A gigantic maypole stretched up toward the sky, tethering audience members to its streamers. It was as if the pirate ship that had set sail at the Acid Tests now traveled onward across Golden Gate Park, banners waving and mast boldly cutting through the wind off the ocean.[95]

This vessel of intensified democratic interaction remained, as Foucault claimed of boats in general, a "reserve of the imagination . . . the heterotopia par excellence." But it was also, like the boats of empire before it, a "great instrument of economic development."[96] As it ploughed through waves of expanding participation during the remainder of the 1960s, the San Francisco counterculture rocked between these two possibilities—civic transformation through the ecstatic imagination and the realization that this pursuit itself might be a strange new kind of imprisonment in systems of control, especially the consumerist one of hip capitalism. In the coming years, the question would become not only "Can You Pass the Acid Test?" but also what to do once one graduated.

2

WE ARE KMPX FM ROCK, COMPLETE WITH

ALL THE CONTRADICTIONS

ON A HANDBILL that made its way around San Francisco in the spring of 1967, a radio tower beamed its signal in all directions, as if it were perched atop the Merry Pranksters' "Dome fantasy" at the Acid Tests.[1] Below the tower, the words "Folk" and "Rock" warped around a photograph of a bearded man in a beret. His head was turned back over his shoulder as if beckoning the viewer to follow. The man's name, the handbill announced, was Larry Miller (figure 2.1). He broadcast on KMPX, 106.9 FM, from midnight to six in the morning.[2] One of the first "underground rock" radio shows, Miller's program fast became a crucial sonic space for the San Francisco counterculture. By the end of 1967, KMPX had expanded its entire schedule to a similar format. One year later, it became the site of a struggle over the stakes of citizenship in the growing counterculture of the Bay Area.

As a radio station broadcasting across the Bay Area, KMPX played a bigger role in forming a sort of countercultural commonwealth than the Acid Tests. Ken Kesey and the Merry Pranksters' events were much mythologized, but only lasted for a brief time. They also only took place in specific locations for a limited audience. By contrast, KMPX was on the air day and night and could be accessed wherever its signal reached. Keen observers such as the Berkeley-based writer and political activist Michael Rossman, who had been much impressed with the Acid Test experience at the Trips Festival, noticed the significance of KMPX to the counterculture. "How long ago," he asked in a 1968 article, "was it when someone turned us on to that odd little station where we could turn for a few hours . . . and

FIGURE 2.1. Freeform community on the radio: Larry Miller KMPX-FM Flier. Larry Miller Personal Collection.

hear some quiet unknown friend playing all those records we'd heard of but hadn't heard?" Answering his own question, Rossman decided, "We knew it had to come, that now a Good Rock Station was appropriate to our dawning community and would appear."[3] KMPX had gained a large audience by the time Rossman's article was published, and it seemed to confirm that the counterculture could create its own communications medium for fostering a sense of commonality and shared civic participation.

KMPX was not only part of the countercultural society that Rossman and others thought they were beginning to develop; it was also a pioneering example of hip capitalism. Its disc jockeys and its sales staff of marijuana dealers and rock hipsters forged a profitable niche market out of the head shops, clothing stores, and rock concert halls that increasingly dotted the Bay Area. The "Good Rock Station" of the counterculture's "dawning community" was a crucial cog in this new commercial apparatus. It also linked San Francisco to the corporate music business by playing and advertising releases from the mainstream labels. Most of all, it perfected a new hip capitalist style through which revolt against mass consumerism could be packaged and sold as a new market segment within consumerism itself. On KMPX, gone was the fast, shrill announcing and the rigid, repetitive song sequencing of AM pop radio; in their place was a slower, mellower approach that embedded psychedelic rock in a wide-ranging, disc jockey–controlled programming format. KMPX was a key example of what became known as "free-form" or "progressive" rock radio. The latest songs from local San Francisco bands, British Invasion groups, and others would flow from radio speakers in what Larry Miller called a "spontanuity" (spontaneous continuity) of sounds that included folk, avant-garde classical music, soul, and traditional music from around the world, as well as comedy sketches, long monologues, and, eventually, news reports with a countercultural slant.[4]

Yet as with Ken Kesey and the Merry Pranksters, the KMPX staff members were not completely co-opted by their refusal to abandon core American values: their insistence on creating a new kind of commercial radio within the existing system rather than opposing capitalism in toto did not mean that they simply acquiesced to the dominant forces of postwar American consumer life. Their place at the cutting edge of hip capitalism meant that they also faced many of the central contradictions of postindustrial labor and its linkages to questions of citizenship. Indeed, the very same week that Rossman described the pleasures of listening to "some quiet unknown friend" on KMPX, the staff of the station noisily walked off the job. Outside their studio, the supposedly mellow, hip capitalist DJs staged a riotous picket line complete with light show and loud rock bands.[5] The disc jockeys, engineers, salesmen, and even the program directorwent on strike not only to demand better wages and working conditions, but also to acquire greater artistic freedom and creative control. Their turn to a classic tactic of industrial labor in pursuit of goals that went beyond the typical demands of post–World War II industrial unions reminds us that countercultural rock music was not only part of American leisure culture; hippies also confronted the meaning of work.

The staff of KMPX struggled with questions of labor and value and went on strike as a result of these questions. They did so in the face of dramatic transformations in the industrial order as it increasingly gave way to a "symbolic" economy driven by services, images, and intangible goods.[6] As culture workers—or, better put, counterculture workers—in the emerging framework of hip capitalism, the KMPX staff members inherited the labor activism found in the entertainment industries of the 1930s and '40s. But whereas these earlier entertainment industry workers helped to foster what historian Michael Denning calls a "laboring of American culture," saturating the artifacts of popular culture with working-class issues and styles during an era of radical industrial unionism, hippies of the 1960s found themselves enmeshed in what is best described as a "leisuring of American culture," an intensification after World War II of the focus on the pleasures of consumption and reception as the key spaces for realizing the American dream.[7] The KMPX DJs tried to make sense of what it meant to work within this new, leisure-dominated context.

KMPX was so indicative of the shift to hip capitalism that sociologist Susan Krieger used the phrase as the title of her 1979 study of the station.[8] The KMPX DJs and staff were certainly proponents of a cultural style that found a place within consumerism as a new market segment. But their strike also offers a story of how rock music inspired radical responses to the very system it helped to spread. From within hip capitalism, the KMPX strike presents us with a lost labor history of hippies. As KMPX became a cultural product in which conventional work had been exchanged for a fantastical world of hedonism and pleasure, the DJs and staff at the station also found themselves fretting about their roles as laboring citizens in the republic of rock. By eventually going on strike, they confounded the binary of labor and leisure, production and consumption, industriousness and play. Their walkout reveals a countercultural engagement with work that has often been ignored.[9] The strikers at KMPX raised pressing questions and generated robust debates about what it meant to labor in the new fields and factories of hip capitalism.

The KPMX walkout presaged later labor clashes in more conventional settings, such as the Lordstown strike of the early 1970s, which found workers in an automobile plant frustrated not only with their wages and benefits, but also with a lack of meaningful work and control over their labor.[10] The KMPX strike, however, was more than just a precursor to conflicts in the industrial sector. It is important not only because it marks one of the sources of countercultural values that later surfaced among the working class, but also because it is an example of the appearance of a working-class consciousness within the counterculture itself.[11] The KMPX strike suggests that during the late 1960s in San Francisco, working-class and middle-class formations collided to the sounds of rock. Out of this collision, the vision of a countercultural civic life at the intersection of the working and middle classes briefly appeared. As such, the KMPX episode proposes the possibility that New Left analysts at the time were not entirely wrong to conceptualize the formation of a New Working Class that brought sectors of the professional-managerial class closer to the world of industrial wage laborers.[12] But this was no easy realignment of class structure in America; it took place within dramatic shifts in capitalist managerial theory itself. In what became popularly known as "Theory Y," corporations discovered that they could accept and even accentuate countercultural ideals of community, individuality, flexibility, and creativity. Without ceding power or control, without fully granting workers full autonomy over their labor, corporations need not cling to the hierarchical rigidity traditionally deployed in industrial capitalism.[13]

The music business was at the forefront of these changes.[14] As the staff of a station at the vanguard of the popular music business, the KMPXers found themselves in a confusing situation. They were at once helping to forge the new corporate style and also found themselves deeply dissatisfied with their co-optation. Frustrated with the owners of KMPX, the KMPX DJs and staff asked probing political and philosophical questions about their situation. Who, they wondered, produced value when it came to the intangible and symbolic products of rock music entertainment? How should workers in this milieu be compensated if their style of labor was, in a sense, the product they sold? Were they themselves increasingly the means of production, the mechanism by which the raw goods of rock music were processed into products of musical enjoyment? What constituted authentic work in this new, playful environment of hedonistic pleasure and fun? If the staff was itself the station's central means of production, should they not ultimately own their own labor power and the means to make use of it? To try to answer these disorienting questions of the postindustrial condition, the KMPX DJs and staff embraced the unlikely form of the industrial union.[15]

Perhaps they did so because it seemed as if everyone was going on strike in the Bay Area during 1968. The walkout at KMPX took place during what journalist and historian Dick Meister calls San Francisco's "year of the strike." Daily newspaper guilds, school teachers, retail clerks, truck drivers, machinists, garment workers, hospital employees, telephone company unions, longshoremen, and other workers in the Bay Area all went on strike during 1968.[16] Radical political protests were in full flight that year too. Not only did the peace movement continue to grow in size in opposition to the Vietnam War, but also the San Francisco State College student strike began that year, as did the first confrontations over People's Park in Berkeley, an undeveloped piece of property owned by the university that radical activists wished to turn into a public commons.[17] These conflicts all brought issues of labor and work into contact with larger civic issues of political power and public space.

Within the counterculture itself, KMPX DJs joined a turn to cooperatives, collectives, and communes.[18] They were not even the only hippie workers to go on strike. One year after the KMPX episode, a similar walkout took place at one of the most radical underground newspapers, *The Berkeley Barb*, resulting in the formation of the Red Mountain Tribe collective, which began to publish a competing publication, *The Berkeley Tribe*.[19] The KMPX strike was merely the most vivid example of how issues of work and labor became linked to countercultural questions of citizenship and civic life. When they started out, the DJs and staff at the station thought they were merely playing rock records for fun, spreading the sound of joyous countercultural community over the airwaves, but this merging of leisure and labor, of enterprise and play, eventually got them worked up enough about their work to go on strike.

"KMPX Appeared, and We Put the Records Up for a While to Give It a Hearing": February 1967–March 1968

By the spring of 1968, when the KMPXers walked out, the station was one of the crucial institutions of the burgeoning Bay Area counterculture. As one of the first stations at which disc jockeys created free-form and underground rock programming, it was also an important part of FM radio's rise during the 1960s. KMPX's place in the development of FM and its new formats helps to explain why the strike at the station would come to matter so much to larger questions of civics and citizenship in the Bay Area. For countercultural participants, FM was appealing because it provided a kind of surreptitious entryway into the mass-communications apparatus of the 1960s; in this way, FM shared qualities with the Acid Tests of 1965 and 1966. Disc jockeys and listeners at a station such as KMPX were oriented toward a civic engagement with dilemmas of individual and collective being, but they did not entirely turn away from what Tom Wolfe called the "incredible postwar American electro-pastel surge . . . of freedom and mobility"; rather, they used the aesthetic atmosphere provided by rock music to probe the democratic possibilities of this new setting.[20] Though KMPX proved far less extreme and avant-garde than the Acid Tests, it remained very much a technological space. What made it appealing to participants in the counterculture was that it was part of the contemporary "technological wonderworld," as Tom Wolfe put it, while simultaneously being marginal and alternative—a space of difference and distinction within the larger consumer marketplace.

Invented in the 1920s and '30s, frequency modulation (the technique that gave FM its name) had lost out to the dominant AM (amplitude modulation) format; moreover, by the 1960s, both AM and FM were increasingly overshadowed by television. Nonetheless, audiophiles considered FM's aural fidelity to be superior; its stereophonic capacities were at once more "fantastic" and more "real." Because of its perceived high audio quality, whatever interest FM had attracted prior to the mid-1960s tended to be oriented toward fine arts programming, precisely the kind of aesthetic category to which rock musicians and their fans were increasingly aspiring by the late 1960s. FM also offered affordable accessibility, particularly after a 1965 Federal Communication Commission ruling that required all FM channels to broadcast at least 50 percent original programming.[21] In San Francisco, KMPX was a perfect incarnation of FM's appeal: broadcasting at 106.9 megahertz, the station was literally at the far edge of a peripheral technology, yet it also still circulated through the mass communications system of the region.[22]

KMPX began in 1959 as jazz station KPUP, created by Bay Area businessman Franklin Mieuli, but in 1960, its call letters became KHIP in an effort to market its "hip" musical programming more effectively. In 1962, Mieuli sold the station to Leon Crosby, who had previously owned the station KHYD in Hayward, California. A believer in the coming popularity of FM, Crosby changed the call letters to KMPX, signifying the "multiplex" stereo technology the station used. But by 1967, his middle-of-the-road pop format gave way, under financial duress, to foreign language programs.[23] In February of 1967, Miller, a young disc jockey from Detroit, joined KMPX's staff and hosted the overnight slot, the infamous "graveyard shift," from midnight until six AM. Miller abandoned the frenetic advertising pitches and repetitive, tightly controlled playlists of typical AM pop radio for a more expansive range of sounds brought together in surprising sequences. He had already begun to experiment with this more adventurous format as the host of *Promenade*, a folk music show on WDTM-FM in Detroit.[24] Influenced by public events in the nascent Bay Area counterculture, such as the Acid Tests and the Human Be-In/Gathering of the Tribes, Miller began to shape his own version of the free-form progressive rock style.

At the core of this new approach was the latest rock music, itself increasingly dedicated to experimentalism and syncretism during the era of the Beatles' *Sgt. Pepper's Lonely Hearts Club Band* and similar long-playing albums. Miller's radio format echoed the efforts at hybridity and diversity within the rock genre itself. Free-form progressive rock radio strived to integrate a multiplicity of sounds. It celebrated difference but also pursued connection. The disc jockey became what Michael Rossman called an "intelligent friend" who provided an unexpected stream of sonic synchronicities and uncanny coincidences through the free-form progressive rock format. Larry Miller explained his approach: "I would pull a dozen albums at the start of a show, and then build from there. Sometimes, word games, sometimes 'sound-alike' sets. As a musician, I could hear when songs were in the same key and would flow together."[25] Free-form emphasized not only the art of the music itself, but also the art of listening to the music. "Our listening habits have changed completely," Rossman excitedly wrote in his March 1968 article. The station had "a happy sense of experiment." And it treated the core sounds of rock as "an art form, like a living art form, as it is, with its changing reaches now rich enough to be worth researching and displaying."[26]

One can hear this new approach on one of the only known recordings of Larry Miller's show, from October 11, 1967. A sitar recording flows into "Los Pescadores" by Buffy Sainte-Marie and back again into the sitar recording, which burbles along under Miller's talk set of commentary. Miller discusses his recent interview with the Grateful Dead and his admiration of Jerry Garcia's vibrato vocal skills, which Miller laughingly comments sound like an electronic effect but in fact are similar to Sainte-Marie's singing style. Then, since the Grateful Dead focus will be "enough devotion" for one night, Miller goes on to reject a listener request for Eric Burdon and the Animals, citing his own distaste for Burdon's vocal style. There is no effort to sell listeners on a particular hit, as on AM radio; rather, Miller invites listeners into an atmosphere of musical inquiry, debate, and discussion. "I'm not gonna lie to you and put you on," Miller explains at one point, "because you've had enough of that listening to the radio."[27]

Miller's style modeled a mode of listening to rock music. It was for both intense pleasure and taking seriously; it was for enjoyment but also provided the aural context for thinking about questions of taste, artistic validity, "phoniness" (which Miller accused Burdon of), and authenticity. As a kind of navigator of the listening experience, Miller was not entirely unlike Ken Kesey at the Acid Tests: through communications systems, the disc jockey became a programmer of experience, an equivalent to Kesey atop his tower of electronic equipment, twisting knobs, rapping into microphones, and scribbling messages across the auditoriums of countercultural assembly. A DJ such as Miller did not seek to control people, but rather to manipulate the technological setting in which others could then explore their own interior selves and the shared feelings of togetherness. But if the Acid Tests were events of highly charged electronic intensity, Larry Miller's show, broadcast in the dead of night, was an amorphous, flickering, transitory mass-mediated commons. It was not confrontational, but rather persistently present. In this way, it challenged distinctions between public and private space. Miller's show, and KMPX in general, provided the soundtrack for what Nick Bromell calls "living to music."[28] While Bromell focuses on his memories of listening directly to long-playing phonograph records, radio may have been even more crucial to the role of music in shaping the lives of countercultural participants. DJs such as Larry Miller not only played music from these LPs, but also organized songs into thought-provoking sequences surrounded by commentary. On the air itself, they produced what French sociologist Bruno Latour calls an "atmosphere of democracy," encouraging a sense of involvement and engagement that linked the individual listener to a larger, if somewhat abstract, collective.[29] As Michael Rossman wrote, "KMPX appeared, and we put the records up for a while to give it a hearing."[30]

KMPX became a key medium both for getting together and trying to get it together. As the media historian Susan Douglas argues, when audiences tuned into the station, "they entered a brand-new auditory, political, and cultural world. And they went there specifically to indulge a newly heightened, much more concentrated mode of listening, fidelity listening." While Douglas goes on, quite rightfully, to emphasize the gendered dimensions of FM rock radio, the ways in which its emphasis on good taste and sonic fidelity contributed to the "remasculinization of rock music" by transforming the supposedly passive act of listening to pop music into a requirement that rock involve the active display of technical mastery and know-how, this was not the only significant aspect of KMPX. Before free-form progressive rock radio grew rigid and brittle, predictable and normative, it was a more amorphous and wide-open entity: one which enlivened issues of work and labor as well as race, ethnicity, and even gender, within the emerging context of late 1960s hip capitalism.[31]

Larry Miller pioneered the free-form progressive rock radio format that would become a signature style at KMPX, but he was no businessman. The prominent AM rock 'n' roll disc jockey Tom "Big Daddy" Donahue (figure 2.2) was, however. In addition to his popular show on KYA, San Francisco's main AM pop music station, Donahue owned Autumn Records, the preeminent Bay Area pop-rock record label, and had promoted the Beatles' Cow Palace concert in 1964. By 1967, Donahue had tired of the limited AM format. "Top-40 radio, as we have known it for the last ten years, is dead," he wrote in a *Rolling Stone* article that year, "and its rotting corpse is stinking up the airways." Observing the blooming Bay Area rock music scene and counterculture and perhaps tuning in Larry Miller's show one night, Donahue also seemed to sense that a new kind of market was developing.

Donahue approached KMPX owner Leon Crosby in March of 1967. He took over as program director and evening disc jockey in early April. Soon thereafter, he moved the entire station from ethnic programming to a rock-centered format with plenty of experimental opportunities for disc jockeys to work in the

FIGURE 2.2. Managing hip capitalism: KMPX station manager Tom Donahue, 1967. Photographer: Baron Wolman.

free-form style.[32] "Suddenly that polyglot ethnic/religious station on the edge of the dial is gone," Michael Rossman recalled, "its mosaic of private messages displaced segment by segment. And KMPX, the Voice of Community, has the largest FM audience in the Bay Area."[33]As Rossman's comments reveal, there was a deep irony to the changes that Donahue undertook at KMPX: meant to diversify the tightly scripted and narrowly conceived format of AM pop radio, the new programming actually decreased the station's prior diversity of ethnic sounds; meant to be available to people of all backgrounds, the station in the end served what rock critic Sandy Darlington evocatively described as a "mostly white alternative"[34]; meant to be the universal "Voice of Community" for the counterculture, KMPX excluded the sonic presence of other marginalized communities.[35] Suffused with a yearning for collective liberation, the strike that unfolded at KMPX in 1968 carried with it these deeply flawed differentials of power and control.

A strike was probably the last thing on the minds of KMPXers during 1967. As San Francisco's Summer of Love became a national event, KMPX continued to grow in popularity. By the end of the year, the station had not only become the

FIGURE 2.3. A vision of countercultural association: KMPX staff photograph, 1968.
Photographer: Baron Wolman.

preeminent countercultural station in the country; under Tom Donahue's leadership, KMPX's gross income grew from $5,000 to $25,000 per month.[36] Donahue
began an equally popular and profitable sister station on KPPC-FM in the Los
Angeles area, which was also owned by Leon Crosby and his associate Lew Avery.
Even successful Top-40 stations such as KYA in San Francisco started to imitate
aspects of the free-form approach. A *Billboard* article described KMPX as "the talk
of the radio industry."[37] Stations in other markets began adopting what many
called the "progressive rock" format.

Much of KMPX's appeal had to do with the ways in which the staff projected a
sense of individual creativity enlivened by a spirit of kinship and community. The
station's studio in the warehouse district of downtown San Francisco literally
became a communal hangout for participants in the counterculture.[38] Symbolically,
the station's staff members presented themselves as a group that brought together
individual flair with communal belonging. A photograph of the staff from early
1968 that circulated in articles and advertisements showed roughly two-dozen men
and women assembled in a kind of yearbook or team group shot (figure 2.3). Various

members of the group sport colorful costumes in this advertorial representation of the kind of shared belonging and individual flair that KMPX sought to project over the airwaves. Tom Donahue's wife Raechel sits on Donahue's lap at the center of the group, wearing a large bowler hat. A man in the front row has large work gloves splayed across his lap, as if he just came in from baling hay. A woman in a kind of fur trapper's outfit leans on a vintage shotgun. The actor Howard Hesseman stands on the left side of the group, wearing a large, pink scarf for a tie. Later a star of *WKRP in Cincinnati*, the 1970s and '80s television sitcom inspired, partly, by the story of KMPX, he was a member of The Committee, a theater troupe that created a number of skits and advertisements for the station. To emphasize the communal, bucolic spirit of KMPX, two dogs sleep peacefully at the front of the group. The photograph presents the staff as a kind of guild or civic association and expresses a sense of pride in working for the country's preeminent hippie station.[39]

The staff at this point included no people of color (it later would), but its mix of men and women hinted at the ways in which questions of women's liberation lurked, in vexed but important ways, within the counterculture.[40] While most of the disc jockeys on the station were men, Donahue often hired female engineers because he preferred their looks. He continued to employ Katie Johnson, who had been at KMPX before he arrived. He also hired Sue Henderson (figure 2.4) aka Suzy Sweet Smile or sometimes Suzie Creamcheese (later Sue Kagan), Dusty Street,

FIGURE 2.4. Sue "Suzie Creamcheese" Henderson (now Kagan) at the control board, KMPX, 1967 or 1968. Sue Kagan Personal Collection. Photographer: Jerry Burchard.

Raechel Donahue, and his daughter Buzzy, among others. These women became known as the "bird engineers" or "chick engineers." They often had to endure the sexism of the counterculture, which could be even more extreme than the dominant culture. Though they were key members of the KMPX staff, the female engineers were sometimes falsely labeled "groupies" only interested in sexual relations with rock stars.[41] However, these women were also able, within the sexist constraints of the hippie counterculture and the radio industry, to acquire technological jobs previously available only to men. As Dusty Street commented on the air, "I just want to say if it weren't for KMPX, I would never have become an engineer because chicks just can't make it in this business."[42] The female engineers had their pulse on the new music that was growing popular in the growing Bay Area counterculture and often served as the actual programmers of music for a number of the older male disc jockeys.[43] Eventually, many were able to acquire their own shows. They even organized their own woman's program on Sunday afternoons. "The Chicks on Sunday" show became a sonic space for the growing second-wave feminist movement in the Bay Area.[44]

The notion of KMPX as a democratic space was crucial to both the staff and the station's listeners. The station was able to provide a "community forum," as Rossman put it, that incorporated discussion of political issues from civil rights and the Vietnam War to drug legalization and prison reform to various local issues within the flow of music, especially rock. This could give the music a political hue even when the disc jockeys refrained from explicit editorializing: "It seemed more effective to play a set of antiwar songs than to do an antiwar rant," Larry Miller recalled.[45] But KMPX was no KPFA, radical pacifist Lewis Hill's innovative listener-supported station based in Berkeley. It was a civic medium underwritten by commercial sponsorship.[46] Donahue sales staff, which combined established radio admen with a few of the Haight-Ashbury's preeminent marijuana dealers, reflected the linkages between a countercultural civic life and the forces of commerce. The staff signed up new businesses that were associated with the counterculture: record stores, concert halls, clothing boutiques, outdoor gear sellers, and other small entrepreneurs within the Bay Area hippie world. KMPX was also able to attract bigger corporations eager to reach young consumers.

While KMPX loosely aligned itself with the radical politics of the New Left, Black Power, and antiwar movements (for instance, the station refused to take enlistment advertisements from the US military), the KMPX staffers were never anticapitalist. Even as KMPX "began to serve . . . as a community Voice" for "an emerging community trying to find and shape its identity," as Michael Rossman wrote, the station also played a crucial role in developing the emerging niche market of the hippie lifestyle.[47] In fact, it may have been precisely because KMPX sought to meet larger civic desires and needs that it was so successful commercially. What the station sold was its noncommercial sensibility: its civic ethos *was* its bill of goods. But so too, as KMPX became the essential sonic medium for the Bay Area counterculture, it also became a place where the tensions between the pleasures of consumption and the energies of civic life collided. Wishing to pursue a more creative and autonomous mode of unalienated labor within the new economy of hip capitalism, the KMPX staff careened between, on the one hand, the countercultural dream of authentic community and enlivened individualism and, on the other, the realities of shaping a new, and extremely profitable, commercial service at the cutting edge of American capitalism's postindustrial turn. Trying to keep it small, but attracted to making it big, KMPX's staff went on strike in the spring of 1968. Their actions opened up radical possibilities for countercultural workers, but also implicated them deeply in the workings of hip capitalism.

"The Ability to Have Creative Growth Here Has Been So Limited": The Strike Begins, March 1968

By spring of 1968, despite all of its success commercially and culturally, conditions had dramatically worsened for the KMPX staff. They had not received wage increases despite the growing advertising revenues at the station. Even the checks for their existing pay repeatedly bounced. Working conditions at the station suffered as well. Owner Leon Crosby refused to install new equipment needed for the kinds of creative innovation that the staff wanted to implement. Worse yet, Crosby increasingly sought to censor the disc jockeys, fearing fines by the FCC.[48] He was a hip capitalist, but as an independent operator, he would only go so far toward allowing the countercultural freedom that KMPX staffers desired.

Crosby's concerns were not entirely unfounded: the KMPX studio was a center of drug experimentation and other indiscretions. Michael Rossman remembered hearing a disc jockey make a "public service" announcement that a marijuana delivery to a dealer had been cancelled, followed by another shocked voice crying out, "But you can't say *that* on the air!" So too, the station reveled in its nonprofessionalism. "KPMX's trademark," according to Rossman, was "the programmer or someone fucking up, blowing something matter-of-factly upfront on the air, backed by a chorus of giggles from the bird engineers."[49] What concerned Crosby was precisely what appealed to Rossman and other participants in the counterculture: the sense of a shared public life that explored new territories over the airwaves and, in the process, broke away from constraining, inauthentic regulations and expectations. Failing to recognize that KMPX was forging a new niche-market of hip consumers, and fearing that the wild behavior of disc jockeys on the air would generate fines by the FCC, Crosby continued to constrain precisely the qualities that made KMPX successful in the minds of the staff—and to the ears of listeners. "Happenings in the station on the air became less frequent," Michael Rossman noted. So too, "the Public Forum programming cut out," and "people weren't allowed to talk so freely on the air any more." Tensions between Donahue and Larry Miller, which would return during the strike itself, led to Miller's removal. "That kid Larry [Miller] with his eccentric sometimes lovely programs was fired," Rossman wrote.[50] Then, during the week of March 11, Crosby and station manager Ron Hunt fired Donahue (or Donahue quit after an argument; accounts differ). "Management," according to Rossman, "had nudged out the people who made KMPX into a creative center."[51]

On Saturday, March 16, 1968, at a meeting of the KMPXers at staff member Bob Prescott's apartment, Donahue suggested that the station's workers go on strike to seek the demands he, as their manager, had been unable to secure. The fact that the manager of the station proposed the strike suggests that this was not to be a dispute that broke down along traditional lines of management and worker. Part of Donahue's motivation for the strike may have been selfish—he possibly had his eye on seizing ownership of the station outright from Crosby—but the fact that he turned to his staff rather than to outside investors and partners indicates the strange alliances forged by countercultural labor politics.[52] The KMPX strike did not spring entirely from Tom Donahue's mind, however; the Bay Area counterculture already had many links to the local labor movement. A number of staff members at KMPX had been involved in the Family Dog collective, which promoted the first psychedelic-rock concerts in the Bay Area by renting Longshoreman's Hall from the International Longshoreman and Warehouse Union (ILWU). Led by the famous radical labor leader Harry Bridges, the ILWU had a long tradition of bohemianism and open-mindedness, making it quite different from more conservative unions. As elsewhere in the United States after the AFL and CIO merged in 1955, there were tensions between older American Federation of Labor (AFL) trade unions and newer industrial ones affiliated with the Congress of Industrial Organizations (CIO). Many Bay Area unions in fact tilted leftward. There was a strong Communist Party presence. Even more obscure sects on the left such as Maoists or the much-romanticized International Workers of the World (IWW) had strong outposts in San Francisco.

Radical unions such as the ILWU supported the growing civil rights movement, fought McCarthyism and red-baiting, and, unlike most of the trade union movement in the United States, were opposed to the war in Vietnam.[53] In the 1960s, they vigorously recruited student activists, often sponsoring gatherings after political protests. According to concert promoter Chet Helms, these unions were partially responsible for the large party circuit that helped to give birth to the local countercultural scene in the Bay Area. For students at the University of California, Berkeley or at San Francisco State College, a day on the picket line would lead to a night of festivities.[54] They were at the very least tolerant of young hippies. Unlike the stereotype of "hard-hat" working-class conservatives that emerged after the famous (and carefully planned) confrontation between construction workers and antiwar protesters in downtown Manhattan in 1970, the members of unions such as the ILWU were generally unthreatened by the long hair, colorful clothes, and looser attitudes toward sex, drugs, and public interaction found among counter-culturalists.[55] When San Francisco police arrested Ken Kesey just prior to the Trips Festival in 1966, for instance, members of the ILWU approached the organizers to express their support for the event, which was to take place at the Longshoreman's Hall. It turned out a number of Hell's Angels were members of the ILWU, and they had developed strong, if controversial, ties to Kesey and the Merry Pranksters.[56]

Among participants in the emerging rock music industry itself, many had direct connections to labor. Grateful Dead guitarist Jerry Garcia was raised by his grandmother, Tillie Clifford, who had helped to found the laundry workers' union in San Francisco. When his band grew successful, Garcia, like many other rock musicians, joined the local Musicians Union.[57] Prior to the influx of hippies to the Haight-Ashbury, the neighborhood had been a home to many labor activists in the 1940s.[58] At KMPX itself, the engineer Dusty Street's father, Emerson Street, was a local labor mediator for the AFL-CIO.[59] Tom Donahue's father had also been a labor journalist and a member of the National Wage Stabilization Board in Washington, D.C. The station manager himself had been active himself in liberal politics on the East Coast. In San Francisco, the counterculture certainly diverged from the conventional labor movement in many ways, but it also maintained ties, shared sympathies, and kept friendly relations.[60] But despite the connections to the labor movement, members of the KMPX staff were quite ambivalent about their strike. Was it the best way to secure what they wanted from Crosby? Could they maintain a strike and encourage others to honor it? Was their walkout even legal, since they were not formally affiliated with a trade union? They were not sure, but despite hesitations, they unanimously decided to form their own trade union: the AAFIFMWW, the Amalgamated American Federation of International FM Workers of the World, North Beach Local No. 1. The FM stood for both Frequency Modulation and Free Men. In solidarity with KMPX's staff, the disc jockeys at sister station KPPC in Pasadena also went on strike, organizing their own branch of the AAFIFMWW.

Forming their own union allowed these countercultural radio workers to maintain control over their strike. It also seemed to revitalize the communal ideals of

the station and the counterculture as a whole.[61] The AAFIFMWW was an inten-
tionally ridiculous name. In one sense the staff was playing at being a union. Their
humor was meant to distinguish them from the conventional labor movement.
This was something different, creative, home-crafted, and absurd. This union was
going to be fun. At the same time, the name referred to the Industrial Workers of
the World (IWW), which suggested an awareness that the strikers joined an older
labor tradition with bohemian inflections.[62] Symbolizing their mix of old and new,
the staff went so far as to create union cards, the quintessential symbol of union
membership. Like the Merry Pranksters, however, the KMPX staff used the cards
playfully, expressing their countercultural flair by decorating the cards with whim-
sical, psychedelic, Age of Aquarius drawings (figure 2.5).[63]

Befitting these hybrid union cards, the strike combined traditional labor grievances with a newfound focus on the art of radio. Speaking on the air in the minutes before the strike began at 3 AM on Monday morning, March 23, 1968, Steven
Hirsh—better known as Edward Bear—told listeners: "The reason we're going out
on strike is not because there is so much black plague running around but that it
seems kind of apparent to all of us that the ability to have creative growth here has
been so limited to the point that the foreseeable future is grim." For Bear, the
strike was about the future of "creative growth" at the station. As fellow DJ Bob
McClay told listeners, "We want to keep KMPX as it has been, and this is the only
way we see that it's going to be possible to do this, because otherwise in a matter
of a short space of time, KMPX will not be the same radio station that you have
come to like to listen to."[64] For these disc jockeys, the KMPX strike certainly related
to quintessential labor issues, such as frustrations about bounced checks and a
lack of salary increases as the station's profits increased. But it also had to do with
what those poor working conditions caused: an environment increasingly lacking
in opportunities for artistic autonomy and the feelings of freedom and community that this creative control fostered. As Jeff Jassen, covering the strike for the
Berkeley Barb, wrote, "Thirty employees of KMPX Radio walked off their jobs in
protest of station policy and poor working conditions," but "the main issue, according to striking employees, is that of 'artistic freedom.'"[65]

In its first weeks, the strike unleashed tremendous support and excitement in
the Bay Area counterculture. As one disc jockey put it just before the staff walked
out, "Okay. This is now radio free San Francisco. Everybody is free to do as they
please."[66] Outside the studio at 50 Green Street, everybody seemed to be doing just
that. The first night of the picket line turned into a veritable rock festival. Rock
bands from the Grateful Dead to the Ace of Cups performed in support of the
strikers. A light show took place in the San Francisco fog.[67] After the initial
evening's turnout, rock bands and promoters continued to hold successful benefit

FIGURES 2.5 "Hippies of the world unite!": The Amalgamated American Federation of International FM Workers of the World union card of Sue "Suzie Creamcheese" Henderson (now Kagan). Sue Kagan personal collection. Artist unknown.

concerts. They asked their record companies to stop KMPX from broadcasting their recordings. Local businesses agreed to honor the strike save for two: United Airlines and the Carousel Ballroom. The staff even received a letter of support from the Rolling Stones in London: "We want you to know that we support your fight against the bureaucracy. We believe in KMPX and KPPC and will keep the faith over here. Love, Mick, Keith, Brian, Charlie, Bill."[68] The strikers would maintain their picket for the duration of the two-month strike, enriching the old-fashioned labor tactic with their own psychedelic stamp of colorful, psychedelic placards, costumes, semi-naked volunteers, and other countercultural touches.[69]

Certain listeners thought that the union presaged things to come. Michael Rossman dreamed that the KMPX strike of March 1968 would lead to a free, community-supported rock station liberated from the constraints of capitalism. "We need some sort of *free* station," he wrote, "a station responsive and responsible to its community in everything from taste to politics." The listening audience would be able to shape the station's content: "I'm convinced that it's important to let everyone who actively listens to the station have some control over it . . . that's part of what free means," Rossman explained. The station would ideally be open and loose in its institutional structure: "Any design for a community *free* rock station should try to provide for that vital flexibility, perhaps even at the risk of not looking like much of a design at all." Such a station could "change the political climate of the Bay Area," Rossman believed, through "Media Organizing" rather than older modes of traditional politics.[70]

Meanwhile, support also emerged in more traditional sectors of the labor movement. The leadership of the local National Association of Broadcast Engineers and Technicians (NABET) chapter, based at the Pacifica station KPFA, voted its support for the strike. The directors of KPFA let the KMPX disc jockeys broadcast on their airwaves during the strike. The American Federation of Television and Radio Artists (AFTRA) sent a letter of support. The ILWU, the National Maritime Union, and the Teamsters and Machinists all offered to incorporate the KMPX staff into their organizations. Progressive political organizations also backed the walkout. The newly formed Peace and Freedom Party endorsed the "Rock Power" strikers at their 1968 convention.[71] But other unions chose to stay out of the conflict. Their reasons speak to the ways in which the KMPX strike diverged from older models and norms of labor activism. One of the predominant radio unions, the International Brotherhood of Electrical Workers (IBEW), an older AFL organization that was quite conservative, refused to support the walk-out, fearing that hippie styles would either offend its members or, worse, that the KMPX action might actually inspire its own rank and file to pursue wildcat strikes. Ed Bird, the business manager of IBEW Local 202, was hesitant to ask his own union or the influential San Francisco Labor Council, an association of established labor organizations, to go on record in support of a strike that featured topless picketers. Perhaps even more troublingly, Bird was deeply suspicious of a group of workers who had staged a walkout without formalizing a contract with management beforehand through an existing trade union.[72]

The KMPX staffers argued that basic material interests such as wages and working conditions went hand in hand with their new countercultural demands for artistic freedom and creative control. They urged San Franciscans to boycott any companies that were, according to one flier, "assisting radio station KMPX in denying us artistic freedom and decent levels of income."[73] Salaries were not unimportant to the striking staff, however much they espoused antimaterialist hippie values on the surface. The staffers certainly wanted their fair share for creating a dramatic increase in revenue. Among their eleven demands, printed and distributed on March 18, 1968 (figure 2.6), they insisted that, "The employees shall share in the increase in profits of the radio station."[74] But higher wages were only one factor in the walkout. The strikers also demanded that Crosby reinstate station manager Donahue, engineer Paul Boucher, and sales manager Milan Melvin and

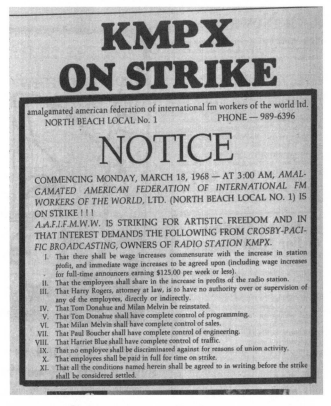

FIGURE 2.6. KMPX strike demands. *San Francisco Express-Times*, March 21, 1968.

that these three men be given "complete control" of their respective departments. Unlike more traditional labor disputes, in the KMPX strike management was not an arm of ownership, but rather of workers. For the staff, Donahue, Boucher, and Melvin had been instrumental in creating the station's sense of community and creativity—its spirit of "artistic freedom"; thus, they were core participants in the strike. Compared to the typical industrial-labor confrontation, in this particular "hip capitalist" conflict, the solidarities between management and workers grew stronger at KMPX, while a clearer demarcation emerged between ownership and management.[75]

As the strike developed, the KMPX staff also began to develop a new perspective on the value of their countercultural labor: the means of production, they argued, were not the technologies that allowed the station to broadcast, but rather the people who gave KMPX its sound and style. Their stations were less "a collection of chairs, desks, tubes, and turntables" than "the living idea of a loving group of people," they wrote in a flier circulated at a press conference on March 20, 1968, and distributed on the picket lines. Leon Crosby, the owner, had been content to employ "long-haired, beaded, or barefoot employees" when the station had been "on the brink of collapse." But now that the labor of these hippies had led to "the success these stations enjoy today," suddenly "management has seen fit to remove and replace some of the people who created the concept of KMPX." Crosby's actions, the strikers claimed, imperiled both the economic growth of the station and its countercultural growth. The "continuing harassment" was driven by "attempts to prevent the artistic and personal freedom that have in themselves made these stations a unique and beautiful experiment."[76] To the strikers, economic expansion and countercultural fulfillment worked in tandem. In the new dynamic of hip capitalism, the serious business of profit and the zany pleasures of countercultural joy were linked. But without the working conditions of "artist and personal freedom" and without the disc jockeys, engineers, sales staff, and managers, both the economic value and the countercultural energy generated by KMPX ceased to exist.

In his influential *San Francisco Chronicle* column, music critic Ralph Gleason developed a kind of hippie labor theory of value to describe KMPX. He favorably called the walkout the "first hippie strike." Gleason considered it a symbol of the shift away from the coldly rational, technocratic style of industrial America to a postindustrial order in which creativity, worker control, absurdist irreverence, and new concepts of normality might blossom. This was a strike, after all, whose workers submitted a proposed contract to owner Leon Crosby that was printed on paisley paper and included the proposition that workers should be paid overtime when the sun or moon was in eclipse.[77] At the same time, the strikers themselves understood that by going on strike they had joined a tradition of more radical and bohemian-friendly labor activism in the Bay Area. Their strike was at once old and new. Demonstrating his awareness of San Francisco's radical labor past, Tom Donahue told *Rolling Stone* magazine, "I do like the idea of having Harry Bridges [of the ILWU] negotiate with Crosby." The notion that Bridges, one of the most colorful labor leaders in the land, might join the hippie strikers was playfully appealing. In the end, however, Donahue expressed a belief that the strike at KMPX demonstrated a break with the past. "We appreciate the offers, but we'd just be walking into another establishment structure."[78] The idea of moving beyond the establishment, whether of business or labor, was crucial to the strikers and generated much debate about the walkout within the counterculture.

"The KMPX Strike Is Not a Simple Case of Workers Fighting Management": The Complexities of Hippie Labor, Spring 1968

By late March 1968, the unlikely strike at KMPX seemed to be succeeding, but Leon Crosby still refused to settle with the staff. The strikers organized a successful benefit concert, the Superball, held at the Winterland Ballroom, on April 3, to commemorate the first year anniversary of the station's switch to its new rock-based format. Larry Miller, who had returned to San Francisco by invitation from Crosby to replace Donahue as station manager, appeared at the Superball, which eased anxieties that he would cross the picket line. Nonetheless, difficulties were developing, in part because of the unconventional nature of the strike, which merged traditional labor demands with a new countercultural ethos.[79] The combination of the older labor form and newer sensibility meant that though negotiations took place between the staff and management, little common ground could be established even though the strikers remained eager to reestablish themselves at the station and stay on good terms with station manager Ron Hunt and even with Leon Crosby. Disc jockey Bob McClay told *Berkley Barb* reporter Jeff Jassen that the initial negotiations had been "very unfruitful, partially due to the fact that as announcers, we aren't really too experienced at collective bargaining procedures." Despite the lack of progress, even Ron Hunt attended the Superball concert. "It's really a family," disc jockey Bob Postle believed. "The only one we really have to get through to is Lee Crosby."[80]

Along with his station manager Ron Hunt, Crosby reopened KMPX using replacement disc jockeys from a local country station and student DJs recruited from the College of San Mateo and elsewhere. The strikers managed to cut down on this scabbing by appealing directly to the students, but KMPX was back on the air. Crosby himself took to the airwaves to fill holes in the broadcast schedule. As the strike dragged on in April and May, the positive mood of the strikers began to wane; the strike grew more complex, its pressures more great, and its purpose more murky. Strategically, with the station back on the air using new disc jockeys, even novice ones, there was the possibility that the original staff were not as valuable to KMPX's identity as they had calculated.[81] In one of the most confusing episodes of the strike, Larry Miller initially supported the strikers at the Superball, but then crossed the picket line. At first, Miller rejected an offer from Leon Crosby to replace Donahue as program director. At the time of the Superball, he felt that he "couldn't accept the offer unless the strike is resolved" because he "couldn't go against public opinion." But a few days later, on April 10, he issued a statement explaining his decision to join KMPX despite the continuing labor protest. "Last week," Miller wrote, "I publicly lent my support to the KMPX strikers and stood with them on the stage at Winterland [for the Superball] because I accepted the validity of their cause." But now, Miller decided, "I have investigated the situation more thoroughly and been forced to re-evaluate my position." Miller, already bitter at Donahue for firing him, believed that the staff at KMPX had been led astray by the former station manager, writing, "The strikers apparently have been misled by irresponsible and self-interested leadership."[82]

Miller took the position that he was not, in fact, crossing a picket line since he was taking over a management position. "Before the strike began," he wrote, "the former program director quit and that position has since stood vacant." To Miller, "the program directorship, being an executive position, is therefore not an issue in this strike." Wanting to judge the strike by traditional labor criteria, Miller did not view accepting the program director job as a rejection of the strike. It was merely a way to preserve what KMPX "has come to stand for." The creative radio format of free-form progressive rock was what mattered most to Miller, along with the idea that he could return to the airwaves in San Francisco. As for the notion that replacing Donahue was scabbing, Miller wrote, "to make it an issue would be clearly a case of placing personalities above the issues" of wages, working conditions, and artistic freedom at KMPX.[83] His stint proved brief: in June, Miller resigned on the air and returned to Detroit in dismay at the entire conflict. Trying to salvage KMPX's new style and approach until the strike could be resolved, he wound up infuriating the strikers and the underground-press writers in the Bay Area, who labeled him with all the anti-union invective they could muster as countercultural-ists. Miller, according to a resignation announcement he read over the air, was called "'scab,' 'strikebreaker,' 'fink,' and some other words which are not even air-able because of, after all, there are some words you just can't say on the radio." The disc jockey felt he had tried "to look at all sides of the situation and evaluate them," but "I have never in my life been confronted with a bunch of thoroughly vicious, thoroughly negative group of people as I am up against in trying to deal with the strikers."[84]

Miller could not grasp why the staff would not take the long view to "prevent this kind of radio from coming to an end forever." He remained committed to the same countercultural radio that the strikers themselves had walked out to preserve; he merely disagreed about tactics. The strikers wanted to stop the station from functioning to preserve KMPX's free-form progressive format, while Miller decided it made more sense to keep the spirit of his original show present on the KMPX airwaves during the walkout so that the station would retain its identity. Miller grounded his opposition to the strike on precisely the same grounds as the strikers. Of course there were also material factors: Miller admitted that he wanted his own chance to get back on the air in the Bay Area in the prestigious position of program director at KMPX, just as the strikers wanted better wages and working conditions. But more importantly, he saw his job just as they did: to preserve the ethos of the free-form progressive approach they had pioneered in 1967, with its commitment to countercultural values of creative freedom and personal expression.[85]

Trying to make sense of Miller's actions, rock critic Sandy Darlington admitted that the strike had its complexities, but he remained positive about the ways in which it was giving birth to a new sense of collective spirit at the station. For him, the strike was far bigger than just a feud between Tom Donahue and Larry Miller. To Darlington, Donahue's own unusual role as a member of management leading the strike was of little concern once the labor action began. "As soon as they struck, Tom Donahue started becoming an important member of the group rather than the leader." This was because, for Darlington, the strikers were "struggling together for an ideal. Their seriousness and equality increase daily. No one man is running the show."[86] Darlington was attracted to the democratic transformations of the strike, which seemed the result of the station's free-form programming ethos itself. He thought the KMPX strike spread a spirit of community far beyond the AAFIFMWW itself, just as its radio signal had when the staff was on the air. "Because of the benefits and the need for help and the general situation of being on the street and visible," he wrote, "all sorts of force lines are reaching from the striking group out into the community and back." Here was the sense of civic engagement that defined the Bay Area counterculture for Darlington and many other participants. The rock critic noticed that the strike had pushed the Bay Area's countercultural community toward imagining new economic institutions born of its growing community ethos. The interaction between the KMPX strikers and the larger Bay Area counterculture "has been strengthened further," Darlington argued, "since various bands, dance hall owners and other advertisers began joining together with the strikers toward the possible purchase of a radio station." Like Michael Rossman, Darlington believed that the strike might lead to new economic institutions such as a hippie-owned radio station. These would operate within the existing system of consumer capitalism, but they would also begin to move beyond its inequities and shortcomings.[87]

Others in the Bay Area counterculture were far more suspicious of the KMPX strike. In the letters section of the April 26 issue of the *Berkeley Barb*, Ernie Barry critiqued the lack of clear boundaries between workers and management in the strike. "As a Wobbly and a fighter for years for workers' rights I can assure you the KMPX strike is not a simple case of workers fighting management," Barry argued. He pointed out that "[m]uch of the strike revolved around the dismissal by management of one of their bosses and his subsequent forceful harassing of the underpaid workers to go out on strike to get him reinstated and seek better wages for themselves and him." Seeking to maintain the demarcations of traditional labor disputes, Barry claimed that "[t]he radical and hip community owes support to the striking workers but not to the striking management."[88]

Barry dismissed the idea that Tom Donahue was some kind of hero in the labor dispute, viewing him as just as bad as other managers in the radio industry. He was less certain that management truly was on the side of labor, even in the new postindustrial, countercultural economy. Barry noted that even though Donahue hired women to engineer shows on KMPX, it was more important for these so-called "bird engineers" to be attractive than talented. Donahue also practiced nepotism, Barry complained, hiring his own family when there might have been more qualified disc jockeys and engineers. And he fired other DJs, such as the original KMPX rock disc jockey Larry Miller, simply because he did not like them personally. For Barry, the KMPX strike was deeply problematic precisely for the ways in which it blurred the boundaries between labor and management. Donahue, from his perspective, was not allied with the staff at KMPX but rather their manipulator.[89]

"Wild and Weird Discussion . . . This Is a Labor Negotiation!": The Corporate Turn and Continued Labor Activism at KSAN

The denouement of the KMPX strike proved Barry correct to some degree. Tom Donahue, who had not participated directly in the strike but had pursued alternative arrangements for the staff throughout the spring of 1968, intervened to move the entire staff to a new radio station: KSAN. This new station was neither collectively owned, nor dedicated to a revolution beyond capitalism. It belonged to Metromedia, a national corporation. The KMPX strikers noted their dismay as they entered the bland, corporate offices of the station on their first day back at work, but believed they had no other choice.[90] At KSAN, they found themselves inhabiting the contradictory roles of hip capitalists even more intensely: they celebrated countercultural liberation from consumer capitalism in order to develop a niche market for a large corporation that flourished within that very economic system. In this position, they ironically collapsed the distance between the only two companies that had refused to honor the 1968 strike at KMPX, United Airlines and the Carousel Ballroom. United Airlines had continued to advertise on KMPX despite fliers that called for it "not to support a scab-operated company. . . ."[91] That a major corporation ignored the strike comes as no surprise, but the other business that did not suspend its advertisements was the Carousel Ballroom, perhaps the most radical of the famous San Francisco ballrooms. Co-operated by the Jefferson Airplane, Grateful Dead, and Quicksilver Messenger Service, the Carousel was a wild environment for experimentation by musicians and audiences alike. Its "anything goes" policy seems to have lent itself to a laissez-faire, libertarian position on labor disputes. Even as bands such as the Dead performed benefits for the KMPX strikers, the ballroom the band helped to run continued to advertise on the station's airwaves.

That both a mainstream corporation and a libertarian rock venue were the holdouts to the KMPX strike and boycott pointed to the dynamic of hip capitalism. Businesses of both types could accommodate laissez-faire attitudes. The counterculture's anarchic rebelliousness ultimately did not threaten mainstream corporate capitalism. Precisely by advocating "artistic and creative freedom" for employees, companies such as United Airlines or Metromedia could sell all that the Carousel Ballroom symbolized and the KMPX strikers desired. They need not fundamentally alter the very system that gave rise to the alienations and exploitations that bothered so many participants in the counterculture.[92] Yet, the legacies of the KMPX strike lingered with the move to KSAN. In going to work for the corporate-owned station, the staff became members of a conventional union. The ex-KMPX staff negotiated contracts with Metromedia in 1969 and again in 1971 through the International Brotherhood of Electrical Workers (IBEW) Local 202, the very union that had not supported their strike in 1968. Even here, the AAFIF-MWW's combination of old-line trade unionism and countercultural ideas persisted. Negotiations with their corporate bosses remained marked by the attitudes, ideas, and approaches of the hippie counterculture. "Wild and weird discussion of economics—philosophy, politics, broadcasting—this is a labor negotiation!" wrote

Metromedia's director of personnel during the 1972 meetings.[93] Even though the KSAN staff ultimately went along with the more conventional union's decisions, sacrificing control over the station for improved wages and benefits, and even as they found themselves caught within the tricky logic of hip capitalism, the countercultural energies of the 1968 strike would continue. Partially absorbed into corporate capitalism, they also buzzed in unruly directions, one of which was toward the Wild West Festival of 1969.

3

THE WILD WEST FESTIVAL IS YOU AND ME

IN A COOPERATIVE ASSOCIATION

ON AUGUST 11, 1969, Joseph L. Alioto, the mayor of San Francisco, issued an unusual proclamation (figure 3.1):

> WHEREAS San Francisco is in the midst of a cultural renaissance centering around the vitality and freedom of expression of music and art, I, Joseph L. Alioto, Mayor of the City and County of San Francisco, do hereby proclaim the week of August 18–24, 1969, as Wild West week in the City and County of San Francisco.

With the city's seal affixed to it, the proclamation announced that "a group of leaders from San Francisco's music and artistic community" known as the San Francisco Music Council, had "established 'The Wild West,' a festival of music and art dedicated to the involvement of the entire community." It explained that "the days of August 22, 23, and 24, 1969, will mark the occasion of this celebration of the arts in our City by free performances, exhibitions, and events centered within our City's own historic monument to our people known as Golden Gate Park."

Wild West was to include prominent musicians and bands—Janis Joplin, the Grateful Dead, Jefferson Airplane, the Youngbloods, and Sly and the Family Stone—but it was more than just a rock festival. It also welcomed attendance by all citizens, not just rock fans, and would include theater, dance, classical music, folk music, puppet shows, hayrides, circus acts, and more. As Mayor Alioto idealistically

OFFICE OF THE MAYOR
SAN FRANCISCO

JOSEPH L. ALIOTO

Proclamation

WHEREAS,   San Francisco is in the midst of a cultural renaissance
centering around the vitality and freedom of expression
of music and art; and

WHEREAS,   The San Francisco Music Council, a group of leaders from
San Francisco's music and artistic community, have established "THE WILD WEST", a festival of music and art dedicated
to the involvement of the entire community; and

WHEREAS,   The Wild West Festival is You and Me in a cooperative
association which recognizes that through the gift of music
and art, people of all ages and backgrounds can share a beauty
of communication; and

WHEREAS,   The days of August 22, 23, 24, 1969, will mark the occasion
of this celebration of the arts in our City by free performances, exhibitions and events centered within our City's own
historic monument to our people known as Golden Gate Park;

NOW, THEREFORE, I, Joseph L. Alioto, Mayor of the City and County of
San Francisco, do hereby proclaim the week of August 18-24,
1969, as Wild West Week in the City and County of San Francisco.

IN WITNESS WHEREOF I have here-
unto set my hand and caused
the seal of the City and County
of San Francisco to be affixed
this eleventh day of August,
nineteen hundred and sixty-nine.

Joseph L. Alioto
Mayor

FIGURE 3.1. Mayor Joseph L. Alioto's Declaration of Wild West Week in San Francisco, August 18–24, 1969. Berkeley Folk Music Festival Collection, Northwestern University Library Special Collections.

proclaimed, "The Wild West Festival is You and Me in a cooperative association." It "recognizes that through the gift of music and art, people of all ages and backgrounds can share a beauty of communication."[1]

Flush with economic success, the rock promoters, band managers, radio disc jockeys, record executives, magazine publishers, and journalists behind the Wild West Festival had formed the San Francisco Music Council. They imagined the festival as both a testament to rock's galvanizing force in the Bay Area and an impetus to new modes of artistic and civic engagement.[2] That the organizers had been able to obtain the mayor's support was no small matter in a municipality whose government remained deeply unsympathetic, if not outright hostile, to the counterculture. The official support that the San Francisco Music Council garnered was remarkably different from the negative response to a rock festival scheduled in upstate New York for the very same month of August 1969: Woodstock.[3] It was in fact Wild West, not Woodstock, that many at the time anticipated would become the definitive countercultural gathering of the era. The San Francisco festival so overshadowed Woodstock that one underground newspaper simply referred to the New York concert as "Wild East."[4] Yet, decades later, Woodstock is intensely commemorated, while Wild West is virtually forgotten. Why is this so?

It is because Wild West never took place. The members of the San Francisco Music Council had to cancel "the landmark event" at the last moment. They did so not under pressure from Alioto's administration or other outside forces. Instead, countercultural participants themselves forced the cancellation by organizing a strike and boycott. Even though the San Francisco Music Council sought to do exactly what protesters demanded—imagine and implement a more robustly civic, public, communal, and ultimately noncommercial purpose for rock music—protesters objected to the festival's admission-only rock concerts in Kezar Stadium (figure 3.2), which they felt went against the spirit of a "cooperative" gathering. To counterculturalists opposed to Wild West, the festival seemed intent on generating profits and acclaim for the rock industry leaders rather than benefiting the larger countercultural milieu in which rock music was so beloved.

The original vision for Wild West and the resulting protests against it carried forward countercultural engagements that had first surfaced at the Acid Tests and the KMPX strike: how were economic issues of production and consumption, ownership and labor value, linked to political questions of shared public life, individual freedom, and collective justice? Even though the festival never happened, what Bay Area writer Joan Holden labeled Wild West's "non-event" became a crucial, if underappreciated, moment in the history of the Bay Area counterculture and its engagement with citizenship.[5] Wild West also sheds light on the narrative of rock music festivals and the counterculture as a whole. This story typically starts in San Francisco with the Human Be-In/Gathering of the Tribes in Golden Gate Park in January of 1967, followed by the announcement of rock's arrival as a powerful new art form at the Monterey Pop Festival of 1967. It concludes with a contrast between Woodstock, a supposedly utopian event, and the counterculture's violent fall from grace during a Rolling Stones concert at Altamont, an event at which the Hell's Angels murdered an African-American audience member while the Rolling Stones

FIGURE 3.2. The Wild West Festival in Kezar Stadium, August 8–10, 1969, cancelled at the last moment. Berkeley Folk Music Festival Collection, Northwestern University Library Special Collections.

performed.[6] But Wild West offers a different narrative. In place of a Garden of Eden narrative, it demonstrates how rock music fostered an arena of spirited debate and disagreement about the limits of democratic citizenship that the counterculture could offer within the framework of hip capitalism.

"San Francisco Is the Place": Origins of the Wild West Festival, Early 1969

Wild West emerged within a worldwide trend of large-scale rock festivals during the late 1960s. These large outdoor gatherings drew upon a tradition of folk music and jazz festivals. They became places for young people to experience the feeling of joining something larger and more communal than their individual everyday lives. They were also, usually, for-profit events.[7] By 1969, many in the counterculture began to question the commercial dimensions of what felt like civic gatherings. If festivals centered on bringing people out of isolation and into shared interaction with each other, why was participation limited by the cost of a ticket? In San Francisco, these debates about festivals intersected with local conflicts in the Bay Area over public institutions and public spaces. The People's Park controversy raged in Berkeley throughout 1969. So too did the San Francisco State College's student strikes.[8] The Wild West brought these international, national, and local debates to a head.

Accentuating the sense of crisis, the Haight-Ashbury neighborhood—the symbolic town commons of the counterculture in San Francisco and around the world—was in serious decline by 1969. "There was a graveyard air about the boarded-up store fronts, the newspaper-shrouded display windows," *Village Voice* journalist Grover Lewis wrote after a visit that spring.[9] Of course, the Haight-Ashbury was never the utopian place that the mainstream media portrayed in the heyday of 1967's Summer of Love.[10] With an influx of people searching for new ways of living and the lack of a fully adequate response by either the city government or even the local "hip" merchants to the need for housing, safety, and other resources, the Haight had always been a darker and more desperate place than admirers were willing to admit. But by 1969 the bloom of flower children, peace, love, and harmony was fully faded.

The growing economic clout of the rock music business, the increased distance between rock stars and their fans, and the decline of the original scene that gave rise to rock's successes troubled participants in the Bay Area counterculture, especially those who were themselves finding economic success. Had the sense of civic renewal promised by rock and the counterculture in its early years been lost? Had they failed in their very success? On Wednesday, March 12, 1969, a group of band managers, promoters, disc jockeys, impresarios, and musicians gathered at the Jefferson Airplane's "mansion" on the edge of Golden Gate Park for an unlikely rock music event: breakfast. They had been summoned by Ron Polte, manager of, among other bands, the Quicksilver Messenger Service. Participants at the meeting included KSAN-FM disc jockey Tom Donahue, promoter Bill Graham, record label executive David Rubinson, LSD-maker Owsley Stanley, Berkeley Folk Festival organizer Barry Olivier, *San Francisco Chronicle* journalist Ralph Gleason, *Rolling Stone* publisher Jann Wenner, and band managers such as Bill Thompson of the Jefferson Airplane and Rock Scully of the Grateful Dead.

Polte offered a plan for how to recover the initial positive energies of the Bay Area counterculture and even, perhaps, propel those energies forward.[11] Inspired by an idea that seems to have first been proposed by Frank Werber, manager of the Kingston Trio and owner of the Trident Restaurant in Sausalito, Polte imagined a festival that would expand from rock music to all art forms, welcome all ages, and even, possibly, reshape the economics of the entertainment industry through a new cooperative structure.[12] The goal of the festival was to create what Tom Donahue called "a tidal wave" of creativity and artistic expression that would transform the Bay Area and spread to other places around the world.[13] With rock music at its core, Wild West would offer a new vision of communal life, of political and personal engagement in society and of economic interaction that moved toward more collective modes of production and consumption.

The festival that Polte and fellow organizers started to imagine would return to the original excitement they had felt when they first attended rock concerts, Acid Tests, and Be-Ins, but it would add greater institutional stability. At a follow-up meeting a few days later, KSAN disc jockey Bob McClay argued that the "Haight-Ashbury failure" was just "a tactical retreat" and "now [a] major advance is coming."[14] Barry Olivier, who would soon be appointed director of the not-yet-named festival, summarized the "concept" that his coconspirators envisioned. Olivier wrote, "San Francisco is the place. Where people are showing the world how to get along together, make music, live with peace and hope. How natural it seems to all of us to celebrate San Francisco and its music with a Festival. The Festival can be both a party and a spiritual statement."[15] As Olivier's summation of the concept for the Wild West Festival suggests, the organizers imagined it as more than just a music festival. They believed that rock was the clarion call of the San Francisco counterculture and that the counterculture, in turn, remained the harbinger of new forms of social, economic, and political organization. These new modes of living were to be participatory. They often involved art-making. They were driven, most of all, by the urge to "get together," as the hit song written by Dino Valenti, a member of the Quicksilver Messenger Service, put it. At one early meeting, the Wild West planners even considered calling the festival "Get Together." This hope for communion—and all the problems it raised—would return repeatedly.[16]

Even promoter Bill Graham, typically a hard-nosed pragmatist focused exclusively on the business of rock concert promotion, thought that Wild West could be more than just a good time. A "party's great," he explained, "but it should be taken one step further."[17] The effort to get to something more meaningful extended to the labor involved in the event. Bert Kanegson, who worked with the Grateful Dead, argued, "What most of people in [the] scene . . . want to do is *work together*."[18] The dream, Tom Donahue would explain at a press conference a few months later, was to "create a celebration of music that the artists would participate in creating." This would spread from rock to other art forms in terms of financial stability and a renewed sense of community.[19] "The idea," Donahue continued, was "that maybe you could have a 'performing arts center' in this community where musicians could practice, where light show people could do their thing, where the film people could show their films, where all aspects of art would be represented."[20] A performing arts center of this nature, the organizers hoped, could be a radically democratic institution. The festival itself could become a model for the American entertainment industry. Wild West would move beyond the separation of production and consumption, them and us, to create a space for imagining a new collective future. All could conceivably join in and "work together" to create and enjoy the event. Never one for understatement when it came to the power of art, critic Ralph Gleason told the attendees at early planning meetings that it was "important to realize that what we do here, it has the potential to change the world." Ron Polte thought that the rock impresarios at least had the "power to make a statement here" by showing how "ethics are being put back into the [entertainment] industry."[21]

These rock impresarios, not the most ethical of businessmen by a long shot, did seem, by and large, to believe that a communal, artist-driven music industry was more principled. Befitting the logic of hip capitalism, they also must have imagined that this in no way would make it less profitable. But they were most intrigued by the ways in which Wild West might offer a new kind of politics: "A lot of people felt that we are in the midst of not only a social revolution [but also] an artistic revolution," Tom Donahue contended. "The artists are going to be the people who are going to be leaders." Rock music was the best example of this, particularly as it symbiotically influenced and was influenced by young people. To Donahue, "a lot of attitudes that exist among young people are being recreated by artists." At the same time, the "attitudes" themselves "were created by the words of people like Bob Dylan and the people like Jefferson Airplane [and] the Grateful Dead, who exist on the local scene."[22] Rock music, for Donahue, was an example of the power of art to alter society as a whole. It was for young rock fans most immediately, but it was not only for them. He and the other organizers envisioned an event that went far beyond rock music audiences—or even just countercultural participants—alone. They could "*not* exclude those people who we've been excluding for 3 years. We have to *invite* them somehow," Ron Polte urged. The goal was to "close the generation gap."[23] Ralph Gleason thought the organizers should "involve all movie makers, jazz, poets, etc." They should "start with core," then "other stuff" would "attach itself to it."[24] If they could create an event that drew upon the "kids' energy and attitude," Polte believed, it would also "do more to turn those people on."[25]

Wild West would position San Francisco as a city on a hill, casting its light-show beacon of a model society out to the world. Thinking about the rest of the United

States, Bert Kanegson expressed his hope that "[t]he country will pick up on it, so one big goal is to make a good festival."[26] Ron Polte went even further, urging his fellow organizers to plan "not a 'hippie' fest in park," but something more "like a World's Fair."[27] Tom Donahue emphasized that the "basic thing" was that "it's a celebration of San Francisco music" precisely because "this is the town where change is going to happen." The festival would be "a statement of the beginning." It would show how the "world can be changed without fighting in the streets."[28] Speaking in similar language to Tom Donahue, who spoke of Wild West as part of a global "tidal wave," poster artist Victor Moscoso imagined Wild West as the "eye of the wave" that would spread around the United States, and perhaps beyond.[29]

"The Wild West Has Taken Off!": Organizing the San Francisco Music Council, March–May 1969

Barry Olivier was chosen as director of Wild West. He had a track record overseeing large festival proceedings as the founder and director of the Berkeley Folk Music Festival, which had taken place on the University of California–Berkeley campus since the late 1950s. Olivier was not deeply involved in the rock business, but he had welcomed rock bands to his folk festival as early as 1966.[30] Olivier began to map out plans for the Wild West Festival to present to the organizers, but very quickly, their ambitions grew beyond just a single event. "We're talking about something that goes a great deal further than [a] festival," Ralph Gleason told Olivier. He pictured the establishment of "a long term Music Council."[31] The idea of this council would be to create a cooperative music and arts association, one that might offer practice space, loans, and other kinds of support for the Bay Area's music and arts communities. Gleason's protégé, *Rolling Stone* editor Jann Wenner, suggested something similar: a "nonprofit corp." with a board of directors.[32] Wild West was taking shape not just as one event, but as a new kind of organizational form that brought the business and art of rock to bear on the encouraging of democratic and civic participation in both the Bay Area and the world.

At the group's second breakfast meeting, Olivier presented a flowchart that might provide an organizational framework for Wild West.[33] Seeking to recover the spontaneous openness of the Acid Tests and the mid-60s Haight-Ashbury scene, his document unwittingly took the form of the very chain-of-command bureaucratic hierarchies that most hippies wanted to escape. But with the counterculture disintegrating into chaos and disarray around them, many of the Wild West organizers endorsed the idea that a bit of institutional order might be necessary.[34] "If we're creating a free situation," Frank Werber told Olivier, "we must be doubly careful to keep it ordered and controlled, so that the freak-out types don't go berserk and scare everybody else away. . ... We must have freedom and control." To Werber, what had started out as a subcultural scene of freaks, hippies, and bohemians in mid-6os San Francisco had the chance to go mainstream, to include the masses, perhaps even to become the dominant culture itself, but only if Wild West, despite its name, did not go too wild. The opportunity was there to go "after straight people" to "turn them onto music, art, etc." But only, Weber believed, if festival could "control the free-est types."[35]

As the ambitions for Wild West grew, the tensions between "freedom and control" quickly encountered economic challenges. If the enormous festival was to be free, how was it to be financed? If it was to give birth to a permanent Music Council, who would fund this new institution? Bill Graham stepped forward in his typical entrepreneurial fashion to handle funds. "Money," he remarked, was "not such a problem as you all think." Graham jotted down a few figures at the meeting, reaching a sum around $25,000. "I'd like to be involved in raising the money," he decided.[36] But soon thereafter he backed out of his commitment due to difficulties in renewing the lease at the Fillmore West, his thriving rock concert hall in San Francisco. He was also tiring of being simultaneously hassled by conservative city officials and politicized radical hippies.[37] In the absence of Graham's leadership, a number of the organizers decided to loan startup money in order to pay Olivier and a small staff.[38] But as they began to assemble a budget, other participants, such as Grateful Dead band manager Rock Scully, imagined an entirely different model for the Wild West Festival. At the next gathering of planners, on March 31 at the KSAN radio studios, Scully suggested, "People should be entertaining themselves."[39] Influenced by the Diggers, the radical theater activists, Scully pictured voluntary labor and participation erasing the distinctions between profit-making rock promoters, musicians and artists taking orders, and passive audiences simply receiving the music.[40]

What emerged in the preliminary meetings about the Wild West Festival was a compromise between "freedom and control." Not only would the events in the park be free, but they would also be organized by artists themselves in a cooperative, participatory framework. The festival would be funded by three admission-only concerts in Golden Gate Park's Kezar Stadium and overseen by the San Francisco Music Council, incorporated as a nonprofit entity. When Barry Olivier, Ron Polte, and Bill Graham met with leaders of the San Francisco Parks and Recreation Committee to explore whether Golden Gate Park might be available for their event, the committee members were receptive to the festival idea, perhaps viewing it as a way to bring together countercultural youth and older San Franciscans in a productive manner. Encouraged by this response, the planning committee moved forward and began to spread the word among musicians and artists. Olivier began to assemble a staff, but the festival, at this point, still lacked an official name.[41] On May 1, organizers gathered to brainstorm. Their discussion revealed how much they were thinking about widening the counterculture's associational life beyond its existing population. "I do like 'Let's Get Together'," Bill Graham commented, saying that the organizers should "keep 'Pop' out" of the title for participants who "don't relate to the young peoples' thing." Polte agreed, "Because it's for all people." Werber also liked this goal of the festival: it "should be abstract," Werber commented, "wide open." Graham also said that he liked another proposed title, "We Are All One," because it "appeals to [the] street or general citizenry."[42]

Though they did not yet have a festival name, the planners decided that when it came to the financial arrangements, the event should be voluntary and not for profit. "All agree [that there should be] free artists," Barry Olivier wrote in his notes. Artists should participate as citizens rather than workers, contributing their music and other forms of arts in a civic celebration. On the question of what to do with any money that might be generated from the event beyond the costs of the festival itself, Oliver wrote, "All agree [to] have a *center*," a music and arts space to expand the energies of the San Francisco rock scene.[43] With the broad outline of their plans in place, the organizers sent out two letters, one to potential participants and the other to a bank. Their differences were indicative of the contradictions lurking in the planning of the Wild West Festival. The first letter focused on the radically democratic, cooperative approach to organizing Wild West, while the second emphasized how music business experts were hierarchically in charge of the event. In the first letter, sent out in early May, the organizers informed musicians and artists that, "Very shortly there will be a general meeting for the managers and members of the bands and the individual artists interested in helping plan the Festival."[44] Power would be in the hands of artists, not music business managers and promoters. The second letter, sent out in early May as well, informed a vice president at Bank of America in San Francisco that "leading figures in San Francisco's booming music industry" were "undertaking [their] first project—the establishment of a major Festival of music and art." The letter mentioned that the overall festival was a "nonprofit" event, but it pointed out that the "income" from ticket sales for the three rock concerts would enable the organizers to repay a potential loan.[45]

How inclusive was Wild West going to be? How democratic? The two questions were not one and the same. To be inclusive was to open up participation to "straights," but this required a more conventional hierarchical organization in order to reach out to a broader population. To be more democratic, by contrast, meant handing over control to the most active countercultural participants; but this meant that the festival might not have as broadly public an appeal—the festival might not even cohere in time. Moreover, the problem of funding remained in whatever framework Wild West took place. Barry Olivier was well aware of these dilemmas. The "problem," he wrote, was "how much can be done to build structure while [the] philosophy [is] still formative."[46] How would he create a functioning festival that combined control with innovation, hierarchical order with fervent participation, and the need to pay the bills with the urge to create something free for all people?

Once the festival dates were set, planning took on new urgency. On May 27, the San Francisco Music Council welcomed representatives of the most prominent Bay Area rock bands to the Stern Grove Clubhouse for the first full artists' meeting for the Wild West Festival. Tom Donahue explained the concept of the festival: "Create the event with 'volunteers' from the Community. . . . People who are involved are the creators of the show." Artists themselves would design Wild West, instead of just performing at it. He urged them to "get musicians and *other* artists together" and "involve all generations" in order to foster "an *open* situation" that "no one [would be] afraid to walk in to." If they did so, Ron Polte stressed, then "SF artists can change the world."[47] At a second meeting, Polte further articulated the dream of civic transformation at the heart of the Wild West Festival: "Collective consciousness is what's going to make this festival happen," he explained, "If we [as] a community get together, we can do whatever we want!"[48]

As June began, Barry Olivier hired additional staff and opened an office at 3044 Pine Street, near the Presidio, to coordinate the planning for the Wild West Festival. In typically colorful countercultural prose, a press release expressed the great optimism organizers felt for the event. "Wild West Circus Jump For Joy We've Caught Fire Colored Cloud Meeting," the press release declared. For counterculturalists, the Wild West was a moment to "celebrate the freedom we've had to develop our life-style, a festival to praise the joy of our lives!" But it was also an opportunity for the "WHOLE CITY" to attend, "sharing our joy." Inviting counterculturalists and others to come together around Wild West, the press release exclaimed: "HEY! THAT'S US! WE'RE DOING IT! HOW FAR CAN WE GO?"[49] Two days after the press release went out, a far more conventional letter written in far less purple prose revealed the complicated private maneuverings behind the public proceedings. Stanley W. Blackfield, Attorney at Law, wrote to Olivier and his fellow organizers that their application to establish a nonprofit corporation in the state of California as part of the Wild West Festival had been accepted. The "name 'San Francisco Music Council' has been approved by the Secretary of State," Blackfield wrote. In an unintended allusion to the controversy that Wild West would soon generate, Blackfield concluded his letter, "So we're in business."[50]

"We Should Start For-Real Organizing": Planning the Wild West Festival, June–July 1969

At a Wild West Festival staff meeting on June 10, new staff member Bruce Grimes "brought up the need to start a definite formation of committees with structures incorporating band members, staff council, artists, etc." The staff, which now included seven people, "decided that this should happen as soon as possible so plans can get under way. . . . Everyone agreed that we should start for-real organizing."[51] On June 16, the San Francisco Music Council held a press conference to announce the festival to the public (figure 3.3). They had come to an agreement with the Parks and Recreation Department to rent Kezar Stadium and use Golden Gate Park. Planning meetings for poster makers, poets, street dramatists, environment, multimedia artists, filmmakers, dancers, symphony, ballet, and opera organizers, and ethnic, country-and-western, jazz, folk, and rock music makers were scheduled, indicating the goal of inclusivity for Wild West (figures 3.4 and 3.5).[52]

Spirits were riding high at the Pine Street offices as artists began to meet to imagine what they might do at the festival. "There are thousands of people now working on actualizing a common fantasy," staff member Joel Selvin wrote in a

FIGURE 3.3. Wild West Festival press conference, June 16, 1969, San Francisco. From left, Barry Olivier, Ron Polte, unidentified Parks and Recreation official, person with head down (possibly John Cipollina), Denise Kaufman, Rock Scully, Jerry Garcia, and Bill Graham. Barry Olivier Personal Collection.

mock-up version of the first Wild West Festival newsletter, *Any Day Now!* (figure 3.6), "and when it comes off, all these people, as well as those that came to see, are going to be drawn together in one, very real community." Selvin was impressed by the effects of the festival planning on the associational life of participants. "What is happening is that people are finding a common project and one large enough to encompass hundreds and hundreds of people. Then they are finding that with this common denominator, they can truly work side by side with the others involved, in fact they find they have to."[53] For Selvin, as for the original organizers of the festival and a growing number of participants, the Wild West promised to be more than just a celebration: it would be a transformation in the social life of the Bay Area. Though it was difficult to understand exactly where this communal energy would lead, he decided that, "What is going on is a lot larger than just a simple festival. . . . The very absence of money, the presence of release, will introduce a new image of how to do it together."[54] Selvin described how he and the "people everywhere" around him began to believe that the Wild West Festival might bring about a new spirit of individual freedom through cooperative creative endeavor: a new kind of citizenship in the San Francisco region that might serve as a model of a postcapitalist economy and culture.[55]

An anonymous letter in the very same issue of *Any Day Now!* provided evidence of the growing eagerness to participate in the Wild West. A woman wrote to ask for support in creating a booth for people to bring clothes for mending. Her idea reflected both the intensely traditional gender roles of the counterculture and the ways in which women began to assert themselves as countercultural leaders:

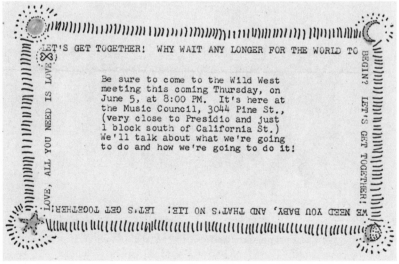

FIGURE 3.4. "Let's Get Together": Wild West Festival meeting invitation, June 5, 1969. Berkeley Folk Music Festival Collection, Northwestern University Library Special Collections.

THURSDAY, JUNE 19, 8:00, THURSDAY

JUNE 19, 8:00 PM, THURSDAY JUNE 19, 8:00 PM, THURSDAY JUNE 19, 8:00 PM

JUNE 19, 8:00 PM, JUNE 19, 8:00 PM, THURSDAY THURSDAY, JUNE 19, 8:00

Artist and poets meeting!
Opera and ballet and rodeo
Meeting!
Rock and folk and tapdance
Meeting!
String quartet and trapeze
Meeting!
All performers meeting!
All non-performers, meeting!

THE WILD WEST
Meeting!

Fellowship Church
2041 Larkin
San Francisco
Thursday, June 19
8:00 PM

San Francisco Music Council

Tom Donahue
Ralph Gleason
Bill Graham
Barry Olivier
Ron Polte
Rock Scully
Bill Thompson
Jann Wenner

Come and plan The Wild West
with us!

See you!

Thursday, June 19

THURSDAY, JUNE 19, 8:00, THURSDAY

FIGURE 3.5. "Come and plan the Wild West with us!": Festival planning meeting, June 19, 1969. Berkeley Folk Music Festival Collection, Northwestern University Library Special Collections.

18 JULY 1969   VOL. 1, NO. 2

festival news from the Wild West

The Wild West is the conglomeration of Bay Area artists in concert with nature, themselves and the people of San Francisco. The three day celebration of creativity planned for the August 22nd weekend will be the most important artistic event of the decade.

As the dynamics of the Festival begin to take shape, it becomes more and more apparent that superlatives are somehow inadequate in describing what promises to be San Francisco's finest hour. The biggest impact of the Festival will be in its presentation.

The staging area will be Golden Gate Park, which will provide more than ample room for the festival to live and breathe. There will be four main stages with a fifth set up for musicians who are feeling a little loose and want to get together and jam. Speedway Meadows, the Polo Fields and the Soccer Fields will be the main staging areas, but the whole park will be filled with various happenings. Everything from classical music and dance to jazz, folk and rock will be played. Sculptors, painters, light show folk, dance troups, poets and artists of all sorts will be plying their respective trades in the Park that weekend. Even San Francisco's grand old man of art, Benny Bufano, has expressed a desire to join in on the festivities.

All (with the exception of three nighttime concerts at Kezar Stadium) will be free and open to all mankind. The Kezar concerts will be from 8 til 12 (Sunday night, 7 to 11) and admission will be $3.00. Advance tickets for those concerts will go on sale July 25th.

The Kezar concerts will be almost the entire festival in miniature. All kinds of music will be presented and some extra-special, exciting events are planned. Spontaneity, as with the entire Festival, will be encouraged, (if not perpetrated).

> The first Festival General Meeting will be held Monday, July 28 at 8:00 P.M., Glide Memorial Church, 230 Ellis Street, San Francisco. All involved or interested people are urged to attend.

Most of the major festival artists will be involved in the Kezar concerts.

Response from the artistic community, as well as everyone else, has been fantastic. Every person contacted has been enthusiastic, excited, and anxious to become involved.

*****

As The Wild West grows in possibilities and deeds, so grows the imagination.

Here are a few images and situations: the lights and sounds of San Francisco orchestrated through Moogs located atop Twin Peaks; an eighty foot bar of Ivory soap floating in the bay; huge helium balloons; hundred foot geodesic domes; a 1200 member marching band from the Summer Youth Project; stages floated from balloons. These are not fantasies, they are projects. But they are only the barest intimations of what is happening in the individual and collective centers of stimulation the Festival has located. The ecologists/Environmentalists/Indians met to understand and develop contexts for these projects.

Gary Snyder drew a ground level question: how will the Festival (250,000 people a day, etc.) effect the ecology of the park? This question stimulated much discussion and exposed some beautiful ideas and new approaches to such problems. The operative agreement reached seemed to suggest that nature could take care of herself when people sought to act in concert with her processes and did not try to rape her for material profit and expedience. Change was identified as an integral function of

nature and by extension a park Nature accommodates us when we accommodate her. Many of those present had researches and ideas that could be sold; but these people seemed to be giving their work to a common pool, for all to draw from.

So much knowledge, insight and inspiration getting together in a cooperative effort reiterates a central image and purpose of the Festival. These cats are getting it ready ... they're not waiting any longer.

*****

A group of Bay Area film makers got together at Wild West Headquarters to discuss plans for filming the festival.

The discussion ran the gamut of film techniques as the various artists described their ideas of what a fantastic festival film should be like.

Tom Donahue, recently of KSAN radio and Festival Council member rapped to the group concerning various ideas regarding a documentary of the festival. He suggested that possibly the film makers could divide into units to cover the many-faceted festival.

Mike Haggerty was selected as chairman of a film committee to coordinate the activities of the group. Haggerty is part of an organization called "Mind Reels" that has been filming light shows.

Persons interested in working on filming the festival are ruged to call the Mind Reels office at 359-4772 or 359-5430.

The general consensus of the meeting was that since Wild West is going to be unlike any festival that's gone down before, the film of the event should be the definitive work in this genre. In other words, a movie far out-distancing "Festival" or "Monterey Pop" should emerge from all this creative energy.

FIGURE 3.6. *Any Day Now* Newsletter, Wild West Festival, July 18, 1969. Berkeley Folk Music Festival Collection, Northwestern University Library Special Collections.

I know there are a lot of guys wandering around without old ladies, many without homes, etc. Anyway, these people probably don't have anyone or any way to sew up ripped jeans, sew on buttons, darn socks, patch knees or asses, etc. I think it would be groovy if a group of chicks got together a whole lot of thread, needles, buttons, material scraps and other things, and set up a sort of booth for people in need of mending. Maybe it could be announced on KSAN so people would be forewarned.[56]

The letter writer shared in the excitement of Wild West, which promised to offer a setting for participation "in which everyone shares their talents." She did not address deeply inequitable gender relations in any sustained way, but the festival did inspire her to imagine an active way that she could foster community and help others through her own "talents"—and do so in public.[57]

A meeting at the KSAN studios on July 10 continued to generate excitement among organizers and new participants about the way that what began as a rock music festival for fans was growing into something larger and more meaningful. "What began as a fairly limited concept has snowballed into an incredible gathering of *all* the arts, a gathering that will bridge all gaps and bring everyone, from the very young to the very old," a press release prepared by the KSAN staff noted. "As it stands now, Wild West involves dancers, actors, poets, sculptors, painters, environmental architects, sound engineers and light show designers, as well as representatives of all music forms. But more and more people are volunteering and becoming involved every day. Wild West's office . . . has been transformed into a message center for all of San Francisco's arts."[58] Barry Olivier himself (figure 3.7) conveyed the hope that Wild West Festival was spreading a feeling of celebration

FIGURE 3.7. Barry Olivier standing and laughing at Wild West Festival's Pine Street Office, summer 1969. Barry Olivier Personal Collection. Photographer unknown.

and inclusion. In an interview with music critic Phil Elwood, he remarked, "'What do you want to do?' that's our theme. . . . We'll have ragtime and ragas going on, sand castles and skin painting . . . it's free, open, and everyone's welcome." To Olivier, the name of the festival itself suggested the goal of openness. Just as importantly for Olivier, "Wild West" conveyed the civic spirit of the event rather than any commercial intent. "We call it the 'Wild West' just to let people know it isn't some promoter's profit-making scheme," he told Elwood. "There is an informal, free-spirit sound to 'Wild West'." A billboard poster that the San Francisco Music Council produced for the event evoked this mix of countercultural wildness and accessible friendliness. Designed by poster artist Robert Fried, the image featured an abstract, space-age scene with the words "Wild West" zooming toward the viewer. It was weird, but also colorful, bright, and alluring (figure 3.8).[59]

The formation of groups such as the Environment Committee raised hopes that Wild West would make a lasting impact as the starting point for ongoing organizing. For the event itself, the committee wished to "convey ecological principles to as broad an audience as possible, to lead people to understand the importance of preserving a balanced ecological system." They would offer nature walks, organize car pool shuttles, and offer "twenty-minute raps" on environmental topics between the rock band performances at Kezar Stadium. They would also "present ecological problems as a 'sensual trip—examples of decayed eggs that can be viewed and touched, etc." and even have the "Fern Glade . . . set up as a shrine to nature with

FIGURE 3.8. Wild West Festival billboard, San Francisco, summer 1969. Barry Olivier Personal Collection. Artists: Robert Fried. Photographer: Barry Olivier.

'nothing happening'."[60] But the committee also viewed Wild West as the beginning of continued collaboration on environmental issues. The planning of Wild West provided a setting for concerned citizens to come together around ecological concerns just as the modern environmental movement was taking shape. Music and arts became a springboard for far more than just entertainment.

"Don't Do Nothing for Free Because You Can't Make Nothing from It": Troubles Begin, July 1969

If committees such as the group focused on the environment seemed to realize, in nascent form, the dreams of the Wild West organizers, other incidents suggested that developments were not as ideal as they hoped. With artists and festival organizers struggling to turn wild ideas into practical possibilities, new problems began to emerge. On July 11, a letter arrived from choreographer Shela Xoregos, who wrote that she "would not participate in your Wild West Festival principally on the grounds that it is immoral to ask dancers to perform for nothing while the staff is getting any salary whatsoever."[61] A similar issue of paying artists arose with the poster artists Wes Wilson and Victor Moscoso. Since they had become involved early on in the meetings for the festival, Wilson and Moscoso had volunteered to oversee promotion. But were they artists or administrators? Should they be paid or not?[62] The same issues of labor, pay, and control that had pitted Tom Donahue's KMPX hippie disc jockeys against station manager Leon Crosby now began to erupt from within the organizational ranks of the Wild West. The festival was not, it turned out, going to be as harmonious as planners believed.

The organizational structure of the festival and the San Francisco Music Council came under scrutiny. Filmmakers and other artists grew concerned that their volunteer labor was being exploited to further the business interests of the rock impresarios. "Fears should be unfounded concerning a power and/or money grab by council members," a July 23 internal memo insisted, "since a provision for expansion to include people from all the arts is very prominent." Moreover, the memo explained, "the council would be more than amenable to such an expansion and involvement by the whole community. Workshops for all artists and future festivals are only two of the possible benefits to derive from films, books, and events like Wild West. In other words, all of the participants in Wild West will gain, not the organizers."[63] But these sorts of reassurances did nothing to deter the growing sense of protest among certain sectors of the Bay Area's counterculture. A general meeting (figure 3.9) on July 28 at the Glide Memorial Church, which had served as a meeting ground for the counterculture since the mid-1960s, brought

FIGURE 3.9. Wild West Festival meeting at Glide Church, July 28, 1969. Barry Olivier Personal Collection. Photographer unknown.

this mounting protest to a head.[64] The Wild West Festival staff planned extensively for the general meeting, but even these meetings became contentious, lasting "some three hours, in the course of which there was much argumentation as to the execution of particular jobs, the need to raise money, the means to raise it; various people volunteered ideas. Nothing specific was decided and it was left up in the air. . . ." The ambitions for Wild West were beginning to meet the reality of creating such a large and unprecedented event. At the planning session, Olivier's assistant director Peter Sharkey "stressed the fact that we all know that our funds have been exhausted, that there is no money, and that the causes for this problem are the responsibility of failures on the part of the Staff."[65] Nonetheless, the Wild West planners sought to move forward. Although they were under growing pressure in terms of time, funds, and unified agreement as to their goals, the staff decided that "the important thing of the meeting was to convey to people the enthusiasm and vibrations of love and unity in the Festival, so that those people in turn, could go out and spread those vibrations and good feelings."[66] Though the staff tried to emphasize positive spirits, the actual implementation of the vision was proving difficult.

At the actual Glide Church meeting, the "vibrations and good feelings" turned truly negative. The San Francisco Mime Troupe, another radical theater group, handed out fliers that protested Wild West, critiquing the blurry lines that the festival established between the commerce of rock and larger civic dimensions of the event:

WILD WEST?
* When San Francisco opened the Haight, who made money off the stories in the big magazines?
* When San Francisco gave birth to the rock concert idea, who made money off the ticket sales?
* When San Francisco sound became a reality in concerts and in the parks, who made money off the records?
* When the records play on the new FM stations, who makes money off the commercials?
* When sound of the West is made and the festival is faded, who writes about it? Who plays it between commercials? Who books it and makes loot on "concerts"?????????
If you don't own a radio station (commercials), a newspaper (ads), or a concert hall (tickets), then don't do nothing for free because you can't make nothing from it. CHANGE IN LIFE-STYLE!!!!!!!!!!!
PAY ALL PERFORMERS DOUBLE THEIR USUAL FEES
LET ALL THE PEOPLE IN FREE!
This message is hand delivered by the S.F. Mime Troupe
Venceremos! Power to the People![67]

With their usual cheek, The Mime Troupe's flier jeered at the murky relationship between those on the San Francisco Music Council, who were all involved in the emerging rock music entertainment industry, and the goals of creating a "people's celebration." After the "sound of the West is made and the festival is faded, who writes about it? Who plays it between commercials? Who books it and makes loot on 'concerts'?" the Mime Troupe asked. A "CHANGE IN LIFE-STYLE!!!!!!!!!!!"—as the flier dramatically called it—meant the impossible task of redistributing wealth from promoters to artists *and* making the entire event free to the public at the same time.

The planners had not anticipated such a raucous spirit of questioning and dissent at the Glide Church meeting. Though many in the audience challenged the plans for the festival, in one sense the organizers had succeeded: they had brought the counterculture of the Bay Area together to engage in a robust debate about their collective endeavors. The discussion kept returning to the question of "the people": who they were, what they wanted, how the festival might belong to them. When Barry Olivier stepped forward to explain that any "profits would go . . . to the S.F. Music Council" from the filming of the Wild West Festival, a storm of criticism rained down on him. "This raised a number of questions as to what the money would be used for, who would be benefiting directly, etc. etc."[68] The reporter for *Good Times* described the scene more damningly: "Important questions about the budget, control of the city cops, legal structure of the council (which is under a state charter), and representation on the council by non-music artists were not adequately answered."[69]

Music coordinator Jon Sagen took the microphone to plead for cooperation and commitment. "He told the people that we need them," general staff notes for the Wild West office explained, "He wanted them to say OK . . . we want this!"[70] But Sagen's hopes were dashed. When Ron Polte was introduced, he was peppered with challenging questions. "Why are we putting it on? Who will benefit from it? Where are we getting the money? Why not give the money to the under-privileged? How can we celebrate a Festival like this when millions people are starving? Who wants this Festival? *Why*? What about the third world people, why aren't they repre-sented?"[71] Bill Graham stepped forward to support Polte. According to the general meeting notes, "Several negative comments as to the need of this Festival were made. Questions were not specifically answered and the people felt they were being put off. . . . The people were very agitated at this point."[72] As *Good Times* described the scene: "The focus swung over to a rap between R.G. [Ronnie] Davis [of the San Francisco Mime Troupe] and Bill Graham. Davis said Wild West was a hype, people should get into Kezar for free, and that Graham was sucking money out of the community. Graham said the council decided not to fund-raise for the festival and so needed the receipts from Kezar to pay for the rest, and he offered a percentage of his own gross if others would do the same."[73]

Others echoed Ronnie Davis's objections to the financial implications of the Wild West Festival, but he also emphasized the lack of representation in the con-trol and planning of the event. "At first their concerns were directed primarily at the financial arrangements of the festival," wrote Joel Selvin. "Then Arnold Townsend of the Neighborhood Arts Council spoke, saying that the festival had 'ignored the Third World community.'" Townsend pointed out that their "role in the forming of the 'San Francisco Sound' has never been properly appreciated." Moreover, he noted, "there wasn't one black person on the Board and that in the festival's meeting with the police, there weren't any blacks present." Continuing to emphasize the issues of race and ethnicity, Townsend argued that the whole notion of a "celebration" would not resonate in the poorer ethnic communities and neigh-borhoods of San Francisco. "When people in the Mission, Fillmore, and China-town hear about the Wild West spending $150,000 to groove for three days, they won't be able to relate to it," Townsend contended.[74] He and Bill Graham began to scream at each other. "This discussion was on Graham's money," general meeting notes explained. Eventually, Townsend relented from demanding the cancellation of Wild West; instead, he "demanded 10,000 free tickets for the more underprivileged people."[75] At Glide Church, the question of how Wild West would balance the needs of multiple constituencies exploded. The festival provided the setting for difficult, unruly debates to burst forth. But as the planning continued, it would not only be self-positioned outsiders to the counterculture, such as Townsend, who objected to the event. Core participants in the counterculture itself began to protest Wild West.

"Stick 'Em Up Wild West, This Is a Strike!": Hippies Protest the Festival, Early August 1969

On July 31, a group calling itself the Haight Commune convened a meeting and proceeded to distribute a flier around the Bay Area: "The *HAIGHT COMMUNE* is the assembly of the people of the Hip Community of San Francisco," the "Strike Bulletin #1" announced. "As of July 31, we are calling for a *NATIONWIDE BOYCOTT & HIP COMMUNITY STRIKE* against the 'WILD WEST FESTIVAL'." Once again, the question about who "the people" were when it came to counterculture, as well as who could legitimately represent them, emerged from the festival planning. The Haight Commune argued that it, not the San Francisco Music Council, represented the "assembly of the people." They thought that the Wild West Festival was an attempt to appropriate and exploit the labor and culture of Bay Areas artists. "The 'Wild West' has been put forth as an event both *for the community* and as a *transformation of consciousness*," the Haight Commune wrote, "but the people of the Hip, Black, and Third World communities of San Francisco have been excluded from all aspects of the Festival." The Wild West promoters had colluded with "the local power structure (police, City Hall, etc.) regarding the arrangements of the event," the Haight Commune complained, "but they have been unable to relate to the people of the communities on even the most basic human levels." Worse yet, the event marked a devious commodification of countercultural forms. "PLEASE HONOR OUR STRIKE," the Hip Commune pleaded in all capital letters, "BY STAYING HOME AND CONTINUING TO CREATE THE TRUE CULTURE AND LIFESTYLE FOR ALL THE PEOPLE."[76] Though they shared the Music Council's belief that San Francisco's counterculture offered a potentially global model of "true culture and lifestyle for all the people," they objected to the ways in which the organizers had failed to democratize the planning for Wild West. Despite the effort to create a cooperative, bottom-up festival, the Haight Commune called the event a "rip-off of the people's culture."[77] The original goal of the commune was to defend the interests of the battered Haight-Ashbury hippie scene, but its focus increasingly shifted toward opposing the Wild West Festival.[78] The next flier from the commune was an "Anti-Official Statement" signed by the Haight Commune, the Mime Troupe, the San Francisco branch of the Detroit-based White Panthers, the High School Union (a group of politically radical Bay Area high school students), the underground newspaper staffs of the *Dock of Bay* and the *Berkeley Tribe*, the Berkeley Liberation Communes, Los Siete de la Raza (a Latino activist group), the radical film collective Newsreel, the Liberation News Service, the Northern California branch of Students for a Democratic Society, the Red Guard, and the mysterious anarchist group the International Werewolf Conspiracy.[79] A transplanted member of the radical New York City anarcho-political activists Up Against the Wall Motherfucker, Johnny Sundstrom, better known as John the Motherfucker, became a spokesman for the various groups calling for a strike against the Wild West Festival.[80]

During the first weeks of August, the strike gained momentum. Fliers continued to emphasize the contradictions of the festival: was it truly an event of "the people" or was it in fact intended to bolster the profiles and power of rock impresarios and businessmen? "This festival is not 'for the people' as has often been claimed by its promoters," the protesters argued. "It is instead an event OF/BY/FOR the Rock Industry."[81] Another flier, colorfully titled "Long Hair Is Not Enough! Is Your Soul Shaggy Too?" (figure 3.10), continued this contrast between "people's culture" and commodified consumer culture. "People's culture comes from the people. IT is the free expression of Life/Imagination/Energy; isolated human beings reacting out to each other with noises/gestures/visions to create a new and common reality." By comparison, "Culture-for-Sale is the rip-off that converts the People's Culture into a synthetic substitute for reality and sells it back to the very people it was stolen from." The real goal of Wild West, protesters argued, was to create "a shit version of our expression" and then "hustle it back to us for incredible profits."[82]

Even the San Francisco Music Council's interest in using profits from Wild West to open a local arts center seemed undemocratic to the protesters. As an article in the *Berkeley Tribe* put it, "These fancy mod businessmen have set up the Festival in such a way that they can tax us, the hip/radical community, for a Cultural Center we have never decided on."[83] To become "truly representative," the protesters argued, not only meant expanding the Council's membership, but also reorienting its very understanding of the civic dimensions of rock music and the counterculture. They called for a more radical event that might "truly belong to the people." They demanded that the organizers to plan in concrete terms for the potential influx of hundreds of thousands of rock music fans rather than relying on the

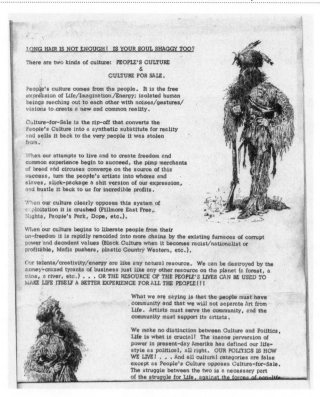

FIGURE 3.10. "Long Hair Is Not Enough! Is Your Soul Shaggy Too?": The Haight Commune protests the Wild West Festival, August 1969. Berkeley Folk Music Festival Collection, Northwestern University Library Special Collections.

police to keep order.[84] When Ron Polte agreed to meet with them and expand membership on the Music Council, they refused his offer. Instead, the Haight Commune dreamed of a gathering with a far more radical goal. They desired "the joyous/serious merging of all our energies, the communication of our discoveries and experiments, the free exchange of our goods and abilities." Their version of the festival would have to be more than just a three-day event. They wanted Wild West to "be part of an ongoing 365 day-a-year celebration and struggle for Life."[85] It was that or nothing.

"STICK 'EM UP 'WILD WEST,' THIS IS A STRIKE!" a Haight Commune leaflet declared (figure 3.11). Drawing upon the very same frontier imagery and language as the festival organizers, it featured an image of Clint Eastwood as the outlaw Blondie from *The Good, The Bad, and the Ugly*, the 1966 "spaghetti western" by Italian director Sergio Leone that was a cult classic in the United States.[86] Dressed in a poncho, with a steely look in his eye, Eastwood points a revolver threateningly toward an unseen opponent. In the mimeographed image, Eastwood's hair was

FIGURE 3.11. "Stick 'Em Up 'Wild West' This is a Strike!": The Haight Commune protests. Berkeley Folk Music Festival Collection, Northwestern University Library Special Collections.

rendered longer and more hippie-ish beneath his hat. The stub in his mouth looked more like a marijuana joint than a cigar.[87] The flier turned the nostalgic, family rodeo vision of the Wild West organizers in a very different direction, emphasizing a far more violent and exploitative American past. "The businessmen, railroad owners, saloon-pimps, sheriffs & marshals of the frontier acted just the same as they do now," the Haight Commune protesters wrote. "They kept the people separated from each other and excluded from the power to create their own lives."[88] Once again emphasizing the concept of "the people," the flier expressed a hope for a different future. "We know that if SQUATTERS / TRAPPERS / OUTLAWS, and the INDIANS had hooked-up with each other instead of fighting among themselves, the WEST would've rid itself of the real criminals and become a truly WILD, WILD PEOPLE'S WEST. . . ."[89]

For the protesters, opposing the festival became a way of overcoming the emerging system of hip capitalism, which feigned authentic communion and individual liberation, but only left people more exploited, isolated, and atomized. "The Wild Waste," as the San Francisco Mime Troupe called the festival, was the "greatest waste of talent, energy, and money in the history of hip capitalism."[90] It was the ultimate example of how "pimp merchants of bread and circuses" took advantage of the counterculture whenever it began "to liberate people from their unfreedom."[91] Hip capitalism "rapidly remolded" this liberation "into more chains" and any "attempts to live and to create freedom and common experience" were deceptively and deviously transformed into publicity and profits for the new class of rock stars whom the Wild West organizers represented.[92] Of course, there was an irony to the Haight Commune's use of Clint Eastwood's image on their leaflets: they appropriated a film-poster image that emanated from the very "culture-for-sale" that they critiqued! Nonetheless, the figure of the outlaw, even from a kitschy Western, effectively symbolized their core argument: only by developing a more critical awareness of the system of hip capitalism could San Francisco counterculturalists achieve the truly egalitarian and democratic social order that Wild West advertised but did not deliver. While the organizers of the festival imagined an event that bracketed politics to celebrate culture, the protesters made "no distinction between Culture and Politics." For the "hip community" that they represented, "OUR POLITICS IS HOW WE LIVE!" Wild West could only succeed by pulling the "People's Culture" out of "Culture-for-Sale" and bringing "LIFE to the LIFE-STYLE."[93] It could not do this in its current form, which saw it too closely associated with both the old power structure of local government and the police and the new class hierarchy of rock star elites and their passive audiences.

At an August 6 news conference called by the San Francisco Music Council, Tom Donahue reiterated that the planners of the festival wanted exactly what the protesters desired: a new kind of event made by, of, and for the people. Admitting that the council members had made mistakes, Donahue insisted that this "was because we were trying to let people do it themselves. We felt that was about the best thing."[94] The disc jockey explained that the civic orientation of the festival was why the organizers "didn't go to the record companies in the first place. That's the reason we didn't go to a foundation; that's the reason we didn't go to rich people and say come up with the bread, because we believe that people could do this thing on a people level and on an artistic level at the same time."[95] Donahue turned the tables on the protesters, claiming that they did not accurately represent the "hip community." "In the two and a half years that I was involved in the so-called underground radio scene in this town, I talked to a whole lot of street people," Donahue explained, but when he attended a meeting of the Haight Commune he "didn't see them there."[96] Instead, he witnessed an undemocratic and uncivil environment. "As we went along, the meeting was as fascistic as anything I have ever been to. . . . There were a lot of people at that meeting last night who were sincerely interested in it and had some questions and some of the questions they brought up were totally legitimate because they were situations that were created through our stupidity." These questions could not be asked. "I think there were a lot of other people there last night that were afraid to stand up because of the way the meeting was being run," Donahue remarked.[97]

Donahue still hoped that Wild West could accommodate the protesters. "I think there were a lot of people there last night who are representative of a good element in the community," he noted, "people who have positive ideas about how the world has to be changed."[98] But he objected to the unwillingness of the protesters to see Wild West as anything but an example of "commercial promoting." To show that the organizers were not simply out for their own economic interests, Donahue explained that they would expand the membership of the San Francisco Music Council "to include representatives from rock musicians, the dance people, the light show people, graphics people, the ecologists, the Panthers, the Third World, Mission Rebels, the Neighborhood Arts Commission, and a representative from the working staff and representative of the Musicians Union, the Parks Department, the Switchboard and Haight-Ashbury Medical Clinic." This expanded council would, in turn, discuss "how profits—which we believe are going to happen—would be spent." It would also "come up with a set of bylaws so we can create a 'firm arts council,' if you will, and find a way that people in this community can instruct the trustees."[99] Legitimately representing "the people" once again became paramount. "I want the Festival Council to be expanded to whatever number is necessary to involve a total participation of the community," Donahue insisted. "If you've got that, that popular participation, and you trust everybody or you at least trust the guy you sent, then you are going to have knowledge of what is happening." Donahue believed that "representation would be there for all the people because we want the representation." He and the other members of the San Francisco Music Council were "willing to trust our brothers." But, Donahue wondered, would the protesters "trust us enough to sit down with us and get this festival on"?[100]

"Wild West Falls In Class Struggle": The Cancellation of the Festival, Mid-August 1969

With the festival dates fast approaching, the Music Council's dream of creating a people's festival that began with rock music and included all the arts was increasingly imperiled. At yet another meeting, on Friday, August 8, the protesters against Wild West threw festival organizer Ron Polte out. "The group voted to continue the strike," an article in the *Dock of Bay* explained, "and committees were set up to work on crash pads, food sources, and legal and medical help."[101] On Monday, August 11, Barry Olivier sent a memo to Polte. He argued that the Haight Commune and other protesters were not going to join a larger Music Council since they viewed such an act as co-optation, so the existing group should carry onward with the event.[102] Nonetheless, Olivier organized an "Expanded Council Committee Meeting" that included representatives of the rock musicians, the San Francisco Neighborhood Arts Council, filmmakers, the Haight-Ashbury Medical Clinic, the S.F. Switchboard, the Mission Rebels, Arribas Juntos, Chinatown–North Beach District Council, Youth for Services, the S.S.F. Opera House, the Musicians Union, and the Black Panthers.[103]

The next day, the Wild West staff issued the final schedule for performances at five stages around Golden Gate Park. At almost the very same moment, however, Ron Polte's resignation from the San Francisco Music Council suddenly arrived on Olivier's desk.[104] Not only had protesters suggested that violence might occur at Wild West, they had also threatened Polte himself in the days leading up to the festival.[105] The next morning, Wednesday, August 13, the original San Francisco Music Council members chose to cancel the event. At a hastily called press conference, they announced their decision. "We have faced difficulties in the past four months that we've been planning this Festival, and we've had a lot of punches— and we've rolled with a lot of punches," they explained. "But we've run into one punch that we just figure we can't roll with. That punch is the threats of violence and bodily harm that have been made to both individuals involved in this thing, and toward the Festival in general."[106] At the press conference, issues of representation once again surfaced. A man interrupted the proceedings. "Who do you represent?" one of the organizers asked. "I represent myself," the man responded. Refusing to engage with the man, one of the organizers ended the press conference.[107] The interruption and the refusal to recognize the young man's right to speak illuminated the distance between the Wild West planners and protesters. For the planners, who were willing to work within the existing economic, political, and social order to bring together all of San Francisco around a celebration of the music and arts and, perhaps, map out a new and more radical future, the difference

between "the people" and "the Press" remained. But the whole point for the protesters was to challenge this and every other old assumption about social roles and
regulations.

That night, San Francisco's public television station, KQED, broadcast an opinion piece about the cancellation of the Wild West Festival by reporter Joe Russin,
who challenged the very claims of the Haight Commune and other protesters to
represent "the people" of the counterculture. Russin questioned the rights of this
countercultural "political leadership" to speak in the name of larger publics. "When
you're talking about power to the people," he told his viewers, "and the Haight
Commune people today for instance were saying the people have shown their
power, and they've called off the show, it's hard to say who are the people and
who's speaking for them."[108] One supporter of the festival, Dorena Wong of Mill-
brae, wrote to Barry Olivier and his staff in agreement with Russin. "Look & see
how many supporters you have, how many volunteers, & how many people would
benefit," she wrote. "Who cares about the minority groups who are selfish. . . . So
please, put the Wild West on."[109] But the festival was cancelled for good. As an
article declared in the *Berkeley Barb*, "Wild West Falls in Class Struggle."[110] To pay
off the San Francisco Music Council's debts and salvage something out of all the
planning, Olivier and his staff organized concerts at the Fillmore Auditorium and
another venue known as the Family Dog on the Great Highway.[111] These seemed to
mark the end of the Wild West affair, but they were in fact only the beginning of a
sustained inquiry into what had happened during the attempt to organize the festival. Essayists in the countercultural press continued to debate the meaning of
the Wild West Festival's demise. The protesters against Wild West celebrated their
victory. "The Natives Were Restless," the San Francisco Mime Troupe triumphantly
announced on a flier distributed after the demise of the festival.[112] Continuing the
frontier theme, the underground newspaper *Good Times* featured a Native American Indian defiantly staring out from the cover, a shotgun in his hand.[113] But others developed a more subtle analysis. Writing in the Communist Party USA
newspaper *People's World*, Judy Baston observed that the festival's cancellation
most of all "prompted a crossfire of rhetoric between what has been loosely defined
as the area's cultural entrepreneurs and its politicos."[114]

For the Mime Troupe and other politically oriented counterculturalists, Wild
West's failure demonstrated the very thing that the festival promoters had sought
to prove: that San Francisco was the wellspring of the counterculture's revolutionary ethos. "San Francisco, birthplace of the psychedelic subculture, has refused to
cooperate with the commercial exploitation of that culture," the Mime Troupe
wrote. "The people the festival purported to represent . . . were sick and tired of a
hardcore handful of operators getting rich off their music and their lifestyle—the

people refused and won. . . . The hip culture of San Francisco remains free in the streets, in the parks, of no use to the mass media, the big record companies, the rock millionaires."[115] But while the Mime Troupe and the Haight Commune celebrated Wild West's failure, others were less certain that victory had been secured. Supporters of the festival thought that protesters failed to see how the organizers sought to turn the commercial appeal of rock toward more civic ends, overcoming divisions between San Franciscans and ushering in a new era in which music and the arts might serve as the seedbed for a new politics. In the *Daily Californian*, the student newspaper at the University of California, an article titled "Public Works" sought to explain "How the West Was Lost."[116] Another article complained, "The Wild West festival died . . . because some segments of the radical community couldn't relax enough to enjoy a festival which had the blessings of the straight world."[117] In the pages of the *Los Angeles Free Press*, Allan Katzman concurred. "The festival," he wrote, "which began as a positive venture to give a shot in the arm to an already heavily distrusted rock scene and disparate related community, was torn apart by paranoia, bad timing, threats of violence, lies, and general all-around bad ego trips."[118] The Wild West organizers had their shortcomings, Katzman admitted, but they were mostly the victims of "a growing fascism on the New Left" that was "being used on the very people that the radical claim to represent." In the end, Katzman believed, the "bid to take over or destroy the Wild West Festival is not a matter of ideology but of simple power grab and takeover."[119]

Perhaps the most bitter of all with regard to the strike against Wild West was Ralph Gleason. "Rock music," he claimed, "has become the single most potent social force for change for several years now," and the protesters were but "musical parasites attempting to steal the power of the music more cynically and corruptly than any agent . . . ever tried to steal the money." They sought to polarize the tensions between the counterculture and mainstream systems of power rather than using rock music to discover a new consciousness. "I had a fruitless conversation with one politico over the San Francisco Wild West Show and his point was how could you have a festival when there were people dying in Vietnam?" For the protester, one had to choose sides. To Gleason, this was "irresponsible reckless bullshit." It reflected "the inability of the politicos to readjust to the new form" of rock music.[120] His sharp words sparked many retorts. Marjorie Heins wrote in *Dock of Bay* that "Gleason's situation is a microcosm of the whole rock music mess," which conflated revolutionary politics and mass consumerism.[121] Peter Wiley agreed: "at the same time that rock is part of the cultural revolution, it is also a hot commodity." This meant that the music could be particularly insidious in subverting the very values it announced, sustaining "a whole raft of promoters, reviewers, and hustlers who" were "not interested in social change; they are interested in the bread and acclaim that can be made from phrase-mongering about social change."[122] Joan Holden, a member of the San Francisco Mime Troupe, echoed Wiley's perspective. Holden theorized in *Ramparts* magazine that "hip culture, in its mass form, is based on two consumer goods, rock music and drugs" and it created "battles between those to whom a 'revolutionary lifestyle' means socialism and those for whom it means profit." To Holden, the music was ultimately detrimental to revolution because it turned protest into commerce. "You could probably start a revolution with rock music," she quipped, but only "if you could get someone to outlaw it."[123]

The debates and discussions after Wild West's cancellation manifested volatile discussions of public life and citizenship within hip capitalism.[124] Could rock music inspire better "exchange between culture and the community" in the Bay Area, Judy Baston wondered.[125] Or was the problem, as Sam Silver noted in *Good Times*, that "you can't take the revolution and package it for the bourgeoisie masses and expect Bobby Seale and Joe Alioto to both dig it."[126] These questions would continue to haunt the San Francisco rock scene after Wild West. As V. I. Lemming hoped, perhaps "an artists' co-op will arise from the ashes of Wild West, enabling all to share in the new culture." Perhaps to the surprise of many, just such a phenomenon arose out at the Family Dog on the Great Highway, at the far western edge of San Francisco.[127]

"Can the Common Extend the Form of WW?": The Family Dog on the Great Highway, Fall 1969

Like the members of the San Francisco Music Council, Chet Helms worried that the original energies of cooperative creativity had faded from San Francisco's booming rock industry. An émigré to San Francisco from Texas and one of the earliest promoters of rock music in the psychedelic ballrooms of San Francisco, Helms had inherited the Family Dog moniker from its originators, a group consisting primarily of San Francisco State College students.[128] Eventually, he relocated the venue to an old ice-skating rink in the Playland amusement park, just off the Great Highway. Helms came closest to realizing the cooperative venture that the Wild West Festival organizers had envisioned. The story of the Family Dog's transformation into "the Commons" would be the final chapter of the Wild West Festival's strange tale.

Considered a kind of anti–Bill Graham in his promoting style, which was more concerned with fostering a festive environment than turning a profit, Helms also wound up ensnared in a strike and boycott during the summer of 1969.[129] During meetings for the Wild West Festival, light show artists who had come of age with the rock scene began to organize a Light Artists Guild. They sought higher wages and better working conditions at San Francisco's concert ballrooms. Like the strikers at KMPX one year earlier, the Light Artists Guild sought to imagine a new mode of collectivism centered around their identities as workers in the emerging rock music industry. As a writer named Tari put it in the *Berkeley Tribe*, the Light Artists Guild was an example of countercultural participants realizing that "in our culture, WE are the means of production." As Art Johnson wrote in the *Berkeley Tribe* the following week, "The San Francisco light shows . . . have come together to work for the development of their art form, and their economic survival."[130]

The growing sense that creative freedom and economic practicality were linked brought a deep sense of radical possibility to the Light Artists Guild. Rock music sparked an effort to grasp—and even to remake—the relationship between the material realities of economic profit and ideas about artistic development and shared communal life. Just as with the KMPX strikers, the guild's "members emphasize that they are not strictly a union," but they could "function in traditional union ways" when they needed to do so. They believed that "the light show is an integral part of the rock environment" and therefore hoped to "expand and embellish the art."[131] After voting to go on strike "if the ballrooms refused to recognize the Guild," they chose to picket Chet Helms and the Family Dog during a Grateful Dead show on August 1. A colorful strike much like the one at KMPX one year earlier featured "a psychedelic picket line, with light show, conga drums, coffee and food." The "scene . . . was absurdly festive," local underground newspapers reported. "Dog staffers passed out carnations . . . Michael Christopher served a trayful of macrobiotic bread to projectionists working from the roof of a van" and "power for the light show . . . supplied . . . partly by extension cord from the Dog." Helms, Jerry Garcia of the Grateful Dead, Jerry Abrams of the Headlights light show, and others retreated to a van to discuss the strike. Their conversation produced a new vision for the Family Dog on the Great Highway: what Helms called "the Commons."[132]

The meeting between Garcia, Abrams, Helms, and other participants in San Francisco rock led to an effort to imagine new modes of collective association that might address ongoing problems that all were having with combining artistic expression and economic survival. It was, in many ways, the same conversation that the San Francisco Music Council members were having. Johnson reported, "When the Dead finally arrived, we all trucked out to their Metro van, 50 yards from the pounding surf, lit the peace pipe, and began to rap. It became clear that all of us are 'out on the edge, hangin' on, trying to live.'" Helms, like the Wild West planners, felt that the strike once again placed San Francisco at the edge of a coming revolution. "It feels like a precursor," he remarked, "of what's going to happen around the country. They're looking at us to see not only what we can do about us, but what they can learn from us." The sense that San Francisco presaged an upheaval around the United States drove the participants to try to imagine alternatives to the existing norms of the commercial rock business. As Nixon, a pseudonymous writer for the *Berkeley Tribe* put it, "There's no reason why the rock bands and ballrooms can't return some of their monies to the community. There's no reason why various communes can't begin to set up a booking network across the nation and take that power and money out of the hands of the hip capitalists. There's no reason why the bands can't stay in the community and use the community's facilities when they come to town."[133] Helms similarly argued, "We started out with the forms that were given, business forms, union forms." But, since the San Francisco psychedelic rock scene had developed in the mid-1960s, "the whole fuckin' world has been looking at us for new solutions."[134] By the end of the talks in the Dead's Metro van, the Light Show Guild members agreed to suspend their strike. In return, Helms called two "community meetings" for Saturday, August 2, and Tuesday, August 5. "The idea I proposed," Helms would later explain, "was that of the Boston Common. Basically, we invited the community. Everyone who had some stake in the ballrooms. We would invite all those voices and try to work out a way of salvaging the ship so we could all survive."[135] Here was an effort to realize what the Wild West Festival also sought to create: a transformation of rock's commercial power into a countercultural civic space.

At the first community meeting, participants in the Bay Area rock world such as Jerry Garcia (figure 3.12) conducted a robust discussion about their individual and collective situations. The glimmerings of a different kind of artistic and economic collective life for the Bay Area counterculture appeared. Many hoped the Commons would recover the initial adventurousness and openness of the early Acid Test gatherings and perhaps even move the energies of those early events forward. But at the Tuesday meeting, Bill Graham appeared, and in an angry confrontation with countercultural mystic preacher Stephen Gaskin and other participants, defiantly rejected the Light Show Guild's requests to pay them more. He also refused to provide a "community subsidy" from his concerts.[136] Nonetheless, the Commons not only continued, but for a time it flourished. Its goal, according to the writer Verne, was "an integrated construct by all artists." Verne believed that "the community is where it must be at for the total scene to further its form." In this vision of the San Francisco rock scene, "there will be jams and parties where everybody contributes to the trip. No longer will one performer work in the corner while everybody else is forced to just sit or stand there because no one can move."[137] It was the Acid Tests all over again: a vision of participatory festivity rather than passive spectacle, democratic partying rather than hierarchical entertainment. But achieving this ideal would require much deliberation and discussion—there would have to be as many meetings as parties. These gatherings often started

FIGURE 3.12. Jerry Garcia joining the conversation at the Family Dog on the Great Highway Commons, Summer 1969. Anne/Berkeley Tribe.

"with what some have called 'Berkeley Bullshit'—confrontation with a march," but slowly, Verne felt, the Commons "evolved into a strong community of artists who want to be able to do their thing together with the people."[138]

When the Wild West Festival was cancelled just days before it was supposed to take place, participants in the Family Dog Commons hoped they could fill the void. "Can the common extend the form of WW?" they asked. Could they "create a 72-hour-plus environment that would really be remembered as a good trip?"[139] When this did not occur, they focused on developing collective possibilities at the Family Dog. "My place was run for three months as a cooperative with my staff staffing it and our salaries coming off the top," Chet Helms explained. "A big calendar was put up so people who wanted to produce shows could do so. It was an open calendar. If anyone stood up and said, 'Hey, let's do *this!*' and there was enough energy on the floor with people saying, 'Well, I'll contribute this and my band will play this' we did it." Helms admitted that "eighty percent of what people bit off never came to fruition." But at the same time, "I will say that some of the most marvelous things happened. . . . It was absolutely one of the most free-form creative periods."[140] What the Commons demonstrated was that rock music unleashed a vibrant associational life in the Bay Area during the late 1960s. Participants sought out radically democratic modes of art-making, collective decision-making, individual self-determination, and critical reflection. They were aware that their efforts required difficult engagements with the system of hip capitalism. As Chet Helms put it, "You gotta get from here to there and anything we do has to start with a capitalist system and evolve to some other point . . . we must evolve that structure so that the cumulative effect of it over a period of years becomes something else."[141] Within the new dynamics of hip capitalism, the Commons became "a sort of parliament and group therapy for everyone interested in the future of the Family Dog at the Beach."[142] Similarly, the Wild West Festival, even in its failure, became an event around which participants confronted difficult questions together.

While the stories of Woodstock and Altamont—the supposed countercultural Garden of Eden and the eventual fall from grace—dominate our historical memory of the 1960s, Wild West and the Commons suggest a more complex story: rock was utopian and sinister in equal parts, but in the key location of the San Francisco Bay Area it most of all provided a sonic framework for thinking, feeling, discussing, and dancing out the vexing problems of democratic togetherness and individual liberation.[143] As Hunter S. Thompson's alter-ego Raoul Duke famously remarked in *Fear and Loathing in Las Vegas*, "History is hard to know . . . but without being sure of 'history' it seems entirely reasonable to think that every now and then the energy of a whole generation comes to a head in a long line flash." Coming out of places like the Fillmore "one or five or maybe forty nights," one "could strike sparks anywhere. . . . We were riding the crest of a high and beautiful wave." But a few years later, looking westward from his alienated debauchery in Las Vegas, Thompson's Duke wrote, "with the right kind of eyes you can almost *see* the high-water mark—that place where the wave finally broke and rolled back."[144]

Thompson's observation suggests that even after the San Francisco counterculture's civic energies waned, the city of the Summer of Love retained an important symbolic power. Wild West did not become the "tidal wave" of cultural revolution that Tom Donahue imagined, but it left tie-dyed swirls wherever it spread.[145] One of those places was across the Pacific Ocean, where, in the midst of the American military intervention in Vietnam, the sounds of rock music splashed across the war zone in startling ways.

Vietnam

4

A SOUNDTRACK FOR THE ENTIRE PROCESS

DURING THE VIETNAM War, an American helicopter gunner named Davies rented an apartment in the Cholon district of Saigon. Living there against military regulations but with the toleration of his commanders, Davies commuted to Tan Son Nhut airbase each day to fly missions to the Cambodian border. As if working a regular nine-to-five job, he returned each night to his building, where his Vietnamese girlfriend and her family resided. Fellow GIs and other friends would gather at Davies's home to socialize. One night they assembled a collage on one of his apartment walls. As journalist Michael Herr observed, it included:

> . . . glimpses of burning monks, stacked Viet Cong dead, wounded Marines screaming and weeping . . . Ronald Reagan, his face halved and separated by a stalk of cannabis; pictures of John Lennon peering through wire-rimmed glasses, Mick Jagger, Jimi Hendrix, Dylan, Eldridge Cleaver, Rap Brown; coffins draped with American flags whose stars were replaced by swastikas and dollar signs; odd parts clipped from *Playboy* pictures . . ., beautiful girls holding flowers, showers of peace symbols; . . . a map of the western United States with the shape of Vietnam reversed and fitted over California and one large long figure that began at the bottom with shiny leather boots and rouged knees and ascended in a microskirt, bare breasts, graceful shoulders and a long neck, topped by the burned, blackened face of a dead Vietnamese woman.[1]

Among the striking juxtapositions of the collage, Davies and his friends included rock icons such as John Lennon of the Beatles, Mick Jagger of the Rolling Stones, and guitarist Jimi Hendrix. Hinting at rock music's presence in Vietnam, these famous musicians "peered out" from a disturbing pastiche of materials whose incongruities seemed to emphasize the great distance between war zone and home front yet also hint at lurking connections between life in "the 'Nam" and "back in the World," the terms GIs used to map their existence. To be sure, there were many forms of music aimed at Americans in Vietnam: country for conservative southern troops; soul for African-American soldiers; mainstream pop and easy listening sounds on AVFN radio; folk music; and even traditional Vietnamese music for GIs who might be interested. But as Herr noted in *Dispatches*, his famous book of reportage about the Vietnam War, rock music mattered immensely to anyone who was trying to make sense of the conflict (figure 4.1).[2] Whether or not one liked the music, its disorienting qualities resonated with the confusing mood of the US military intervention in Southeast Asia.

In the collage that Herr described on Davies's wall, California and Vietnam featured prominently. They were "reversed and fitted" over each other. The land of "beautiful girls holding flowers," "showers of peace symbols," Governor Ronald Reagan, the Black Panther Party, and a burgeoning psychedelic drug culture served not only as the antithesis to Vietnam, but also as its strangely overlapping equivalent. Herr went one step further: it was not just California, but San Francisco and

FIGURE 4.1. American servicemen relaxing with marijuana and music; note the stereo speakers and psychedelic posters in the background, Quan Tri Province, South Vietnam, July 13, 1971. CORBIS. Photographer unknown.

its burgeoning rock scene that both stood in contrast and related to Vietnam. During the Battle of Khe Sanh in 1967, Herr recalled a US marine disconcertingly humming the lyrics of "San Francisco (Be Sure to Wear Flowers in Your Hair)" outside a triage tent where a fellow solider was dying.[3] At another moment during the war, he glimpsed how a GI's "face was painted up for night walking now like a bad hallucination, not like the painted faces I'd seen in San Francisco only a few weeks before, the other extreme of the same theater."[4] In both cases, San Francisco was the reference point for making sense of the war.

At first, Herr's use of San Francisco suggested that the City by the Bay and Vietnam were leagues apart. Dying in a Vietnam triage tent could not be more different from going to San Francisco with flowers in your hair; a young GI painting his face for a search-and-destroy mission in the Vietnam highlands was fundamentally dissimilar from a young woman dotting her cheeks with peace symbols to go to the Fillmore. But these antagonisms were also dialectically connected. Herr's marine was humming "San Francisco" not only because it was a hit song from the home front during 1967, but also because the coffins of dead GIs usually traveled through Bay Area military installations on their way to their final destinations.[5] The theater of war could even look eerily like the theaters of rock entertainment. Vietnam veteran Roger Steffens described the flares and mortars of the Tet Offensive of 1968 as "the wickedest light show west of the Fillmore."[6] Peace, love, and flowers in San Francisco and war, hate, and violence in Vietnam were perhaps not as different as one might first think.

Rock was a crucial cultural form that linked the two places. From the escalation of American intervention in Indochina in the middle of the 1960s to the end of the war in 1975, the music circulated from the home front to the war zone. GIs brought recordings, instruments, and rock paraphernalia with them, plugging rock into the daily waging of war at unofficial levels (figure 4.2). Michael Herr remembered riding in helicopters and listening to "cassette rock and roll in one ear and door-gun fire in the other."[7] The music also arrived on official frequencies: on the airwaves of the Armed Forces Vietnam Network (AFVN), in programs organized by the Entertainment Branch, and even among non-Americans who listened to and played the music. Never banned or forbidden, rock was encouraged as a leisure activity. Tolerance, even support, for it by the Armed Forced revealed how the managers of the US military transferred the latest consumer strategies from domestic culture to military life. Paralleling the appearance of hip capitalism at home, what I call hip militarism emerged in Vietnam as a tactic for raising morale within the US Armed Forces. It turned out there was much more to entertainment during the war than just Bob Hope's famous Christmas tours.[8] The Armed Forces also actively imported the latest "acid rock," so called for its associations with the

FIGURE 4.2. An American GI listens to LP records on his portable phonograph; The Beatles' *Revolver* leans against the wall in the background. Credit unknown. Photographer unknown.

hallucinogenic drug LSD, into Vietnam in hopes of keeping GIs who liked the music engaged in the war effort. That the US military would use a music often associated with disengagement from—and sometimes even opposition to—hierarchical modes of authority in order to try desperately to maintain control over a failing war effort would produce many ironic effects in Vietnam.[9]

Using entertainment to buoy the spirits of American GIs had long been a part of the American military's self-perceived mission, but during the Vietnam War, investment in providing troops with "rest and relaxation" grew to unprecedented levels.[10] The Special Services division, charged with providing troops with entertainment, had what one staff member described, early in the conflict, as "an almost unlimited budget."[11] At the height of spending in 1970, the budget of appropriated funds (taxpayer dollars) for Special Services was $14.9 million, with additional funding in nonappropriated funds (monies generated by soliders themselves) at $3.5 million. Between 1966 and the first half of 1971, the Special Services budget totaled almost $35 million in appropriated funds and roughly $10 million in nonappropriated funds.[12] If antiwar protesters in the Bay Area and elsewhere sought to "bring the war home," as a popular antiwar slogan of the time went, then the commanders and managers of the United States Armed Forces sought to "bring home to the war" as never before.

Because of a manpower and promotion system that exacerbated generational differences, racial tensions, and dissent among American fighters, Special Services sought to import and create leisure opportunities for particular groups rather than for personnel as a whole.[13] Rock surfaced in Vietnam as part of the effort to cater to younger GIs in lower-level positions, the "grunts" who distinguished themselves from "lifers," who tended to be older, career military officers.[14] Paralleling the turn toward hip capitalism in the domestic consumer market, the Armed Forces tried to get hip by offering a robust and variegated leisure culture for American fighters. Other factors also contributed to the embrace of rock. While Vietnam remained largely a "working-class war" in terms of the socioeconomic backgrounds of American GIs, changes in the draft after 1967 brought more middle-class, college-educated troops to Vietnam, precisely the demographic that constituted the main part of the rock market.[15] Additionally, after 1968 newly elected president Richard Nixon endorsed recommendations to relax military standards and even allow for a decentralization of control over the command structure as he and his administration began to imagine ending the draft and creating an all-volunteer military.[16] These changes meant that the US military appropriated rock music even though the music seemed associated with the antiwar movement, the counterculture, and a general sense of rebellion on the home front.

Hip militarism marked an effective new strategy of incorporation and co-optation. As film scholar David E. James argues, while "on many levels rock music supplied the libidinal and imaginative energy of contestation . . . by the same terms, the music was equally functional in social quietism and indeed the prosecution of the war itself."[17] Rock could communicate antiwar energies, but not in any stable ideological way. As a form of domestic consumer culture, it was easily accommodated into the continued functioning of the military. But rock also intensified experiences of Vietnam as a place of disarray and confusion, of blurred lines between official and unofficial knowledge, and of questionings of the role of the citizen-soldier. For GIs attracted to the music, it illuminated the intersections and disconnections between personal, micropolitical, and existential experiences and large geopolitical concerns.[18] It did so not because the music was outside American cultural and military empire, but rather because it was within it. Rock accentuated a surreal collage of startling incongruities. It evoked the immediacy of battle but also numbed participants. It seemed, on the surface, to be antiwar music, but many troops drew upon rock's aesthetic *Sturm und Drang* to inspire themselves for fighting. Or they used quieter rock tracks to cool down and numb themselves to the war around them and their involvement in waging it. Particularly in combination with drugs, rock desensitized participants in the Vietnam War.[19] But it could also, in certain contexts, awaken empathy, even solidarity, with those suffering from the war. Rock could go either way, which allowed it to render the military intervention in Vietnam an object of critical inquiry at both sensual and intellectual levels. In its continual evocation of juxtapositions, its use of electronic technologies that paralleled modern military weaponry, its distancing effects within the immersive intensity of the war zone, and its rapid oscillations between home front and battlefield, rock also allowed those caught up in the conflict to perceive and examine its powerful grip on their lives.[20] Propelled into the lives of GIs through the tactic of hip militarism, rock made the relationship between contestation and complicity, entrance into the war and escape from it, no simple matter.

Certain rock songs became anthems in Vietnam because they represented the experience of simultaneously getting away from the war and taking pleasure in its spaces of leisure and entertainment. "We Gotta Get Outta This Place," a 1965 hit written by Brill Building songwriters Carole King and Gerry Goffin and performed by Eric Burdon and the Animals was one such song. As AFVN-TV "weather girl" Bobbie Keith recollected to historians Doug Bradley and Craig Werner, "'we listened and danced to the tune in a state of heightened awareness that many of us might not make it out." For Keith, "The song conjures up the fire flares and rockets that illuminated the sky each night . . . as helicopters whirled overhead, creating an ominous musical cacophony that the war, ever present, was all around us." But within this dangerous environment, Americans in Vietnam also "'danced, listened and sang along.'" As they yelled out the lines "We gotta get out of this place, if it's the last thing we ever do," Americans in Vietnam conveyed a kind of war sublime. In a form at once embodied by their singing and mediated by recorded sound, they articulated an incongruous mingling of feelings: panic and revelry, fear and amusement, worry and calmness, intimacy and enormity.[21] Sometimes, American GIs expressed this mix of emotions about the war by placing rock lyrics on their helmets.[22] One soldier even scrawled "San Francisco City of Love" across his government-issued camouflage helmet cover (figure 0.4).[23] This was not exactly protest against the war, but something more self-reflective. At its core, helmet graffiti registered the duel identity of the citizen-soldier. It inscribed, quite literally, the tensions between individual expression and institutional role on the heads of GIs.[24] Even pro-war soldiers drew upon the hippie counterculture to articulate their awareness that the very civic legitimacy of the war was up for debate. "Make war not love," a GI sardonically scrawled in 1967. This soldier reversed the classic hippie slogan, but he also arranged the words in an ambiguous (one might even say psychedelic) X pattern, so that they might be read in any order or direction, as on a psychedelic rock poster: make war not love, make love not war, make not love war, make not war love.[25]

FIGURE 4.3. War and peace in Vietnam: A GI with "peace" helmet graffiti during mission into Cambodia, 1970. AP Photo. Photographer unknown.

Another GI wrote "Peace" across the back of his helmet, his letters vaguely resembling the typography of rock poster art (figure 4.3). In another photograph, an American GI sat in uniform atop a tank turret. He audaciously held a pink umbrella over his head, as if it might protect him from sniper fire. On his helmet, in large capital letters, he had labeled himself a "HIPPIE" (figure 0.3).[26] It was as if since he couldn't go to San Francisco with flowers in his hair, he had simply used a felt-tip marker to bring a bit of San Francisco with him to Vietnam.

As with helmets, the radio airwaves became particularly powerful sonic spaces in which rock mediated the confusions of serving as US citizen-soldiers in Vietnam. Listening to music on the Armed Forces Radio Network and other channels, GIs were able, at least aurally, to be at home and at war all at once. They could occupy ambiguous positions between their roles as American soldiers in the midst of battle and civilians enjoying the latest domestic consumer culture (figure 4.4). Because domestic consumer culture increasingly included the hip anti-consumerism emanating from places such as San Francisco, GIs also had access to the sounds and moods of the counterculture. Just as San Francisco countercultur-alists caught up within hip capitalism used rock's commodified qualities to confront questions of citizenship in the United States, so too GIs actively used rock for more than just entertainment. Beyond tuning into rock on AFVN, they also plugged turntables and tape recorders into the audio apparatus of the US military.

FIGURE 4.4. A GI resting with his transistor radio, Vietnam, date unknown. Photographer unknown.

On what became known as the "bullshit band," the unused frequencies on military radios, GIs dialed over from the official audio channels of the military command structure to self-generated sonic spaces of soldier camaraderie and fellowship. In these zones of rock music, friendly chatter, and GI sociality, new modes of listening emerged. With them, new kinds of criticality and new sorts of solidarity arose as well. Eventually, even pirate and "underground rock" radio stations surfaced on the airwaves, just as they were doing on KMPX in San Francisco and elsewhere beyond the theater of war. By the last years of the Vietnam conflict, the cultural bandwidth of hip militarism had erupted into a sonic space of discontent and questioning far beyond what the Armed Forces intended.

Rock helped GIs temporarily escape from the war, to be sure, but in its distancing effects, the music also introduced disruptive static into the war effort. As American GIs encountered rock as both a commodity imported by the military and a vernacular form of expression enjoyed outside mechanisms of official control, a dizzying feedback loop emerged, a circuit of confusing sounds, feelings, attitudes, and sensibilities. America's citizen-soldiers found themselves dancing between the domestic counterculture's war-shaped pursuits of civic inquiry and their own counterculturally-influenced experiences of fighting in Vietnam. Neither entirely outside the existing system of domination, nor utterly incorporated into the war machine, rock flowed through the conflict, becoming a "soundtrack for the entire process," as veteran Lee Ballinger put it.[27] At once sanctioned and illicit, it offered pleasurable release from the war at times; in other moments, it provided sonic vistas from which to critically peer down at the bombed-out surroundings; and in still other moments, the music immersed participants in aesthetic representations of the violence, alienation, chaos, and boredom of the military occupation in which GIs participated. No wonder Davies and his friends portrayed the military involvement of the United States in Southeast Asia as a collage of burned bodies and peace symbols, governmental officials and Playboy centerfolds, California and Vietnam, with rock musicians floating through the mess. In a war zone where, through music, the countercultural energies of San Francisco could suddenly erupt in the middle of Saigon, a churning, swirling, fragmented war culture emerged. In this context, rock became a means for feeling one's way along the jagged edges of US imperial power. Within the jarring bricolage of the war, out of the new tactic of hip militarism, American GIs and others in Vietnam taped together their understandings of citizenship.

The Sgt. Pepper Show: Rock on AFVN

For many American troops, the Armed Forces Radio Network became part of the everyday sounds of war in Indochina (figure 4.5). "Radio was the medium that meant the most to those in combat during the Vietnam War," AFVN disc jockey Billy Williams contended. "To many, radio offered a touch of home in a hostile environment. And music on the radio provided escape from a frightening, dangerous world."[28] The network grew from a small channel in Saigon to a multibase operation that broadcast on nine stations spanning all of the Republic of Vietnam. In terms of size and scope of programming, the AFVN network headquarters in Saigon came to resemble a typical regional broadcast facility in the United States.[29] It was also part of a global American military and governmental radio network that included stations in other parts of Asia as well as Europe and Africa. The Armed Forces Radio and Television Services (AFRTS), based in Los Angeles, licensed domestic commercial shows to this worldwide network and created in-house productions for distribution. The main Saigon station and a number of the relay stations sometimes offered their own original programming too.[30] AFVN reached over half a million GIs in Vietnam, along with what a 1956 military report had called the "ghost audience" of non-American nationals.

While many GIs criticized AFVN for not airing more rock, the music surfaced on the official military radio network in Vietnam quite often, particularly after 1968,

FIGURE 4.5. American GI Francisco Ghydirotti, Jr., listening to AFVN on his transistor radio, South Vietnam, January 6, 1969. NARA. Photographer: Kenneth L. Powell.

as part of the effort to bring the latest sounds of home to the battle zone.[31] AFVN was not, contrary to the film *Good Morning, Vietnam*, devoid of rock sounds.[32] "One of the last things freshly-arrived soldiers expect to hear in Vietnam is acid rock, but it is played nightly over AFVN radio," James P. Sterba wrote in a 1970 *New York Times* article.[33] By 1970, AFVN regularly broadcast the genre on general programs of popular music and on shows dedicated exclusively to "acid rock" and "underground" music. After surveys of GI listening desires were completed in 1968, 1970, and 1971, *Pacific Stars & Stripes* correspondent Stephen F. Kroft reported that "[t]he 'Sergeant Pepper Show,' an hour and a half of 'underground' music broadcast on Sunday evening over AFVN-AM, has been expanded to two hours following its strong showing in the survey."[34] The show featured psychedelic songs such as Donovan's "Hurdy Gurdy Man." Two other tracks that were played, The Who's "Talkin' 'Bout My Generation," with its famous lyric, "Hope I die before I get old," and the Guess Who's "Hang on to Your Life," were typical in that they had the potential to take on entirely different meanings in the context of the war.[35] In addition to the *Sergeant Pepper Show*, produced from Saigon, countless programs from AFRTS in Los Angeles delivered the sounds of the domestic counterculture to Vietnam. While it is possible that a number of these shows, distributed to stations on long-playing phonograph records, were banned, no evidence suggests that censorship was systematic.[36] One AFRTS program, *The Pop Chronicles*, even explored the sounds of San Francisco rock. As a series that examined the history of American popular music in the twentieth century, *The Pop Chronicles* featured two episodes about the Acid Tests, replete with psychedelic recordings from the Merry Pranksters themselves. "John Gilliland presents Part One of 'The Acid Test'," the *AFRTS Radio Round-Up* instructed disc jockeys to announce in October of 1970. "Pop music hops aboard the hallucinogenic roller coaster for a joy-ride to the outer limits and beyond. Almost simultaneously, rock and roll and a sub-culture come of age in San Francisco, U.S.A."

The *Pop Chronicles* about the Acid Tests demonstrated the military's willingness to let countercultural music and stories be broadcast over AFVN. The *Round-Up* continued, "Two perceptive firsthand observers of the San Francisco scene, Ralph Gleason and Jann Wenner help conduct this tour of the pulsating epicenter of 'hippiedom.' There are guest appearances by Jefferson Airplane and Janis Joplin and a lot of choice music by the San Francisco bands."[37] The episode was to be "a no holds barred examination of some of the oft-misused subcultural terminology, like 'psychedelic,' 'hippy' and 'acid trip' through rockin' San Francisco." As if to note the oddness of the US military broadcasting the sounds of the Acid Tests over its communications network, the *Round-Up* concluded with a parenthetical comment. The program would be "complete with built-in disclaimer and some equal time for anti-drug material."[38]

By the later years of the Vietnam War, AFRTS not only produced its own counterculturally oriented rock programming, but also syndicated corporate media shows that aimed to capture the hippie market. The ABC program *Love*, a mainstream imitation of the free-form underground rock radio stylings pioneered at KMPX in San Francisco, was sent out to AFRTS stations during 1970 and 1971. A series of *Love* episodes, hosted by the Lutheran minister John Rydgren, featured music from the 1970 soundtrack recording for the film *Woodstock: Three Days of Peace and Music*, even including Country Joe and the Fish's satirical anti–Vietnam War protest song, "Feel Like I'm Fixin' to Die Rag" and Jimi Hendrix's painful, searing rendition of "The Star-Spangled Banner."[39] Countercultural rebellion seemed easily accommodated by the US military's broadcast system. Yet, because rock both appeared on AFVN and was brought in by GIs themselves, it spoke to issues of civics and citizenship in Vietnam despite its incorporation into the Armed Forces. Hip militarism was as much an opening for counterhegemonic beliefs and attitudes as it was a strategy of containing dissent or rebellion.[40] As the music appeared on the officially sanctioned channel of the US military, it dramatized the disorienting oppositions and overlaps between the domestic counterculture and the war itself. Boundaries blurred and contradictions intensified. The music never ended the war, but if, by the logic of hip militarism, it was meant to tame dissent and raise morale, it did so in the strangest of ways. Listening to one broadcast from October of 1968 indicates how this was so.

"All Along the Watchtower": Jimi Hendrix on AFVN

The *Stateside Top Thirty Countdown*, broadcast on AFVN in October 1968, provided a pastiche of pop hits from the home front. But when rock songs appeared among the placid music, something disconcerting began to take shape over the airwaves. It was the aural equivalent of Davies's collage, with the everyday faux-normality of domestic consumer culture interrupted by countercultural visions, feelings, and moods. Alongside far less confrontational music by the Archies, Frank Sinatra, The Fifth Dimension, and Mary Hopkin, listeners to the *Stateside Top Thirty Countdown* heard songs such as "Piece of My Heart," originally recorded by soul singer Erma Franklin but made famous by Janis Joplin and her San Francisco band Big Brother and the Holding Company. They also heard songs by Steppenwolf and Vanilla Fudge. Most strikingly, Jimi Hendrix's version of Bob Dylan's "All Along the Watchtower" roared out over the military's official broadcast channel.[41]

Hendrix's appearance on AFVN is worth closer scrutiny. Many GIs greatly admired the rock guitarist, who, prior to Vietnam, was himself an ex-member of the 101st Airborne Division.[42] Many GIs claimed Hendrix as their own, believing that he was more important to them in Vietnam than to any civilians back in America. As Special Private 4 Jack Martin remembered, "being there and listening to him, no matter what the kids back home thought his music meant, they could never connect at the level we did."[43] Hendrix's music, one veteran explained, was the "melody of war."[44] Another veteran remarked, "Jimi Hendrix in 'Nam? That's affirmative, bro! Hell, he wrote the fuckin' soundtrack!"[45] Hendrix's version of "All Along the Watchtower," piped in from the domestic top of the charts, seemed even to articulate the meaning of the war in Vietnam itself.[46] As music historian Craig Werner writes, it became "the national anthem of America-in-Vietnam and Vietnam-in-America."[47]

The song first appeared on Dylan's album *John Wesley Harding*, released in December 1967.[48] One influential rock critic heard Dylan's quiet, mostly acoustic record as suffused with the Vietnam conflict. But "All Along the Watchtower" only refers to the war obliquely, in a disjointed, collage-like story with its beginning, middle, and end shuffled into an uncertain order.[49] A joker and a thief console each other in the midst of an impending battle. The joker wonders if "there must be some kind of way out of here," while the thief urges calm. "No reason to get excited," he remarks, for "there are many here among us who feel that life is but a joke." In the song, there are women, foot servants, princes, and businessmen who "drink my wine" while "plowmen dig my earth." Danger, paranoia, ominous brooding, even death are present in the uneasy movement between minor and major chords and in Dylan's shrill vocals. But there is something taut, exciting, clenched, and full of adrenaline in the song too. "Two riders" approach in the night "as the wind began to howl." They might be two grunts in Vietnam, the names Joker and Thief graffitied on their helmets. Or perhaps these are two soldiers gone "AWOL," deserting the US military to become fugitives somewhere in Southeast Asia. Whatever fantasy one wanted to explore when listening to "All Along the Watchtower," it could easily become an allegory for the Vietnam conflict.

Released the year after Dylan's version, Hendrix's amped-up take on "All Along the Watchtower" viscerally communicates the experience of modern, technological warfare. Whatever quiet, reflective qualities of the original arrangement vanish in a maelstrom of clattering, reverberating, martial drums, piercing acoustic strumming, and Hendrix's electric-guitar howls. The song evokes a sense of vertiginous space, as if one were flying through the air, glimpsing vast horizons; at the same time, its warbling, slightly distorted, hyper-electronic quality is slightly claustrophobic, wobbly, almost oppressive. Hendrix's acoustic-guitar track strums in partial collision with Mitchell's snare drum, creating a flamenco-like pattern, creating a kind of exoticized mood of danger, at once terrifying and alluring.[50] Dylan's lyrics hint at impending violence and disaster, but only when Hendix's electric-guitar solo swoops in does the song's full power erupt. His guitar becomes a helicopter gunship, its rotor blades spinning, its nose dipping and soaring, its automatic weaponry blazing. The electric bass, played by Hendrix himself on the recording, drops bombs that seem to leave huge craters in the hypnotic major-minor harmonic progression, which rolls along ceaselessly, like an endless landscape of deltas, rice paddies, straw huts, muddy roads, and deep forests.[51] This version of the song performs, in representational form, technological violence on an exoticized people and place. But it also comments on this figurative violence. Hendrix's singing, whose bluesy note-bending contains a grain of hesitation and doubt, and his guitar playing, which is almost frighteningly virtuosic yet also remains grounded in the articulate grittiness of the blues, undercut the assault of the song. Hendrix seems to bemoan the very technological horror that his song expresses.

As "the national anthem of America-in-Vietnam and Vietnam-in-America," Hendrix's version of "All Along the Watchtower" reveals the ways in which rock sparked questions about citizenship for American citizen-soldiers. The song was much like another famous Hendrix recording, "Machine Gun," which also seemed to be about Vietnam without ever mentioning the war directly. As with "All Along the Watchtower," "Machine Gun" is told from the perspective of a soldier, a "foot servant," caught up in larger political confusions and technological fury. But the lyrics kaleidoscopically shift points of view as they move from a soldier firing a machine gun to a "farmer" who tries to "pick up his axe." The term axe was, of course, also a nickname for the electric guitar. It linked Hendrix simultaneously to the soldier and the farmer. In the song, he enacted the violent actions of a soldier, making his guitar sound like an automatic machine gun, but he also reached out to see things from the farmer's perspective. "The same way you shoot me down, baby," Hendrix sings, "you'll be goin' just the same."[52] Perhaps this farmer was a Vietnamese peasant by day who at night became an insurgent, fighting against American imperialism. Merging and blending multiple, on-the-ground perspectives of war, "Machine Gun" also expressed a yearning to transcend this violence: "I ain't afraid of your bullets no more, baby," Hendrix declares, "I ain't afraid no more." Singing from both sides of the gun, the guitarist notes that, "we're only families apart." "Machine Gun" took the sound and message of "All Along the Watchtower" to an extreme level: it was a kind of feeling-experiment, an uncertain inquiry into the meaning of war. It explored the power of an American GI and the terrible dehumanizations of technological warfare. Because of this, musical and cultural theorists have often returned to both of these songs to make sense of Hendrix's role as a kind of public intellectual for the counterculture: a rock star with a serious point and a former GI who became a hippie. As cultural theorist Paul Gilroy argues, "we should always remember that Hendrix was a soldier and think of him as an ex-paratrooper who became a hippie in an act of profound and complete treason."[53] While this might not have been the case literally—after all, many Americans join the Armed Forces for any number of reasons without committing to it ideologically—Gilroy's point is an important one: Hendrix drew upon militaristic references and sounds to evoke a psychedelically informed dream of peace.

Hendrix's self-presentation and musical expression pointed to the distinctions between citizen and soldier identities, but his music and style also returned repeatedly to the connections between the two.[54] Like many at the time, he noticed how the domestic counterculture in places such as the San Francisco Bay Area was not separate from the war raging in Vietnam. When Hendrix performed "Machine Gun" in the Bay Area during a 1970 concert, he went so far as to dedicate the song to the "soldiers fighting in Berkeley—you know what soldiers I'm talking about—and oh yeah, the soldiers fighting in Vietnam too."[55] For the rock guitarist, the links between the Bay Area and the war in Southeast Asia were many. Rock music provided a way to make sense of the dizzying overlaps, to gain a perspective that both soared above the confusion he and others felt about the world around them and, at the same time, dive straight into the mess. As Gilroy contends by referencing Hendrix's lyric about riding a dragonfly in the song "Spanish Castle Magic," the guitarist offered an "update in the poetics of world citizenship" by imagining people "taming the U.S. military industrial complex in the subversive act of traveling by dragonfly rather than warplane or helicopter."[56] In the context of Vietnam, Hendrix musically evoked the countercultural encounter with eroticized violence but then reached past it toward a "planetary" consciousness of shared global citizenship. Similarly, the film director Oliver Stone wrote that "[f]reedom was an important concept for everyone there, and Jimi evoked a sense of breaking to another reality."[57] But even as Hendrix tried to communicate a liberating transcendence, he also rendered the violence of Vietnam palpable and immediate in his songs. "There was something about his music that was very much a downer, and it fitted with what was going on out there," Stone remembered about listening to Hendrix during the war. Hendrix's music did so, as one veteran remembered, not by announcing public opposition to the war, but rather by penetrating deeply into the subjective core of the citizen-soldier identity. There, it generated doubts, hesitations, and questions. Hendrix's music pointed to the need to look within as well as without for liberation. "Jimi was the point at which you went inside, and stopped listening to the bastards in charge," veteran Jack Martin recalled.[58] "Machine Gun" did this by merging the identities of soldier and farmer around the lyrical and musical blurring of guns, guitars, and axes in a fury of technological violence that questioned clear distinctions between individual power and larger forces and structures. But that song was heard mostly by more committed rock fans who purchased Hendrix's 1970 album, *Band of Gypsys*. "All Along the Watchtower," a much bigger hit, had a far wider impact.

On the *Stateside Top Thirty Countdown* and other shows on AFVN, the intensity of "All Along the Watchtower" only increased due to its position within the show's disorienting combination of musical genres and styles. In the sonic collage of the *Stateside Countdown*, the song followed "Bang Shang-A-Lang," a tune whose title only begins to communicate its sugary bubblegum sound and hypercommodified content. "Bang Shang-A-Lang" was not even credited to actual people; it was performed by anonymous studio musicians for the television animated-cartoon band The Archies. "My heart went bang-shang-a-lang . . . Bang! Bang!" the chorus of male and female singers chanted with good cheer, though in the context of Vietnam, the lyric, like so many other seemingly innocent ones, could take on a very different meaning for close listeners. At spot fifteen, one ahead of Hendrix on the charts, was a white rock group Vanilla Fudge, who, like Hendrix, represented the growing criss-cross between soul and rock on the pop charts. Vanilla Fudge sang "Take Me for a Little While," a soul-tinged song first performed by the white Brooklyn singer Evie Sands. The track was Vanilla Fudge's follow-up to the group's drugged-out, psychedelic version of "You Keep Me Hangin' On," originally a hit by the Motown superstars Diana Ross and the Supremes. Other songs on the *Stateside Top Thirty Countdown* similarly reflected the collage-like mix of pop, rock, soul, and other genres. Frank Sinatra appeared alongside Janis Joplin. The British rock supergroup Cream wailed out their eerie "White Room" after O. C. Smith crooned "Little Green Apples." Jose Feliciano, who generated an outcry for his supposedly unpatriotic version of the "Star-Spangled Banner" at a baseball game earlier in the year, sang about putting on your "High Heel Sneakers" over Latin rhythms, flute, and strings, while Curtis Mayfield and the Impressions soulfully declared, "I'm a Fool for You."[59] One of Manning's "favorite groups," the druggily named Grass Roots, performed "Midnight Confessions." At number one, Mary Hopkin celebrated how "Those Were the Days," a non-rock song that had been released by the Beatles' Apple Records. But while Hopkin's song turned nostalgic, just before her the rock group Steppenwolf invited listeners to accompany them on a psychedelic "Magic Carpet Ride" into a futuristic hallucination.

The *Stateside Top Thirty Countdown* showed how, by 1968, countercultural energies that challenged the military's official narrative of the war erupted within official channels. To be sure, it is difficult to document what a song beamed across the invisible airwaves of AFVN meant in particular moments and settings, but when Stateside Countdown host Scott Manning introduced "All Along the Watchtower," he was eager to emphasize the sheer energy and power of the song. Manning stumbled through his introduction: "The electric Jimi Hendrix and . . . Electric Ladyland . . . and his Experience." Then, ambiguously, Manning warned his listeners that Hendrix was "watching for you, all along the watchtower." What the disc jockey meant was a bit unclear: was Hendrix another GI on lookout for his fellow soldiers? Or was he a member of the Vietcong, lurking out in the darkness, a rider approaching to mount a guerrilla attack? The ways in which Manning presented Hendrix on AFVN called attention to the song's unfixing of stable perspectives on the Vietnam conflict.

With songs such as "All Along the Watchtower," rock mediated the collapsing binary between home front and war zone. The music did not necessarily transmit explicit antiwar positions; instead, it arrived as part of the importation of domestic popular culture, which bundled countercultural flavors into the taste of home. Rock also complicated distinctions between official channels of communication and unofficial levels of disquiet, dissatisfaction, and even dissent in Vietnam. The music never threatened the US intervention enough to ban the genre outright, but the integration of psychedelic sounds into AFVN broadcasts hinted at how much the domestic counterculture and its zones of democratic inquiry into citizenship resonated in Vietnam.

Hendrix's music touched questions of democratic citizenship at another level as well: through the guitarist's complex relationship to race. As a person of mixed ethnic background who was usually identified as African-American, Hendrix grappled with his relationship to the black nationalist turn in the civil rights movement during the late 1960s. At times, he identified with the turn away from an inclusive vision of American citizenship toward black separatism; in other moments, he developed a pluralistic theory of global social belonging in what he called the "electric sky church."[60] Hendrix's investigations of blackness in relation to both American citizenship and world citizenship made him a crucial figure to African-American GIs in Vietnam. That Hendrix himself was an ex-soldier made him all the more appealing.[61] To know about and like Jimi Hendrix was a means both of asserting blackness in Vietnam and connecting across racial affiliations. "That music meant a lot to them," Michael Herr wrote of Hendrix's popularity among African-American soldiers. "In a war where a lot of people talked about Aretha [Franklin]'s 'Satisfaction' the way other people speak of Brahms' Fourth," appreciating Hendrix was "Credentials." When Herr told black GIs about hearing Hendrix for the first time while under enemy fire, they would often reply, "Say, that Jimi Hendrix is my main man. . . . He has definitely got his shit together!"[62] Indeed, one reason why Hendrix may have appeared on AFVN after 1968 was in fact that African-American GIs had protested the lack of black music on the official station.[63] Veteran Jack Martin recalled that, "For awhile, all the souls [black soldiers] wanted to have a 'fro [an afro haircut] like Jimi's, and lots of them wore wigs off duty."[64] Oliver Stone remembered that while not all African-American GIs liked Hendrix, the ones who smoked marijuana did. "A lot of the black druggies really understood his guitar style," Stone reminisced, and "they also appreciated the fact that he managed to look so great and be ex-army at the same time."[65]

Even as Hendrix appealed to many African-American GIs in Vietnam as a black artist, he simultaneously provided common ground among young GIs of all races who were curious about the counterculture. The guitarist's music proposed a shared generational identity that cut across ethnic or racial divisions. He "brought the races together with the consciousness behind the music, and his lyrics," Jack Martin claimed.[66] This was appealing to the managers of the United States Armed

Forces because it seemed like a way to overcome racial tensions among troops in-country. Accepting Hendrix's countercultural music on the official airwaves marked an effort by the Armed Forces to harness the power of cohesion in Hendrix's songs. "It was unusual in the unit I was in for whites to be listening to soul music," remembered Vietnam veteran R. Guy Slater, "just as it was for blacks to be listening to country music. But we all agreed that Jimi Hendrix was great (all us kids, that is.)"[67] Slater's parenthetical aside spoke volumes about the challenge the Armed Forces faced: to raise morale by repairing deteriorating race relations among American GIs meant establishing a new shared identity based on age and rank. Countercultural rock exacerbated the generational tensions between "grunts" and "lifers" that were lowering morale in Vietnam even as it brought subgroups of GIs together.

Moreover, the terms by which Hendrix was "great" had to do as much with the guitarist's assertions of dissolute hedonism as with his music's affirmative qualities. Particularly in association with illegal activities such as psychedelic drug use, Hendrix's songs and style cracked open countercultural possibilities within its very acceptance and incorporation on AFVN. The music was part of "sort of a common bond" between black and white rock fans "because . . . at least a certain percentage of the black guys were getting high—smoking pot," veteran Dave Cline noted. "You had the heads. You had the juicers. You had the brothers," Cline explained about the leisure culture of Vietnam. "The juicers would be more into country music, and the heads would be more into the latest Jefferson Airplane, or Janis Joplin, or Hendrix." For Cline, a soldier in the 4th Battalion, 9th Infantry, 25th Division near Cu Chi, Hendrix was part of the appearance of the counterculture within the war zone. "See '67 was when San Francisco—the hippie—all that type of stuff was coming up," he recalled. Listening to someone like Hendrix, there developed "a pretty good relationship between the heads and the brothers, even culturally."[68] For many of these GIs, rock mattered not because it raised morale, but because it suggested that a new and different social order was blossoming on the home front in direct contrast to the war. "We were in a situation of extreme brutality," Cline remarked, "and I think that we used to look at the whole hippie thing—or at least I did—as being an alternative where people were living more in harmony. . . . Like, here are people living just the opposite of us. . . . And I used to really be attracted to that."[69]

With Hendrix's guitar careening across the official airwaves, rock was incorporated into the war machine, but its incorporation also brought the counterculture's unruly energies of civic questioning into military command and communication structures. One helicopter door gunner, Jim Peachin, recalled that he would listen to combat commands on one radio channel, but another of "the channels that we always had available to us, and we always kept tuned to it, was AFVN, was the Armed Forces radio station." For Peachin, "What was nice about that was, I got pop music," but this was "what made it so weird sometimes." Peachin explained how "we would take off in the morning, and we'd be flying low level across these rice paddies and I'd hear Diana Ross singing 'Everybody I Love You,' and the sky is beautiful, the sun's glistening off the waters. Rice paddies look like felt on a pool table, from a certain altitude. I mean, it looks like you could jump into it. You just couldn't possibly get hurt. And then you hear this music, that is enjoyable at the same time." Then, Peachin noted, "three minutes later, you might be shooting your gun at somebody. Or three minutes later you might be going in to pick up some wounded soldiers. Or three minutes later you might be landing in a place where people are shooting at you." For Peachin, the eerie mix of consumer pleasure and sudden terror encouraged a sense of surreal dissociation.

From this experience, rock could even generate spirit of antiauthoritarian dissent. The music formed a crucial part of a soundscape of rebellion against those in command. Peachin believed that "listening to the radio" and "listening to other people" allowed a soldier to "tune in on different things." Pop, rock, and soul on AFVN might be in one channel, making one feel "like Superman," but on another radio channel, "You would hear someone, like a colonel or a general giving somebody orders, and you'd hear somebody else come on the same line and say, 'Aw, fuck you.'" Because "there was the anonymity of being on a radio," music occasionally provided the background soundtrack for GIs to challenge the authority of the chain of command and the legitimacy of the entire war effort.[70] The acceptance of Hendrix and other rock songs on the official wavelengths of AFVN was part of the shift toward hip militarism by the bureaucracy of the US military, but it also meant that American GIs could, both literally and figuratively, flip a switch between sanctioned broadcasts and sanctuaries of dissent. When they did so, they used rock to foster a counterpublic in the unlikely space of a war zone. But this counterpublic was not a coherent one. Rather, it was comprised of streaks, eddies, fissures, and shards. It consisted of uneven accelerations and decelerations of engagement, sudden lines of inquiry and blurts of anger followed by periods of passivity, numbness, and acquiescence. It was atmospheric, a lurking commons for civic inquiry rather than an open space for outright democratic deliberation. The music allowed GIs to grapple with the relationship between the individual citizen-soldier and the American war machine by being part of the war machine. Broadcast from the official relay towers of AFVN, the music let American fighters stand "all along the watchtower," wondering but unsure if there might be "someway out of here."

"An Open Conference Line among Enlisted Men": The Bullshit Band

Hip militarism—the effort of the United States Armed Forces to incorporate countercultural sounds and styles into the war effort itself—meant that rock music moved through the official channels of AFVN, but this was not the only broadcast medium on which rock arrived in Vietnam. The music also surfaced on unauthorized broadcasts, ranging from the bullshit band, the term for unused radio frequencies on which GIs would play rock music for each other, to more elaborately produced "pirate" and "underground" radio shows. These unofficial broadcasts sometimes allowed GIs to anonymously and outrageously say "aw, fuck you" to a colonel or general, as Jim Peachin recollected. But more crucially, they offered a sonic space for GIs to probe the war's complex milieu of angst and pleasure, anxiety and camaraderie.

On the bullshit band, GIs wired phonograph players, cassette decks, and hi-fi stereos to their radio equipment to send the latest recordings of rock along with other popular sounds from home across the air in Vietnam. They became instant disc jockeys, while rock turned into the soundtrack for mediated public exchanges that pushed beyond military structures toward alternative configurations of citizen-soldier identity and community. GI DJs welcomed communication from troops out in the field and often took requests, just as radio hosts did on radio stations back on the home front. On the bullshit band, rock helped to push hip militarism to the brink, creating a milieu of connection, affiliation, and shared expression that turned the technological infrastructure of the US war machine's communications systems against the orderly waging of the war itself.

This does not mean that the bullshit band stopped the war or was even explicitly antiwar; rather, the bullshit band created a space of open, contradictory, murky, and swirling inquiry at multiple levels, from the ideological to the affective. In what folklorist Lydia Fish evocatively calls the "informal communications systems" of the Vietnam War, the bullshit band generated a flickering counterpublic, a network of buzzing static within the technological infrastructure of the American military intervention.[71] As marine Jay Peterson remembered, "Every night, they'd have these channels" on "a certain part of the low bands of a radio." There a GI would find that "all these people are sitting back in Danang An Hoac, with these tanks or real units, stuff like that, have these fantastic setups that broadcast from An Hoac to the United States or something—are sitting back there at An Hoac in bunkers and stuff, with their stereos. And they're plugging their stereos into these fantastic units, and we're picking these guys up, you know." Peterson's company would "switch over to these freqs, you know, and listen to these guys all night, playing really hard rock music."[72] Though Peterson himself preferred country and western, he was struck that one could hear all the songs "that you wouldn't get on the AFVN."

Of course, one could get many of them on AFVN, but Peterson's memory suggests that the Armed Forces' strategy of hip militarism could only go so far toward incorporating the urge among GIs to connect to the domestic counterculture in places such as San Francisco. Many wanted to get closer to the music than simply hearing it among other bits of domestic pop culture on the official airwaves. To do so, they took to the airwaves themselves. Perhaps their efforts even raised morale just as the military hoped broadcasting rock on AFVN would accomplish. But this camaraderie was laced with alternative possibilities for community that pulled GIs away from the war and toward other perspectives. Marine John Imsdahl, for instance, broadcast over the bullshit band. He remembered how "we had a lot of disc jockeys at night" because "a lot of the artillery guys that were waiting up all night, to fire, and stuff, had electricity on mortars, and they'd play music on their tape decks, and make special requests and, you know, things like that."[73] As they did so, other messages insinuated themselves into the broadcasts. In Imsdahl's case, he adopted his DJ moniker from a Jefferson Airplane song. "I was White Rabbit," he recalled. The connotations of Imsdahl's pseudonym were many. An anthem of the counterculture, the 1967 hit by the San Francisco band was not only about taking psychedelic drugs, but also about seeing past the authority of parents and leaders whose "logic and proportion" had "fallen sloppy dead."[74] For Imsdahl, taking on the anonymous identity of "White Rabbit" allowed him to join an invisible community that used the very channels of command structure and communication to forge more colorful, egalitarian, and even, at times, antiauthoritarian relationships among individuals.

Occasionally, the bullshit band actually interfered with the war effort itself. Jay Peterson recollected one incident in which a GI was "stoned out of his mind" and so busy tuning in the bullshit band that he neglected to radio in reports of potential Vietnamese attacks. "He had the radio on . . . on the underground channels," Peterson explained, "and this is the radio they're supposed to be using to call in when they see artillery flashes from the Vietnamese outside the wires and everything."[75] Instead of fighting the war, this GI fell asleep to the sounds of rock and GI banter on the bullshit band, transforming the realities of war into the dreams of countercultural bliss. This particular GI numbed himself to the war using drugs and music, but in tuning out the war, he did not just tune out altogether; he also tuned in to another channel of sound, meaning, and shared experience.

The bullshit band reached deep into individual lives and, from there, reworked the connections among GIs. As the poet and former marine W. D. Erhart remembered, it "was regularly used . . . as an open conference line among enlisted men."[76]

The radio allowed GIs to converse with each other about the war and it provided a soundtrack for reflection, discussion, and momentary escapes into alternative modes of being. "Partying" to rock music often led to more than just a good time; it also led to a deepening consciousness of the war's absurdities and fundamental injustices. Hearing the music one night over the bullshit band, Ehrhart remembered how he and his company decided to relax, even if it meant that they might suffer a guerrilla attack while doing so. Ehrhart smoked marijuana for the first time, and while neither the music nor the drugs instantly turned him against the war, they provided a setting in which Ehrhart and his fellow troops began to reflect upon their experiences in Vietnam. "Who am I?" a voice asked over the bullshit band after the end of a song, "Why, I'm Dancin' Jack, your Armed Forces Bullshit Network DJ, comin' to you from somewhere deep in the heart of the heart of the country." Listening in, Ehrhart remembered hearing the Beatles, Otis Redding, and Martha and the Vandellas. Talk among his platoon turned to the legality and illegality of the war. While listening to the broadcast, a fellow GI asked Ehrhart how he liked his marijuana. "Oh, wow," Ehrhart replied. "But it's illegal, ain't it?" His friend responded, "What have you done in the last ten months that ain't illegal, Ehrhart?" The GIs all broke up in laughter at the question of legality.[77] The combination of an illegal broadcast of music and the illicit use of marijuana was a way to let off steam and to bond. But rock and marijuana also created the setting for expressing the sense that something was terribly wrong with the larger US mission in Vietnam and even with their own personal actions as fighters. The illegality of the bullshit band seemed to open up a critical awareness of the questionable ethics of the American state's military intervention in Southeast Asia.

Along with drugs, rock music on the bullshit band allowed GIs to simply escape from the war for a time. "The music was playing and playing, and fingers popped in time, and bodies swayed, and the laughter and the night and the smoke rolled on and on like waves against a beach on a far-off tropical island inhabited by Dancin' Jack," Ehrhart recalled. Similarly, a member of the 75th Rangers Regiment, Jon Seikula, remembered that, "We used music to cope with the stress of war.... Music allowed us to detach ourselves from the havoc we were wreaking." For this GI, rock music numbed American fighters to the destruction they unleashed. But in his detachment from the war, Seikula also articulated his awareness that something was amiss in the Vietnam War: "When we were dropping white phosphorous rounds on the enemy... we knew that was pretty lethal stuff."[78] Rock on the bullshit band offered escape—from the official military, from the war itself—but its distancing effect also led to civic questions: was the war just? Was the individual American citizen-soldier complicit in its violent injustices? Listening to rock on the bullshit band anesthetized American GIs, but even as the music carried them far away to Dancin' Jack's tropical island, it also gave them a vista on the war and their individual roles in it.[79] As rock moved between AFVN and the bullshit band, the music brought into question the seemingly arbitrary boundary between legality and illegality in Vietnam. It generated a counterpublic space not by rejecting the technological systems through which the American Armed Forces waged war, but rather by seizing and reorienting the communications system, for moments at a time, toward another aural environment: the sounds of the counterculture back on the home front. The bullshit band did this in fleeting ways. But, if memoirs and memories of Vietnam veterans are to be believed, they nonetheless left their mark. Perhaps their very ephemerality even, paradoxically, increased their impact. This certainly was the case when one GI got more serious about creating an unauthorized pirate radio program and the sounds of the counterculture from home took on a whole new cast in Vietnam.

"The Purpose of This Program Is to Bring Vital News, Information, and Hard Acid-Rock Music": Radio First Termer

In the back room of a Saigon house of prostitution, microphones, a mixing board, and three large Akai reel-to-reel tape decks stood at the ready. The room had been soundproofed behind one-inch thick cork tiles and mattresses. A relay switch clicked. Suddenly, for anyone near Tan Son Nhut Air Base, on the outskirts of Saigon, a voice interrupted the programming on the Armed Forces Vietnam Network, broadcasting at 99.9 megahertz. "Vietnam," the anonymous voice announced, "in thirty seconds, your radio experience will change forever. Turn on your radios to 69 megacycles on your FM dial. If you don't we are going to re-up you for another tour of Vietnam."

If, at that moment, a GI turned the radio dial down to the purposefully naughty frequency number, he would have heard a female voice speak over a flourish of Indian sitar music:

> The following program is in living color and has been rated X by the Vietnam academy of maggots. This is Radio First Termer, operating on Dave Rabbit's own frequency of sixty-nine megacycles on your FM dial. The purpose of this program is to bring vital news, information, and hard acid-rock music to the first termers and non-reenlistees in the Republic of Vietnam. Radio First Termer operates under no Air Force regulations or manuals. In the event of a vice-squad raid, this program will automatically self-destruct. Your host tonight is Dave Rabbit. . . .[80]

FIGURE 4.6. Dave DeLay, Jr., soon to become "Dave Rabbit," at Radio Phan Rang, Vietnam, circa 1970. Estate of C. Dave DeLay, Jr. Photographer unknown.

So began Radio First Termer, an underground rock radio show broadcast from the depths of the Vietnam War. Hosted by Air Force sergeant C. David Delay, Jr., who borrowed his pseudonym Rabbit from a famous stateside DJ, the program appeared on the air for three weeks in January of 1971 (figure 4.6).[81]

Appropriating the underground rock radio format that had first appeared on KMPX and other stations back in the United States, Rabbit claimed that Radio First Termer was "an underground radio station here, and we say what we feel like saying." His show used satirical skits, Rabbit's ominous baritone, and what the DJ called "hard acid-rock music" to represent its version of what life was really like for GIs. The program was especially directed at newcomers to the theater of war. It would bring "the truth to the first termers in the Republic of Vietnam," Rabbit repeatedly noted. We cannot ascertain how many GIs actually heard Radio First Termer in January 1971, nor can we know what they made of the program. But the program itself offers a window onto the reception of rock music in the war zone. Radio First Termer showed how the genre connected GIs to the domestic counter-culture and, at the same time, helped to represent the anomie felt by low-level troops in Vietnam. With "hard acid-rock music" thundering in the background, Radio First Termer poked a finger at the authority and legitimacy of the United States Armed Forces. In the process, it took the logic of hip militarism to its brink. But the program did not break out of hip militarism. It was not overtly antiwar, at least not in any straightforward way, and it did not reject US involvement in Vietnam. It was also misogynist, homophobic, and racist. Radio First Termer did not transcend the war in Vietnam; rather, it registered the fraught, ambivalent, and bitter culture of American citizen-soldiers serving in a war gone terribly awry.[82]

By 1971, the United States Armed Forces was coming apart at the seams. There were cases of GIs refusing to follow orders and flagrantly disobeying what many referred to as the "Mickey Mouse" rules of the military, which demanded a formality that did not seem to match the confusing context of the war. Corruption was rampant, as was drug use. There were even "fraggings," assassinations of commanding officers—though just how many occurred is difficult to ascertain.[83] The Armed Forces Vietnam Network increasingly included rock music, but it did not communicate how rock connected to feelings of disenchantment among lower-level GIs in the war zone. Pirate radio broadcasts, however, did. Radio First Termer was part of a panoply of such programs that appeared in Vietnam by 1970. Jim Scheukler remembered a pirate station "run by the 192nd [Infantry Brigade]'s avionics techs" who "played rock music from open-reel tapes." This station focused on broadcasting the music itself. "While I was there," Scheukler explained, "they purposely were not doing vocal announcing to minimize the risk of pissing-off somebody who could shut them down."[84] Other pirate radio stations positioned rock within messages that were more explicitly antiwar. Jay Peterson recalls "a thing called the Wizard of Oz, that used to have a regular program only . . . (off tape) . . . and it was such a small frequency that you couldn't hardly ever pick it up. These guys are in the rear, with these fantastic set ups, could pick it up and they'd broadcast it over the regular frequencies so you had a real underground, you know, 'Stop the war' campaign going on."[85]

Even the North Vietnamese participated in the pirate radio phenomenon, sending broadcasts of American popular music into South Vietnam. These featured a female announcer, who American GIs famously labeled Hanoi Hannah. Between rock and pop music from the United States, she exhorted GIs to desert the United States Armed Forces.[86] At one point, the antiwar movement in the United States sent "underground" rock radio shows to the North Vietnamese to broadcast to American troops. It is not clear whether they were actually broadcast, but political and countercultural icons such as Abbie Hoffman produced programs for a mock-station called WPAX. "The first show should go on the air in Hanoi on March 8th," disc jockey John Gabree told *Rolling Stone* reporter Peter McCabe in 1971. "We'll be starting with Jimi Hendrix's version of 'The Star Spangled Banner': don't you think that's appropriate?"[87]

Radio First Termer joined these broadcasts, undercutting the official sound of AFVN with unauthorized messages and moods. The program presented a different soundscape of Vietnam than the one the Armed Forces wished to project. In place of a highly efficient and effective fighting machine whose troops were all the more motivated because they were free to enjoy the latest, hippest "mod sounds" from the home front, Radio First Termer instead evoked a world of boredom, sin, inequity, and rage within an alienating bureaucracy. This was not a setting of hardened troops on the front lines, but a decadent leisure culture on the huge military bases in and around Saigon. As a space for taking stock of citizenship, it was a highly gendered and racialized framework, not so much an idealized vision of universal social belonging as an effort to make sense of the evaporation of both the rights and the obligations of citizenship within the Vietnam War.

This was not a show interested in projecting a better world of equality and justice, but rather in measuring and representing experiences of bitter dissatisfaction and desperate hedonism. Dave Rabbit and his cohost, engineer Pete Sadler (figure 4.7), established a puerile, adolescent banter, full of hypersexualized male innuendo. There were countless jokes about local prostitutes and plenty of homophobic commentary. There were endless gags about male and female sexual parts, sexually transmitted diseases, and commanders wearing women's clothing. The show presented the homosocial energies of the military as sick pleasures, as a kind of abject self-immiseration, as if the war were ruining the potentially dignified and noble

FIGURE 4.7. Underground rock radio in Vietnam: Radio First Termer's host Dave Rabbit (Dave DeLay, Jr.) and "Engineer Pete Sadler" (actual name unknown) in Vietnam, 1971. Estate of C. Dave DeLay, Jr. Photographer unknown.

identity of the male citizen-soldier.[88] By making a joke of the cheap, seedy pleasures that were all GIs had to get through their terms of service in what amounted to an American imperial occupation, the program sought to put the lie to portrayals of a healthy, functioning military. Sometimes skits even directly critiqued the fighting abilities of the United States Armed Forces. One featured an Air Force emergency crew mistakenly spraying a pilot with sticky, rancid antiflammable foam. This provided "a living example of how fucked up the Air Force really is," according to Dave Rabbit. Most of the satire did not attack the military's technical prowess directly, but rather focused on the inauthenticity of AFVN. Radio First Termer proposed an alternative soundscape to the war through its burlesques of the official Armed Forces station. Mock newscasts warned about vice-squad raids; an absurdist weather report was given by an effete "Captain Ivan Pansy"; an obscene "swap shop of the air" advertised dildos for sale; an angry send-up of an AFVN announcement encouraged GIs to purchase drugs such as acid, pot, and heroin at stores on US military bases; and a skit featured two GIs securing the services of a Vietnamese prostitute. Rabbit even went so far as to make the comparison of Radio First Termer to AFVN explicit: "We're now going to return you to the regular crappy programming of the American Forces Vietnamese [sic] Network," he explained at the end of one of his pirate broadcasts.[89]

By establishing a very different soundscape for the war zone than the one AFVN projected, Radio First Termer came close to articulating an outright antiwar position. But it did so using humor rather than sincerity, undercutting any stable ideological position on the war. Most of the antiwar focus centered on the unhappiness of GIs as individuals rather than on a larger geopolitical vision of whether the intervention by the United States was just or not. This was a close-up view of life for American citizen-soldiers, not a macroscopic perspective on the war. A mock advertisement for the popular program *Mission Impossible*, which was licensed for broadcast on AFVN, featured an anonymous announcer declaring, "These episodes just go to show that to try to get first-termers to reenlist in the Air Force is truly . . . *mission impossible.*" When Rabbit played "Gotta Find a Way" by the band Bloodrock, he explained to his listeners, "What they're really trying to say is: 'I gotta find a way to get out of fucking Vietnam'." The dedication for Led Zeppelin's "Heartbreaker" went out to "the new troops who have just recently come into the Republic of Vietnam and every day sit and watch those Freedom Birds fly back to the world again." A parody of an AFVN public service announcement featured female announcer Nguyen suggesting that GIs run over other troops who needed rides rather than pick them up. "After all," Nguyen asks, "what are they gonna do? Send you to Vietnam?" "Fooled you, sister," Rabbit responds, "They already did! Ha ha!"[90]

In the most explicit political commentary on the war, Rabbit quoted a soldier's anonymous musings. "Here's another quickie from the latrine walls," he announced. "This joker writes, 'eighteen days until I can go home to picket and protest this fucking waste of human lives that lifers and the government call a war.'" By labeling the graffiti writer a "joker" (shades of "All Along the Watchtower"?), Rabbit left uncertain whether he agreed with the graffiti's antiwar sentiment or not. Was the problem the Vietnam War itself or the presence of "jokers" such as this graffiti writer among GIs? Was the problem that the war was unjust or that the military and government were waging it ineffectively? Radio First Termer's ambiguous framing of antiwar sentiment revealed an ambivalence and complexity of emotions that teetered on outright opposition, but never quite fell into such a position. This kept the program within hip militarism's logic. It also meant that the show perhaps resonated with GIs in a way that a clearly stated and earnest antiwar position could not.[91]

The vexed, almost disoriented mood of the Radio First Termer skits and talksets was continually reinforced by the program's soundtrack, which pulled GIs away from the war toward the domestic counterculture and, at the same time, resonated with life in Vietnam itself. On the one hand, Dave Rabbit wanted to bring "the up-to-date music of today's American youth" to GIs on Radio First Termer. The music was a fantastical if temporary escape back to the home front. But once again through satire and adolescent trench humor, Rabbit also made the music about everyday life in the war. Even the way he referred to the music—as "hard acid-rock music"—connected rock to GI experiences in the military. Rabbit purposefully pronounced the phrase "hard acid" as "hard *ass*-id," as if to emphasize how the music captured the toughness and cruelty of a military drill sergeant or a GI in-country. Rock was a temporary release from war back to civic life in the United States, but at the same time it was an affirmation of a GI's soldier identity in Vietnam.[92]

Rabbit's uses of rock music were often multifaceted. For instance, when he played "I'm a Man" by the Spencer Davis Group, he offered a mock "dedication to the United States Army. Army Sucks!" that was "called in by General Creighton W. Abrams," the head of American Forces in Vietnam. The title of the song and the satire of Abrams implied an antiwar sentiment, but the gag could just as easily have been a critique of the Army by an Air Force sergeant, an example of intramilitary competitiveness. It could even be heard as an effort to raise troop morale by poking fun at the distance between low-level GIs and their supposed leaders. What the dedication most of all demonstrates is the spirit of outlandishness in the name of capturing the complex of emotions that many American servicemen might have felt in Vietnam.[93] Other songs similarly registered conflicting feelings. The program opened with Bloodrock's "Double Cross," a song with a hard Led Zeppelin-esque riff and lyrics about a man seized by anger and rage at a lover. "You deserve everything you get," vocalist Jim Rutledge sings about someone deserving to die.[94] Heard in Vietnam, this statement might have been meant for the military brass or the Vietnamese. It could even have a message GIs were telling themselves. The lyric, as with the song as a whole, was animated most of all by emotions of betrayal, resentfulness, frustration, anger, self-loathing, and self-disgust. Other songs echoed this mood, either through their lyrics or their "heavy" sounds: Santana's "Evil Ways"; Vanilla Fudge's heavy, sluggish version of the Supremes' "You Keep Me Hangin' On"; Cream's "White Room"; Steppenwolf's "The Pusher"; Iron Butterfly's "Soul Experience"; Three Dog Night's "Rock and Roll Widow"; and the same group's version of "Chest Fever," a song originally by The Band. These were hits on the home front that took on a whole new meaning in the context of Vietnam.[95]

Songs that were less ominous in mood, less obsessed with death, rage, or the abject, seemed meant to connect GIs "back to the world" of domestic civilian life; but they too could easily become about the war. Certain selections were most of all about the woozy thrills and illegal pleasures of psychedelic drug use. Hits such as the Byrds' "Eight Miles High," Donovan's "Hurdy Gurdy Man," and Three Dog Night's "Don't Step on the Grass, Sam" connected the experimentation with drugs in the domestic counterculture to the use of them in Vietnam. Buffalo Springfield's "For What It's Worth," released in early 1967, began as a commentary on the so-called "Sunset Strip Riots" in Hollywood during November of 1966, but it quickly became an anthem of countercultural upheaval and questioning in general.[96] Heard in Vietnam in early 1971, the song's chorus—"Stop, children, what's that sound / Everybody look what's going down"—could easily have been about the war.[97]

Jimi Hendrix turned up once again on Radio First Termer, not once but three times, singing "Fire," "Purple Haze," and performing on his drummer Buddy Miles's song "Changes." On Radio First Termer, the guitarist and rock star did not join the collage of pop hits that surrounded his music on AFVN; rather, his songs appeared in a mix of angry sounds and styles. They took on whole new meanings and intensities in the raunchier, starker context of Radio First Termer. Rabbit called out higher-ranking officials in the Armed Forces when he dedicated "Purple Haze" to the "lifers around the Republic of Vietnam, who during the day act Establishment and during the night turn into swingers." The comment was once again multidimensional: a critique of the out-of-touch military bureaucrats who were not only hypocritical, but also uncool, listening to a rock song already four years old—they weren't hippies but swingers. At the end of the song, however, Rabbit

FIGURE 4.8. Engineer Pete Sadler, along with DJ Dave Rabbit and his raised middle finger gold necklace, Vietnam, 1971. Estate of C. Dave DeLay, Jr. Photographer unknown.

shifted tone to explore racial tensions within the United States Armed Forces. "Cookin' with the number one soul man . . . Jimi Hendrix," he remarked. In its strange, satirical way, Radio First Termer's attempted to connect across racial boundaries that were splitting the American military. Rabbit's sidekick Pete Sadler (figure 4.8) continually declared "Right on!" throughout the show. At one level, the appropriation of the phrase from African-Americans was offensive, but it also signaled that Radio First Termer recognized the counterculture's intersections with African-American culture in Vietnam.[98] The broadcast ended with Dave Rabbit jokingly referring to the growing political activism among African-Americans in Vietnam, who were among the most active embracers of black nationalism. "Remember," Rabbit declared to close his program, "there is no black power or white power in Vietnam. There's only one power. And that's rabbit power." Here was an admission that GIs were split by racial divisions, but also an attempt to use countercultural sounds and styles to cut across them.[99] With the satirical call for "rabbit power," Radio First Termer signed off with a sly call for a shared, cross-racial, antiauthoritarian GI culture in Vietnam. But its humor never fully disentangled the program from the larger logic of hip militarism. The effort to bridge racial divides ironically mirrored the Armed Forces' official efforts to do so.

In fact, certain Vietnam veterans believe that pirate radio shows may have sometimes been purposefully tolerated by the Armed Forces. "The powers that be correctly assumed that the VC would not attack and/or destroy any of the pirate stations since they had a slightly anti-war or anti-military [message] at times," psychological operations (PSY-OPS) radio engineer Steve Robbins argues. "This may also account for the reason that many of the pirate stations were left in operation, instead of being closed down by the military as some of the brass wanted to do."[100] No corroborating evidence has ever surfaced to support Robbins' claim that the US military tolerated pirate rock stations for strategic purposes, but the very existence of his theory suggests how hip militarism functioned to undercut the war effort even though the United States Armed Forces hoped that it would raise morale. Reflecting back on the war, Robbins wondered where the lines blurred among official military policy, vernacular troop culture, and covert operations. Rock formed the soundtrack, both within the war and even more so in memories of it, for a crisis of legitimacy, a festering sense of doubt, and a questioning of anything and everything.

So too, the afterlife of Dave Rabbit's program indicates the ways in which hip militarism fostered a dizzying, confusing sense of the Vietnam War. Rabbit shut the program down by the end of January 1971 when the technicians helping him broadcast the show came under threat of exposure. His show survived on bootlegged cassette tapes and, eventually, on the Internet as a historical document of uncertain provenance. It even made an appearance in a National Public Radio *All Things Considered* report in 1987.[101] There were rumors that Dave Rabbit was conspiracy theorist and cult-DJ Art Bell or *Wheel of Fortune* game show host Pat Sajak, who had served in Vietnam as an AFVN disc jockey.[102] Many veterans disputed whether the recordings were in fact ever broadcast in Vietnam, noting their complex use of cross-fading techniques—perhaps they were made by AFVN DJs in their off-time or perhaps a veteran had made them after the war in an act of historical imagining.[103] Then, in 2006, Dave Rabbit resurfaced. Living in Dallas, Texas, he heard recordings of his program when his son was working on a high school term paper. Rabbit had indeed been involved in radio during his time in Vietnam, and he claimed he had indeed broadcast the show in January of 1971 from Tan Son Nhut Air Force Base. He told his story in a series of articles and interviews. Then, later that year, something even stranger occurred. Rabbit decided to revive the Radio First Termer program for the Iraq War. This time, however, he traveled with official press credentials and broadcast the show with the approval of the United States Armed Forces. In 2011, he made a similar trip to Afghanistan to present another Radio First Termer program. Full of the same hard rock music soundtrack and disgruntled trench humor that bordered on antiwar rhetoric but never quite fully delivered it, Radio First Termer Iraq and Afghanistan demonstrated that the logic of hip militarism was alive and well years after the Vietnam War had ended.[104]

Yet it is also worth remembering that Radio First Termer provided a medium for measuring feelings of disenchantment and even beginning to think critically about them. Within hip militarism, the program proposed a temporary, fluctuating commons of the air for GIs struggling to come to terms with the Vietnam War and the multiple senses of fragmentation it brought them. The show evoked both the pains and the pleasures—and the troubling mix of the two—that comprised life in Vietnam for many American citizen-soldiers. And it offered them a script for surviving and perhaps even making sense of their experiences. Radio First Termer's humor and "hard acid-rock music" soundtrack told GIs they were welcome. It oriented them by dramatizing their disorientations.

Surveying Rock in Vietnam

The more pirate radio and the bullshit band blared rock music and its countercultural ethos into Vietnam, the more the Armed Forces recognized that GIs wanted to hear such music in Vietnam. Concerned with measuring troop opinion in order to serve them best, and also to justify military expenditure on AFVN, the network conducted audience surveys in 1968, 1970, and 1971. These surveys were rich with information about the official military stance on music brought to the war zone: they indicated a willingness to bring to Vietnam any music popular on the domestic airwaves, but they also revealed an anxiety about maintaining the legitimacy of the American intervention.

Author James Wentz wrote in the 1968 report, which was issued at the beginning of 1969, "The exclusion of any music from military broadcasting outlets can be damaging to the credibility and reputation of the network. This is not to say that absolutely no restrictions should be placed on music forwarded to field activities. However, exceptional care must be taken when the matter of exclusion is considered." As Wentz's comments suggested, the military did not ignore the antiwar dimensions of popular music on the home front. Wentz himself noted, somewhat vaguely, that "[t]he matter of music selection has become a more delicate issue in today's environment of social and moral conflict."[105] But overall, Wentz took the position that since most of this music made it to Vietnam in other forms, the military was better off including it. The AFVN surveys also registered shifts that were occurring in domestic consumer capitalism as the American mass market transitioned from a mingling of pop culture styles to segmented niche markets. On the 1968 *Stateside Top Thirty Countdown*, rock music exploded from a swirl of disparate sounds all collaged together, but by 1970, "acid rock" and "soul" were becoming niche market genres, each with a small but substantive presence on AFVN. In 1968 and 1970, soul had consistently been approved by roughly ten percent of survey respondents, with a bit higher ranking among younger servicemen; by 1971, twenty two percent deemed soul their "most listened to" form of music. Acid rock grew from not existing at all as a category in 1968 to being the first, second, or third choice of 30 percent of respondents in 1970 (figure 4.9). By 1971, this niche market among GIs continued to exist at roughly the same level: 31 percent of troops deemed acid rock their "most listened to" form of music.[106]

Whether the inclusion of rock actually improved GI morale or, by contrast, undercut the war effort with antiwar messages and moods remains up for debate, but what is perhaps more important is the manner in which rock entered Vietnam simultaneously "above ground" and "underground," part of the official military effort to bring a taste of home to troops but also as the music of the domestic counterculture. In his official 1971 AFVN survey, Gunar Grubaums referred to acid rock as "underground" music, noting that the military had decided, based on its survey, to increase the broadcast time of this music over the Armed Forces radio network in Vietnam for a prime time hour on Saturday nights.[107] The emergence of acid rock as a distinctive category of music on the official airwaves of AFVN hinted at the ways in which American public culture, increasingly driven by hip capitalism, was shifting from a mass market to ever-more-granular subgroups.

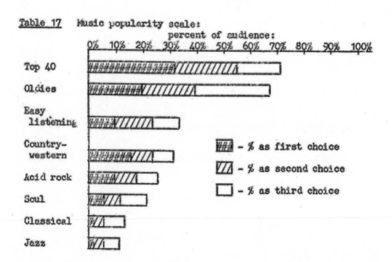

FIGURE 4.9. The nichification of Armed Forces Vietnam Network radio and the emergence of "acid rock": The 1970 survey of audience opinion by AFVN.

"Underground" had a proper place now on the officially sanctioned airwaves. Even in the military, where service to country and the threat of death had the potential to render a common civic identity, rock music's changing place on the official military airwaves bespoke fragmentation. The unified, mass-market collage of American public life was breaking up. Absorbed into the official broadcast channel of the military but continuing its presence on unofficial frequencies, rock circulated a mood of psychedelic discontinuity and disruption. From this swirl of co-optation and continued static, GIs drew upon rock to ask what kind of American citizenship was possible halfway around the world when a unified civic life was disintegrating at home.[108] They did so on the radio airwaves, as they both tuned into AFVN and created their own pirate rock radio shows. When they started playing rock music themselves, the strategies of hip militarism once again surfaced. So too, once again, did questions of citizenship.

5

WELCOME TO ENTERTAINMENT VIETNAM!

THE FRONTISPIECE FOR an Entertainment Branch scrapbook created at the end of 1968 featured images of soldier-entertainers among music notes, tragedy and comedy masks, and the names of music genres such as jazz and soul (figure 5.1). The word "rock" was cut out from construction paper and angled to fit right into the pastiche. "Welcome to Entertainment Vietnam!" the title page incongruously announced. "Turn the pages and view that which is the greatest morale booster today!"[1]

The scrapbook commemorated an unusual program called the Command Military Touring Shows (CMTS), which organized GIs into music and theater groups and sent them out into the field on temporary duty to raise the spirits of fellow troops. Celebrating the ability of the Entertainment Branch to draw upon the talents of GIs themselves to deliver leisure activities to each other, the book was part of an enormous effort by the United States Armed Forces to improve troop morale in Vietnam.[2] Within CMTS, rock appeared as merely another genre, fully incorporated into the war machine. Yet, as much as the CMTS scrapbook marked the military's absorption of rock, with all its countercultural associations, into its apparatus of wartime entertainment, far more was at stake in the military's official sanctioning of soldier bands performing the music. Once groups went out into the field to perform, other experiences, ideas, representations, and sensibilities arose: as GIs played and listened to rock, they not only entered into the logic of hip militarism, the tactic by which the Armed Forces accepted, even cultivated, rebellious modes of expression, they were also touched by the civic energies and ideas of the counterculture. A little bit of San Francisco traveled with rock wherever it

FIGURE 5.1. Welcome to Entertainment Vietnam!: The CMTS Scrapbook, South Vietnam, 1968. NARA.

went and whoever performed it. Whenever CMTS groups performed the music, GIs not only entertained themselves, they also heightened the tensions between the two halves of their citizen-soldier identities and, in the process, made pressing questions about the Vietnam War available for scrutiny.

The CMTS grew out of the Black Patches talent shows organized in 1966. These had been put together from Air Force and Army personnel in late 1966 "to provide live entertainment in places where USO shows were forbidden for security reasons."[3] The USO, or United Service Organization, was a private, nonprofit organization that had provided entertainment to American GIs since World War II.[4] But the growing antiwar movement on the home front and complicated politics and military arrangements in Vietnam meant that the USO was unable to bring a steady stream of domestic culture to the war zone. This was particularly the case with rock music. While Bob Hope continued to perform his famous Christmas shows for GIs and even James Brown toured the Republic of Vietnam (without the support of the Armed Forces), rock bands from the San Francisco scene and elsewhere were far less likely to cooperate with the American government and travel to Southeast Asia.[5] Into the breach, the military itself stepped, particularly after the war escalated in the mid-1960s. "During the period May 1966–January 1968," an official history of CMTS from 1970 explained, the entire Entertainment Branch "had the 'big, happy family' flavor" with all it units "working as a pioneering family, roughing it and loving it." Using a phrase that oddly evoked the imperial role that the United States inherited from French colonizers, the memo celebrated how members of the Entertainment Branch were "empire-building together." Even after the Tet Offensive of January 1968 and Richard Nixon's decision to begin withdrawing American troops the next year, the CMTS program continued to expand. "The Big Tet of 1968 brought about a less idealistic, more naturalistic set of operational circumstances," the official history contended.[6] Even mainstream celebrities were less likely to visit Vietnam on USO tours. But given the continued failure of the United States to secure victory for the ruling government of South Vietnam, there was an even greater need to lift sagging morale among troops.

The CMTS marked a response to this situation and revealed two underlying assumptions about rock music in its circulation between the home front and Vietnam. First, Entertainment Branch officials seemed to believe that if CMTS could provide a "taste of home" to GIs everywhere in the war zone, no matter what their particular tastes or where they were located, then this demonstrated not the pampered weakness of US fighting forces, but rather the power of the military to maintain morale. Second, the Entertainment Branch was keen to elevate the status of GIs in an effort to keep them happy despite the distractions of a war gone increasingly awry. On the first count, the penetration of domestic consumer culture, especially the most cutting-edge forms of entertainment, to the most remote reaches of Vietnam was equated with military prowess itself. If this meant training soldiers themselves to perform the latest sounds from home and coordinating their travels around the war zone, sometimes with over 800 pounds of equipment, this was not an example of the bureaucratic bloat or imperial extravagance of the United States Armed Forces, but rather a sign of its mission effectiveness and logistical skill. Officials in the Entertainment Branch often focused on CMTS's ability to provide all servicemen with leisure activities no matter how remote their locale in Vietnam (figure 5.2). "A primary concern of the branch," a report from 1971 explained, "has been to locate and provide live entertainment for military units whose missions have isolated them from normal recreation circuits."[7] As Major Edward J. Jones, Saigon Support Command Special Services Officer, had put it two years earlier, in 1969, "For the troops far out in the field we have touring soldier shows." Jones explained that while the USO shows were available in the rearguard, CMTS groups could go anywhere. "They go where the pros can't" (figure 5.3).[8] The idea that the military could provide entertainment—anywhere, anytime—to lift morale was understood to be a triumph of military logistics. Never mind that morale might be suffering for reasons beyond the lack of entertainment, such as the drift of American goals in Vietnam, official distortions of truth, or the lack of clarity about the reasons for the mission in Vietnam in the first place.

The second underlying assumption behind CMTS went even further than just proving how effectively the military could deliver consumer entertainment from the home front. Particularly after 1968, as the United States Armed Forces faced sagging morale and the possibility of needing to recruit an all-volunteer force if the draft ended, officials in the Entertainment Branch increasingly fostered a GI-generated leisure culture.[9] The CMTS program was not just about bringing rock to war, but about making warriors into rock stars. This new emphasis on encouraging GIs to take up electric guitars and amplifiers paralleled the changing management and marketing strategies on the home front. At American corporations, the 1960s saw a transformation from top-down bureaucracy to more democratic, bottom-up organizational models that encouraged individualism, creativity, even eccentricity instead of conformity, hierarchy, and order.[10] The CMTS echoed these changes within the institutional culture of the Armed Forces. Never was the effort to encourage and coordinate GI-generated entertainment so intensive. Indeed, by the early 1970s, a decentralized and participatory form of hip militarism appeared in Vietnam to rival anything corporations offered on the home front. The Entertainment Branch devoted considerable resources to hosting talent shows and "music happenings,"

"And my sergeant will be in the lead ship. He makes the final decision to land or not, okay?"

FIGURE 5.2. *Army Times* cartoon poking fun at CMTS bands, undated. NARA.

FIGURE 5.3. "They go where the pros can't": CMTS group Page Six loading amplifiers and drums onto a helicopter, South Vietnam, 1970. NARA.

providing instruments and practice rooms, and encouraging commanders to allow musically oriented soldiers to serve in CMTS groups. In place of slick commercial presentations, CMTS emphasized countercultural values of vernacular, do-it-yourself musical creation. The goal of the program was not only to entertain troops, but also "to provide an outlet for the performers' talents," as one memorandum explained.[11] "The theme of entertainment . . . predominates this program," the 1968 CMTS scrapbook noted, but it also celebrated the quality of "top GI talent."[12] A Special Services memorandum entitled "Entertainment as a Tool of Public Relations" emphasized the goal of getting servicemen involved in making their own entertainment. "All [military] installations have their share of performers, some of considerable talent and experience," the document noted. "With effective technical backing, these people can represent the installation to great advantage."[13]

Picking up on the countercultural values placed on authenticity and self-expression, the Entertainment Branch especially embraced the idea of self-generated GI entertainment when it came to rock music. A speech prepared for a 1970 staff conference explained that among GIs with musical ability, "certainly the most numerous are those who help make the loud, rhythmic music which is most popular with the vast majority of the young servicemen." But, "even with their large numbers and the demand for their performing abilities, getting them organized for performances gets to be quite a project. That's where our Entertainment Directors can be most useful."[14] The job of the Entertainment Branch was to encourage GIs to play that "loud, rhythmic music" no matter what its ideological content. Even when audience evaluation forms reported back to the Entertainment Branch that the favorite song performed by a CMTS band was Edwin Starr's soul-rock hit song "War! (What Is It Good For? Absolutely Nothing!)," the show went on—both the war itself and rock's accepted presence in it.[15] By the logic of hip militarism, the Entertainment Branch eventually considered even CMTS to be too professionalized a program. "Now that civilian entertainment directors are operating in each Corps area," an Entertainment Branch report announced in 1972, "the number of Command Military Touring Shows will gradually decrease as locally produced activities gain their rightful emphasis."[16] At this late date in the American intervention in Vietnam, the Entertainment Branch was still "empire-building." Officials hoped that each part of the Republic of Vietnam might became a localized zone of participation and bottom-up morale-building through non-professional music-making (figure 5.4). "Musical and technical equipment has become available in all military regions for use by an increasing number of military personnel," a 1970 Entertainment Branch report had claimed. This "availability for rehearsals and performances encourages recreational entertainment for participants and local spectators." There would one day, the Entertainment Branch officers hoped, be a high density of "Entertainment Centers" across South Vietnam where GIs could check out electric guitars, form "rock combos," rehearse, and entertain themselves and their fellow servicemen.[17] It was as if the San Francisco Music Council had joined the US military to organize a Wild Southeast Asia Festival.

The dream of a fully realized "Entertainment Vietnam" in which troops could make ample use of local arts centers never came fully to fruition, but the CMTS program was indicative of a larger turn in the military toward hip militarism at the end of the 1960s. In the Navy, for instance, the sideburn-wearing Admiral Elmo R. Zumwalt took over in 1970 as the new chief of naval operations and instituted a new policy: relaxed regulations for hair length, facial hair, and uniforms, along with the "establishment of five 'hard rock clubs' at naval stations as pilot projects."

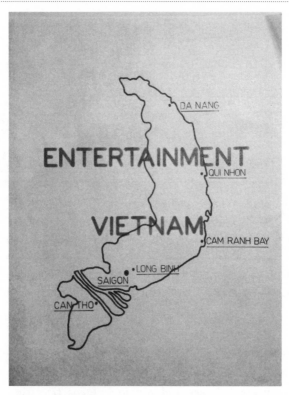

FIGURE 5.4. Entertainment Vietnam: A map from the Entertainment Branch of the United States Army in Vietnam, circa 1970. NARA.

These clubs opened "so the Navy's now-generation of under-thirty officers can have a place of their own to really rock it."[18] The Army also sought to relax what Zumwalt called "Mickey Mouse" regulations and requirements. "We will keep up to—and try to stay ahead of—changes in society which involve developing the dignity and inherent value of every man," Lieutenant General George I. Forsythe explained to a reporter.[19] "The Navy has reached the point," Zumwalt argued, "where we can no longer drift with the tides and winds of change oblivious to the . . . needs of our civilian society."[20] Of course, Forsythe never mentioned that the goal of the Army was to be an effective killing machine, something that might be in contradiction with "developing the dignity and inherent value of every man," but his comments nonetheless pointed to the ways in which the military itself had gone countercultural by 1970.

A cartoon on the front cover of an "underground" newspaper that circulated in Vietnam called the *Grunt Free Press*—never overtly antiwar but also, like the Entertainment Branch, dedicated to raising troop morale through humor and satire—poked fun at hip militarism (figure 5.5).[21] A high-ranking officer from the

FIGURE 5.5. "Don't you want to be a growing part of that swingin' group, the U.S. Army?": Responding ambiguously to hip militarism in the *Grunt Free Press*, August 1971. Estate of Kenneth Sams.

Pentagon addresses troops in Vietnam: "Hi, men! I'm here . . . to tell you that you've got a place in today's mod, hep, on the go-go, with it, got it together Army!" The officer, wearing sunglasses and not looking particularly countercultural himself, continues, "You like the Army now, and you're gonna find it even better as you go along! Get this—L-O-N-G hair, with sideburns even! No more unnecessary formations and details! And if you're man enough, you can keep your moustaches! Waddya say, don't you want to be a growing part of that swingin' group, the U.S. Army?" In the final panel of the cartoon, this representative from the Pentagon gets his response: an anonymous raised middle-finger shoots up from the mass of helmeted troops.[22] The gesture is ambiguous: is it a radical critique of hip militarism, a refusal by GIs to be co-opted by the military brass's pseudo-cool? Or is it just the opposite: an expression of longing for the traditional military and its rigid regulations? The cartoonist for the *Grunt Free Press* leaves the meaning unclear, but either way, the cover suggests that there is more to the story of hip militarism than its adoption by the managers of the Armed Forces. Just as hip capitalism in late-60s San Francisco was the starting point for a robust engagement with questions of democratic citizenship and shared public life in a shifting domestic American consumer culture, so too in Vietnam, hip militarism was not the end result of the importation of countercultural styles from the home front. Rather, hip militarism marked the beginning of a story of highway salutes and flipped birds, an ethos of democratic anger and desperation rife with tensions and contradictions.

"The Entertainment Branch Invites You to Submerge Yourself in the Pulsating Rhythm of the Peace-Pac": Publicity Materials and Public Life

In San Francisco, live performances of rock music offered a new mode of citizenship and public life within the context of hip capitalism, but in Vietnam, CMTS rock shows remained much more inchoate in their civic import. Certainly, rock was not tied to antiwar politics in any direct way. No GIs instantaneously beat their automatic guns into electric guitars when they heard a CMTS group perform its version of a Jimi Hendrix, Creedence Clearwater Revival, Jefferson Airplane, Beatles, or Rolling Stones song. Not only was the genre not a stable communicator of antiwar sentiment, but in CMTS shows it did not create public spheres of civic inquiry in any straightforward sense. After all, these were events for GIs to let off steam, get drunk, and lose themselves in music. They were political in the sense that they represented a temporary suspension of military norms and regulations, but they were not spaces in which soldiers engaged in overt antiwar critique. Yet, in their own way, they became environments for registering the many dissonances of life in Vietnam.

Publicity materials created by the Entertainment Branch especially suggest that even when CMTS bands actually succeeded at raising morale in the short run by playing rock music and bringing a taste of home to the war, they also, in the same instance, transported the energies of the domestic counterculture to Vietnam. Even though it was for leisure and entertainment, rock introduced proxies of the investigations of individual identity and collective belonging in places such as San Francisco. While the music may have improved spirits temporarily, it undermined morale in the long run by importing countercultural dissonance, engagement, and civic questioning. With CMTS, hip militarism proved to be an uncertain and unruly strategy of control. Like hip capitalism, it rendered obsolete old assumptions about simplistic binaries of cultural opposition. Rebellion and co-optation were no longer easily sorted out.

Publicity materials for CMTS easily appropriated the exaggerated language of marketing domestic rock on the home front, but in doing so they introduced potential connections between the counterculture and GI audiences. The disruptive, disorienting loudness of the groups was emphasized. If troops wanted to "blow their minds" with deafening sounds when they were taking a break from the roar of mortars, bombs, and automatic rounds, then the Entertainment Branch would provide it. The "CMTS is proud to present 'BUZZ'," one press release declared, "a rock group with 3 outstanding musicians who get it together in a distinctive bag. . . . When 'Buzz' comes on stage and begins to play hard rock music, the walls will shake, feet will stomp, and hands will clap!" To further link rock music in Vietnam to the counterculture of places like San Francisco, Buzz's

FIGURE 5.6. A GI in faux–R. Crumb comic style: Poster for CMTS group Buzz, South Vietnam, December 1971. NARA.

publicity poster imitated the iconic countercultural R. Crumb icon "Keep On Truckin'," a series of men with their shoes extended toward the viewer in an exaggerated stride (figure 5.6). Never copyrighted by Crumb, the "Keep On Truckin'" figures were popular on LSD "blotter art" as well as on rolling papers for marijuana. The Buzz poster featured a similar character to Crumb's, but this time with a crew cut, as if he were a GI who wanted to march right alongside R. Crumb's characters down Haight Street in San Francisco.[23] He also seems to be holding a joint and breathing out the druggy name of the band in lightning bolts of smoke.

Other CMTS groups emphasized the ability of the Entertainment Branch to sponsor the most sonically aggressive and confrontational forms of rock music to troops. A press release for Burning Spear announced that the band played "hard hitting, ear shattering rock 'n' roll." Peace-Pac "is not for the Lawrence Welk fans," CMTS announced. "These boys are heavy. . . . The Entertainment Branch invites you to submerge yourself in the pulsating rhythm of The Peace-Pac."[24] Another group, Fresh Air, was celebrated for the sheer volume of its sound. "Advance reports state that this is the loudest rock band USARV Entertainment has ever sent out to entertain American servicemen," a CMTS press release noted. "So have your ear plugs ready when 'Fresh Air' comes to entertain." As if to impress upon troops the military commitment of resources and power being devoted to entertaining them, the press release ended by noting that Fresh Air was traveling with more than "800 pounds of equipment."[25]

Like these other groups, Fixed Water was sent out on tour with a press release that emphasized the band's psychedelic *bona fides*. "USARV Special Services Entertainment Branch is proud to present the mind-bending psychedelic sounds of the 'Fixed Water'," according to the group's publicity materials.[26] The band was so successful during their first tour in the summer of 1969, they were sent out again in the fall with a slightly different lineup. The Entertainment Branch publicity once again announced, "Strong and heavy, the 'Fixed Water' is the ultimate in psychedelic now-sounds. Prepare yourself!" The publicity poster connected the group even more explicitly to the rock sounds and styles from home. Imitating the flourishing poster art styles for which San Francisco's rock ballrooms had become renowned, the Fixed Water poster featured mesmerizing swirls and stripes in a simplified version of the ornate Op-Art style that sometimes appeared on posters for the Fillmore and Avalon Ballrooms, among other venues. In bubble letters, askew and slanted across the page, the poster announced that "Fixed Water" was a "psychedelic band" (figure 5.7).[27]

By design, the sound of bands such as Fixed Water appealed to grunts, the younger draftees and enlistees who often felt alienated from their ostensible mission in Vietnam. Doing so through the mode of hip militarism ended up accentuating their disenchantment with the military hierarchy and the war itself. Positive reviews of Fixed Water concealed negative impacts on the American war machine. One soldier, WM Smith Jr., praised Fixed Water for a performance at Chu Lai: "There are thousands of young men fighting over here that like this type of music would give anything to be able to hear it played by four outstanding young men who know it and how to play it."[28] An Army advanced team member who signed his name Eben E. P. Trevor saw a show at the Ben Tre NCO/EM Open Mess on November 28, 1969, and wrote, "I think personally that this show is what is needed

FIGURE 5.7. A "Psychedelic Band": CMTS group Fixed Water, South Vietnam, August 1969. NARA.

in Vietnam. More of this for the younger people would be great."[29] Both these comments confirm the ways in which the Entertainment Branch so successfully co-opted rock. Yet buried within the approval is a sense that the "thousands of young men" were desperately longing to participate in the counterculture back at home and not be stuck in a war halfway around the world. Morale raised was also morale weakened.

William D. Founds, 1st Lieutenant, wrote the most telling description of a Fixed Water show at the Phu Bai amphitheater on October 3, 1969: "Performances scheduled in the Amphitheater draw crowds of all age groups. Fifteen minutes after show got underway a large number of the older men walked out. Music is one thing and noise is another. Psychedelic Band apparently was not their thing. Those who stayed enjoyed the show."[30] The "mind-bending sounds" of Fixed Water firmed up the boundaries of difference between young and old, hip and unhip, grunts and lifers. The group was not the only band to have this effect. The CMTS band Fresh Air also noted the ways in which rock music marked distinctions of identity in Vietnam. The group's After-Action Report described a concert at the Phu Cat Officer's Club: "I was told that these people had been wanting a hard rock band for approximately 5 months. They complained about the music being too loud after we had turned our volume down about three times. The AC power was then turned off in the middle of a song and we were told that the music was still too loud. Maybe they would have rather had dinner music. We were told that our effort was greatly appreciated, but no thank you."[31] Donna Douglas, the Entertainment Branch officer for Phu Cat, also wrote a letter to CMTS director Brad Arrington that the band was drinking onstage and refused to cooperate when asked to turn their volume down.[32] So too, the group Ace Trucking Company was similarly "very loud but the troops loved it.

They appealed to the young troops."[33] Once again, raising the morale of young GIs meant exacerbating the lack of cohesion between troops and their commanders.

If certain CMTS rock bands seemed designed to bring the latest sounds, styles, and civic energies of the "mind-bending psychedelic" home front to Southeast Asia, other groups were meant to appeal more directly to the experiences of GIs themselves in Vietnam. One group, the aptly-named Electric Grunts, were "five men with music designed for the man on the line." Since they were "coming from the field, they know what songs need hearing and how they must be played." These included "'Springfield: "For What It's Worth'; Beatles: A Day in the Life'; Sweat and Tears: 'I Love You More Than You'll Ever Know'; Animals, 'Sky Pilot'" and ranged "from Acid Rock to Heavy Blues." While the band's publicity release emphasized the band's ability to "bring it all home," it was unclear where exactly home was: it certainly was not small-town conservative America But was it back in the groovy streets of the Haight-Ashbury or was home now deep in the jungles of Vietnam?

The Entertainment Branch presented the Electric Grunts as a band that demonstrated how the military brass had become hip to the experiences of being a low-level infantryman in "the 'Nam."[34] But many of the songs that the Electric Grunts included in their show were fraught with ambivalence about the Vietnam War. If these were the songs that GIs "need hearing," as the press release put it, then hip militarism unleashed unruly antiwar energies into the entertainment mix even as it seemed to contain them through a kind of repressive tolerance. Buffalo Springfield's "For What It's Worth" and the Beatles' "A Day in the Life" were anthems of the domestic counterculture, songs filled with a mood of change, dread, and wonder. As Buffalo Springfield's Stephen Stills famously sang, "There's something happening here / what it is ain't exactly clear." The Beatles' "A Day in the Life" was the climactic track of the quintessential psychedelic album *Sgt. Pepper's Lonely Hearts Club Band*. Though a bit dated by 1970, when the Electric Grunts toured Vietnam, "For What It's Worth" and "A Day In the Life" remained signal countercultural songs. The inclusion of "Sky Pilot" in the press release is even more surprising. Eric Burdon and the Animals' trippy epic went to fourteen on the US pop charts in 1968 and seemed almost an outright antiwar song. Referring indirectly to the intensive American bombing campaigns of North Vietnam, Burdon sang: "In the morning they return / With tears in their eyes / The stench of death / Drifts up to the skies / A young soldier so ill / Looks at the Sky Pilot / Remembers the words / 'Thou Shall Not Kill'." That the Entertainment Branch sponsored the performance of this type of material suggests how much the logic of hip militarism penetrated the officer corps, at least in the Special Services division.[35]

As with other CMTS rock bands, when bands such as the Electric Grunts or OD Circus (figure 5.8) performed, their music divided American GIs. At a show near Vinh Long, generational conflicts once again erupted: "We caused a verbal battle

CMTS DECEMBER – JANUARY 1970
The O D Circus

FIGURE 5.8. The CMTS group OD Circus performing at a GI club, South Vietnam, January 1970. NARA.

between the younger officers who grooved on the acid-rock and the older ones who thought we ought to go back where we came from," the members of the Electric Grunts reported. Often these differences took place through competing genre styles: acid rock and country and western symbolized opposing worldviews, values, and modes of being. Even in 1970, when even the most successful psychedelic rock bands such as the Grateful Dead and the Byrds were well on their way toward adopting country sounds as their own, CMTS bands in Vietnam were forced to choose between the two. When the Electric Grunts "flew out to Duc Hoa for a performance," the band members explained that, "The order for the day was for country-western music. It wasn't our bag, but we managed to fake 'Your Cheatin' Heart' and 'Sweet Georgia Brown.'" A few days later, however, when the band played at Firebase Jamie, the group reported that the audience, "seem to like our acid-rock numbers the best."[36]

The tensions between GIs who were country fans and those who liked acid rock continued to haunt the Electric Grunts' tour. When the band performed for Special Forces B-51, they "wouldn't settle for anything less than stone cold country-western music." By contrast, when the Electric Grunts played in an enlisted men's club a few nights after that, "The men were really friendly and appreciated our acid-rock numbers." At a naval station, Vinh Long NAVSUP, the Electric Grunts reported that, "Acid rock was appreciated the most here," and a transportation company in Qui Nhon, "was *not* a country-western crowd and our first c and w numbers drew jeers." Instead, "the acid-rock seemed to be the most popular part of the show."[37] Like good soldiers, the Electric Grunts adjusted to what their particular audiences needed to boost spirits, but performing a song such as "Sky Pilot" was certainly a strange way to do it.

"Rock n' Soul": Race and Music for "Everyday People" in Vietnam

Country and acid rock were not the only genres that made their way from the home front to the war zone. Soul music was increasingly prominent as well. It was a particularly important genre for African-American soldiers serving in the war effort. When the Electric Grunts performed at the Long My Depot at Qui Nhon, it was not what they played, but what they did not play that caused trouble. "When we wouldn't do another soul number at the end," the band reported, "a brother raced up on the stage determined to fight the guitar player. A short scuffle took place before his buddies pulled him off stage." A few days later, at a Plieku Enlisted Men–Non-Commissioned Officer Club, the band noticed outright segregation among attendees. "Strangely," the Electric Grunts wrote in their after-action report, "the blacks and whites in the audience sat in different sections of the room."[38] These divisions were most starkly distinguished by country-western and soul; rock, however, played a more ambiguous role in the racial tensions of the Vietnam War.

Racial conflicts in Vietnam often revolved around the perceived lack of cultural options for African-American GIs at military clubs and bases. Historian Ron Spector cites a "Report of Inquiry Concerning a Petition of Redress of Grievances by a Group of Soldiers of the 71st Transportation Battalion One" to explain that "a common cause of arguments was music, with blacks frequently demanding that the clubs provide more soul music. One club at Cam Ranh Bay that featured almost exclusively country and western music was the scene of a near riot and 'threats to burn the club down.'"[39] While the racial distinctions between country and soul were more clearly marked, rock and soul overlapped in ways that the military tried to utilize in order to maintain troop morale.

The CMTS responded to the tensions over the lack of entertainment for African-American troops by organizing GI bands that played, as the poster for the group Jimmy and the Everyday People put it, "Rock n' Soul" (figure 5.9).[40] As their name rather obviously suggested, Jimmy and the Everyday People were modeled after

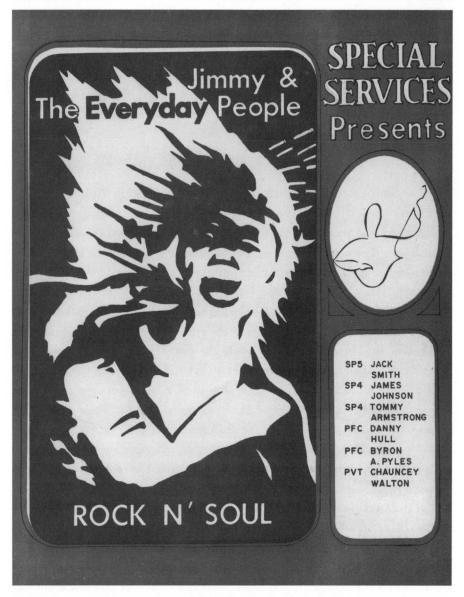

FIGURE 5.9. The CMTS group Jimmy and the Everyday People, Rock n' Soul poster, August 1971. NARA.

the integrated band Sly and the Family Stone, whose hit song "Everyday People" had been gone to number one in 1968 on both the *Billboard* soul chart and the Hot 100 pop chart—the first song to ever do so. Until their darker album *There's A Riot Goin' On*, released in late 1971, the Bay Area–based band offered a vision of a harmonious multicultural America (though often with an undercurrent of bluesy doubt in even their most happy songs).[41] Like Sly and the Family Stone on the home front, the members of Jimmy and the Everyday People (figure 5.10)—two

FIGURE 5.10. Jimmy and the Everyday People publicity photograph, South Vietnam, date unknown. NARA.

Caucasian and three African-American GIs—projected a sense of Americans coming together around the latest popular music regardless of race.

Touring Vietnam during 1970–71, the band garnered attention for its ability to bring GIs together for moments of harmony and "togetherness" despite the tensions of the war. As Commanding Officer A. E. Rowe Jr. wrote of a concert "under floodlights" on the main deck of the USS *Windham County*, the audience for Jimmy and the Everyday People was "very appreciative. The group, especially Jimmy, seemed to know the mood of the audience and was able to react to it."[42] The band did this by borrowing from the African-American musical tradition of call and response, emphasizing—even demanding—audience participation when they performed. Lead singer Special Private 4 Jimmy Johnson explained to audiences that with his group, "You have to put something in to get anything out."[43] Evaluation forms suggest that Johnson's approach worked. "Performers were very 'together,'" one Entertainment Branch assistant reported, "and succeeded very well in securing audience participation."[44] "Audience participation was tremendous," another wrote.[45]

Exchanging their military uniforms for fringe vests and headbands, Jimmy and the Everyday People seemed to accomplish just what CMTS hoped: the band improved morale by providing a contemporary black performance style. But this example of hip militarism—an attempt by the Armed Forces to satisfy the demands of a particular demographic segment of GIs by demonstrating how "with it" the US military was—generated other surprising energies. Imitating Sly and the Family Stone, Jimmy and the Everyday People imported a version of counter-cultural communion from the home front. The highlight of the CMTS band's performances was their version of Sly and the Family Stone's "(I Want to Take You) Higher." "This is the song that brings people over the top," one of the members of the group noted.[46] "(I Want to Take You) Higher" was a hit in 1969 and, even more famously, was performed as the climax of the Woodstock film and soundtrack.[47] Positioned at the center of the counterculture's most public and symbolic event, the song became, in Vietnam, a portal to something besides the war. Jimmy and the Everyday People did not cause GIs to instantly lay down their arms and become hippies, but rather, by referencing a key event in rock music history, they allowed American GIs to inhabit, for a moment, what Abbie Hoffman termed Woodstock Nation.[48] The managers of the Armed Forces were trying to bridge racial divides in Vietnam by sponsoring soul music, but GIs found a bridge to something else: the domestic counterculture.

Performed by a band that CMTS intended to satisfy black GIs with a taste of soul, "(I Want to Take You) Higher" pulled GI listeners into rock's orbit of counter-cultural citizenship. Jimmy and the Everyday People raised morale, but they did so by invading the normal order of the American military with an alternative vision of social freedom and affiliation appropriated from the home front. The band was "competing with the realities of war" and "brought hard hitting sounds and messages everywhere they played."[49] But what were these "hard hitting sounds and messages"? In many respects, they were outpourings of more tender and human emotions than typically permitted in official military culture: sadness, ecstasy, pain, sorrow, and, most of all, participatory involvement. Raising morale by allowing for the unleashing of human emotion, Jimmy and the Everyday People raised morale by weakening military discipline. So, too, they connected the races but on terms that were not necessarily conducive to the hierarchical command structure of the military. Many GIs bonded through the sounds of Jimmy and the Everyday People, but those bonds were not one and the same as the mechanisms that might hold the US war machine together.

The counter-military energies unleashed at Jimmy and the Everyday People's military-sponsored shows were most noticeable when the band performed another counterculturally tinged rock song, "Let It Be" by the Beatles. This song, observers noted, moved audiences deeply. Lead singer Jimmy Johnson's version "was beautiful," M. D. Magette wrote. "The audience was quickly captivated by Jimmy's

superb performance which was quite unique and most of all sincere." For this com-
menter, the song was part of a "devastating" show. An anthem of solace in the face
of failure, "Let It Be" seemed to help discontented GIs feel a bit less miserable. It
was a key part of how Jimmy and the Everyday People were "making people
happy!"[50] But happiness on what terms? Happiness came to GIs as "people" rather
than soldiers, and it came from relishing a song whose sound and lyrics were at
their core about failure, fatigue, and resignation.

Strange were the ways of hip militarism: striving to make the military more hip
for African-American GIs, CMTS wound up ushering in a kind of cross-racial mini-
Woodstock in the midst of Vietnam. Jimmy and the Everyday People created a
space filled with reflection, contemplative release, ecstatic togetherness, and calls
for communal transformation. It raised morale in the immediate moment, but it
did so by delivering music to GIs that accentuated their alienation from the war
effort. While the Entertainment Branch hoped to encourage cross-racial harmony
while also delivering more soul music to African-American GIs, troops themselves
tried to get themselves taken higher on an ecstatic sense of countercultural communion that worked against military order. The Entertainment Branch sought to
bring the latest sounds of the home front to the war, but these sounds did not
confirm the American mission. Rather, they undermined it when GI audiences,
singing together, pondered what it might mean in the midst of a frustrating and
confusing military conflict to simply let it be.

A Flower-Covered Cargo Van of Love: Visions of Countercultural Life in Vietnam

Many of the CMTS rock groups created temporary spaces suffused with the civic
energies of places such as San Francisco's Haight-Ashbury. One band, the Local
Board, went so far as to present their concerts as a kind of mini-San Francisco
appearing within the war zone. On a poster that CMTS circulated to publicize
appearances by the Local Board around Vietnam, battle raged on the margins as a
bomb exploded in the distant hills (figure 0.2). At the center of the poster, a city
appeared to have gone utterly psychedelic. A van, decorated in paisley, flowers, and
hearts, had the word "Love" written on its cargo-hold (figure 5.11). It was parked in
front of an "Art Mart" store. A café sold "Pot Dogs." A hot air balloon dropped
"Peace" fliers on the street and buildings. On all corners, artists painted portraits,
drawing on or carrying easels. A closer look revealed that they were all smoking
large marijuana joints. Naked classical female statues appeared throughout the
streetscape. A totem pole stood on the corner among drug-punning signs: "Speed,"

FIGURE 5.11. "Love" van: Detail of Cav Touring Show Poster, South Vietnam, date unknown. NARA.

"Go," and "120 MPH." A building seemed to be selling American flags, another advertised soup, as if to lampoon the strange mix of military might and consumer goods in Vietnam.[51]

The poster, merely a primitive line drawing advertising musical entertainment that was meant to foster troop morale, positioned the Local Board's concert as a way to escape the Vietnam War and arrive, if only for a few hours, in the midst of the counterculture back in the United States. Or, even more daringly, the poster suggested that this counterculture might spring up within Vietnam itself, even as the war lurked on the edges, just beyond the hills. The Local Board's name further insinuated the notion that the band might draft GIs into a different social arrangement than the military. First, it was a pun on being "bored," the predominant experience for most GIs in Vietnam, who mostly worked in the rearguard or faced combat infrequently between long stretches when they had nothing to do.[52] Second, local boards were the institutions through which draftees began their journey from the United States to Southeast Asia, from civilian to military identities. When the band performed, perhaps the reverse happened:

GIs halfway around the world processed their military roles through styles and attitudes influenced by rock and the counterculture. This local board turned soldiers back into civilians, and hippie ones at that. Here was an outpost of Paul Williams's Fillmore Auditorium "induction center" where one least expected to find it.

The Local Board's name and publicity materials suggested a vision of the Vietnam War as a space in which uncertain, countercultural inquiry took place. Within the cartoonish hedonism and licentious behavior of leisure and down time in Vietnam, a vision of what GIs were missing back at home, in countercultural spaces such as San Francisco, appeared. This was certainly not the traditional public sphere of rational debate and discussion or the idealized civic space of a New England town commons. But within the irrational context of the Vietnam War, the Local Board's poster suggested that countercultural visions permeated the war zone. The Local Board poster positioned the music as a gateway to deeper individual and collective truth—to a commons in a place torn apart in an absurd collage of pleasure and suffering.

By inserting a countercultural sensibility into the war, CMTS rock shows perhaps raised morale, but only by threatening to lower military discipline. The Local Board was praised for maintaining "military discipline and appearance" by one Entertainment Branch official (who liked their country and western numbers best).[53] But other officials criticized the band for their "ragged" performances, which were not always professionally slick and often featured an "uncertain" flow of songs.[54] Other CMTS groups were criticized for not maintaining proper military decorum, either by altering their uniforms or getting drunk while they played.[55] The continual relief when CMTS bands displayed good discipline and the occasional report of disciplinary problems suggests that there was an undercurrent of anxiety among military officials about bringing rock music to Vietnam. One musician eventually crossed the line. In July of 1971, Fresh Air guitarist Johnny Flynn was cited by US military police for sewing a California state flag to the back of his uniform (figure 5.12).[56] Flynn's Golden Bear flag transformed his body into the equivalent of the collage on the Saigon house wall of helicopter gunner Davies. Flynn had not become a hippie exactly, either in his photograph or in other reports about his behavior, but making a patchwork of his military uniform while playing rock music in Vietnam, he registered the confusing experiences of indulgence and discipline that hip militarism generated. Was the Vietnam War a theater of war or just a theater? Were American GIs there to participate in the same experiences as attendees at Woodstock or Haight-Ashbury *flaneurs* with flowers in their hair, or were they tough and noble warriors fighting for their nation? Which nation was that by the early 1970s? Was it the United States or Woodstock Nation or some combination of the two?

FIGURE 5.12. California Dreamin': John P. Flynn, Special Private 4, member of the CMTS band Fresh Air, arrested by US Military Police, July 1971. NARA.

Rock music, as part of CMTS's hip militarism, introduced the possibility of these questions in the very same gesture that it strove to allay them by bringing a taste of domestic culture to Vietnam. But in the case of Johnny Flynn's uniform, the ambiguous permissiveness of hip militarism seemed to hit a crisis point. Paul Englestad, Entertainment Director for the northernmost sector of the Republic of Vietnam, wrote to CMTS director Brad Arrington that GIs such as Flynn "must know that as long as they are in the service they will remain soldiers first and entertainers second."[57] The letter was a reminder that as much as CMTS was designed to show how the US military wanted to raise morale by sponsoring the music of the domestic counterculture, in the end the Armed Forces had a war to fight. In an inchoate but provocative way, the mood of self-expression, collective inquiry, and uncertain questioning that rock music unleashed through CMTS performances worked against this effort. When the sounds and visions of Woodstock Nation or the Haight-Ashbury suddenly burst forth through guitars and amplifiers played by GIs themselves, hip militarism gave way to the possibility of civic engagement by citizen-soldiers stuck in the fundamentally uncivil setting of Vietnam.

"You Realize that They Lied to You in Civics Class": Countercultural Affiliation and Military Disenchantment

Recalling everyday life in a 101st Airborne Division platoon stationed near Phu Bai, Vietnam veteran John Imsdahl remembered that "[w]e listened to Janis Joplin and, you know, home music—you know. So definitely, we were—we were antiwar. It's odd to say that."[58] Interviewed in the late 1970s, Imsdahl's memories indicate the ambiguous role of rock in Vietnam. On the one hand, listening to the music of the San Francisco rock star Janis Joplin seemed to transform, as if by magic, Imsdahl into an antiwar GI. But his hesitations and his own self-reflexive awareness indicate that even Imsdahl remained uncertain as to whether this was really the case. Hearing Joplin belt out songs about taking a piece of her heart or listening to her announce that freedom was just another word for nothing left to lose, Imsdahl and his fellow GIs connected to the domestic counterculture's sense of personal and collective inquiry through rock music. But what the music actually achieved ideologically was uncertain. Imsdahl may have felt like he was joining the antiwar movement by listening to rock, but he never stopped fighting in the US war machine.

Rock continually marked the incongruities of distance and connection between home front and war zone. As Drill Sergeant Steve Hassna remembered, "I was totally out of touch with news, music, any kind of culture, You know, I was—I got back and I was like three years behind on all the rock music." Hassna felt a tremendous difference between his identity and the identity of a peer with a "Stateside nine to fiver job, that was all hip to the latest groups, you know, and was hip to what was happening in Haight-Ashbury and all this other bullshit—where I was totally alienated."[59] But for others, rock went along with the war seamlessly. "It was like the beginning of the whole acid rock thing, and it infiltrated the Army," recalled nurse Betty Wilkinson. She noticed how GIs would "have, you know, the psychedelic posters on the walls of their barracks, and their rooms."[60]

Rock music was a kind of sonic measuring stick in Vietnam, a ruler by which Vietnam veterans calibrated their senses of the war zone and its relationship to the fast-changing culture of life "back in the World." A survey of American GIs conducted in the fall of 1968 by *Rolling Stone* magazine, the San Francisco publication that was quickly becoming the premier chronicler of the counterculture and rock music in the United States, suggested as much. A countercultural equivalent to the radio survey of GIs by AFVN officials (see the end of chapter 4), the *Rolling Stone* questionnaire's responses revealed the ways in which American fighters were not always becoming politically radicalized in any simple and direct way, but rather were using both drugs and rock music to escape their roles as soldiers and enter into civilian identities. Reporter Charles Perry went so far as to write that "incredible numbers of enlisted men are smoking grass to 'get away,' and more than that, to reinforce their feelings of solidarity with other unwilling conscripts." Not only numbing themselves to their jobs as GIs, but also using rock to feel connected to other draftees, American fighters cultivated small moments of civic questioning and even resistance to the war machine. As a corporal in Phu Bai wrote, "Guys have mustaches and long sideburns that the average citizen would never believe they were soldiers. We are anxious to get back and grow wild hair and beards without any restrictions. Beads and Peace symbols are worn with the uniform."[61] And when rock gave GIs access to the new kind of civilian life emerging in the domestic counterculture, it also introduced them to issues of citizenship.

A number of GIs moved from a rock-inspired, generalized sense of countercultural participation to outright political activism. Veteran John Lindquist, for example, rooted his eventual involvement in the GI antiwar movement in his listening to rock songs with fellow soldiers, explaining in reference to a famous British rock group, "We'd listen to Cream and talk about how the war was messed up. . . ."[62] Lindquist moved from rock music to overt political action. But for other fighters in Vietnam, rock existed on the level of vernacular troop culture as a means to experience, feel, and meditate on the confusing situations in which the war positioned them, and from this, to begin to confront the issue of their precise relationship to America. Veteran Michael Rodriquez remembered about Bay Area group Country Joe and the Fish's famously sardonic antiwar song, "I Feel Like I'm Fixin' to Die Rag" that it "became, for many of us, the song for Vietnam. Bitter, sarcastic, angry at a government some of us felt we didn't understand, the 'Rag' became the battle standard for too many Grunts in the Bush."[63] Rodriquez and others did not adopt the song as an anthem of antiwar resistance, but rather as a song that expressed the uncertainties they felt, the anger at being pulled from their civilian lives into the Vietnam conflict, and the longing to join the individual freedom and communal festivity of the burgeoning domestic counterculture.

As it circulated to Vietnam, rock unleashed energies of civic awareness. Amorphous, hedonistic, unpredictable, electronic, sounding out the war by beckoning to the home front and imitating the sounds of the Vietnam conflict itself, rock did not deliver truths so much as cut through any false pretenses with the feeling that something had come unglued in Vietnam. It provided temporary escape or respite from war, but in doing so, it also undercut the authority of the official American position. As veteran Jim Heiden recalled, "You realize that they lied to you in civics class."[64] Rock did not stop the war, but it transported to Vietnam countercultural questionings of authority and legitimacy. Even when CMTS

FIGURE 5.13. "Watch for Volume 2–Another Chapter of Entertainment Vietnam": CMTS Scrapbook, 1968. NARA.

bands raised the morale of GIs in the moment, they did so in ways that challenged the coherence of the American military mission and the shared clarity of American civic purpose (figure 5.13). The music was part of an infusion of countercultural sounds that were supposed to buoy spirits, but wound up communicating a different story.

Ken Sams, who both published the *Grunt Free Press* and worked for the United States Air Force's Project for the Contemporary Historical Evaluation of Combat Operations (CHECO), contended decades later about the cultural context in which GIs listened to rock in Vietnam: "I'm convinced that the answer to why we lost the war in Vietnam is more likely to be found in my comic stories and cartoons than in all my reports for CHECO."[65] As with comedy and cartoons, so too with rock music: drawing upon the sound of the domestic American counterculture as channeled through the military's appropriations of hip capitalism, it spoke the truth not about what was right or wrong in Vietnam, but rather about how difficult it was to discern right or wrong and yet how individual GIs still felt the obligation to do so. The music's ability to connect individuals to the geopolitics of war would eventually make it important not only to GIs, but also to young Vietnamese in the South who found themselves coming of age as citizens of both the Republic of Vietnam and the republic of rock.

6

A LITTLE PEACE MESSAGE, LIKE STRAIGHT FROM SAIGON

SPREAD ACROSS TWO pages in the September–October 1970 issue of Ken Sams's *Grunt Free Press*, a photographic collage rivaled the images Michael Herr glimpsed in the apartment of Davies the Marine as well as the front of the CMTS scrapbook: artist Tran Dinh Thuc turned pictures of the CBC Band, a Vietnamese rock group, into a psychedelic Mount Rushmore (figure 6.1). The group, whose name stood for Con Bà Cu, "Mother's Children" in Vietnamese, consisted of siblings in the Phan family as well as a number of other musicians. They wore their hair long and in t-shirts, sunglasses, and floppy hats they looked like Western hippies. In silhouette at the lower right of the collage, a young Vietnamese boy gave the "V" peace sign. Other pictures in the collage featured the musicians grinning at the camera and playfully raising their middle fingers. A peace symbol floated up from the images, like a sun shining above the chaos of faces. Splotches of black ink cast a more ominous mood, as if an explosion had occurred. Frilly psychedelic lettering curled out from the top of the collage, declaring: "Happiness is Acid Rock on Plantation Road."[1]

The article described how the CBC Band created a kind of Haight-Ashbury-in-exile at the Kim Kim Club. Playing covers of the latest rock hits from the West at venues on Plantation Road, the GI entertainment district by the massive Tan Son Nhut Air Force Base, as well as at other clubs, bars, and military installations around South Vietnam, CBC made a living in the wartime economy primarily by entertaining American GIs.[2] But rock was more than just a means to economic survival. While it arrived in Vietnam as part of American consumer culture imported to the war zone to give GIs a taste of home, the music also gave the members of CBC themselves access to

FIGURE 6.1. Collage of CBC Band, *Grunt Free Press*, September/October 1970. Estate of Kenneth Sams. Artist: Tran Dinh Thuc.

HAPPINESS AND ROCK

(FOLLOWED FROM PAGE 3.)

« I've come here every night for the last four months, » a young airman said. « I just wouldn't miss it. » Another said he came down from Cu Chi just to hear the CBC. The CBC is the number one Vietnamese rock group that packs them into the Kim Kim — the fabulous group of brothers and sisters who get their music taped right off of AFVN or from grunts who buy tapes and records in the PX.

The CBC are known throughout the Saigon area. The letters used to stand for Con Ba Cu, Vietnamese for « Mother's children », but to the grunts CBC has been re-named to mean « Come Blow Can Sao ». They are four boys and two girls and four are from one family — two boys and two girls. They wear broken peace symbols, with the metal removed from the bottom of the inverted « Y » to indicate the lack of peace in Vietnam. Their hair is long enough to bring harassment from Vietnamese MPs who keep threatening to cut it off and US MPs who call them « dirty people ». The musicians call the

police « pigs ». They chafe under the harassment, but they know that every GI in that audience would go to bat for them if there were real trouble. On one occasion, when the MPs harassed the group, every grunt walked out of the place.

« We understand the problem, » the group's leader, a 21 year old named Linh said. « In Vietnam today, there is a war and we must expect controls. But I hope when it is over, we can be as free as young people everywhere. I hope that one day, we can have a Woodstock in Saigon, maybe in the Zoo, with some rock groups from America and England, playing together with us. It would be the greatest day in Saigon — for our young people and your young GIs. »

« Yeah, man », a grunt interrupted. « Like they ought to give Bob Hope and Billy Graham a year off and send us the Doors or the Jefferson Airplane or the Mamas and Papas. »

« You writing a story on this band », another GI chimed in, « and it better be good. Cause these guys made this tour worthwhile. They got it. They just got it — and I ain't found it anywhere else ».

During an intermission, the grunts file out of the low ceilinged, 20-by-40-foot room, packed with foot-high red stools and low tables where the GIs sit and drink, mainly Coca Cola. They go outside to have a smoke, and bat the breeze and they all file in. « Hell, yes, we all know each other, » an aiman from Tan Son Nhut, explained, « when a guy comes here, he's one of us. »

There have been nights when the CBC could not appear for the eight o'clock show (possibly a police delay) and the 200 or so grunts who show up just stand around. They don't go anywhere else, but they sit around and smoke and have a beer or coke. The Kim Kim is their thing and they don't dig the regular bars with the tea-drinking hustlers or the assembly line massage parlors. They come from Bien Hoa and Cu Chi and Phuoc Vinh and Long Binh and from all over Saigon to hear the CBC. Troops on their R & R spend most of their time in Saigon at Kim Kim.

« You know, it's like this. Some GIs bitch and moan about Vietnam but man, it ain't as bad as all that. Gimme a place like this and it don't matter I'm in Saigon or Sioux City. There's some good thing going for us here, man, but you got to know where it's at. »

The CBC at the Kim Kim Club on Nguyen Van Toal St., Plantation Road, is « where it's at », for the grunt who's out looking. It's managed by a young Indian, owned by a young Chinese, and frequented by young Americans and Vietnamese. It's a « together » place where you forget the war and where you're cool. There's no counts is if you're pro-American or anti-Vietnam or anti-American or anti-black or anti-white or anti-anything is the pound of those drums, the frenetic guitar, the cymbals, the screams, the white flashing light and with it all the beat — one solid beat that links every man in the room to everybody else. »

« I come out of the place, and this cyclo driver sees me and says « where you go? » I tell him I'm broke but have to go to Tan Son Nhut. He says « Get in. He took me for free. I ain't shittin you. He didn't take no money. »

Four years ago, Plantation Road was a street lined with tin and straw shacks and the remnants of a rubber plantation. Today, it is a glittering neon-lit row of modern buildings, housing a dozen buildings for billeting Army and Air Force troops, scores of bars, massage parlors, restaurants, hotels. In May 1968, the VC marched up the street toward Tan Son Nhut but got stopped in a French cemetery. Since that time, the ten o'clock curfew took effect and Plantation Road took over from Tu Do as the « great White Way » of Saigon. It's near the hotel quarters and the sprawling air base of Tan Son Nhut and there's plenty of parking and the girls are as good-looking as they are downtown. And it's as close to a rock festival as anything you can find in Vietnam.

« I got this buddy, see, who was over here six months and never left the base, and I bring him down here. He goes completely ape and star is kicking himself in the ass for not getting out earlier. That's true with a lot of guys, you know. »

When the performance is over at 9:45 p.m. (curfew preparation), the band and some of the GIs clown about together. They dig each other. The posters for the club, the tapes and records for the band to copy, the ideas for new numbers, all come from the grunts. The band learned their English from the GIs and the GIs picked up their « need to know » phrases from the Vietnamese at the club. You'd be hard put to find a place in Vietnam where there is as much admiration and respect for Vietnamese performers among GIs. And vice versa. The guys who patronize the Kim Kim aren't violating any Vietnamese taboos and they're as peaceful and gentle as anyone you could find west of San Francisco.

« It's the vibrations, man. I dig the vibrations here, that's all I can say. There's something mellow about these people when I come in here. And I don't get it anywhere else. »

At ten o'clock, it's over at the Kim Kim. The customers are back at their quarters or dodging MP patrols or maybe in the sack with one of the hundreds of girls who make their living on the streets and, bars of this new Broadway. The musicians hop in their small pick-up with their instruments and head for home. The cyclos and taxi drivers outside the club pull out for greener pastures. The lights go out in the club and the muddy street becomes just another dark alley. But between eight o'clock and ten o'clock every night, the building houses a few hundred young Americans and Vietnamese who forget there's a war on and groove together. A rock festival in Saigon with American and Vietnamese groups playing to young Americans and young Vietnamese?

197

what was becoming, by the end of the 1960s, a global counterculture. Performing for a mixed audience of Americans, nationals from other countries, and young Vietnamese, CBC reproduced rock's aesthetics of hedonistic, individualistic personal expression. At their concerts, the band members and their audiences seemed to escape the Republic of Vietnam for the republic of rock.

This seemed, at first glance, to be an abandonment of their Vietnamese identity. But putting on the costumes of hippies and playing rock music was something more complex and daring. It was not an abandonment of being Vietnamese so much as a reworking of that identity. Like many young people around the world in the decolonizing context of the post–World War II decades, the members of CBC combined Western culture with their own heritage to fashion something new and hybridized.[3] In their case, they were drawn to the countercultural ideals of togetherness and fellowship that they heard in rock. These values offered a way both to join the cosmopolitan modernity of the counterculture as individuals and, at the same time, to reaffirm the primary Vietnamese commitment to family as the building block of society.[4] The CBC was, after all, a family band. Playing rock was a means of keeping the Phan family together even as the group embraced the countercultural ideal of creating a universal family. In the United States, they would have been part of Woodstock Nation. Taken from the famed festival in upstate New York during August of 1969, this was the shorthand name for the imagined utopian country of the counterculture. In Vietnam, it makes more sense to think of CBC as joining—indeed helping to constitute—what is more accurately called the Woodstock Transnational.[5]

The story of CBC took place within the dynamic of the war in Vietnam after the Tet Offensive of 1968. With the election of Richard Nixon in the United States later that year, and the growing sense in America that the Vietnam War was unwinnable, the actual number of American troops declined rapidly in the late 1960s and early 1970s. This did not mean, however, that the side effects of the US intervention faded. American consumer products saturated South Vietnam as never before, and the American presence continued to undercut the development of a stable economy independent of American involvement.[6] Moreover, after 1969, Nixon's administration adopted the policy of "Vietnamization," which sought to shift fighting responsibility to South Vietnam.[7] For the men in CBC and other young male Vietnamese, this meant that they were under increased pressure of conscription into the Army of the Republic of Vietnam. In this context, rock, emanating from overseas, became a cultural way to address the continued influence of shifting American policy in Vietnam.

For members of the "cowboy" (pronounced KO-boy) youth culture of Saigon, rock was the soundtrack for rejecting traditional Vietnamese culture. Gloria Emerson reported in the New York Times that the music was part of a generational rebellion against older generations. Noting that it was hard to hear him over "a tape recording of 'The Age of Aquarius'," Emerson learned that sixteen-year-old Cang, the son of a construction worker, loved "the latest popular American music." He told her, "'I have a record player at home, but I have stopped listening to music because my parents cannot bear my kind of music while I can't bear to hear theirs.'"[8] This was quite different from the hybridization of tradition and modernity that CBC pursued. Cang used rock to position himself against his parents; the siblings in CBC had been encouraged by their mother to start a band. This does not mean that there were no tensions in CBC's family, but rather that their love of rock complicates the story of responses to Western culture and American imperialism during the last stages of the war.

Many in South Vietnam did not approve of "Cowboy" youth culture, or even of the in-between, hybrid spaces that CBC established. They heard "nhac tre," the name for the new Westernized music that was popular among young Vietnamese, as an abandonment of Vietnamese identity.[9] Worst yet, the government in the South was threatened by rock's antiwar associations. As David Butler reported in *Rolling Stone*, the South Vietnamese government would not allow one performer, Trinh Cong Son, to publish his antiwar songs.[10] But just because the South Vietnamese state found rock threatening did not mean that the opposition forces in Vietnam—the North Vietnamese communist government or the Viet Cong—heard rock as affiliated with their cause. The North Vietnamese government went so far as to decry rock's influx into Vietnam as part of a coherent tactic of psychological warfare by the very South Vietnamese government that banned the music. "Among the cultural methods used by the neo-colonial regime," Nguyen Khac Vien and Phong Hien wrote in a 1982 article on the war years, "music was one of the most effective." It kept "youth aloof from the revolutionary path by leading them to avenues of escape or to the exultation of low instincts and finally to corruption." They argued that "[i]n Saigon, crushed by the war and sinking into corruption, the psywar services as well as the record and cassette dealers knew perfectly how to use the rhythms and melodies [of rock music] to lull scruples to sleep, whilst stirring up the worst instincts."[11] Neither the North, nor the South Vietnamese governments liked rock. Both believed it threatened traditional Vietnamese culture.

For CBC, rock was neither the music of capitalism or communism; rather, within a nightmarish setting of war, it was a way to dream of peace and connect to a mass-mediated image of togetherness and imagined kinship. Woodstock Nation, they hoped, had a place for them. The CBC was not alone in using rock to seek out a countercultural alternative that confounded the existing political and cultural contexts of the Vietnam War. Nyugen Giang Cao, a musician who played many of the same venues as CBC, recalled "the feel of togetherness" when he learned about the

Woodstock festival. Though he believed that he and his peers "weren't real hippies," they still "loved the look of hippies." Most crucially, Nyugen remembered, "We can feel freedom as any other hippies." He felt "that we are part of it."[12] For Nyugen, rock in Vietnam led to dreams of joining a worldwide youth culture in which he and other young Vietnamese could both be modern individuals and recreate a feeling of family togetherness. Rock may have arrived through the imperialistic channels of American consumer culture as part of the new military tactic of hip militarism, but for musicians such as Cao and the CBC, it also provided access to countercultural experiences of social belonging that tenuously but evocatively balanced old and new, tradition and modernity, individuality and community, freedom and obligation.

"It's a Warm Scene, as Mellow as Any Found in Haight-Ashbury": CBC and the Making of a Counterculture in Vietnam

When CBC performed, the symbolic antipodes of Vietnam and San Francisco seemed especially magnetized. At the Kim Kim Club (figure 6.2), the *Grunt Free Press* described "a warm scene, as mellow as any found in Haight-Ashbury."

FIGURE 6.2. Love, peace, Hendrix, and "Weedies": The CBC Band at the Kim Kim Club, circa 1970/1971. CBC Archive. Photographer: Phan Lien.

The GIs in attendance became as "peaceful and gentle as anyone you could find west of San Francisco." On a typical night at the Kim Kim Club, the band drew an audience of roughly two hundred American GIs and fifty young South Vietnamese citizens. "On the stage," the *Grunt Free Press* reported, "there are five young Vietnamese musicians . . . all with unisexed hair. Behind them is a bright orange and red peace symbol, psychedelic posters . . . showing the finger V for peace, a black militant, a cereal box marked 'Weedies,' and the Jefferson Airplane." As "black light flashes on the players and the signs," the musicians and posters blurred together in "half second slow motion glimpses." In Vietnam, within a setting that marked the most violent dimensions of American imperialism, CBC and their audiences longed to recreate the Haight-Ashbury within the war zone. In doing so, they constituted an important space for engagements with countercultural citizenship.[13] For American GIs, the Kim Kim Club became a place where racist hostilities toward civilian Vietnamese ceased and they instead sought out the utopian and universalist fellowship found in the mythos of the Bay Area's Summer of Love. For CBC and the Vietnamese in the audience, rock music offered similar access to a vision of community and commonality. As guitarist Phan Linh put it, "We understand the problem" that "there is a war . . . but I hope when it is over, we can be as free as young people everywhere."[14]

Phan Linh and his siblings, who comprised the heart of the group, were from a family of eleven children. Their mother was from a rural village in the south; their father had come to Saigon from Hanoi prior to the end of French rule to work as an embassy chef.[15] He died, possibly after harassment and imprisonment by the French. An older brother, Lan, who was a musician himself, plotted out a strategy for the youngest siblings to work as musicians after he was drafted into the South Vietnamese military. With the support of their mother, Lan and another older sister Ly taught the younger children—Linh, Loan, and Van—to play music. Playing popular music from both Vietnam and the West became a way to sustain their family rather than an abandonment of it. The trio performed in the streets of Saigon as early as 1961. By 1963, they appeared on a Sunday radio program broadcast in the city.[16] A few years later another sister, Lien, joined the group. So did Linh's wife, Marie Louise, who along with her husband would eventually come to be known, playfully, as the Yoko Ono and John Lennon of Vietnamese rock music (figure 6.3).

The years between the end of French colonialism in 1954 and the escalation of American military involvement in 1965 were known as the "Golden Period," a time of relative peace that found many Vietnamese moving between countryside and urban areas as they strove to fuse commitments to family and tradition with new, cosmopolitan modes of economic and cultural modernism.[17] The CBC gained access

FIGURE 6.3. The Yoko Ono and John Lennon of Vietnamese rock music: Phan Linh and Phan Marie Louise at the Saigon Zoo, circa 1973. Frank Ford Personal Collection. Photographer: Allen Quinn.

to Western music in Cholon, where they could listen to the latest records from the West in the shops of Chinese businessmen. Connections to non-Vietnamese businessmen in Saigon also gave them access to electronic instruments and amplifiers. Later, American friends would order them equipment.[18] The band first performed for American forces in 1964, on a base at Can Tho in the Mekong Delta. CBC won over GIs with a version of "Wipe Out." Band members were amazed by the free Dr. Pepper and fried chicken, which they had never had before, as well as getting paid in MPC (military payment certificate). As the United States escalated its presence in Vietnam, CBC grew quite popular. They performed at base clubs, occasionally at NCO (Non-Commissioned Officers) or Officer Clubs, but more often for lower-echelon troops at venues such as the Airman's Club at Tan Son Nhut. They also played at private venues in the entertainment districts of Saigon, such as on the rooftop of the Tai Hotel, Maxims, the Sherwood Forest, and the Fillmore Far East. They eventually ran their own bar near Me Linh Square and To Do Street called the My Phung Club. Typically, young Vietnamese would see the band perform in the afternoons, then CBC would perform for GIs at night, but more often than not the audiences were mixed.[19]

To learn new songs, the group would ask Americans to give them recordings of songs they wanted CBC to play. One hears this in the existing recordings of CBC from the early 1970s, which reflected the rise of rock as the dominant genre of popular music. They also revealed the importance of the long-playing album. The band performed many of the songs on the latest hard rock LPs by Grand Funk Railroad and the James Gang. The CBC also covered softer sounds, such the hits from singer-songwriter Carole King's best-selling *Tapestry* album. The group also played classic rock songs of the last few years, including hits by Jimi Hendrix, Janis Joplin, Santana, and the Beatles.[20] As a teenager in Saigon during the mid- and late 1960s, guitarist Linh fell in love with these earlier rock sounds, as well as soul music from Motown. "I still remember the first 45, the small discs, by the Beatles," he recalled, "It flipped me out." John Lennon became an especially important inspiration to him. Linh would spend hours listening to and memorizing words, arrangements, and especially the guitar parts. It was important to him to learn rock songs note for note. This was a way of honoring music that had moved him emotionally. Escaping from the war into his earphones, Linh remembered how he would "just sit in front of my real small stereo cassette with the headset . . . and whatever song I learn, I try to play exactly like the way that the original artist play because I respect them so much. . . . I enjoy them so much." The pleasure of hearing this music from afar, being able to make it his own, and then being able to share it with others and make them happy was, for Linh, his "gift."[21] By 1970, he was famous around Vietnam for being able to play songs with difficult guitar parts, such as Jimi Hendrix's "Star-Spangled Banner." His sister

Loan shared Linh's gift of imitation and appropriation. She was especially good at learning the words to songs even though neither she nor her siblings spoke English fluently. Many GIs would tell her that they could not understand her when she spoke but that she sounded American when she sang.[22]

Though CBC was far from the only non-American group to perform rock in Vietnam, they were among the most explicitly countercultural. The band performed among a panoply of commercial "floor shows" that the United States Armed Forces hired. A 1972 list of "Approved Commercial Entertainment" by the United States Army's Entertainment Branch featured almost twenty groups, including the Electric Lollipops Band, six males and three females, who performed for $350 per show. The Australian/New Zealand/Malta Electric Flower Floor Show performed for $425 a night. Other groups included the Korean/Vietnamese Last Change Floor Show, and the Sound and Fury Band, from the Philippines.[23] In his memoir, *My Rock 'n' Roll War*, drummer Don Morrison recalls touring Vietnam with his Australian band, Xanadu.[24] And a young Australian guitarist named Rick Springfield, who would find fame in the 1980s with the song "Jesse's Girl" and an acting role on the soap opera *General Hospital*, toured Vietnam entertaining GIs.[25] While their job was to bring pleasure and escape, performers in floor shows and commercial entertainment in Vietnam faced dangers and difficulties. Agents took a large percentage of performance fees. Certain Vietnamese government officials and American military officers charged with running entertainment clubs were corrupt.[26] Bands were sent to dangerous areas of Vietnam without proper protection. Even getting around Saigon could be difficult due to harassment by Vietnamese police, American military police, or both. Female performers often faced the worst conditions. As Vietnam veteran Peter Cameron recalled of fights, brawls, and worse at venues, "If you get a room full of very horny, very frustrated, bored men, some from the roughest streets in the cities, and give them a lot of beer and let them get fucked up, and bring on these Filipino and Korean girls, in these sequins and these bands, that was playing the imitation American rock, and get the heat going—and what are you going to do with all that energy?"[27] Leisure spaces may have been far from the front lines of the war, but they had their own violent atmosphere.

For the CBC Band, the world of floor shows was something to be endured in order to be able to generate a countercultural environment. The group was unlike any of the most performing groups. The female members of CBC did not appear in scantily-clad bikinis to gyrate provocatively like go-go dancers, as with most floor shows, but rather imitated the self-expressive, internally driven performance styles of rockers such as Janis Joplin. They wore pants and shirts in the more unisex look of hippies in the United States (figure 6.4). Hippie fashion

FIGURE 6.4. The CBC Band at the Saigon Zoo, circa 1973. Frank Ford Personal Collection. Photographer: Allen Quinn.

allowed them to be more modest in personal presentation. It also created a means of more suggestive political expression. The sisters in the band often wore American flag t-shirts while singing antiwar songs such as Grand Funk Railroad's "People, Let's Stop the War." It was as if they sought to shift the focus from their female bodies to questions of the civic body. Singing, "Hey all you people, for goodness sake / Let's get together, what does it take," lead singer Phan Loan used the American flag in ways that echoed Ken Kesey and the Merry Pranksters; one might say that she clothed herself in questions of American power in the setting of Vietnam.[28] As the band wailed and the psychedelic light show flashed around her at the Sherwood Forest Club (figure 6.5), Loan's words, borrowed from a hard rock Detroit band, asked what the relationship was to be between the American nation and Woodstock Nation. Much like Jimi Hendrix performing the American national anthem at Woodstock, Phan Loan and CBC used rock to dramatize the ambiguities of the presence of the United States military in Southeast Asia. Was the United States of America, whose flag appeared on her shirt, the country of military occupation and senseless destruction or was it a beacon of openness and democratic freedom? Was it an imperial power or

FIGURE 6.5. The CBC Band performs at the Sherwood Forest Club, circa 1973. Frank Ford Personal Collection. Photographer: Allen Quinn.

the land in which Woodstock Nation had been founded? When CBC performed rock, especially a song such as "People, Let's Stop the War," the band intensified these questions. As *Grunt Free Press* publisher Ken Sams would later recall, CBC's concerts "drew a sizable following among young Vietnamese who formed the closest thing you could find to a hippie-style peace movement in Saigon."[29] As the *Grunt Free Press* put it, the band's shows became "as close to a rock festival as anything you can find in Vietnam."[30]

What one American GI called the "vibrations" of the CBC rock music reshaped, if only for moments at a time, the very contours of people and nation in South Vietnam. Rock music, when "played with Woodstock intensity," seemed capable of generating surprising moods of togetherness that redefined the social underpinnings of citizenship in the war zone. In a war suffused with racial intolerance and bigotry, the *Grunt Free Press* reporter noticed that at the Kim Kim Club "you'd be hard put to find a place in Vietnam where there is so much respect for Vietnamese performers among GIs. And vice-versa." The club became "a 'together' place where you forget the war. . . . There's no anti-Vietnam or anti-American or anti-black or anti-white or anti-anything in the place." Rock music, considered unruly by many, established civil interaction within the uncivil context of a military conflict. There was "empathy between these young Vietnamese and young Americans found nowhere else in Vietnam," the *Grunt Free Press* explained. When CBC performed, "all that counts is the pound of those drums, the frenetic guitar, the cymbals, the screams, the white flashing light and with it the beat—one solid beat that links every man in the room to everybody else."[31]

A sense of fellowship erupted from CBC's adaptations of Western rock music. Recognition across boundaries of difference flourished. A spirit of inquiry and even a mechanism for reflection on self and society arose. The roar of the music was certainly a way to dull the pain and anxiety of living in a war zone, but it also provided an atmosphere of connection in which the "one solid beat" generated a proliferation of critical questions and ideas. The CBC's performances of rock music most of all allowed for reflections on the contradictions of life within the reach of American imperialism, which seemed so oppressive in Vietnam when it was not outright deadly, yet also ironically brought with it the energies of the counterculture to the war zone. As CBC lead singer Phan Loan evocatively put it, reflecting on her simultaneous love of rock music and horror at the destruction wrought by America in her homeland, "The United States must be the greatest paradox in the history of the world. . . . It puts out the best conceivable sounds in its music and the worst conceivable sounds in its weapons. Its children want peace but fight a war against an aggressor who has never really threatened the soil of the United States. A mixed-up country."[32] For Loan, playing American rock not only involved making and enjoying musical sound, but also registering the "mixed-up" context of war in which rock resounded. The CBC's performances placed the paradoxes of the American intervention front and center. At the start of every show, Loan would announce from the stage, "Yea, we're the CBC Band, and we'd like to turn you on . . . We got a little peace message, like straight from Saigon. Waaaaaaah yeaaa!"[33] Declaring this was a political act in its own way, but neither CBC, nor the band's fans, challenged state power directly. Rather they used countercultural rock to register the dissonances of life during wartime while also asserting their right to have a space to dream and take pleasure within the context of their country's suffering. As if to symbolize these two desires, the members of CBC wore "broken peace symbols, with the metal removed from the bottom of the 'Y' to indicate the lack of peace in Vietnam."[34]

Despite efforts to stay out of the governmental political struggles of the Vietnam War, the members of CBC found themselves pulled into the cultural politics of the counterculture. As in the United States, conscription brought the power of the state directly into personal lives. The young men in the band were under constant threat of being drafted into the Army of the Republic of Vietnam. The group's countercultural look also made them targets in everyday life. "Their hair is long enough to bring harassment from Vietnamese MPs [military police] and US PM's call them 'dirty people'," the *Grunt Free Press* reported.[35] Responding to these pressures, the CBC created concert environments that asserted a different sense of social affiliation than what the Republic of Vietnam could offer them. Their versions of the latest Western rock linked the pleasures of musical sound (and drugs, since GIs often smoked marijuana at their perform-ances) to the refashioning of emotions of national belonging. The power of this cultural politics came most of all from connecting with audiences through music. This is what mattered most to the members of CBC. A recording that CBC made for GIs in the early 1970s captured the way that the band used rock to both offer temporary escape from Vietnam while also creating a sonic space for reflecting on the war and connecting across lines of race, nationality, distance, and time. "Peo-ple," Loan explains, "we have make [sic] this tape in hopes that wherever you go after the 'Nam, you will always remember us. And maybe, someday soon, we'll be in the world to play for you once again."[36] The introduction set the music across global space, contrasting but also connecting "the 'Nam" to "back in the world." It also hinted at how rock became a music of heightened memory and historical consciousness. Because of the uncertainties of life in Vietnam during wartime, CBC at once spoke to experiences of the war and to a time when it would be in the past. From the depths of the conflict itself, Loan's sister Lien remarked: "Well, I just want to say that I hope someday you will play this tape and you will think of us and the good times we all had together, okay?"

The band played two Grand Funk Railroad songs: "Sin's a Good Man's Brother" and "Nothing is the Same."[37] As with so many rock songs during the Vietnam War years, the lyrics arrived from the home front, but seemed tailor made for the war. "Ain't seen a day / That I don't hear people say / They know they're gonna die," Loan sang with extra emotion on "Sin's a Good Man's Brother." The last verse of the song was more ambiguous in its political references: "Some folks say we need an education / Don't give up or we'll lose the nation / You say we need a revolu-tion / It seems to be the only solution." But if Loan was thinking about the civil war in the Vietnam nation while she sang these lines, her words were quickly swallowed up by Linh's lead guitar. He used an overdrive pedal to replicate the heavy riffs and frantic solo of guitarist Mark Farner, while brother Van bashed out the beat on the drums. On the rest of the recording, the band performed other hit songs from the early 1970s, as well as a few songs that reached back into the 1960s. A number were remarkable copies of the original versions, while others bore the mark of translation. A few were core acid-rock and hard-rock songs, but others were softer, reflecting of the rise of singer-songwriters in the early 1970s. All gave a sense of CBC's interest in performing songs that were important to them and to their audiences in Vietnam. They included "Walk Away" by the James Gang, Carole King's "It's Too Late" and "You've Got a Friend," Santana's "Soul Sacrifice," Janis Joplin's "Mercedes Benz," Jimi Hendrix's "Star Spangled Banner" and "Purple Haze," "Paranoid" by Black Sabbath, a medley of Beatles' songs, and John Lennon's "Imagine."[38]

The most revealing moments were when the members of the band spoke. Addressing GIs on the tape, they not only communicated musically, but also by using the lingo of the counterculture. With a psychedelic echo on their voices, they chanted together: "Peace is something we all want." As they appropriated typical American rock sound effects to create this chant, the members of the group also expressed their wish to end the war and join the global counterculture. Later on the recording, Loan introduced the band. Her style and the responses of the other band members further signaled their sense of participating in a counterculture along with American GIs. "Hey people," Loan playfully announced. "Well let's take a little time to let them know who we are." She starts with her younger brother. "Come over here brother Van. Van he is 14. He's our drummer. Say something little brother." Van giggled, imitating phrases he had learned from hip GIs: "Lifer, lifer, lifer, so many lifers, where do they come from? I hope they go back. Dig it, dig." Van made the language of "grunts" in Vietnam his own. Other members also referenced the sensibilities and phraseology of the counterculture to express their own dreams of peace among the suffering of the Vietnam War. Loan introduced the group's bass player: "Hien is our bass player," she says, "what do you got to say for yourself, baby?" Hien responds, "Peace man, that's all I want, that's all I say." Loan then introduced the other Hien in the band, the guitarist whom everyone called Hien Rhythm. "Well let's see now, oh yeah, Hien Rhythm, he's 19 now, on guitar a couple of years, say something brother." Hien Rhythm responded, "What's happening brother? Let's get our stuff together, brothers, man, it's the way." "Right on," brother Linh said in the background. Finally, Loan introduced herself as "the little lady up front" and explained, "I just want to let you know that we all love you, man."

At the end of the tape, as the organ began the song "Imagine" in the background, Loan offered a final, countercultural message from Vietnam: "As you all sometime soon will be leaving the 'Nam and heading back to the world, we hope that you will take with you the understanding that someday, somehow, we must all come together as brothers and sisters bound together in the name of humanity to bring forth a peace universal to all." The CBC's expressions of love in the group's appropriations of countercultural rock were complex. The members of the band were entertainers, of course, and made their living channeling the latest hits from the home front to American GIs and other internationals in Saigon. As good performers, they showed that they knew how to situate the music in the sensibilities of peace, love, and harmony it was associated with "back in the world." But they also made the music and its messages relevant to their own lives. Rock from the late 1960s and early 1970s carried the weight of their sadness about the war around them, but it also represented their dreams of transforming the world through music. When Loan introduced "our leader, big brother Linh, he's been playing guitar for just 2 years" and said, playfully, "Come here, lifer, say something," Linh responded: "Wow. Talk, talk, talk. Only talk, no music man. Talk tire me, music blows me. Right on."[39] He wanted to make his adaptations of rock music count as his participation in and contribution to developing a sense of social belonging that transcended the war not by ignoring it, but by using rock to recognize pain and perhaps move past anger into a new spirit of gathering together. From their place as a Vietnamese family band, CBC communicated the vision of a universal human family.

When CBC performed songs such as "Soul Sacrifice" or Jimi Hendrix's version of "The Star Spangled Banner," both featured in the film of the Woodstock festival, when Loan sang like Janis Joplin or did her best to reach the high notes of Led Zeppelin's Robert Plant, when drummer Phan Van tried to replicate the long drum solo from Iron Butterfly's "Inna Gotta Da Vita," or when the band had GI audiences join them in imitating the obscene cheer of Country Joe and the Fish ("Gimme an F . . ."), the group felt free of the war for a time—and the band members felt as though they were passing along that freedom to their audiences.[40] From this musical communion, the cultural underpinnings of a new nation, a new family, a new "people" flickered into being. "It's the vibrations, man," one GI remarked about hearing CBC at the Kim Kim Club. "I dig the vibrations here and that's all I can say. There's something mellow about these people when I come in here. And I don't get it anywhere else."[41] Musical communion offered entrance into new, more harmonious social relationships among different peoples. American fighters changed their racist perceptions of Vietnamese. "Most GIs," Phan Linh commented, "before they hear us play, look at us as long-haired gooks. . . . But after they hear us play, they don't look at us as gooks anymore. They realize that we are people."[42] At the same time, the music allowed the members of CBC to perceive Americans in new ways. As Linh told Rolling Stone, "Americans in the United States must be groovy people, the ones who went to Woodstock I mean."[43] Rock music fostered feelings of commonality and affinity, of connections across different identities, peoples, and places around the world. From the connections established through music, a new sense of global collectivity seemed to be born from the depths of war. In this way, CBC and their audiences refashioned what anthropologist Benedict Anderson calls the "imagined community" of the nation-state during a time in Vietnam when both nation and state were up for grabs. They did so through commercial music imported from the United States, but their use of the music took rock in directions beyond its imperial origins and commodified properties.

With the future of Vietnam at stake in a long and confusing civil war that itself took place in the aftermath of colonial influence by the Chinese, French, and

United States, CBC and their fans interrupted existing configurations of the Vietnam War by introducing the sounds of the global counterculture. Rock created a different sense of simultaneity, a different sense of individual identity, and a new alignment of familial social belonging for South Vietnamese and Americans alike.[44] Unleashed through the strategies of hip militarism by the American Armed Forces in South Vietnam, rock became a way to escape to a transnational, cosmopolitan community in which global fellowship replaced national distinctions.[45] It was the borders of Woodstock Nation that CBC and their fans wished to cross. In their own way, they reached this strange country when the band participated in the Saigon International Rock Festival of 1971.

"Woodstock in Saigon": The Paradoxes of the Woodstock Transnational

The legacy of San Francisco and its Summer of Love still mattered in Vietnam, but in the aftermath of the Woodstock Festival in August of 1969 and especially with the worldwide release of the film and soundtrack about the event in 1970, Woodstock became the key reference point for those interested in joining the counterculture. Abbie Hoffman's term "Woodstock Nation" became shorthand for the sense of altered social belonging that the rock festival inspired. It was equal parts sophisticated conceptual theory, simplistic political slogan, and effective marketing tagline, but what is easy to forget is that the idea of Woodstock Nation arose most of all from Hoffman's musings about the relationship between rock music and citizenship.[46]

Even though he had infamously been kicked off the stage by Pete Townsend, the guitarist for The Who, for attempting to make a political speech in support of marijuana activist and White Panther Party founder John Sinclair, Hoffman wrote a largely positive book about Woodstock. For him, the event signified the American counterculture's ability to constitute, at least for a weekend, a "new society in the vacant lots of the old." Woodstock Nation became a sort of placeless place defined most of all by the feeling that rock music was generating a new sense of belonging. "Rock music," Hoffman believed, would "provide the energy" for a "soulful socialism" to emerge. This nascent civic order, however, required more than just rock music's ability to spread awareness among its "people"; it also, to Hoffman's mind, needed an "army" if it was to challenge existing state power.[47]

Thinking in military as well as civil terms, Hoffman noticed how Woodstock Nation's origins were to be found precisely in the interactions between the Vietnam War and the San Francisco counterculture. "Once upon a time," he recalled, "right after the thirteen-thousand-seven-hundred-and-sixty-fourth demonstration against the war in Vietnam, young people started to congregate in an area of San Francisco known as the Haight-Ashbury." Emphasizing the links between the antiwar movement in the United States and the emergence of the counterculture in the City by the Bay, Hoffman then commented that, by 1969, "napalming villages in Vietnam is not the only kind of imperialism the country is into."[48] The Nixon administration not only continued the war in Southeast Asia, but also attacked Americans at home, whether it be civil rights activists or hippies or antiwar protesters. Hoffman believed that these oppressions brought young Americans into potential solidarity with other young people around the world. Though Hoffman never put it this way, Woodstock Nation was really the Woodstock Transnational.

For Hoffman, in this context, rock would "provide the energy" for imagining an alternative body politic, a new nation, that would ultimately diverge from the existing political order of the United States. But the activist thought that this nascent Woodstock Nation needed an "army" to defend it. And Hoffman observed that something like a citizen's brigade was indeed coming into being when, at the actual rock festival, "a sort of instant people's militia was formed" in response to authority figures who attempted to intervene in the spontaneous self-governing of the event. For Hoffman, Woodstock Nation was a new homeland that was paradoxically "built on electricity" from the existing commercial and political order of mass consumerism. Yet if "the people will provide the power," Woodstock Nation might eventually turn the circuits toward a new republic.[49] Caught up in the increasingly militant antiwar movement in the United States, Hoffman imagined the counterculture of Woodstock Nation itself developing a military force. "Music can make the walls shake," Hoffman wrote, referring to a quotation from Plato that was popular in the 1960s, "but you need an army to take the city." It was his version of what John Sinclair termed the "guitar army" of the counterculture.[50]

In Vietnam, however, young citizens such as the members of CBC wanted nothing to do with armies of any sort; they wanted to connect to the feeling of global countercultural participation. Because the band members looked like hippies and embraced rock music from the West, they drew the ire of Vietnamese traditionalists, but for the very same reasons they were harassed by the American military apparatus as well. Pursuing a kind of third way beyond Vietnamese nationalism and American imperialism, the band used rock to escape the war and enter a different realm of social and cultural belonging. They did not wish to make a statement about politics, but their very effort to reach Woodstock Nation was inevitably political. This became violently apparent on April 8, 1971, when a bomb detonated in a club on Tu Do Street in downtown Saigon while the band was playing Jimi Hendrix's "Purple

Haze" (figures 6.6 and 6.7).[51] Probably planted by the Viet Cong, the bomb killed one American GI and one Vietnamese woman, the girlfriend of drummer Phan Van.[52] When their music pointed so powerfully to other configurations of social relations than those available in the war, the members of CBC were ultimately unable to exist outside the hardened binaries of a civil war.

CBC kept performing in the aftermath of the Tu Do Street bombing, still seeking a path to Woodstock Nation. The members of CBC were deeply affected by the images and sounds of the festival when they saw the 1970 documentary film about it.[53] Phan Linh even dreamt of organizing a Woodstock-like event in Vietnam. "I hope," the guitarist told the *Grunt Free Press*, "that one day we can have a Woodstock in Saigon . . . with some rock groups from America and England, playing together with us. It would be the greatest day in Saigon—for our young people and your young GIs."[54] Not one month after the bombing of the CBC concert on Tu Do Street, Linh's dream came true. In May of 1971, the Saigon International Rock Festival took place. But the details of this event only further revealed the paradoxes of constituting the Woodstock Transnational—the global, cross-cultural

FIGURE 6.6. Entrance to My Phung Club, Saigon, 1971. Scott Roberts Personal Collection. Photographer: Scott Roberts.

FIGURE 6.7. My Phung Club after bombing, April 8 1971. Scott Roberts Personal Collection. Photographer: Scott Roberts.

version of Woodstock Nation. For one day, the Saigon International Rock Festival offered a kind of temporary asylum and citizenship in Woodstock Nation. Bands from South Vietnam, Australia, the Philippines, Malaysia, Japan, South Korea, Thailand, and elsewhere performed at the Saigon Zoo for roughly 7,000 fans. It was one of a number of rock festivals that eventually took place in South Vietnam at venues such as the Saigon Zoo, the city's soccer stadium, and at Taberd High School, which had featured Western pop music at festivals as early as 1965.[55] But the Saigon International Rock Festival was particularly odd because the organizers of the event were neither hippies, nor antiwar activists, nor even hip capitalist entrepreneurs, as was the case with the original Woodstock. The most conservative, pro-American, pro-war wing of South Vietnamese society sponsored the festival. According to Gloria Emerson, "The Vietnamese weekly magazine *Dieu Hau* *(The Hawk)*" whose "writers are nearly all military men, and its editorial policies support the South Vietnamese Army," promoted the festival.[56] Profits from the event went to the families of South Vietnamese who had served in the South Vietnamese Army, the very military that the members of CBC hoped to evade joining.

This was a particularly surreal form of hip militarism in which pro-war advocates in the Republic of Vietnam sponsored music associated with the antiwar movement in the United States. Yet the festival was not merely an example of co-optation. As with other instances of hip militarism, it also generated fervent debate about the war itself. The event met with protests by those who bemoaned the smothering of traditional Vietnamese traditions by imported American consumer culture. Gloria Emerson reported that "[c]ritics who said they represented teachers, parents of students, religious, cultural, and educational groups" sent a letter to the opposition newspaper *Tin Sang*, in which they claimed that the Saigon International Rock Festival "'legalizes a degenerate foreign culture which is harmful to Vietnamese culture and tradition.'" A Vietnamese professor added class to the critique. He wrote that, "a hippie or pop festival is . . . a festival of children of the privileged and powerful who are trying to turn themselves into yellow-skinned Americans."[57] The North Vietnamese did not approve of the event either. On a clandestine broadcast of Liberation Radio to the South, on May 29, 1971, an announcer called the festival "a scheme to morally poison southern youths and teenagers. It is a wicked, evil act to sabotage the Vietnamese national culture. This is a great crime not against a certain group alone but against our entire people. It is an unpardonable crime."[58] These critics took Woodstock Nation to be nothing more than a form of American consumerism that once again privileged the individual over social structures such as the traditional family. And on one level, they were correct in this assessment. As a television reporter for an American news broadcast remarked of the festival, "The fact that it's here at all underlines the lust of the urban youth here to join with other youths across the world in enjoying the freedom, even the license, of the youth culture."[59] The irony, of course, was that for the siblings in CBC rock music allowed them to keep their family together and intact. Perhaps this was part of why Phan Linh dreamed of a Woodstock Festival in Saigon. The event, with its emphasis on fellowship, communal obligation, and thinking of all people as brothers and sisters, offered a way to project the traditional Vietnamese emphasis on family into a modern, cosmopolitan global context. The Woodstock Transnational beckoned from within Vietnam because it offered a vision of combining traditional ideals with modern possibilities.[60]

Rock music, blasting out across a muddy field reminiscent of Woodstock, offered "freedom" and "even license," as the American television reporter claimed, but more than a feeling of individual liberation, it provided a small, temporary space of togetherness among the confusions of war. "About 500 GI's attended," Emerson reported, "many wearing headbands and antiwar or black-power jewelry." Emerson's figure suggests that the bulk of the audience consisted of South Vietnamese youth. She reported that "[i]t seemed that many of them—with their long sideburns, far-out sunglasses, open skirts and flared trousers—might want to be hippies but that life in South Vietnam did not permit it."[61] Except that for that afternoon, it did. With its temporary sonic passage to a wider world, the Saigon International Rock Festival paradoxically generated a sanctuary, a refuge, a safe harbor within the claustrophobic pressures of wartime Vietnam. As Gloria Emerson wrote, "In the rain, GI's and Vietnamese huddled together under the big umbrellas on the festival grounds or inside tents put up by the army, many of them laughing at how wet they were."[62] As Emerson suggested, the umbrellas at the Saigon International Rock Festival provided more than just shelter from the weather. They also provided cover for public expressions of fellowship and community that addressed experiences of the war and, at the same time, reached beyond it to new configurations of both private and public life. The umbrellas were impermanent and provisional, erected by the very military forces so many in the audience longed to escape, but under them, communal laughter blended with the reverberations of amplified guitars and drums. The dim outlines of the republic of rock appeared in the shadows of hip militarism in the Republic of Vietnam.

"I've Been Waiting for so Long, To Be Where I'm Going": Stateless in the Woodstock Transnational

Phan Linh's dream came true: CBC performed at the Saigon International Rock Festival in 1971. But the dream had its costs. By seeking out the Woodstock Nation within the military struggle over the Vietnam nation, the members of CBC eventually found themselves stateless, without a country. Fearful that the North Vietnamese communist government would persecute them for associating with Americans and adopting American culture, the Phan family fled to Thailand. But the visas for the men in the group ran out.[63] Rather than return to South Vietnam, the group made their way to Malaysia, Bali, and then to a Tibetan monastery in northern India.[64] Footage from a 1975 NBC news report showed the band in India, citizens without a state and lacking the electric guitars and amplifiers that gave them access to Woodstock Nation. Still, music remained crucial to their lives. Sitting in the monastery courtyard, they performed a song they had written in English about their experiences: "We love the South and we love the North," Phan Loan sings as her brother Linh strums chords on an acoustic guitar and her brother Van, without a drum set, hammers out the beat with sticks, "We love our music and for this we ran / our land was Vietnam." She and her family then sing together in tight harmony: "We just want to see our people free."[65]

By the end of 1975, CBC was able to resettle in the United States, largely through the help of a group of supportive American GIs who had been fans of the group in

Saigon during the war. With the financial assistance of one GI's parents and the governmental assistance of the Inter-Agency Task Force on Indochinese Refugee Resettlement, they first moved to Fort Wayne, Indiana.[66] After purchasing instruments in Chicago, they embarked on tours of the Midwest and South, performing on a booking contract at Ramada Inn hotels, with occasional trips to the Vietnamese refugee enclave of Los Angeles and other parts of the West Coast.[67] As with any hotel or bar band, CBC played the latest hits or anything else that entertained their audiences, but they remained in love most of all with the sounds of psychedelic rock. As if to make this point, in one publicity photograph taken of the group in 1975, just after they had arrived in the United States, CBC's members stood by the side of a dirt road outside Fort Wayne as if waiting for a passing car or truck (or perhaps the psychedelic bus of the Merry Pranksters) to pick them up. Where did they wish to go? Almost ten years after Paul Williams walked out of the "induction center" of the Fillmore Auditorium into what he thought might be a new counterculture *civitas* in the streets of San Francisco, CBC held up a sign indicating their hoped-for destination: "Filmore" (figure 6.8).[68]

FIGURE 6.8. Searching for the "Filmore" Auditorium: The Vietnamese band CBC as hitchhikers on the road to San Francisco, 1975. Frank Ford Personal Collection. Photographer: Allen Quinn.

FIGURE 6.9. The Phan family/CBC Band with Vietnam veteran friends, Houston, Texas, April 2011: from left in back, Rich Cameron, Quang Minh, Phan Marie Louise, Phan Linh; from left in front, Phan Van, Phan Lan, Phan Loan, and Phan Lien. Photographer: Michael J. Kramer.

The CBC stayed on the road until the early 1980s in search of this rock music goal, finally settling in Houston, Texas, where the group continues to perform to this day (figure 6.9).[69] In a video from the late 2000s, the ensemble can be seen playing a version of Cream's 1968 hit "Sunshine of Your Love" at a club they opened in the city, CBC Mini-Club. Phan Linh's guitar still blazes, snarls, pleads, and soars. Wearing a black-and-white, go-go style, checkered miniskirt dress and white boots, Phan Loan steps out front. She leans forward into the microphone, eyes closed: "I've been waiting for so long / To be where I'm going," she sings, rocking back and forth. The music seems to propel her and CBC backward and forward all at once, cast deep into the blurry memories of a long gone war and, at the same time, launched into the pixilated stream of a global countercultural circuit whose possibilities for transnational connection still beckon even as CBC's rock notes fade into history.[70]

Epilogue

IN 1979, THE playwright Václav Havel, who would go on after the fall of communism to become president of Czechoslovakia, wrote critically of the arrest and trial of a largely apolitical group of young musicians who called themselves the Plastic People of the Universe. The Czech state's incursions on the band's freedom to play rock had inspired Havel and others to sign Charter 77, a document that lamented the limitations on civil society behind the Iron Curtain. "Who would have foreseen," Havel asked in his essay, "The Power of the Powerless," "that the prosecution of one or two obscure rock groups would have such far-reaching consequences?"[1]

Havel was most interested in the "pre-political" ethos that the Plastic People found in playing rock music.[2] The Plastics, to Havel, cared not about the political implications of their cultural experiences. Theirs was instead a kind of libertarian withdrawal, a request to be left alone. But this libertarian streak sparked a communitarian response. It gave rise to what Havel described as a kind of "parallel *polis*" to the official government, a space of more open and democratic relations in the pursuit of truth, justice, dignity, togetherness, and community. The right of the Plastic People to play rock music without harassment was eventually "understood as a human freedom" that required protection, according to Havel. It was equivalent of the right "to engage in philosophical and political reflection, the freedom to write, the freedom to express and defend various social and political interests of society."[3] The music became an avenue to questions of citizenship that could not be answered by straightforward political activity in Czechoslovakia.[4]

This was a kind of existential politics, and Havel was one of many around the world who noticed how rock was part of it during the 1960s and in the decade's aftermath.[5] When *bossa nova* star Caetano Veloso strung electrical wires around his neck and sang the rock-inflected "É proibido proibir (Prohibiting is prohibited)" at the 1968 Globo Music Festival in Brazil, when Mexican youth gathered at the Woodstock-like *Avándaro* rock festival in 1971, when Malian adolescents named their social clubs after rock bands and dreamed of organizing a Woodstock in the capital of Bamako, and in many other places and settings, rock fostered outposts of Woodstock Nation.[6] A Woodstock Transnational emerged as people around the globe adopted rock music for their own needs. But the fact that they pursued the nature of truth and freedom using a music that was so much a part of American consumer and military empire suggests that the appropriation of rock was never pure, never transcendent. The logics of hip capitalism and militarism meant that even as rock brought civic energies of engagement to people around the world, it always did so in relation to the spread of American global hegemony.

Even in the Soviet Union, the competing superpower of the Cold War, rock delivered a heightened engagement with citizenship. After the publication of an article about hippie culture in 1968, young people sought out the latest rock from the West and adopted many of the styles and practices of hippies. They grew their hair long, adopted hippie fashion styles, and experimented with drugs. The *hippi*, as they were called, gathered in Moscow at the Hippodrome near Moscow University, and at the Nevsky Prospekt near the Kazan Cathedral in Leningrad (St. Petersburg). In the summer, they traveled to rural areas of the Soviet Union, where they "bartered clothing, records, and other accoutrements of Western-style youth culture."[7] As historian Timothy Ryback notes in *Rock Around the Bloc*, "The Soviet system, equipped to combat political dissent and ideological deviation, offered few mechanisms for confronting the emerging Soviet hippie culture." Local-level militias and the *druzhinniki* (volunteer police) sometimes dragged in male *hippi* and cut their hair off, but other than strong penalties for drug use, a rock counterculture flourished among Soviet youth.[8] It did so in the same "hidden sphere" of civil society that Havel noticed in Czechoslovakia.

Long after the heyday of the 1960s counterculture passed in the United States and Western Europe, it continued in the Soviet Union. "Thousands of *hippi* continued to litter Soviet society long after their counterparts in the West had disappeared," Ryback observed. "As late as 1978, . . . hundreds of Soviet *hippi* still gathered" to listen to rock or wander the country.[9] As Andrea Lee, an American living in Leningrad, reported in her book *Russian Journal*: "It was strange for me to see and hear all around me vestiges of the American drug culture of a decade ago—the psychedelic drawings, the fantastic clothes, Grace Slick wailing on a tape player."[10] Consigned to the memory chambers of nostalgia in the United States by 1978, Grace Slick's "wail on a tape player" continued to circulate around the world as a harbinger of civic possibilities. First resonating in San Francisco in the mid-1960s, where Slick found fame with the Jefferson Airplane, rock music traveled to Vietnam by the late 1960s, where Phan Loan gained renown with the CBC Band as the Grace Slick of the war zone. Many dubbed copies later, the music sustained countercultural energies deep within the Soviet Union, where *hippi* listened to rock long after the counterculture had faded elsewhere.

They were drawn to the alluring freedom and flashy modernity of Western leisure culture, to be sure (even Grace Slick and the Jefferson Airplane in their own way). But more than that, they tuned in the sounds of rock because it represented the smuggled ciphers of a global counterculture that they longed to join. Even as the counterculture vanished into the historical background, rock summoned dreams of an openness that was difficult to locate in their immediate surroundings. However, by the time of the Soviet *hippi* in the late 1970s, a crucial reversal had taken place: the relationship between private and public experience that had first defined the power of rock for listeners in the mid-1960s had flipped. As Nick Bromell writes (and as Stephen Spender noticed before him), rock originally provided a soundtrack for going public with private revelations.[11] This was a driving desire in the counterculture—think of Slick and the Jefferson Airplane singing about their experiences with drugs in the band's hit song "White Rabbit" or Ken Kesey and the Merry Pranksters as they widened their LSD-fueled inquiries to include an ever-larger swathe of participants.[12] By the late 1970s, in the hinterlands of the Soviet Union, the music did not move from private to public; instead, it retreated from public into semi-secret, private realms away from public scrutiny—from Acid Tests to *samizdat*.

This can be understood less as a mark of failure than as indicative of a shift in the dialectic between public and private within the changing structures of global consumer capitalism. While rock originally drew much of its power from the feeling that citizenship could be improved by bringing the intimate into the commons, now the music seemed charged with the urge to preserve within private lives a lost sense of community. Rock music compacted the open, free sense of citizenship that had defined the sixties counterculture into a few songs that were passed along hand to hand, ear to ear, tape reel to tape reel—recorded and re-recorded and re-recorded again. Why was this so? Perhaps the economic underpinnings for civic life and citizenship changed. On the one hand, consumer capitalism grew ever more expansive, increasingly linking together a public so vast and dispersed as to be almost unimaginable in its scope and diversity. Commercialized rock from America even breached the boundaries of the communist motherland. On the other hand, the way in which consumer capitalism achieved this feat was by subdividing into niche markets. Rock was an example of how capitalism went micro even as it went macro, how its commodities reached deeply into the seemingly free spaces of intimate lives even as capitalism as a system took hold with an ever-firmer grip globally.

Rock in the countercultural moment was a harbinger of what would come to be called post-Fordism, disorganized capitalism, the New Economy, liquid modernity, and simply postmodernism.[13] The music most of all encapsulated the operations of hip capitalism, in which people purchased the feeling of not being sold a bill of goods and thus were sold a bill of goods; they were incorporated into capitalism by buying the very experience of feeling outside capitalism. This "conquest of cool," as historian Thomas Frank called it, began in the 1960s. It produced what he evocatively describes as a "perpetual motion machine" of transgressive rebellion in much of the popular culture to follow.[14] The more that genres of popular music and culture—punk rock, indie rock, hip-hop—followed in the rock tradition of shouting out their rebelliousness, the more easily they were appropriated by consumer capitalism. It was as if Grace Slick's wail, first heard in San Francisco, later through the hip militarism of Vietnam, and eventually on the bootlegged recordings of Soviet *hippi*, had been placed on endless repeat. This was a rebel yell that merely faded into the tape hiss of capitalism's whirring cassette wheels—and soon after that entered into the sleek, frictionless fluidity of the digital age. Rock became the clarion call not of a rebel yell, but of what philosophers Joseph Heath and Andrew Potter call the "rebel sell." Woodstock Nation became a "nation of rebels" whose stylized but empty protest merely expanded consumer culture's alienations, inadequacies, and injustices by, paradoxically, seeming to oppose them.[15]

Yet despite the truth of rock's complicity in hip capitalism (and its surreal extension, hip militarism), it is worth remembering how *hippi* in the Soviet Union and hippies around the world were drawn to rock. They liked the music not only because it felt transgressive, but also because it offered access to core dilemmas of citizenship. The *hippi* did not tune in to Grace Slick's bootlegged wail simply to become hip American capitalists, nor did they do so to fight American capitalism. What they wished to do was "to share experiences and wander the length and breadth of the Soviet Union," as Timothy Ryback pointed out.[16] They wanted to follow the sounds of rock to the lost territory of Woodstock Nation, a place where the systems of capitalism and communism both gave way, in fleeting moments, to a potentially more democratic and cosmopolitan global commons, a place where participants might deeply and movingly investigate how self and society might flourish together.

The puzzles of individual liberation and collective belonging in a globalizing world were ultimately never realized in this Woodstock Transnational, but that does not mean that the song of rock and the counterculture should be forgotten—or, worse yet, forsaken. As Václav Havel remarked of rock in the Czechoslovakian context, "Everyone understood that an attack on the Czech musical underground was an attack on a most elementary and important thing . . . it was an attack on the very notion of 'living within the truth,' on the real aims of life." The hope of grasping what life was about, or at least trying, "in fact bound everyone together," Havel argued.[17] The Plastics borrowed from what turned out to be some of the hippest 1960s American rock—Frank Zappa, the Velvet Underground, the Fugs—but they used these sounds not just to get hip, but for their own pleasures and struggles.

Participants in the global counterculture may have donned American flag t-shirts, as the CBC Band did in Vietnam, but what they used rock to sing about— their own hopes, dreams, desires, and questions—went far beyond what the United States had to offer with either hip capitalism or hip militarism. The "conquest of cool" did not mean total domination. It did not even mean the perfection of hegemonic control. In the United States and around the world, many experienced rock as access to modernity, to technology, and to power of both the electronic and the political sort. As rock critic and radical feminist Ellen Willis wrote, "The history of the sixties strongly suggests that the impulse to buy a new car and tool down the freeway with the radio blasting rock-and-roll is not unconnected to the impulse to fuck outside marriage, get high, stand up to men or white people or bosses, join dissident movements."[18] Consumer experiences that traded on heightened critical awareness could not be vacuum-sealed from actual critical awareness. Economics and politics could not be so simply separated. In culture—and especially the counterculture—they intersected in profound ways. To be sure, rock was compromised by its place within larger structures of power, but it also gave listeners an embedded medium in which to face this complicity. The music invited listeners to enter into its truth-seeking sounds and make them their own. From Ken Kesey and the Merry Pranksters to the CBC Band, they did just that, turning listening into playing, hearing into action, call into response.

This back and forth never really ended, even though the sixties counterculture itself did. So it is that the members of the CBC still sing to us now from a nightclub in Saigon during the Vietnam War. They appear on a computer screen, processed into bits and bytes, channeling a Grand Funk Railroad lyric into their own story, which is increasingly everyone's tale an era of rampant consumer capitalism matched only by seemingly endless militarized conflicts and ongoing crises of democratic representation. From a dank, starkly lit stage thousands of miles from the multicolored splendor of San Francisco's rock halls and now dozens of years removed from the sixties counterculture, they ask a question we still need to answer: "Hey all you people, for goodness sake / Let's get together, what does it take?"[19]

Notes

1. Paul Williams, "The Golden Road: A Report on San Francisco," *Crawdaddy!*, July–August 1967, 6. Williams was the founding editor of *Crawdaddy!*, which was one of the first rock music publications in the United States.

2. It is helpful to contextualize Williams's vision of the Fillmore: antiwar protesters had attempted to close down the actual military induction center in Oakland since 1965; during the autumn 1967 Stop the Draft week, some 10,000 protesters succeeded in shutting down the Oakland induction center during violent conflicts with the police; see W. J. Rorabaugh, *Berkeley At War: The 1960s* (New York: Oxford University Press, 1989), 116–19.

3. Williams, "Golden Road," 7.

4. N. A., "From the Haight," *Berkeley Barb*, October 26, 1967, in *The New Left: A Documentary History*, ed. Massimo Teodori (Indianapolis: Bobbs Merrill, 1969), 363.

5. Allen Cohen and Ron Thelin, Letter to Art Kunkin, Editor of the *Los Angeles Free Press*, January 1, 1967, in Allen Cohen and San Francisco Oracle, Correspondence and Written Material, 1966–1967 Folder, Hippies Collection, San Francisco Historical Center, San Francisco Public Library.

6. Chester Anderson, "Uncle Tim'$ Children," *The Communication Company*, April 16, 1967, The Communication Company (San Francisco, CA) April 1967 Folder, Chester Anderson Papers, Bancroft Manuscript Collection, University of California, Berkeley. Also published in *The Digger Archives*, http://www.diggers.org/comco/ccpaps2b.html [accessed October 1, 2011].

7. Publicity poster, Ent Viet V. 3 Tours, January–March 1970 Folder, RG 472, Records of the United States Army in Vietnam (USARV), Special Services Agency (Provisional), Entertainment Branch, History Files, "Entertainment Vietnam," V. 3, May 1969–December 1970, National Archives—College Park, Maryland [hereafter NARA].

8. Tim Page, photograph of a United States soldier from 8th Regiment, riding atop a 9th Division armored personnel carrier, May 1968, http://www.vietnampix.com/hippie3.htm [accessed January 13, 2003].

9. Gunbunny, photograph of helmet cover marked "ETS January 6, 1970," U.S. Militaria Forum: Collectors Preserving History, http://www.usmilitariaforum.com/forums/index.php?showtopic=46108&st=20 [accessed January 3, 2012].

10. See images on U.S. Militaria Forum: Collectors Preserving History, http://www.usmilitariaforum.com/forums/index.php [accessed January 3, 2012]; and Sherry Buchanan, *Vietnam Zippos: American Soldiers' Engravings and Stories, 1965–1973* (Chicago: University of Chicago Press, 2007).

11. Tim Page, photograph of a United States soldier attached to a mechanized unit posted just below the DMZ, January 29, 1968, http://www.vietnampix.com/hippie2a.htm [accessed January 13, 2003].

12. See Mary Dudziak, *War Time: An Idea, Its History, Its Consequences* (New York: Oxford University Press, 2012).

13. Phan Linh, Phan Loan, Phan Van, Phan Marie Louise, and other Phan family members, interview with author, Houston, TX, April 11, 2011.

14. Howard Brick, *Age of Contradiction: American Thought and Culture in the 1960's* (1998; reprint, Ithaca, NY: Cornell University Press, 2000), 114. Among the many studies of the counterculture, see Charles Reich, *The Greening of America: How the Youth Revolution Is Trying To Make America Livable* (1970; reprint, New York: Crown, 1995); Timothy Miller, *The Hippies and American Values* (Knoxville: University of Tennessee Press, 1991); George Lipsitz, "Who'll Stop the Rain? Youth Culture, Rock 'n' Roll, and Social Crises," in *The Sixties: From Memory to History*, ed. David Farber (Chapel Hill: University of North Carolina Press, 1994), 206–34; Julie Stephens, *Anti-Disciplinary Protest: Sixties Radicalism and Postmodernism* (New York: Cambridge University Press, 1998); Dominick Cavallo, *A Fiction of the Past: The Sixties in American History* (New York: St. Martin's Press, 1999); Peter Braunstein and Michael William Doyle, eds., *Imagine Nation: The American Counterculture of the 1960s and 70s* (New York: Routledge, 2001); Sean McCann and Michael Szalary, eds., "Countercultural Capital: Essays on the Sixties from Some Who Weren't There," *Yale Journal of Criticism* 18, 2 (Fall 2005); Christoph Grunenberg and Jonathan Harris, eds., *Summer of Love: Psychedelic Art, Social Crisis, and Counterculture in the 1960s* (Liverpool: Liverpool University Press–Tate Liverpool Critical Forum, 2005); Fred Turner, *From Counterculture to Cyberculture: Stewart Brand, the Whole Earth Network, and the Rise of Digital Utopianism* (Chicago: University of Chicago Press, 2006); Christopher Gair, *The American Counterculture* (Edinburgh: Edinburgh University Press, 2007); Gretchen Lempke-Santagelo, *Daughters of Aquarius: Women of the Sixties Counterculture* (Lawrence: University Press of Kansas, 2009); and Elissa Auther and Adam Lerner, eds., *West of Center: Art and the Counterculture Experiment in America, 1965–1977* (Minneapolis: University of Minnesota Press, 2012).

For overviews of the sixties, see Todd Gitlin, *The Sixties: Years of Hope, Days of Rage* (New York: Bantam, 1987); David Farber, *The Age of Great Dreams: America In the 1960s* (New York: Hill & Wang, 1994); Arthur Marwick, *The Sixties: Cultural Revolution in Britain, France, Italy, and the United States, c.1958–c.1974* (New York: Oxford University Press, 1998); Maurice Isserman and Michael Kazin, *America Divided: The Civil War of the 1960s* (New York: Oxford University Press, 2000); Mark Lytle, *America's Uncivil Wars: The Sixties Era from Elvis to the Fall of Richard Nixon* (New York: Oxford University Press, 2005); and Klaus P. Fischer, *America in White, Black, and Gray: The Stormy 1960s* (New York: Continuum, 2006).

15. For overviews of democratic citizenship in the United States, see Rogers M. Smith, *Civic Ideals: Conflicting Visions of Citizenship in U.S. History* (New Haven, CT: Yale University Press, 1997); Michael Schudson, *The Good Citizen: A History of American Civic Life* (Cambridge, MA: Harvard University Press, 1998); David M. Ricci, *Good Citizenship in America* (New York: Cambridge University Press, 2004); and Judith Shklar, *American Citizenship: The Quest for Inclusion* (Cambridge, MA: Harvard University Press, 1991). The foundational study of democratic citizenship in the United States is, of course, Alexis de Tocqueville, *Democracy in America* (1835/1840; reprint, New York: Vintage, 1990). Studies on the relationship between democratic citizenship and the arts (both high art and popular art) include Peter Dahlgren, *Television and the Public Sphere: Citizenship, Democracy, and the Media* (Thousand Oaks, CA: Sage Publications, 1995); Arthur M. Melzer, Jerry Weinberger, M. Richard Zinman, eds., *Democracy and the Arts* (Ithaca, NY: Cornell University Press, 1999); Lambert Zuidervaart and Henry Luttikhuizen, eds., *The Arts, Community, and Cultural Democracy* (New York: St. Martin's Press, 2000); *Entertaining the Citizen: When Politics and Popular Culture Converge* (Lanham, MD: Rowman & Littlefield, 2004); James Bau Graves, *Cultural Democracy: The Arts, Community, and the Public Purpose* (Urbana: University of Illinois Press, 2005); Toby Miller, "What Is Cultural Citizenship?," in *Cultural Citizenship: Cosmopolitanism, Consumerism, and Television in a Neoliberal Age* (Philadelphia, PA: Temple University Press, 2006), 27–73; Casey Blake, ed., *The Arts of Democracy: Art, Public Culture, and the State* (Philadelphia: University of Pennsylvania Press, 2007); Richard Butsch, *The Citizen Audience: Crowds, Publics, and Individuals* (New York: Routledge, 2007); and Richard Cándida Smith, *The Modern Moves West: California Artists and Democratic Culture in the Twentieth Century* (Philadelphia: University of Pennsylvania Press, 2009).

For more on citizenship and consumption, see Bryan S. Turner, *Citizenship and Capitalism: The Debate over Reformism* (Boston: Allen & Unwin, 1986); John Urry, *Consuming Places* (New York: Routledge, 1995); Martin Daunton and Matthew Hilton, eds., *The Politics of Consumption: Material Culture and Citizenship in Europe and America* (Oxford: Berg, 2001); and Nestor Garcia Canclini, *Consumers and Citizens: Globalization and Multicultural Conflicts* (Minneapolis: University of Minnesota Press, 2001). For more on global and transnational perspectives on citizenship, see May Joseph, *Nomadic Identities: The Performance of Citizenship* (Minneapolis: University of Minnesota Press, 1999); Aihwa Ong, *Flexible Citizenship: The Cultural Logics of Transnationality* (Durham, NC: Duke University Press, 1999). See also Thomas H. Marshall, *Citizenship and Social Class and Other Essays* (1950; reprint: Concord, MA: Pluto Press, 1992); Hannah Arendt, *The Human Condition* (Chicago: University of Chicago Press, 1958); Hannah Arendt, *On Revolution* (1963; reprint, New York: Penguin, 1990); Raymond Aron, "Is Multinational Citizenship Possible?," *Social Research* 41, 4 (Winter 1974): 638–56; Richard Sennett, *The Fall of Public Man* (1977; reprint, New York: Norton, 1992); J. M. Barbalet, *Citizenship: Rights, Struggle, and Class Inequality* (Minneapolis: University of Minnesota Press, 1988); Adrian Oldfield, *Citizenship and Community: Civic Republicanism and the Modern World* (New York: Routledge, 1990); Maurice Roche, *Rethinking Citizenship: Welfare, Ideology, and Change in Modern Society* (Boston: Polity, 1992); Toby Miller, *Well-Tempered Self: Citizenship, Culture, and the Postmodern Subject* (Baltimore, MD: Johns Hopkins University Press, 1993); Bryan Turner, ed., *Citizenship and Social Theory* (Thousand Oaks, CA: Sage, 1993); Bart van Steenbergen, ed., *The Condition of Citizenship* (Thousand Oaks, CA: Sage, 1994); Gershon Shafir, ed., *The Citizenship Debates: A Reader* (Minneapolis: University of Minnesota Press, 1998); Engin F. Isin and Patricia K. Wood, *Citizenship and Identity* (Thousand Oaks, CA: Sage, 1999); David Selbourne, *The Principle of Duty: An Essay on the Foundation of Civic Order* (South Bend, IN: University of Notre Dame Press, 2000); Renato Rosaldo, "Cultural Citizenship and Educational Democracy,"

Cultural Anthropology 9, 3 (August 1994): 402–11; Ronald Beiner, ed., *Theorizing Citizenship* (Albany: State University of New York Press, 1995); Jan Pakulski, "Cultural Citizenship," *Citizenship Studies* 1, 1 (February 1997): 73–86; Ruth Lister, *Citizenship: Feminist Perspectives* (1997; 2nd ed., New York: New York University Press, 2003); Herman R. van Gunsteren, *A Theory of Citizenship: Organizing Plurality in Contemporary Democracies* (Boulder, CO: Westview Press, 1998); Derek Heater, *What Is Citizenship?* (Boston: Polity, 1999); Keith Faulks, *Citizenship* (New York: Routledge, 2000); Will Kymlicka, *Politics in the Vernacular: Nationalism, Multiculturalism, Citizenship* (New York: Oxford University Press, 2001); Paul Magnette, *Citizenship: The History of an Idea* (Colchester, UK: ECPR, 2005); Engin Fahri Isin, ed., *Recasting the Social in Citizenship* (Toronto: University of Toronto Press, 2008); and Peter Dahlgren, *Media and Political Engagement: Citizens, Communication, and Democracy* (New York: Cambridge University Press, 2009). On the related concept of civil society, see Jay Mechling, "Folklore and Civil Sphere," *Western Folklore* 56, 2 (Spring 1997): 113–37; John Ehrenberg, *Civil Society: The Critical History of an Idea* (New York: New York University Press, 1999); Michael Edwards, *Civil Society* (Malden, MA: Blackwell, 2004); and Jeffrey C. Alexander, *The Civil Sphere* (New York: Oxford University Press, 2006).

16. In 1968, promoter Bill Graham moved his concert company from the original Fillmore Auditorium, located in the Fillmore district of San Francisco, to the former Carousel Ballroom in downtown San Francisco, calling it the Fillmore West; he opened a sister club in New York City called the Fillmore East that same year, but had nothing to do with the Fillmore Far East. See Bill Graham and Robert Greenfield, *Bill Graham Presents: My Life Inside Rock and Out* (New York: Doubleday, 1992), 241–42.

17. There are, of course, many books on the Enlightenment republic of letters: see, for instance, Dena Goodman, *The Republic of Letters: A Cultural History of the French Enlightenment* (Ithaca, NY: Cornell University Press, 1994). Many draw upon the conceptual framework mapped out by Jürgen Habermas in *The Structural Transformation of the Public Sphere: An Inquiry into a Category of Bourgeois Society*, trans. Thomas Burger with Frederick Lawrence (1962; Cambridge, MA: MIT Press, 1989).

18. The republic of rock that I describe is similar to the "invisible republic" that Greil Marcus hears on the "Basement Tapes" recorded by Bob Dylan and the Band in 1967; Marcus pictures the invisible republic as a kind of timeless, subaltern American nation, while I identify the republic of rock as part of a transnational counterculture during the 1960s and '70s; see Greil Marcus, *Invisible Republic: Bob Dylan's Basement Tapes* (New York: Henry Holt, 1997); retitled *The Old, Weird America: The World of Bob Dylan's Basement Tapes* when released in paperback (New York: Picador, 2001).

19. Popular music scholar Simon Frith makes the important point that popular music does not reveal who "the people" are, but rather actively constructs them; see Simon Frith, "Towards an Aesthetic of Popular Music," in *Music and Society: The Politics of Composition, Performance, and Reception*, ed. Richard Leppert and Susan McClary (New York: Cambridge University Press, 1987), 133–49. Drawing upon the work of Zygmunt Bauman, Josh Kun makes a similar point to Frith about popular music and citizenship; for Kun, music offers a contested space for struggles over cultural difference in relation to political rights and social belonging; see Josh Kun, *Audiotopia: Music, Race, and America* (Berkeley: University of California Press, 2005), 10–11; see also Zygmunt Bauman, "Modernity and Ambivalence," *Theory, Culture and Society: Explorations in Critical Social Science* 7, 2 (June 1990): 143–69. On the concept of "the people" as a category of political rhetoric, see Pierre Bourdieu, "The Uses of 'The People,'" in *In Other Words: Essays Toward a Reflexive Sociology* (Palo Alto: Stanford University Press, 1990), 150–155. See also, Ernesto Laclau,

On Populist Reason (New York: Verso, 2005); Laclau treats the people as a constructed "floating signifier" utilized in populist political struggles. Among the many other works on theories of democratic practice, my argument is particularly informed by Ernesto Laclau and Chantal Mouffe, *Hegemony and Socialist Strategy: Towards a Radical Democratic Politics* (1985; 2nd ed., New York: Verso, 2001); Claude Lefort, *Democracy and Political Theory*, trans. David Macey (Minneapolis: University of Minnesota Press, 1988); Chantal Mouffe, ed., *Dimensions of Radical Democracy: Pluralism, Citizenship, Community* (New York: Verso, 1992); and Chantal Mouffe, *The Democratic Paradox* (New York: Verso, 2000).

20. Talcott Parsons, *The Social System* (New York: Free Press, 1951), 522. J. Milton Yinger, "Contraculture and Subculture," *American Sociological Review* 25, 4 (October 1960): 625–35; see also J. Milton Yinger, *Countercultures: The Promise and Peril of a World Turned Upside Down* (New York: Free Press, 1982). For more on the academic origins of the term counterculture, see Peter Braunstein and William Michael Doyle, "Introduction," in Braunstein and Doyle, *Imagine Nation*, 6–7; and Howard Brick, "Talcott Parsons's 'Shift Away from Economics,' 1937–1946," *Journal of American History* 87, 2 (September 2000): 490–514.

21. Theodore Roszak, *The Making of a Counter Culture: Reflections on the Technocratic Society and Its Youthful Opposition* (1969; reprint, Berkeley: University of California Press, 1995). A number of the chapters were adopted from essays written in 1968 and published in *The Nation*. Many lump Roszak's analysis in with utopian books such as Charles Reich's *The Greening of America*; however Roszak was far less optimistic about and far more critical of the counterculture. Furthermore, he placed citizenship front and center as the key issue of the countercultural response to technocratic social practices; see Roszak, *Making of a Counter Culture*, 7.

22. On the struggles over the popular memory of the 1960s, see Bernard von Bothmer, *Framing the Sixties: The Uses and Abuses of a Decade from Ronald Reagan to George W. Bush* (Amherst: University of Massachusetts Press, 2010).

23. Braunstein and Doyle, "Introduction," in Braunstein and Doyle, *Imagine Nation*, 10. Arthur Marwick and Klaus Fischer similarly picture the counterculture as a cluster of overlapping subcultures and political movements rather than a coherent phenomenon. See Marwick, *The Sixties*, 11–13; Fischer, *America in White, Black, and Gray*, 335.

24. Brick, *Age of Contradiction*, 114.

25. Lipsitz, "Who'll Stop the Rain?"; and Farber, *Age of Great Dreams*, 169. On popular music, politics, and space, see Kun, *Audiotopia*, 21–26; and Ray Pratt, "Popular Music, Free Space, and the Quest for Community," *Popular Music and Society* 13, 4 (1989): 59–76. More broadly, see Harry Boyte and Sara Evans, *Free Spaces: The Sources of Democratic Change in America* (New York: Harper & Row, 1986; Gaston Bachelard, *The Poetics of Space* (1958; reprint, Boston, MA: Beacon Press, 1994); Michel Foucault, "Of Other Spaces (1967)," *Diacritics* 16 (Spring 1986), 22–27; Henri Lefebvre, *The Production of Space* (1974; trans., Cambridge, MA: Blackwell, 1991); Lawrence Grossberg, "The Space of Culture, The Power of Space," in *The Post-Colonial Question: Common Skies, Divided Horizons*, ed. Iain Chambers and Lidia Curt (New York: Routledge, 1996); and Edward W. Soja, *Postmodern Geographies: The Reassertion of Space in Critical Social Theory* (New York: Verso, 1997).

26. Brick draws upon Talcott Parsons for this interpretation. See Brick, *Age of Contradiction*, 118–19; Talcott Parsons, "Kinship and Associational Aspects of Social Structure," in *Kinship and Culture*, ed. Francis L. K. Hsu (Chicago: Aldine, 1971), 409–38. See also Harvey Cox's book, *The Secular City: Secularization and Urbanization in Theological Perspective* (New York: Macmillan, 1965), which made a similar argument about the liberating potential of the long-term shift from small, closely knit communities to a more cosmopolitan framework.

27. Braunstein and Doyle, "Introduction," in Braunstein and Doyle, *Imagine Nation*, 10.

28. Nick Stevenson, "Culture and Citizenship: An Introduction," in *Culture and Citizenship*, ed. Nick Stevenson (Thousand Oaks, CA: Sage, 2001), 2.

29. Counterculturalists were part of a more conscious critical awareness of the politics of everyday life that arose in the decades after World War II. See Henri Lefebvre, *Critique of Everyday Life*, vol. 1–3, trans. John Moore (1961; trans., New York: Verso, 2002); Henri Lefebvre, *Rhythmanalysis: Space, Time, and Everyday Life*, trans. Stuart Elden (1992; trans., New York: Continuum, 2004); Michel de Certeau, *The Practice of Everyday Life*, trans. Steven Rendall (Berkeley: University of California Press, 1984); Jürgen Habermas, *The Theory of Communicative Action*, vol. 2: *Lifeworld and System-A Critique of Functionalist Reason*, trans. Thomas McCarthy (1981; trans., Boston: Beacon Press, 1987); and Tony Bennett and Diane Watson, eds., *Understanding Everyday Life* (Cambridge, MA: Blackwell, 2002). For a sonic exploration of everyday life, see Brandon Labelle, *Acoustic Territories: Sound Culture and Everyday Life* (New York: Continuum, 2010).

30. My study emphasizes that the cultural politics of rock are best understood through the lens of citizenship. For studies that similarly address the cultural politics of rock and popular music, see Peter Doggett, *There's a Riot Going On: Revolutionaries, Rock Stars, and the Rise and Fall of the '60s* (Edinburgh: Canongate Books, 2008); Robin Denselow, *When the Music's Over: The Story of Political Pop* (London: Faber & Faber, 1989); Ray Pratt, *Rhythm and Resistance: Explorations in the Political Uses of Music* (New York: Praeger, 1990); Ron Eyerman and Andrew Jamison, eds., *Music and Social Movements: Mobilizing Traditions in the Twentieth Century* (Cambridge: Cambridge University Press, 1998); Mark Mattern, *Acting in Concert: Music, Community, and Political Action* (New Brunswick, NJ: Rutgers University Press, 1998); Reebee Garofalo, ed., *Rockin' the Boat: Mass Music and Mass Movement* (Boston: South End Press, 1999); and Tom Turino, "Music and Political Movements," in *Music as Social Life: The Politics of Participation* (Chicago: University of Chicago Press, 2008), 189–224.

31. For more on rock music and the politics of "incorporation," see the work of Lawrence Grossberg, especially his essay, "Another Boring Day in Paradise: Rock and Roll and the Empowerment of Everyday Life," *Popular Music* 4 (January 1984): 225–58.

32. In this sense, the counterculture had much in common with the theory of "participatory democracy" in the more political New Left. This relationship between cultural ferment and political activism has been a central point of contention in studies of "the sixties." Many have argued that the counterculture marked a diversion away from politics. See former rock critic James Miller's study of Students for a Democratic Society (SDS), *Democracy Is in the Streets: From Port Huron to the Siege of Chicago* (1987; reprint, Cambridge, MA: Harvard University Press, 1994); and Todd Gitlin's magisterial memoir-history, *The Sixties*, for examples of this interpretation. Other scholars contend that the New Left's politics must be placed in the broader milieu of a "movement culture" that included the counterculture. See Wini Breines, *Community and Organization in the New Left, 1962–1968* (1982; reprint, New Brunswick, NJ: Rutgers University Press, 1989); Sohnya Sayres et al., eds., *The 60s Without Apology* (Minneapolis: University of Minnesota Press in cooperation with *Social Text*, 1984); Gregory Calvert, *Democracy From the Heart: Spiritual Values, Decentralism, and Democratic Idealism in the Movement of the 1960's* (Novato, CA: Communitas Press, 1991); Barbara L. Tischler, ed., *Sights on the Sixties* (New Brunswick, NJ: Rutgers University Press, 1992); Van Gosse, *Where the Boys Are: Cuba, Cold War America and the Making of a New Left* (New York: Verso, 1993); James J. Farrell, *The Spirit of the Sixties: Making Postwar Radicalism* (New York: Routledge, 1997); Doug Rossinow, "'The Revolution Is About Our Lives': The New Left's Counterculture," in Braunstein

and Doyle, *Imagine Nation*, 99–124; Van Gosse, *Rethinking the New Left: An Interpretive History* (New York: Palgrave MacMillan, 2005); and Alice Echols, *Shaky Ground: The '60s and Its After-shocks* (New York: Columbia University Press, 2002). For more on SDS and New Left politics, see Richard Flacks, *Youth and Social Change* (Chicago: University of Chicago Press, 1971); Greg Calvert and Carol Neiman, *A Disrupted History: The New Left and the New Capitalism* (New York: Random House, 1971); James P. O'Brien, "The Development of a New Left in the United States, 1960–1965" (Ph.D. diss., Madison: University of Wisconsin, 1971); Kirkpatrick Sale, *SDS* (New York: Vintage, 1973); George Vickers, *The Formation of the New Left: The Early Years* (Lexington, MA: Lexington Books, 1975); Paul Buhle, ed., *History and the New Left: Madison, Wisconsin, 1950–1970* (Philadelphia, PA: Temple University Press, 1990); Paul Berman, *A Tale of Two Utopias: The Political Journey of the Generation of 1968* (New York: W.W. Norton, 1996); John McMillian and Paul Buhle, eds., *The New Left Revisited* (Philadelphia, PA: Temple University Press, 2003); Geoff Bailey, "The Making of a New Left: The Rise and Fall of SDS," *International Socialist Review* 31 (September–October 2003), http://www.isreview.org/issues/31/sds.shtml [accessed September 1, 2011]; and David Barber, *A Hard Rain Fell: SDS and Why It Failed* (Oxford: University Press of Mississippi, 2008).

33. In this sense, rock fits with arguments about how culture shapes spaces of political activity; see Harry Boyte and Sara Evans, *Free Spaces*. Culture had always been a crucial arena of engagement in the various political movements for expanded civil rights during the 1960s. For examples from the modern African-American civil rights movement, see William Chafe, *Civilities and Civil Rights: Greensboro, North Carolina, and the Black Struggle for Freedom* (New York: Oxford University Press, 1980); Charles Payne, *I've Got the Light of Freedom: The Organizing Tradition and the Mississippi Freedom Struggle* (Berkeley: University of California Press, 1996); James C. Hall, *Mercy, Mercy, Me: African American Culture and the American Sixties* (New York: Oxford University Press, 2001); Barbara Ransby, *Ella Baker and the Black Freedom Movement: A Radical Democratic Vision* (Chapel Hill: University of North Carolina Press, 2003); Cynthia Young, *Soul Power: Culture, Radicalism, and the Making of a U.S. Third World Left* (Durham, NC: Duke University Press, 2006); Scot Brown, *Fighting for US: Maulana Karenga, the US Organization, and Black Cultural Nationalism* (New York: New York University Press, 2004); Brian Ward, *Radio and the Struggle for Civil Rights in the South* (Gainesville: University Press of Florida, 2004); James Smethurst, *The Black Arts Movement: Literary Nationalism in the 1960s and 1970s* (Chapel Hill: University of North Carolina Press, 2005); and Thomas Sugrue, *Sweet Land of Liberty: The Forgotten Struggle for Civil Rights in the North* (New York: Random House, 2008). For an overview of the African-American civil rights movement, see Steven F. Lawson and Charles Payne, *Debating the Civil Rights Movement, 1945–1968* (Rowan & Littlefield, 1998). On culture and second-wave feminism, see Sara Evans, *Personal Politics: The Roots of Women's Liberation in the Civil Rights Movement* (New York: Knopf, 1980); Alice Echols, *Daring to be Bad: Radical Feminism in America, 1967–1975* (Minneapolis: University of Minnesota Press, 1990); and Ruth Rosen, *The World Split Open: How the Modern Women's Movement Changed America* (New York: Viking, 2000). See also David Eisenbach, *Gay Power: An American Revolution* (New York: Carroll & Graf Publishers, 2006); Carlos Munoz, Jr., *Youth, Identity, Power: The Chicano Movement* (London: Verso, 1989); Doug Rossinow, *The Politics of Authenticity: Liberalism, Christianity, and the New Left in America* (New York: Columbia University Press, 1998); Beth Bailey, *Sex in the Heartland* (Cambridge, MA: Harvard University Press, 1999) and Van Gosse, *Where the Boys Are.*

34. Steven Feld, "Communication, Music, and Speech about Music," in Charles Keil and Steven Feld, *Music Grooves: Essays and Dialogues* (Chicago, IL: University of Chicago Press,

1994), 77–91. Lawrence Grossberg's work is also useful here: rather than emphasize the ideological content of rock, Grossberg focuses on the political dimensions of the music's ability to generate emotional and corporeal connectedness, which he terms "affective alliances"; these, he argues, can be "articulated" in multiple ideological ways depending on their contexts, or what Grossberg calls the "apparatus" in which the music is produced and received. See Lawrence Grossberg, *We Gotta Get Out of This Place: Popular Conservatism and Postmodern Culture* (New York: Routledge, 1992); and Lawrence Grossberg, *Dancing In Spite of Myself: Essays on Popular Culture* (Durham, NC: Duke University Press, 1997), especially the section "Dancing . . . (Popular Music)," 27–122.

35. The scholarship on the crisis of liberalism during the 1960s is voluminous. For a good overview, see Allen J. Matusow, *The Unraveling of America: A History of Liberalism in the 1960s* (New York: Harper & Row, 1984). For more recent scholarship on the topic, see Jeremi Suri, *Power and Protest: Global Revolution and the Rise of Détente* (Cambridge, MA: Harvard University Press, 2004); Michael Flamm, *Law and Order: Street Crime, Civil Unrest, and the Crisis of Liberalism in the 1960s* (New York: Columbia University Press, 2005); Rick Perlstein, *Before the Storm: Barry Goldwater and the Unmaking of the American Consensus* (New York: Hill & Wang, 2001); and Rick Perlstein, *Nixonland: The Rise of a President and the Fracturing of America* (New York: Scribner, 2008). Certain commentators, such as Daniel Bell (see Introduction, n. 41), went so far as to attribute the demise of liberalism causally to the rise of rock music, but the evidence I examine suggests it is more accurately described as providing a milieu for responding to larger political crises.

36. I use libertarian rather than liberal to distinguish the radically antiauthoritarian, individualist streak of the counterculture from the dominant post–New Deal liberalism of the Cold War era. Historical debates about the counterculture continue to revolve around assigning it one of these two ideological currents, either anti-statist pursuits of individual liberation or intensely communal visions of cooperative commitment. What responses to rock in San Francisco and Vietnam suggest is that the counterculture was most of all about the tangled intersection of libertarianism and communitarianism: rock served as a resource for articulating demands for individual freedom from constraining social and political institutions such as the military and the state, but it also provided a framework for citizens to ask what they owed each other once they threw off these restrictions. On libertarianism in the counterculture, see Rossinow, *Politics of Authenticity*; Rebecca Klatch, "The Counterculture, the New Left, and the New Right," *Qualitative Sociology* 17, 3 (Fall 1994): 199–214, republished in *Cultural Politics and Social Movements*, ed. Marcy Darnovksy, Barbara Epstein, and Richard Flacks (Philadelphia, PA: Temple University Press, 1995), 74–89; and David Farber, "The Intoxicated State/Illegal Nation: Drugs and the Counterculture," in Braunstein and Doyle, *Imagine Nation*, 17–40. Among the many references to communitarianism in the counterculture, see Laurence Veysey, *The Communal Experience: Anarchist and Mystical Counter-Cultures in America* (New York: Harper & Row, 1973); John Case and Rosemary C. R. Taylor, eds., *Co-ops, Communes, & Collectives: Experiments in Social Change in the 1960s and 1970s* (New York: Pantheon, 1979); Gregory Calvert, *Democracy From the Heart: Spiritual Values, Decentralism, and Democratic Idealism in the Movement of the 1960's* (Novato, CA: Communitas Press, 1991); and Timothy Miller, *The 60s Communes: Hippies and Beyond* (Syracuse: Syracuse University Press, 1999). On liberalism, libertarianism, and communitarianism in rock music, see Theodore Gracyk, *Rhythm and Noise: An Aesthetics of Rock* (Durham, NC: Duke University Press, 1996); Theodore Gracyk, *I Wanna Be Me: Rock Music and the Politics of Identity* (Philadelphia, PA: Temple University Press, 2001); Lawrence Grossberg, *We Gotta Get Out Of This Place*; Lawrence Grossberg, *Dancing In Spite of*

Myself; Robert Pattison, *The Triumph of Vulgarity* (New York: Oxford University Press, 1987); and Carson Holloway, *All Shook Up: Music, Passion, Politics* (Dallas: Spence Publishing Company, 2001). Gracyk argues that rock was ultimately an expression of liberal, multicultural ideas; Grossberg searches for the socialist possibilities in rock, but ultimately sees the music being utilized for reactionary ends; surveying understandings of music from the classics to contemporary thinkers, Holloway interprets rock as a form of republicanism. For an overview of debates about liberalism, libertarianism, and communitarianism, see Michael J. Sandel, ed., *Liberalism and Its Critics* (New York: New York University Press, 1984); Charles Taylor, "Cross Purposes: The Liberal-Communitarian Debate," in *Liberalism and the Moral Life*, ed. Nancy L. Rosenblum (Cambridge, MA: Harvard University Press, 1989), 159–82; Gunsteren, *Theory of Citizenship*, 16–30; and Cornelius F. Delaney, ed., *The Liberalism-Communitarianism Debate: Liberty and Community Values* (Lanham, MD: Rowman & Littlefield, 1994).

37. Irving Bernstein, *Guns or Butter: The Presidency of Lyndon Johnson* (New York: Oxford University Press, 1996). On monetary policy during the 1960s, see Robert Collins, "The Economic Crisis of 1968 and the Waning of the 'American Century,'" *American Historical Review* 101, 2 (April 1996): 396–422; and Robert Collins, *More: The Politics of Economic Growth in Postwar America* (New York: Oxford University Press, 2001).

38. On the shift to post-Fordism, see David Harvey, *The Condition of Postmodernity: An Enquiry into the Origins of Cultural Change* (Cambridge, MA: Blackwell, 1990). See also Daniel Bell, "Post-Industrial Society, the Evolution of an Idea," *Survey* (Spring 1971), 102–68; Daniel Bell, *The Coming of Post-Industrial Society: A Venture in Social Forecasting* (New York: Basic Books, 1973); Jean-Francois Lyotard, *The Postmodern Condition: A Report on Knowledge*, trans. Geoff Bennington and Brian Massumi (Minneapolis: University of Minnesota, 1984); Claus Offe, *Disorganized Capitalism: Contemporary Transformations of Work and Politics*, ed. John Keane (Cambridge, MA: MIT Press, 1985); Scott Lash and John Urry, *The End of Organized Capitalism* (Cambridge: Polity Press, 1987); Mike Featherstone, *Consumer Culture and Postmodernism* (Thousand Oaks, CA: Sage, 1991); Howard Brick, "Imagining Postindustrial Society in the 1960s and 1970s," *American Quarterly* 44, 3 (September 1992): 348–80; Zygmunt Bauman, *Liquid Modernity* (Malden, MA: Polity Press, 2000); Linda Hutcheon, *The Politics of Postmodernism* (New York: Routledge, 1989); Margaret Rose, *The Post-Modern and the Post-Industrial* (New York: Cambridge University Press, 1991); Fredric Jameson, *Postmodernism, Or, the Cultural Logic of Late Capitalism* (Durham, NC: Duke University Press, 1992); Douglas Kellner, *Media Culture: Cultural Studies, Identity, and Politics Between the Modern and the Postmodern* (New York: Routledge, 1995); Steven Best and Douglas Kellner, *The Postmodern Turn* (New York: Guilford Press, 1997); Perry Anderson, *The Origins of Postmodernity* (New York: Verso, 1998); Luc Boltanski and Eve Chiapello, *The New Spirit of Capitalism*, trans. Gregory Elliott (1999; New York: Verso, 2005). On the 1960s and the New Economy, see Fred Turner, "Where the Counterculture Met the New Economy: The WELL and the Origins of Virtual Community," *Technology and Culture* 46, 3 (July 2005): 485–512. For an overview of the cultural shift from modernism to postmodernism during this time, see David Steigerwald, *The Sixties and the End of Modern America* (New York: St. Martin's Press, 1995); and Marianne DeKoven, *Utopia Limited: The Sixties and the Emergence of the Postmodern* (Durham, NC: Duke University Press, 2004). On the music industry, see David Hesmondhalgh, "Post-Fordism, Flexibility and the Music Industries," *Media Culture Society* 18 (1996): 469–88, reprinted in *Popular Music: Critical Concepts*, vol. 2, ed. Simon Frith (New York, Routledge, 2004), 42–61.

39. Lizabeth Cohen, *A Consumers' Republic: The Politics of Mass Consumption in Postwar America* (New York: Knopf, 2003). For a good overview of the scholarship on citizenship and consumerism, see the introduction to Charles McGovern, *Sold American: Consumption and*

Citizenship, 1890–1945 (Chapel Hill: University of North Carolina, 2006), 1–22. See also, Gary S. Cross, *An All-Consuming Century: Why Commercialism Won in Modern America* (New York: Columbia University Press, 2000); Lawrence B. Glickman, *Consumer Society in American History: A Reader* (Ithaca, NY: Cornell University Press, 1999); and Thomas Hine, *Populuxe* (New York: Knopf, 1986). A number of scholars focus on the links between citizenship and consumerism as the repercussions of Romanticism: see especially Colin Campbell, *The Romantic Ethic and the Spirit of Modern Consumerism* (Cambridge, MA: Blackwell, 1987).

40. In making this argument, I diverge from Cohen's declensionist model of the consumers' republic. I draw upon the work of George Lipsitz and Julie Stephens, among others, to do so. Lipsitz uses Gramscian theories of hegemony to identify a struggle between an authentic counterculture and its parallel commercial counterpart. In a similar vein, Julie Stephens uses a Foucauldian analysis of the relationship between knowledge and power to argue that a kind of political resistance persisted despite cooptation. See Lipsitz, "Who'll Stop the Rain?"; and Stephens, *Anti-Disciplinary Protest*, especially her analysis of "coopting cooptation," 94–95. See also Josh Kun's adaptation of Chela Sandoval's concept of "differential consciousness" to popular music in *Audiotopias*, 17; and Chela Sandoval, *Methodology of the Oppressed* (Minneapolis: University of Minnesota Press, 2000).

41. Daniel Bell, *The Cultural Contradictions of Capitalism* (New York: Basic Books, 1978). David Farber uses Bell's thesis as the organizing argument for his survey of the 1960s; see Farber, *Age of Great Dreams*.

42. Bell, *Cultural Contradictions of Capitalism*, xxvi.

43. Bell, *Cultural Contradictions of Capitalism*, 122.

44. While the earlier generation of modernist bohemians wished to merge art and life in the name of self-realization and cultural revolution, counterculturalists tended to want to fuse not art and life, but rather work and play into a new "holistic lifestyle." In doing so, they did not replicate modernist efforts to *épater le bourgeoisie*. Instead, they grappled with postmodern dilemmas of how to discover a nontraditional, nonhierarchical sense of self and society when shock had been so absorbed and accepted as a cultural style that it no longer carried much force. For more on the countercultural effort to fuse work and play into a more free, but ultimately commodified "lifestyle," see Sam Binkley, *Getting Loose: Lifestyle Consumption in the 1970s* (Durham, NC: Duke University Press, 2007); Fred Turner, *From Counterculture to Cyberculture*; and Lonny J. Brooks and Geoffrey Bowker, "Playing at Work: Understanding the Future of Work Practices at the Institute for the Future," *Information, Communication and Society* 5, 1 (March 2002): 109–36. On rock's relationship to work and play, see Cavallo, "Rock and Work: Another Side of Sixties Music," in *A Fiction of the Past*, 145–84. For a collection of essays that captured the effort to merge work and play during the time period itself, see Richard Neville, *Play Power: Exploring the International Underground* (New York: Random House, 1970). A deeper history of play can be found in the classic cultural study by Johan Huizinga, *Homo Ludens: A Study of the Play Element in Human Culture* (1938; reprint, Boston: Beacon Press, 1955). For the history of this earlier bohemian movement, see Henry May, *The End of American Innocence: A Study of the First Years of Our Own Time, 1912–1917* (1959; reprint, New York: Oxford University Press, 1994); Christopher Lasch, *The New Radicalism in America 1889–1963: The Intellectual as a Social Type* (1965; reprint, New York: W. W. Norton, 1997); Daniel Joseph Singal, ed., *Modernist Culture in America* (Belmont, CA: Wadsworth, 1991); Rick Beard and Leslie Cohen Berlowitz, eds., *Greenwich Village: Culture and Counterculture* (New Brunswick, NJ: Rutgers University Press, 1993); Ann Douglas, *Terrible Honesty: Mongrel Manhattan in the 1920s* (New York: Farrar, Straus, & Giroux, 1995); and

Christine Stansell, *American Moderns: Bohemian New York and the Creation of a New Century* (New York: Metropolitan Books, 2000).

45. The phrase "hip capitalism" seems to have originated in the underground press of the 1960s. See, for instance, Craig Karpel, "Das Hip Capital," *Creem* 3, 1 (March 1971). See also Susan Krieger, *Hip Capitalism* (Beverly Hills, CA: Sage Publications, 1979); Thomas Frank, *The Conquest of Cool: Business Culture, Counterculture and the Rise of Hip Consumerism* (Chicago: University of Chicago Press, 1997). Terry H. Anderson refers to it as "hippie capitalism" in "The New American Revolution," in Farber, *The Sixties*, 175–205. For the origins of hipness itself in postwar jazz culture, see Scott Saul, *Freedom Is, Freedom Ain't: Jazz and the Making of the Sixties* (Cambridge, MA: Harvard University Press, 2003), 29–96. See also John Lleland, *Hip: A History* (New York: Ecco/HarperCollins, 2004).

46. See Beth Bailey, *America's Army: Making the All-Volunteer Force* (Cambridge, MA: Harvard University Press, 2009), 1–65.

47. The Diggers, "Let Me Live in a World Pure," Fall 1966, Communication Company, San Francisco, 1967 Folder, Social Protest Collection, Counter Culture, Box 6. Also published in *The Digger Archives*, http://www.diggers.org/digger_sheets.htm [accessed October 1, 2011]. For more on the Diggers, see Emmett Grogan, *Ringolevio: A Life Played for Keeps* (1972; reprint, New York: New York Review Books Classics, 1990); Peter Coyote, *Sleeping Where I Fall* (Washington, D.C.: Counterpoint Press, 1998); William Michael Doyle, "Staging the Revolution: Guerrilla Theater as a Countercultural Practice," in Braunstein and Doyle, *Imagine Nation*, 71–98; Dominick Cavallo, "'It's Free Because It's Yours': The Diggers and the San Francisco Music Scene, 1964–1968," in *A Fiction of the Past: The Sixties in American History*, 97–144; Bradford Martin, "The Diggers: Politicizing the Counterculture," in *The Theater Is in the Street: Politics and Public Performance in Sixties America* (Amherst: University of Massachusetts Press, 2004), 86–124; and Timothy Hodgdon, *Manhood in the Age of Aquarius: Masculinity in Two Countercultural Communities, 1965–1983* (New York: Columbia University Press, 2007). See, also, the magnificent online archive http://www.diggers.org [accessed June 11, 2011].

48. Anderson, "Uncle Tim'$ Children." Chester Anderson, "Notes for the New Geology," *Crawdaddy!* 20 (November–December 1968), 3–7. An earlier version appears in *The San Francisco Oracle* 1 (March 1967), 2, 23, San Francisco Oracle Archives, Department of Special Collections, University of California Library, Davis; also published in Allen Cohen, ed., *The San Francisco Oracle /The Psychedelic Newspaper of the Haight-Ashbury CD-ROM and DVD* (Berkeley, CA: Regent Press, 2005).

49. In this way, rock provided a lens on what philosopher Herbert Marcuse, popular with many counterculturalists, called the "repressive tolerance" of the American consumer society, the ways in which its seeming willingness to accept difference masked a new kind of stifling oppression. While at times the music and its countercultural milieu seemed to be examples of a limiting permissiveness, they also sparked self-reflexive questioning that led to dissent and what Marcuse celebrated as the "great refusal." See Herbert Marcuse, "Repressive Tolerance," in Robert Paul Wolff, Barrington Moore, Jr., and Herbert Marcuse, *A Critique of Pure Tolerance* (Boston: Beacon Press, 1969), 95–137. See also Herbert Marcuse, *One Dimensional Man: Studies in the Ideology of Advanced Industrial Society* (Boston: Beacon Press, 1964); Herbert Marcuse, *An Essay on Liberation* (Boston: Beacon Press, 1969); and Herbert Marcuse, *Counterrevolution and Revolt* (Boston: Beacon Press, 1972).

50. Sandy Darlington, "Creem at Winterland," in *Rock and Roll Will Stand*, ed. Greil Marcus (Boston, MA: Beacon Press, 1969), 80, 77.

51. Greil Marcus, "A Singer and a Rock and Roll Band," in *Rock and Roll Will Stand*, 94.

52. Reg E. Williams, "Fillmore Nights," in *The Straight on the Haight: A True Life Saga from*

the Psychedelic Era of Love, Drugs, and Rock and Roll, excerpted on http://www.thestraight.com [accessed February 3, 2002].

53. There were important differences and tensions between political activists and counterculturalists. Todd Gitlin evocatively explains the conflicts between "freaks" and "politicos" in the Bay Area in Gitlin, *Sixties*, 206–41, 353–61. While overly celebratory at times, the documentary film *Berkeley in the Sixties*, dir. Mark Kitchell (New York: First Run Features, 1990) also provides a vivid overview of the Bay Area milieu in which the counterculture emerged. The more radical position of the International Longshoreman and Warehouse Union (ILWU) and other in the Bay Area unions meant that the traditional industrial labor movement connected much more intensively to young activists, supporting civil rights protests, antiwar rallies, and often funding the parties that would take place after daytime political events; on the labor movement and the New Left, see Peter Levy, *The New Left and Labor in the 1960s* (Champaign-Urbana: University of Illinois Press, 1994), 15, 46–63; on the interactions between labor unions and counterculturalists, see Alice Echols, "Hope and Hype in Sixties Haight-Ashbury," in *Shaky Ground*, 27–28.

54. Ronald Reagan, Speech at the Cow Palace, San Francisco, CA, May 12, 1966, Tape 154, Ronald Reagan Gubernatorial Audiotape Collection, Ronald Reagan Presidential Library, Simi Valley, CA. "Vietnam Day Committee Peace Trip: Rock and Roll Dance Benefit," March 25, 1966, Harmon Gym, University of California–Berkeley, *Berkeley in the Sixties* website, http://berkeleyfolk.blogspot.com/2010/02/berkeley-and-east-bay-rock-concerts.html [accessed June 1, 2011].

55. See Gerald J. DeGroot, "Ronald Reagan and Student Unrest in California, 1966–1970," *Pacific Historical Review* 65, 1 (February 1966): 107–29. For a broader overview of the intersection between the counterculture and the antiwar movement, see David Farber, "The Counterculture and the Antiwar Movement," in *Give Peace a Chance: Exploring the Vietnam Antiwar Movement*, ed. Melvin Small and William D. Hoover (Syracuse, NY: Syracuse University Press, 1992), 7–21. In recent years, historians have begun to focus more intently on the history of conservatism in the 1960s. In my view, the most illuminating work on conservatism and the counterculture remains Rebecca Klatch, "The Counterculture, the New Left, and the New Right." Two important essays on citizenship, the politics of civility, and the rise of modern conservatism in the 1960s are Kenneth Cmeil, "The Politics of Civility," in Farber, *The Sixties*, 263–90 and David Farber, "The Silent Majority and Talk About Revolution," in Farber, *The Sixties*, 291–316. See also Rebecca E. Klatch, *A Generation Divided: The New Left, The New Right, and the 1960s* (Berkeley: University of California Press, 1999); John A. Andrew III, *The Other Side of the Sixties: Young Americans for Freedom and the Rise of Conservative Politics* (New Brunswick, NJ: Rutgers University Press, 1997); Gregory Schneider, *Cadres for Conservatism: Young Americans for Freedom and the Rise of the Contemporary Right* (New York: New York University Press, 1999); Lisa McGirr, *Suburban Warriors: The Origins of the New American Right* (Princeton, NJ: Princeton University Press, 2001); and David Farber and Jeff Roche, eds., *The Conservative Sixties* (New York: Peter Lang, 2003).

56. "Peace Rock 3" poster, a benefit for The Vietnam Peace Day Committee, May 7, 1966, Harmon Gym, University of California–Berkeley, featuring the Grateful Dead, Jaywalkers, Billy Moses Blues Band, *Berkeley in the Sixties* website, http://berkeleyfolk.blogspot.com/2010/02/berkeley-and-east-bay-rock-concerts_24.html [accessed June 1, 2011]; "Angry Arts Week West" poster, April 9–14, 1967, Student Mobilization Committee, San Francisco Folder, Social Protest Collection, Anti-Vietnam War, Box 3, Bancroft Library, University of

California–Berkeley [hereafter materials from the Social Protest Collection will be cited as SPC]; "Dance: The Loading Zone," Provo-VDC Happening, Legal Fund Poster, Steppenwolf Club, San Pablo Avenue, January 8, 1967, Vietnam Day Committee, Berkeley Campus Folder, SPC, Box 3.

57. Most famously, the Free Speech Movement on the University of California–Berkeley campus in 1964 and 1965 became a lightning rod for questions of citizenship among students at the flagship public university of the state of California; see Rorabaugh, *Berkeley At War*, 8–47; Robert Cohen and Reginald E. Zelnik, eds., *The Free Speech Movement: Reflections on Berkeley in the 1960s* (Berkeley: University of California Press, 2002); and David Lance Goines, *The Free Speech Movement: Coming of Age in the 1960s* (Berkeley: Ten Speed Press, 1993).

58. See Robert O. Self, *American Babylon: Race and the Struggle for Postwar Oakland* (Princeton, NJ: Princeton University Press, 2003); and Bruce Nelson, *Workers on the Waterfront: Seamen, Longshoremen, and Unionism in the 1930s* (Urbana: University of Illinois Press, 1988). For more on the bohemian and artistic history of San Francisco, see Richard Cándida Smith, *Utopia and Dissent: Art, Poetry, and Politics in California* (Berkeley: University of California Press, 1995). For a broader sense of the presence of the military in San Francisco and California as a whole during the 1960s, see James L. Clayton, "The Impact of the Cold War on the Economies of California and Utah, 1946–1965," *Pacific Historical Review* 36, 4 (November 1967): 449–73; and Rebecca Lowen, *Creating the Cold War University: The Transformation of Stanford* (Berkeley: University of California Press, 1997).

59. Marcia A. Eymann and Charles Wollenberg, eds., *What's Going On? California and the Vietnam Era* (Berkeley: University of California Press, 2005).

60. Charles Wollenberg, "California and the Vietnam War: Microcosm and Magnification," in *What's Going On?*, 13.

61. For overarching surveys of the Vietnam War, see Guenter Lewy, *America In Vietnam* (New York: Oxford University Press, 1980); Stanley Karnow, *Vietnam: A History* (New York: Viking, 1983); Phillip B. Davidson, *Vietnam at War: The History, 1946–1975* (Novato, CA: Presidio Press, 1988); Marilyn B. Young, *The Vietnam Wars, 1945–1990* (New York: Harper Perennial, 1991); David Elliot, *The Vietnam War: Revolution and Change in the Mekong Delta, 1930–1975* (New York: M.E. Sharpe, 2003); George Herring, *America's Longest War: The United States and Vietnam 1950–1975* (New York: McGraw-Hill, 1995); John Prados, *Vietnam: The History of an Unwinnable War, 1945–1975* (Lawrence: University Press of Kansas, 2009); and Mark Philip Bradley, *Vietnam At War* (New York: Oxford University Press, 2009).

62. Dale Van Atta, *With Honor: Melvin Laird in War, Peace, and Politics* (Madison: University of Wisconsin Press, 2008), 314–15.

63. Charles Perry, "Is This Any Way to Run the Army?," *Rolling Stone*, November 9, 1968, 5.

64. Robert Heinl, "The Collapse of the Armed Forces," *Armed Forces Journal*, June 7, 1971; quoted in Christian G. Appy, *Working-Class War: American Combat Soldiers and Vietnam* (Chapel Hill: University of North Carolina Press, 1993), 247. For more on overt GI resistance, see Larry G. Waterhouse and Mariann G. Wizard, *Turning the Guns Around: Notes on the GI Movement* (New York: Praeger, 1971); Richard Boyle, *GI Revolts: The Breakdown of the U.S. Army in Vietnam* (San Francisco: United Front Press, 1972), 171–200; John Helmer, *Bringing the War Home: The American Soldier in Vietnam and After* (New York: Free Press, 1974); David Cortright, *Soldiers in Revolt: The American Military Today* (New York: Anchor Press, 1975); Melvin Small and William D. Hoover, eds., *Give Peace A Chance: Exploring the Vietnam Antiwar Movement* (Syracuse,

NY: Syracuse University Press, 1992), 91–156; Richard Moser, *The New Winter Soldiers: GI and Veteran Dissent During the Vietnam Era* (New Brunswick, NJ: Rutgers University Press, 1996); James Lewes, *Protest and Survive: Underground GI Newspapers During the Vietnam War* (New York: Praeger, 2003); and the documentary film, *Sir! No Sir!*, DVD, dir.David Zeiger (Los Angeles: Displaced Films, 2005).

65. My argument builds upon the framework in David Lloyd and Lisa Lowe, eds., *The Politics of Culture in the Shadow of Capital* (Durham, NC: Duke University Press, 1997).

66. By the 1960s, almost all Americans had electricity and at least one television. They were plugged in to a grid of electronic media. Mobility in an already-restless country also increased dramatically through the construction of the interstate highway system during the 1950s, and air travel surpassed railways the main mode of long distance transport during the 1960s. Within this context, rock was one among many new kinds of "consumption communities," as historian Daniel Boorstin called them. Statistics from Matusow, *Unraveling of America*, xiii; see also William E. Leuchtenburg, *A Troubled Feast: American Society Since 1945* (Boston, MA: Little, Brown, & Co., 1973), 37–69. Leuchtenburg makes the point that the military budget dwarfed the growing leisure economy in the decades after World War II; he also notes that the trillion-dollar mark was reached partially through inflation. But both Matusow and Leuchtenburg emphasize how substantial real growth in both the overall economy and the leisure economy was crucial to the postwar era. On "consumption communities," see Daniel Boorstin, *The Americans: The Democratic Experience* (New York: Random House, 1973), 89–90.

67. Scott MacKenzie, "San Francisco (Be Sure to Wear Flowers in Your Hair)" (Los Angeles: Ode Records, 1967). The song went to number four on the United States Billboard charts and number one in the United Kingdom and much of Europe.

68. The folk revival played a formative role in shaping rock music, both musically and ideologically. Phillips and MacKenzie tilted toward the more commercially oriented styles of the Kingston Trio, while many (though not all) of the San Francisco musicians were purists. See Simon Frith, "'The Magic That Can Set You Free': The Ideology of Folk and the Myth of the Rock Community," *Popular Music* 1 (1981): 159–68, which remains an illuminating investigation of the influence of the folk revival on rock music. On folk and rock music in San Francisco, see Bruce M. Harrah-Conforth, "The Rise and Fall of a Modern Folk Community: Haight-Ashbury 1965–1967" (Ph.D. diss., Bloomington: Indiana University, 1985) and Warren Bareiss, "Middlebrow Knowingness in 1950s San Francisco: The Kingston Trio, Beat Counterculture, and the Production of 'Authenticity,'" *Popular Music and Society* 33, 1 (February 2010): 9–33. For histories of the folk revival that address the music's intersection with more commercial modes of popular music, see Archie Green's concept of "poplore" in *Only a Miner: Studies in Recorded Coal-Mining Songs* (Urbana: University of Illinois Press, 1972), 3, 14. See also Bruce Jackson, "The Folksong Revival," *New York Folklore* 11 (1985): 195–203, reprinted in Neil V. Rosenberg, ed., *Transforming Tradition: Folk Music Revivals Examined* (Urbana: University of Illinois Press, 1993), 73–83; Archie Green, "Vernacular Music: A Naming Compass," *Musical Quarterly* 77, 1 (Spring 1993): 35–46; Gene Bluestein, *Poplore: Folk and Pop in American Culture* (Amherst: University of Massachusetts Press, 1994); Robert Cantwell, *When We Were Good: The Folk Revival* (Cambridge, MA: Harvard University Press, 1996); Ronald D. Cohen, *Rainbow Quest: The Folk Music Revival and American Society, 1940–1970* (Amherst: University of Massachusetts Press, 2002); Michael F. Scully, *The Never-Ending Revival: Rounder Records and the Folk* (Urbana: University of Illinois Press, 2008); and Ray Allen, *Gone to the Country: The New Lost City Ramblers and the Folk Music Revival* (Urbana: University of Illinois Press, 2010).

69. http://www.scottmckenzie.info/the-sixties.html [accessed October 10, 2011].

70. See *The Complete Monterey Pop*, dir. D.A. Pennebaker (1968; expanded and rereleased, New York: Criterion Collection, 2009); Joel Selvin, *Monterey Pop* (San Francisco: Chronicle Books, 1992); Harvey and Kenneth Kubernik, *A Perfect Haze: The Illustrated History of the Monterey International Pop Festival* (Santa Monica, CA: Santa Monica Press, 2011).

71. There is a rich and provocative literature on the question of genre boundaries in popular music, particularly in terms of issues of race and authenticity. For more on genre boundaries within rock music itself, see Kevin Dettmar and William Richey, eds., *Reading Rock and Roll: Authenticity, Appropriation, Aesthetics* (New York: Columbia University Press, 1999); Roger Beebe, Denise Fulbrook, and Ben Saunders, eds., *Rock Over the Edge: Transformations in Popular Music Culture* (Durham, NC: Duke University Press, 2002); Kevin Dettmar, *Is Rock Dead?* (New York: Routledge, 2005); and Steve Waksman, *This Ain't the Summer of Love: Conflict and Crossover in Heavy Metal and Punk* (Berkeley: University of California Press, 2009). On popular music and genre more broadly, see Fabian Holt, *Genre in Popular Music* (Chicago: University of Chicago Press, 2007); Stuart Borthwick and Ron Moy, *Popular Music Genres: An Introduction* (New York: Routledge, 2004); and Keith Negus, *Music Genres and Corporate Cultures* (New York: Routledge, 1999). For books on the interplay between folk, country, blues, rock, and pop in the United States, see Karl Hagstrom Miller, *Segregating Sound: Inventing Folk and Pop in the Age of Jim Crow* (Durham, NC: Duke University Press, 2010); David Suisman, *Selling Sounds: The Commercial Revolution in American Music* (Cambridge, MA: Harvard University Press, 2009); Diane Pecknold, *The Selling Sound: The Rise of the Country Music Industry* (Durham, NC: Duke University Press, 2007); Richard Peterson, *Creating Country Music: Fabricating Authenticity* (Chicago: University of Chicago Press, 1997); Bernard Gendron, *Between Montmartre and the Mudd Club*; Josh Kun, *Audiotopia*; Ron Radano, ed., *Racial Imagination and Music* (Chicago: University of Chicago Press, 2000); and Guthrie P. Ramsey, Jr., *Race Music: Black Cultures from Bebop to Hip-Hop* (Berkeley: University of California Press, 2003). For overviews of popular music history and theory, see David Brackett, *Interpreting Popular Music* (1995; reprint, Berkeley: University of California Press, 2000); Richard Middleton, *Studying Popular Music* (Philadelphia, PA: Open University Press, 1990); Martin Clayton, Richard Middleton, and Trevor Herbert, eds., *The Cultural Study of Music* (New York: Routledge, 2003); Keith Negus, *Popular Music in Theory: An Introduction* (Hanover, NH: University Press of New England / Wesleyan University Press, 1996); John Shepherd, *Music as Social Text* (Cambridge: Polity Press, 1991); John Shepherd and Peter Wicke, *Music and Cultural Theory* (Malden, MA: Blackwell, 1997); and Keil and Feld, *Music Grooves*.

72. Sheila Whiteley, *The Space Between the Notes: Rock and the Counter-Culture* (New York: Routledge, 1992), 2.

73. Ellen Willis, "Dylan," in *Out of the Vinyl Deeps: Ellen Willis on Rock Music*, ed. Nona Willis Aronowitz (Minneapolis: University of Minnesota Press, 2011), 14; originally published as "The Sound of Bob Dylan," *Commentary* (November 1967), 71–78 and expanded in *Cheetah* (March 1968).

74. On the aesthetics and ideology of sixties rock as a genre, see Frith, "'The Magic That Can Set You Free'"; Simon Frith, *Sound Effects: Youth, Leisure, and the Politics of Rock 'n' Roll* (New York: Pantheon, 1981); Simon Frith and Howard Horne, *Art Into Pop* (New York: Methuen Press, 1987); James Henke with Parke Puterbaugh, Barry Miles, and Charles Perry, eds., *I Want to Take You Higher: The Psychedelic Era, 1965–1969* (San Francisco: Chronicle Books, 1997); and Michael Hicks, *Sixties Rock: Garage, Psychedelic, and Other Satisfactions* (Urbana: University of Illinois, 1999). For overarching histories of rock music that offer differing definitions of the genre and its significance, see Carl Belz, *The Story of Rock* (New York: Oxford University

Press, 1969); Nik Cohn, *Awopbopaloobop Alopbamboom: The Golden Age of Rock* (1970; reprint, New York: Da Capo, 1996); Charlie Gillett, *The Sound of the City: The Rise of Rock and Roll* (1970; reprint, New York: Da Capo Press, 1996); Greil Marcus, *Mystery Train: Images of America in Rock 'n' Roll Music* (1975; reprint, New York: Plume, 1997); David Pichaske, *A Generation in Motion: Popular Music and Culture in the Sixties* (New York: Schirmer Books, 1979); Bernice Martin, "The Sacralization of Disorder: Symbolism in Rock Music," *Sociological Analysis* 40, 2 (1979): 87–124; Bernice Martin, "Rock Music: Narcissus Among the Plebs," in *A Sociology of Contemporary Cultural Change* (Oxford, UK: Blackwell, 1981), 153–84; John Orman, *The Politics of Rock Music* (Chicago, IL: Nelson-Hall, 1984); Herbert I. London, *Closing the Circle: A Cultural History of the Rock Revolution* (Chicago: Nelson-Hall, 1984); Iain Chambers, *Urban Rhythms: Pop Music and Popular Culture* (New York: St. Martin's Press, 1985); Robert Pielke, *You Say You Want a Revolution: Rock Music in American Culture* (Chicago: Nelson-Hall, 1986); Peter Wicke, *Rock Music: Culture, Aesthetics, and Sociology* (New York: Cambridge University Press, 1990); Anthony De-Curtis, ed., *Present Tense: Rock & Roll and Culture* (Durham, NC: Duke University Press, 1992); Philip H. Ennis, *The Seventh Stream: The Emergence of Rock 'n' Roll in American Popular Music* (Hanover, NH: University Press of New England / Wesleyan University Press, 1992); Robert Palmer, *Rock and Roll: An Unruly History* (New York: Harmony Books, 1995); Steve Waksman, *Instruments of Desire: The Electric Guitar and the Shaping of Musical Experience* (Cambridge, MA: Harvard University Press, 1999); Paul Friedlander, *Rock and Roll: A Social History* (Boulder, CO: Westview Press, 2006); and John Covach, *What's That Sound: An Introduction to Rock and Its History* (New York: W. W. Norton, 2006).

75. Statistics from Lipsitz, "Who'll Stop the Rain?," 212; and Ennis, *Seventh Stream*, 286, 345.

76. On the rock music business, see Steve Chapple and Reebee Garofalo, *Rock 'n' Roll Is Here to Pay: The History and Politics of the Music Industry* (Chicago: Nelson-Hall, 1977); and Fred Goodman, *The Mansion on the Hill: Dylan, Young, Geffen, Springsteen, and the Head-On Collision of Rock and Commerce* (New York: Times Books, 1997). For an overview of debates about the role of the recording industry in shaping the reception of popular music, see David Sanjek, "Funkentelechy vs. the Stockholm Syndrome: The Place of Industrial Analysis in Popular Music Studies," *Popular Music and Society* 21, 1 (Spring 1997): 77–98. See also Keith Negus, *Producing Pop: Culture and Conflict in the Popular Music Industry* (New York: Routledge, 1992).

77. Statistic from Lipsitz, "Who'll Stop the Rain?," 212; and Ennis, *Seventh Stream*, 286, 345. On the Baby Boom Generation, see Paul C. Light, *Baby Boomers* (New York: W. W. Norton, 1988) and Grace Palladino, *Teenagers: An American History* (New York: Basic Books, 1996), 191–245.

78. Columbia Records, "The Man Can't Bust Our Music" advertisement, *Rolling Stone*, December 7, 1968, 23. Richard Manglesdorff, "Jimi and Otis; The Yardbirds," *Creem* 2, 16 (September 1970): 38.

79. Robert Christgau, "Anatomy of a Love Festival," *Any Old Way You Choose It: Rock and Other Pop Music, 1967–1973* (1973; exp. ed., New York: Cooper Square Press, 2000), 32. Originally published in *Esquire*, January 1968, in which, according to Christgau, the editors insisted Christgau substitute "just another Uncle Tom" for "psychedelic Uncle Tom"; see author's note, "Anatomy of a Love Festival," *Robert Christgau: Dean of American Rock Critics*, http://www.robertchristgau. com/xg/music/monterey-69.php [accessed October 7, 2011]. On representations of Janis Joplin, see Ellen Willis, "Janis Joplin," in *The Rolling Stone Illustrated History of Rock 'n' Roll* (New York: Rolling Stone Press, 1980), reprinted in Aronowitz, *Out of the Vinyl Deeps*, 125–30; and Alice Echols, *Scars of Sweet Paradise: The Life and Times of Janis Joplin* (New York: Metropolitan Books, 1999).

80. One thinks of Eldridge Cleaver's famous comments about the dance craze of the twist in *Soul On Ice* (1967; reprint, New York: Random House, 1991), 174–79. Some of the best rock criticism was written by young African-American teenagers from Detroit such as Geoffrey Jacques and Richard Allen Pinkston IV, as well as by Samuel Delany, who would go on to a career as a science-fiction novelist. The Asian-American journalist Ben Fong-Torres became a central editor, reporter, and writer at *Rolling Stone*. For more on rock, race, and ethnicity, see Kandia Crazy Horse, ed., *Rip It Up: The Black Experience in Rock 'n' Roll* (New York: Palgrave Macmillan, 2003). In this sense, rock fits into a deeper history of American popular culture, which since blackface minstrelsy has been defined by what Eric Lott famously called "love and theft" by privileged citizens of romanticized others; see Eric Lott, *Love and Theft: Blackface Minstrelsy and the American Working Class* (New York: Oxford University Press, 1995). See also W. T. Lhamon, Jr., *Raising Cain: Blackface Performance from Jim Crow to Hip Hop* (Cambridge, MA: Harvard University Press, 1998); Lynn Abbott and Doug Seroff, *Ragged but Right: Black Traveling Shows, Coon Songs, and the Dark Pathway to Blues and Jazz* (Oxford: University Press of Mississippi, 2007); Leroi Jones (Amiri Baraka)'s comments in *Blues People: Negro Music in White America* (1963; reprint, New York: William & Morrow, 1983), 84–86; and the observations in Robert Cantwell, *Bluegrass Breakdown: The Making of the Old Southern Sound* (Urbana: University of Illinois Press, 1984), 249–74.

81. See Alice Echols, "We Gotta Get Out of This Place: Notes Toward a Remapping of the Sixties," *Socialist Review* 22 (Spring 1992): 11–33, reprinted in *Shaky Ground*, 61–74; Simon Reynolds and Joy Press, *The Sex Revolts: Gender, Rebellion, and Rock 'n' Roll* (Cambridge, MA: Harvard University Press, 1995); Sheila Whiteley, *Women and Popular Music: Sexuality, Identity, and Subjectivity* (New York: Routledge, 2000); Debra Michels, "From 'Consciousness Expansion' to 'Consciousness Raising': Feminism and the Countercultural Politics of the Self," in Braunstein and Doyle, *Imagine Nation*, 41–68; Kathyrn Kerr Fenn, "Daughters of the Revolution, Mothers of the Counterculture: Rock and Roll Groupies In the 1960s" (Ph.D. diss., Duke University, 2002); Lisa Rhodes, *Electric Ladyland: Women and Rock Culture* (Philadelphia, PA: University of Pennsylvania Press, 2005); and Gretchen Lemke-Santangelo, *Daughters of Aquarius: Women of the Sixties Counterculture* (Lawrence: University Press of Kansas, 2009); and Laurie Stas, ed., *She's So Fine: Reflections on Whiteness, Femininity, Adolescence and Class in 1960s Music* (Burlington, VT: Ashgate, 2010).

82. I draw upon Frith, "'The Magic That Can Set You Free,'" to describe the cross-class affiliations of rock music; however, Frith argues that rock resolved contradictions of class, while I contend that rock sustained engagements with these contradictions as they related to questions of cultural and political citizenship. Also see Dominick Cavallo, "Rock and Work: Another Side of Sixties Music," in *Fiction of the Past*, 145–84. For more on rock music and class during the decades after World War II, see Grace Elizabeth Hale, *A Nation of Outsiders: How the White Middle Class Fell in Love with Rebellion in Postwar America* (New York: Oxford University Press, 2011); and Leerom Medovoi, "Transcommodification: Rock 'n' Roll and the Suburban Counterimaginary," in *Rebels: Youth and the Cold War Origins of Identity* (Durham, NC: Duke University Press, 2005), 91–134. For a longer history of the interplay between popular music and avant-garde art, see Gendron, *Between Montmartre and the Mudd Club*.

83. For more on rock music and theories of the public sphere, see Michael J. Kramer, "The Psychedelic Public and Its Problems: Rock Music Festivals and Civil Society in the Sixties Counterculture," in *Media and Public Spheres*, ed. Richard Butsch (New York: Palgrave McMillan, 2007), 270–93. The concept of a "counterpublic" draws upon the work of John Dewey, Walter Lippmann, C. Wright Mills, Jürgen Habermas, and others, but it first emerged

as an explicit term in Rita Felski's studies of feminism. Since then, it has often been invoked in attempts to grasp the political and cultural dynamics of citizenship and civil society between, on the one hand, dominant institutions and ideologies, and on the other hand, aggrieved populations. See Rita Felski, *Beyond Feminist Aesthetics: Feminist Literature and Social Change* (Cambridge, MA: Harvard University Press, 1989); Walter Lippmann, *The Phantom Public* (New York: Harcourt, Brace, 1925); John Dewey, *The Public and Its Problems* (New York: Macmillan, 1927); C. Wright Mills, "The Cultural Apparatus (1959)" in *The Politics of Truth: Selected Writings of C. Wright Mills*, ed. John H. Summers (New York: Oxford University Press, 2008), 203–12; Jürgen Habermas, *Structural Transformation of the Public Sphere*; Jürgen Habermas, "The Public Sphere: An Encyclopedia Article (1964)," trans. Sara Lennox and Frank Lennox, *New German Critique* 3 (Fall 1974): 49–55; and Jürgen Habermas, *Between Facts and Norms: Contributions to a Discourse Theory of Law and Democracy*, trans. William Rehg (Cambridge, MA: MIT Press, 1996). Habermas includes rock concerts in his hierarchy of publics; see *Between Facts and Norms*, 374.

See also Alexander Kluge and Oskar Negt, *Public Sphere and Experience: Toward an Analysis of the Bourgeois and Proletarian Public Sphere*, trans. Peter Labanyi, Owen Daniel, and Assenka Oksiloff (1972; Minneapolis: University of Minnesota Press, 1993); Nancy Fraser, *Unruly Practices: Power, Discourse, and Gender in Contemporary Social Theory* (Minneapolis: University of Minnesota, 1989); The Black Public Sphere Collective, *The Black Public Sphere* (Chicago: University of Chicago Press, 1995); Jim McGuigan, *Culture and the Public Sphere* (New York: Cambridge University Press, 1996); Catherine Squires, "Rethinking the Black Public Sphere: An Alternative Vocabulary for Multiple Public Spheres," *Communication Theory* 12, 4 (November 2002): 446–68; Lauren Berlant, *The Queen of America Goes to Washington City: Essays on Sex and Citizenship* (Durham, NC: Duke University Press, 1997); Lauren Berlant, ed., *Intimacy* (Chicago: University of Chicago Press, 2000); Michael Warner, *Publics and Counterpublics* (Cambridge, MA: MIT Press, 2002); John L. Brooke, "Reason and Passion in the Public Sphere: Habermas and the Cultural Historians," *Journal of Interdisciplinary History* 29, 1 (Summer 1998): 43–67; Harold Mah, "Phantasies of the Public Sphere: Rethinking the Habermas of Historians," *Journal of Modern History* 72, 1 (Summer 2000): 153–82; and Alan McKee, *An Introduction to the Public Sphere* (New York: Cambridge University Press, 2005). See, also, the following essay collections: Richard J. Bernstein, ed., *Habermas and Modernity* (Cambridge, MA: Harvard University Press, 1985); Michael Kelly, ed., *Critique and Power: Recasting the Habermas/Foucault Debate* (Cambridge, MA: MIT Press, 1994); Passerin Maurizio d'Entrèves and Seyla Benhabib, *Habermas and the Unfinished Project of Modernity: Critical Essays on the Philosophical Discourse of Modernity* (Cambridge, MA: MIT Press, 1997); Craig Calhoun, ed. *Habermas and the Public Sphere* (Cambridge, MA: MIT Press, 1992); W. J. T. Mitchell, ed., *Art and the Public Sphere* (Chicago: Chicago University Press, 1992); Bruce Robbins, ed., *The Phantom Public Sphere* (Minneapolis: University of Minnesota Press, 1993); Mike Hill and Warren Montag, eds., *Masses, Classes, and the Public Sphere* (New York: Verso, 2000); Robert Asen and Daniel C. Brouwer, eds., *Counterpublics and the State* (Albany: State University of New York Press, 2001); and Nick Crossley and John Michael Roberts, eds., *After Habermas: New Perspectives on the Public Sphere* (Malden, MA: Blackwell, 2004).

84. Dave Hickey, "Freaks," *Air Guitar: Essays on Art and Democracy* (Los Angeles: Art Issues Press, 1997), 62.

85. In *Counterculture Kaleidoscope: Musical and Cultural Perspectives on Late Sixties San Francisco* (Ann Arbor: University of Michigan Press, 2008), music historian Nadya Zimmerman

treats rock as an example of a kind of watered-down pluralism, in which tolerance rendered oppositional politics impossible. Gerard J. DeGroot treats the entire decade in much the same way in *The Sixties Unplugged: A Kaleidoscopic History of a Disorderly Decade* (Cambridge, MA: Harvard University Press, 2008). But as Nick Bromell argues, rock and the counterculture might best be understood in the tradition of "radical pluralism" dating back to the pragmatist philosophical tradition and politics of William James (himself an experimenter with hallucinogenic drugs). See Nicholas Bromell, *Tomorrow Never Knows: Rock and Psychedelics in the 1960s* (Chicago: University of Chicago Press, 2000), 68–72.

86. My position is influenced by Nicholas Bromell's interpretation of rock and the counterculture in *Tomorrow Never Knows*; see especially, pp. 14–35 and 157–65.

87. Elizabeth Gips, *Scrapbook of a Haight-Ashbury Pilgrim: Spirit, Sacraments and Sex in 1967/68* (Santa Cruz, CA: Changes Press, 1991), ii, 214.

88. For contemporaneous interpretations of religion, ritutal, liminality, and festivity, see Victor Turner, *The Ritual Process: Structure and Anti-Structure* (Chicago: Aldine, 1969) and Harvey Cox, *The Feast of Fools: A Theological Essay on Festivity and Fantasy* (Cambridge, MA: Harvard University Press, 1969). See also Mikhail Bakhtin's ideas about the carnivalesque in *Rabelais and His World*, trans. Hélène Iswolsky (1941; reprint, Bloomington: Indiana University Press, 1993).

89. Gips, *Scrapbook*, 214.

90. Chester Anderson, "Bedrock One," Communication Company, San Francisco 1967 Counter Culture Folder, Box 6, SPC.

91. Many historians argue that rock, the counterculture, and the New Left formulated a "prefigurative politics," in which they sought to model the social relations of a post-revolutionary world. "Live the revolution," after all, was a popular countercultural saying (and one that led to hip capitalist advertising slogans such as Nike's "Just Do It"). Lost in the consensus about prefigurative politics, I contend, is the evidence of a counterculture forged out of engaged figuration and representation of the dilemmas and the possibilities of the 1960s in its moment. On prefigurative politics, see Breines, *Community and Organization in the New Left*, 6–7; Gitlin, *Sixties*, 214; Echols, *Daring to be Bad*, 16–17, 33; and Rossinow, *Politics of Authenticity*, 248, 263. On the larger politics and poetics of utopia, see Ernest Bloch, *The Spirit of Utopia* (1923; reprint, Palo Alto, CA: Stanford University Press, 2000); Frederic Jameson, "Reification and Utopia in Mass Culture," *Social Text* 1, 1 (Winter 1979): 130–48; Richard Dyer, *Only Entertainment* (New York: Routledge, 1992), 19–35; Cándida Smith, *Utopia and Dissent*; David Harvey, *Spaces of Hope* (Berkeley: University of California Press, 2000); Jill Dolan, "Performance, Utopia, and the 'Utopian Performance,'" *Theatre Journal* 55, 3 (October 2001): 455–79; Russell Jacoby, *Picture Imperfect: Utopian Thought for an Anti-Utopian Age* (New York: University of Columbia Press, 2005); and Fredric Jameson, *Archaeologies of the Future: The Desire Called Utopia and Other Science Fictions* (New York: Verso, 2005).

92. Walter Benjamin, "Surrealism: The Last Snapshot of the European Intelligentsia (1929)," in *Reflections: Essays Aphorisms, Autobiographical Writings*, ed. Peter Demetz (New York: Harcourt Brace Jovanovich, 1978), 179. If Walter Benjamin had been able to wander from the arcades of Paris into the Fillmore Auditorium, he might have heard rock not only as a troubling aestheticization of politics, but also as a promising politicization of art; see Walter Benjamin, "The Work of Art in the Age of Mechanical Reproduction," in *Illuminations: Essays and Reflections*, ed. Hannah Arendt (New York: Harcourt Brace Jovanovich, 1968): 217–52.

93. Rock in the 1960s suggests an update to Raymond Williams's formulation of culture as part of the "structures of feeling" that shape power relations. Rock instead constituted a "seizure of feeling" in both senses of the word seizure: the music marked an effort by countercultural participants to seize the means of production as they dematerialized into the symbolic economy of hip capitalism; but this effort took place through seizures of emotional, corporeal, and intellectual intensification that shook, rattled, and rolled power relations without ever fully displacing them. See Raymond Williams, *Marxism and Literature* (New York: Oxford University Press, 1977), 128–35.

94. Stuart Hall, "The Hippies: an American Movement," in *Student Power*, ed. Julian Nagel (London: Merlin Press, 1969), 180.

95. My interpretation of the counterculture as a mediated sphere of civic engagement is inspired by the framework laid out by Arjun Appadurai. See Arjun Appadurai, *Modernity at Large: Cultural Dimensions of Globalization* (Minneapolis: University of Minnesota Press, 1996).

96. Bromell, *Tomorrow Never Knows*, 16.

97. Other important places in the formation of the counterculture were swinging London, the Motor City of Detroit, the heart of the culture industry in Los Angeles, the long-running bohemian enclaves, advertising firms, and publishing companies of New York City, or the Southern soul center of Memphis. For London, see Shawn Levy, *Ready, Steady, Go! The Smashing Rise and Giddy Fall of Swinging London* (New York: Broadway Books, 2002); and Andrew Loog Oldham, *Stoned: A Memoir of London in the 1960s* (New York: St. Martin's Press, 2001). For the history of Detroit rock, see Michael Cary, "The Rise and Fall of the MC5: Rock Music and Counterculture Politics in the Sixties" (Ph.D. diss., Lehigh University, 1985); Van Cagle, *Reconstructing Pop/Subculture: Art, Rock, and Andy Warhol* (Thousand Oaks, CA: Sage Publications, 1995), 96–110; Steve Waksman, "Kick Out the Jams! The MC5 and the Politics of Noise," in *Instruments of Desire*, 207–36; Suzanne Smith, *Dancing in the Street: Motown and the Cultural Politics of Detroit* (Cambridge, MA: Harvard University Press, 2000); Jeff A. Hale, "The White Panthers' 'Total Assault on the Culture,'" in Braunstein and Doyle, *Imagine Nation*, 125–56; David A. Carson, *Grit, Noise, and Revolution: The Birth of Detroit Rock 'n' Roll* (Ann Arbor: University of Michigan Press, 2005); and Matthew J. Bartkowiak, *The MC5 and Social Change: A Study in Rock and Revolution* (Jefferson, NC: McFarland & Company, 2009). For Los Angeles, see David McBride, "On The Fault Line of Mass Culture and Counterculture: A Social History of the Hippie Counterculture in 1960s Los Angeles" (Ph.D. diss., University of California–Los Angeles, 1998) and David McBride, "Death City Radicals: The Counterculture in Los Angeles," in *The New Left Revisited*, ed. John McMillian and Paul Buhle (Philadelphia, PA: Temple University Press, 2003), 110–38. For New York, see Cagle, *Reconstructing Pop/Subculture*, 49–95; and Branden W. Joseph, "'My Mind Split Open': Andy Warhol's Exploding Plastic Inevitable," *Grey Room* (Summer 2002): 80–107. For Memphis and other important parts of the South, see Peter Garulnick, *Sweet Soul Music: Rhythm and Blues and the Southern Dream of Freedom* (1986; reprint: New York: Little, Brown, & Co., 1999); Brian Ward, *Just My Soul Responding: Rhythm and Blues, Black Consciousness, and Race Relations* (Berkeley: University of California Press, 1998); and Craig Werner, *A Change Is Gonna Come: Music, Race and the Soul of America* (New York: Plume, 1998).

98. See Miller, *The 60s Communes*; Turner, *From Counterculture to Cyberculture*; John Markoff, *What the Dormouse Said: How the 60s Counterculture Shaped the Personal Computer*

(New York: Viking, 2005); Andrew G. Kirk, *Counterculture Green: The* Whole Earth Catalog *and American Environmentalism* (Lawrence: University Press of Kansas, 2007); and Rossinow, "Revolution," in Braunstein and Doyle, *Imagine Nation*, 99–124.

99. For more on the concept of the imaginary, see Charles Taylor, *Modern Social Imaginaries* (Durham, NC: Duke University Press, 2004).

100. J. Hoberman, *The Dream Life: Movies, Media, and the Mythology of the Sixties* (New York: New Press, 2003).

101. See Susan Jeffords, *The Remasculinization of America: Gender and the Vietnam War* (Bloomington: Indiana University Press, 1989). For more on women in Vietnam, see Dan Freeman and Jacqueline Rhoads, eds., *Nurses in Vietnam: The Forgotten Veterans* (Austin: Texas Monthly Press, 1987); Kara Dixon Vuic, *Officer, Nurse, Woman: The Army Nurse Corps in the Vietnam War* (Baltimore, MD: Johns Hopkins University Press, 2010); and Heather Stur, *Beyond Combat: Women and Gender in the Vietnam War Era* (New York: Cambridge University Press, 2011).

102. See James William Gibson, *The Perfect War: Technowar in Vietnam* (Boston: Atlantic Monthly Press, 1986); and Christopher Lasch, *The Culture of Narcissism: American Life in an Age of Diminishing Expectations* (New York: W. W. Norton, 1978), 78–81.

103. *Good Morning, Vietnam*, dir. Barry Levinson (Burbank, CA: Touchstone Pictures, 1987).

104. Entertainment Evaluation, Venable Service Club, Sp Svces Entertainment Director, May 1, 1971 and Entertainment Evaluation, FSB Mace, FSB Evelyn, 3rd Base, 1 Cav Div (Am) Special Services, May 7, 71, The Symbols, April 25, 1971 Folder, RG 472, Records of the United States Army in Vietnam (USARV), Special Services Agency (Provisional), Entertainment Branch, After Action Reports Re: USO Tours in Vietnam, April–May 1971, NARA.

105. I concentrate on archival sources for the most part in these chapters rather than rely extensively on oral history interviews with Vietnam veterans. In a reversal of the typical pattern, oral histories have actually dominated historical memories of the Vietnam War. While oral history interviews with Vietnam veterans are an essential part of the historical record, at times they have overshadowed archival materials, which are also worthy of close scrutiny and interpretation. For an overview of the role of oral history in popular memories of the Vietnam War, see Richard Moser, "Talkin' the Vietnam Blues: Vietnam Oral History and Our Popular Memory of War," in *The Legacy: The Vietnam War in the American Imagination*, ed. D. Michael Shafer (Boston: Beacon Press, 1990), 104–21.

106. CBC Band, "People, Let's Stop The War," recorded at The Sherwood Forest Club, Saigon, Republic of Vietnam, May 9, 1973, http://www.youtube.com/watch?v=0ph4q63QRRU [accessed October 10, 2008]. Tom Marlow, "Yea, We're the CBC Band . . .," *Rolling Stone*, November 24, 1970, 29.

107. The phrase was coined by political activist Abbie Hoffman in his book *Woodstock Nation: A Talk-Rock Album* (New York: Vintage, 1969).

108. The transnational community that CBC and their fans established presaged the global cultural affinities described by Arjun Appadurai; see especially Appadurai's explorations of postnational "tribalism" (a concept that fascinated counterculturalists), a "delocalized transnation," and a "federation of diasporas" in *Modernity at Large*, 171–72. See, also, Benedict Anderson, *Imagined Communities: Reflections on the Origin and Spread of Nationalism* (New York: Verso, 1991); Anderson writes of how music has been a powerful cultural tool for nation-building when it has provided an "experience of simultaneity," of "unisonance" in

which "nothing connects us all but imagined sound," 145. For more on the concept of transnationalism, see Sanjeev Khamgram and Peggy Levitt, eds., *The Transnational Studies Reader: Intersections and Innovations* (New York: Routledge, 2007); and Steven Vertovec, *Transnationalism* (New York: Routledge, 2009).

109. The ways in which rock was part American commercial culture and also summoned into being a transnational sense of alternative citizenship has led libertarians to argue that rock contributed to the fall of the Berlin Wall and the end of communism in the East Bloc. This position, however, belies the communitarian longings that rock expressed as a global cultural form informed by the counterculture of the 1960s. For the conservative-libertarian position, see Larry Schweikart, "A Steel Guitar Rocks the Iron Curtain," in *Seven Events That Made America America: And Proved That the Founding Fathers Were Right All Along* (New York: Sentinel, 2010). For more nuanced interpretations of rock and the ghost of the 1960s counterculture during the momentous political events of 1989 and 1990, see Peter Wicke, "Popular Music and Processes of Social Transformation: The Case of Rock Music in Former East Germany," *Music, Culture and Society in Europe* 2 (1996): 77–84; and Joshua Clover, *1989: Bob Dylan Didn't Have This to Sing About* (Berkeley: University of California Press, 2009).

110. Václav Havel, "The Power of the Powerless," originally published in 1979, republished in *The Power of the Powerless: Citizens Against the State in Central-Eastern Europe*, ed. John Keane (London: Hutchinson & Co., 1985), 41, 48, 39, 27, 90. For more on the global existential crisis in relation to the counterculture and the geopolitics of the Cold War, see Jeremi Suri, "The Rise and Fall of an International Counterculture, 1960–1975," *American Historical Review* 114, 1 (February 2009): 45–68.

111. Richard Goldstein, "C. J. Fish on Saturday," in *Reporting the Counterculture* (Boston: Unwin Hyman, 1989), 147.

112. Bill Belmont, "Country Joe and the Fish: A History," http://www.well.com/~cjfish/bandbio.htm [accessed July 1, 2010].

113. Goldstein, "C. J. Fish on Saturday," 146, 147.

114. Janis Joplin, "Me and Bobby McGee," released posthumously on *Pearl* (New York: Columbia Records, 1971).

CHAPTER 1

1. Tom Wolfe, *The Electric Kool-Aid Acid Test* (1969; reprint, New York: Picador, 2008), 411.

2. Wolfe, *Electric Kool-Aid*, 126–30.

3. Ken Kesey and the Pranksters resemble many countercultural figures in their effort to resolve the tensions between attractions and rejections of Cold War American abundance and power. See Fred Turner, "Buckminster Fuller: A Technocrat for the Counterculture," in *New Views on R. Buckminster Fuller*, ed. Hsiao-Yun Chu and Roberto Trujillo (Palo Alto, CA: Stanford University Press, 2009), 146–59.

4. Wolfe, *Electric Kool-Aid*, 12.

5. Mark Christensen, *Acid Christ: Ken Kesey, LSD, and the Politics of Ecstasy* (Tucson, AZ: Schaffner Press, 2010), 16.

6. Wolfe, *Electric Kool-Aid*, 68.

7. Ken Kesey, *One Flew Over the Cuckoo's Nest* (New York: Viking, 1962); Ken Kesey, *Sometimes a Great Notion* (New York: Viking, 1964).

8. Gus Blaisdell, "Shazam and the Neon Renaissance," *Author and Journalist* (June 1963): 7–8.

9. See Tony Tanner, "Edge City," in *City of Words: American Fiction, 1950–1970* (New York: Harper & Row, 1971), 372–91; Scott MacFarlane, *The Hippie Narrative: A Literary Perspective on the Counterculture* (Jefferson, NC: McFarland & Co., 2007), 22–53.

10. Only years later did Kesey and other volunteers learn that the Menlo Park laboratory where they were given LSD was sponsored by the Central Intelligence Agency's covert Project MK-ULTRA program. See Martin Lee and Bruce Shalin, *Acid Dreams: The CIA, LSD, and the Sixties Rebellion* (New York: Grove Press, 1985) and Jay Stevens, *Storming Heaven: LSD and the American Dream* (New York: Grove Press, 1987).

11. Wolfe, *Electric Kool-Aid*, 3, 4, 35–39. Robert Greenfield, *Dark Star: An Oral Biography of Jerry Garcia* (New York: William Morrow & Co., 1996), 70–71. See also the documentary film *Magic Trip*, DVD, dir. Alison Ellwood and Alex Gibney (Austin, TX: Magnolia Home Entertainment, 2011).

12. The events created by Kesey and his compatriots were exemplars of a robust Bay Area artistic milieu during the postwar decades. For more on the emergence of the broader San Francisco arts and psychedelic scene, see Charles Perry, *The Haight-Ashbury: A History* (1984; reprint, New York: Wenner Books, 2005); Joel Selvin, *Summer of Love: The Inside Story of LSD, Rock & Roll, Free Love and High Times in the Wild West* (New York: Dutton, 1994); Barney Hoskyns, *Beneath the Diamond Sky: Haight-Ashbury, 1965–1970* (New York: Simon & Schuster, 1997); John Storey, "Rockin' Hegemony: West Coast Rock and Amerika's War in Vietnam," in *Tell Me Lies About Vietnam*, ed. Alf Louvre and Jeffrey Walsh (Milton Keynes, UK: Open University Press, 1988), 181–97; Alice Echols, "Hope and Hype in Sixties Haight-Ashbury," in *Shaky Ground*, 17–50; Claudia Orenstein, *Festive Revolutions: The Politics of Popular Theater and the San Francisco Mime Troupe* (Oxford: University Press of Mississippi, 1998); Bradford Martin, "The Diggers: Politicizing the Counterculture," in *The Theater Is in the Street*; Michael William Doyle, "Staging the Revolution: Guerrilla Theater as a Countercultural Practice, 1965–1968," in Braunstein and Doyle, *Imagine Nation*, 71–98; Dominick Cavallo, "'It's Free Because It's Yours': The Diggers and the San Francisco Scene, 1964–1968" and "Rock and Work: Another Side of Sixties Music," in *A Fiction of the Past: The Sixties in American History* (New York: St. Martin's Press, 1999), 97–184; David W. Bernstein, ed., *The San Francisco Tape Music Center: 1960s Counterculture and the Avant-Garde* (Berkeley: University of California Press, 2008); Craig Morrison, "Psychedelic Music in San Francisco: Style, Context, Evolution" (Montreal: Ph.D. diss., Concordia University, 2008); and Nadya Zimmerman, *Counterculture Kaleidoscope*.

13. Wolfe, *Electric Kool-Aid*, 194.

14. The Pranksters would go on to present Acid Tests in Portland, Oregon, Los Angeles, and Texas before their efforts gave out in late 1966.

15. Wolfe, *Electric Kool-Aid*, 250.

16. Blair Jackson, *Garcia: An American Life* (New York: Penguin Putnam, 1999), 102.

17. Brent Whelan, "'Furthur': Reflections on the Counter-Culture and the Postmodern," *Cultural Critique* (Winter 1988–89): 63–86.

18. Wolfe, *Electric Kool-Aid*, 251.

19. In this sense the Acid Tests witnessed strangers coming together to form a counter-public. As literary scholar Michael Warner writes, counterpublics might be understood as "spaces of circulation in which it is hoped that the *poesis* of scene-making will be transformative, not replicative merely." See Michael Warner, *Publics and Counterpublics* (Cambridge, MA: MIT Press, 2002), 88. On music and scenes, see Will Straw, "Systems of Articulation, Logics

of Change: Communities and Scenes in Popular Music," *Cultural Studies* 5, 3 (October 1991): 368–88; Barry Shank, *Dissonant Identities: The Rock 'n' Roll Scene in Austin, Texas* (Hanover, NH: University Press of New England / Wesleyan University Press, 1994); Andy Bennett and Richard Peterson, eds., *Music Scenes: Local, Translocal, and Virtual* (Nashville, TN: Vanderbilt University Press, 2004).

20. Wolfe, *Electric Kool-Aid*, 205–7.

21. Wolfe, *Electric Kool-Aid*, 231–32.

22. The very first Acid Test was held at Ken Babbs's farm in Santa Cruz, known as "The Spread."

23. Wolfe, *Electric Kool-Aid*, 236.

24. Some accounts place the Muir Beach Acid Test the following weekend, on December 18, 1965, after an Acid Test that took place at the Big Beat Club in Palo Alto on the 11th, but the most recent research suggests that the Muir Beach Acid Test came first. The website Poster Trip contains a carefully researched account of the Acid Tests; see "The Acid Test Chronicles," http://www.postertrip.com/public/department37.cfm [accessed May 10, 2010].

25. Muir Beach Acid Test Handbill, Chicken on a Unicycle, http://www.chickenonaunicycle. com/Acid Test 19651211-5.jpg [accessed May 11, 2010].

26. Burton H. Wolfe, *The Hippies* (New York: Signet, 1968), 31.

27. "Can You Pass the Acid Test???," Big Beat Club handbill, http://www.postertrip.com/ public/5575.cfm [accessed May 10, 2010].

28. Wolfe, *Electric Kool-Aid*, 241.

29. A later event inspired by the Pranksters, "Trips 196?" continued this emphasis on historical possibility through festive interaction. See Trips 196? Poster, Chicken on a Unicycle, http://www.chickenonaunicycle.com/Longshore 19660422.jpeg [accessed May 10, 2010]. The pursuit of festive liminality corresponds to the theories being developed by anthropologist Victor Turner during the very same time period of the 1960s. One crucial difference is that while Kesey and the Pranksters hoped that liminal experiences might lead to larger social transformations, Turner believed that they resolved back into the existing hierarchical structures. See Victor Turner, "Liminality and Communitas," in *The Ritual Process: Structure and Anti-Structure* (1969; reprint, Piscataway, NJ: Transaction, 2008), 94–130.

30. Uncle Sam "Can You Pass the Acid Test?" Flier, Chicken on a Unicycle, http://www. chickenonaunicycle.com/Acid%20Test%20%2019651204.jpg [accessed May 11, 2010]. On "hailing" and interpellation by state power, see Louis Althusser, "Ideology and Ideological State Apparatuses," in *Lenin and Philosophy and other Essays*, trans. Ben Brewster (1970; published in English, New York: Monthly Review Press, 1971), 121–76.

31. Jackson, *Garcia*, 92.

32. The inspiration here, via modernism and the Beats, is poet Arthur Rimbaud, who called upon artists to pursue a "derangement of all the senses" in order to perceive truth, though Kesey and the Pranksters took a more communal and less individualistic approach to the project.

33. Ben Van Meter quoted in Bonus Features: Panel Discussion, *The Trips Festival Movie* DVD, dir. Eric Christensen (San Francisco: The Trips Festival LLC, 2007). Robert Faggen, "The Art of Fiction," interview with Ken Kesey, *Paris Review* 130 (Spring 1994).

34. For more on radical pluralism and anti-foundationalism in relation to rock and the counterculture, see Bromell, *Tomorrow Never Knows*, 8, 68; see also Barry Shank, "'That Wild Mercury Sound': Bob Dylan and the Illusion of American Culture," *Boundary* 2, 29 (Spring 2002): 97–123.

35. Richard Alpert (Ram Dass), quoted in Paul Perry, *On the Bus: The Complete Guide to the Legendary Trip of Ken Kesey and the Merry Pranksters and the Birth of the Counterculture* (New York: Thunder's Mouth Press, 1990), 149; Also see Blair, *Garcia*, 91. Bromell, *Tomorrow Never Knows*, 68–70; William James, *The Principles of Psychology* (1890; Cambridge, MA: Harvard University Press, 1983), 462.

36. Mountain Girl, quoted in Blair, *Garcia: An American Life* website, chapter 5: Can YOU Pass the Acid Test?, http://www.blairjackson.com/chapter_five_additions.htm [accessed May 10, 2010]; Wolfe, *Electric Kool-Aid*, 245–48; Mountain Girl on Owlsey at Muir Beach Acid Test, quoted in Jerilyn Lee Branelius, *Grateful Dead Family Album* (New York: Warner Books, 1992), 30.

37. Ken Kesey, "The Lives They Lived: Jerry Garcia, The False Notes He Never Played," *New York Times Magazine*, December 31, 1995, http://www.nytimes.com/1995/12/31/magazine/the-lives-they-lived-jerry-garcia-the-false-notes-he-never-played.html [accessed April 30, 2005].

38. Paul Perry, *On the Bus*, 115.

39. Charles Perry, *Haight-Ashbury*, 41–42.

40. For the history of the Fillmore Auditorium, see the public television documentary *The Fillmore*, dir. Peter L. Stein (San Francisco: KQED, 2001), and program website, http://www.pbs.org/kqed/fillmore/index.html [accessed May 10, 2010].

41. Norman Mailer, "The White Negro: Superficial Reflections on the Hipster," *Dissent* (Summer 1957), reprinted in *Advertisements for Myself* (New York: G.P. Putnam & Sons, 1959), 331–58. Marshall McLuhan, *War and Peace in the Global Village: An Inventory of Some of the Current Spastic Situations that Could Be Eliminated by More Feedforward* (New York, McGraw-Hill, 1968).

42. Jerry Garcia quoted from a radio interview in Sandy Troy, *Captain Trips: A Biography of Jerry Garcia* (New York: Thunder's Mouth Press, 1994), 78–80.

43. Michael Rossman quoted in Ralph Gleason, *The Jefferson Airplane and the San Francisco Sound* (New York: Ballantine, 1969), 15–16.

44. Rossman quoted in Gleason, *Jefferson Airplane and the San Francisco Sound*, 16.

45. Tony Martin, "Composing with Light," in *San Francisco Tape Music Center*, 143.

46. Garcia quoted from *The Acid Test* CD; Garcia, quoted in Jerry Garcia, Charles Reich, and Jann Wenner, *A Signpost to New Space: Jerry Garcia, Charles Reich, and Jann Wenner, The* Rolling Stone *Interview, Plus a Stoned Sunday Rap* (1972; reprint, New York: Da Capo Press, 2003), 101.

47. Babbs, quoted from *The Acid Test* CD.

48. Michel Foucault, "Of Other Spaces (1967)," *Diacritics* 16 (Spring 1986): 22–27.

49. Turner, "Buckminster Fuller."

50. Phil Lesh, *Searching for the Sound: My Life with the Grateful Dead* (New York: Little, Brown, & Co., 2005), 69.

51. Lesh, *Searching for the Sound*, 69.

52. See Allan Kaprow, *Essays on the Blurring of Art and Life*, ed. Jeff Kelley (Berkeley: University of California Press, 1993).

53. This effort echoes Marshall McLuhan's theories of the media, which were growing in popularity by the mid-1960s and were certainly absorbed by the Pranksters, Lesh, and others. Michael Callahan, the first technical director of the San Francisco Tape Center and a member of USCO, another multimedia group, recalls talking with fellow-USCO-member Gerd Stern about reading McLuhan's early work. See Bernstein, ed., *The San Francisco Tape Center*, 187. See also Marshall McLuhan, *Understanding Media: The Extensions of Man* (New York: McGraw-Hill, 1964).

54. Though it is very doubtful that Lesh or any of the Merry Pranksters read Antonio Gramsci, Lesh's evocative phrase brings to mind Gramsci's theory of "spontaneous consent." Writing in the late 1920s and early 1930s, the Italian Marxist believed that elites maintained power over the masses not only through brute economic or military force, but also in the more elastic and ambiguous realm of modern civil society. They did so, in particular, by continually securing control over what seemed like "common sense" to the masses. The Acid Tests certainly challenged dominant notions of "common sense" in 1960s America. As such, one might even conceptualize the events as efforts to rethink and even remake "spontaneous consent"—what Lesh calls "spontaneous consensus"—in a space of associational life, of civil society. By manipulating the technologies of subject-formation (art, electronics, drugs, dancing, costumes) to challenge assumptions about common sense, the Acid Tests marked an attempt to democratize the social order itself. See Antonio Gramsci, *Selections from the Prison Notebooks of Antonio Gramsci*, ed. Quintin Hoare and Geoffrey Nowell-Smith (New York: International Publishers, 1971), 12–13.

55. Lesh, *Searching for the Sound*, 69.

56. "Trips Festival" Handbill, Box 1, September 1, 1966 Folder, Hippies Collection, San Francisco History Museum, San Francisco Public Library.

57. For more on Stewart Brand and computing, see Fred Turner, *From Counterculture to Cyberculture*; for Brand's connections to the *Whole Earth Catalog* and environmentalism, see Kirk, *Counterculture Green*.

58. Foucault, "Of Other Spaces," 27.

59. Lesh, *Searching for the Sound*, 69.

60. Carolyn "Mountain Girl" Adams Garcia, "Foreword," in Rosie McGee, *Dancing with the Dead—A Photographic Memoir: My Good Old Days with the Grateful Dead and the San Francisco Scene, 1964–1974* (Rohnert Park: Tioli Press & Bytes, 2012), 10.

61. Quoted in Wolfe, *Electric Kool-Aid*, 275.

62. McGee, *Dancing with the Dead*, 52.

63. McGee, *Dancing with the Dead*, 88.

64. See Rhodes, *Electric Ladyland*.

65. Bromell, *Tomorrow Never Knows*, 68–70. In taking Lesh's memories of the Acid Tests seriously, I disagree with Nadya Zimmerman's argument in *Counterculture Kaleidoscope* that the San Francisco rock scene's pluralism should be understood entirely in negative terms, as merely a kind of laissez-faire respect for difference that lacked any oppositional politics at all. The Acid Tests suggest that San Francisco's rock involved more than just anything-goes relativism. As Nick Bromell argues, there was an ethical dimension, and a critical perspective, that was unleashed in the pursuit of freedom at both individual and collective levels. See Zimmerman, *Counterculture Kaleidoscope*, 5.

66. Babbs, quoted from *The Acid Test* CD.

67. Jay Stevens, *Storming Heaven: LSD and the American Dream* (New York: Grove Press, 1987), 326.

68. Nick Bromell also notes the comic dimensions—in the classic Greek sense—of the 1960s counterculture. See Bromell, *Tomorrow Never Knows*, 164.

69. Bob Weir and others, quoted from *The Acid Test* CD.

70. For more on the role of musical anthems as shapers of nationalism, see Anderson, *Imagined Communities*, 145.

71. Wolfe, *Electric Kool-Aid*, 187–88.

72. *Woodstock: Music from the Original Soundtrack and More*, LP (New York: Cotillion/Atlantic Records, 1970). *Woodstock*, dir. Michael Wadleigh (Burbank, CA: Warner Brothers, 1970).

73. Wolfe, *Electric Kool-Aid*, 224–25.

74. Jackson, *Garcia*, 94.

75. Graham and Greenfield, *Bill Graham Presents*, 170.

76. Ken Kesey, recorded on *Acid Test Vol. 2: San Francisco State 10/1/66* CD (Pleasant Hill, OR: Key-Z Productions, 2002).

77. John Sinclair, *Guitar Army: Street Writings/Prison Writings* (New York: Douglas Books, 1972). Osha Neumann, *Up Against the Wall Motherf**ker: A Memoir of the Sixties with Notes for Next Time* (New York: Seven Stories Press, 2008); see also Patrick Burke, "Tear Down the Walls: Jefferson Airplane, Race, and Revolutionary Rhetoric in 1960s Rock," *Popular Music* 29, 1 (February 2010): 61–79.

78. Kesey, *Acid Test Vol. 2*.

79. See Turner, "Liminality and Communitas."

80. Carol Brightman, *Sweet Chaos: The Grateful Dead's American Adventure* (New York: Crown, 1998), 167.

81. Wolfe, *Electric Kool-Aid*, 63, 12.

82. Wolfe, *Electric Kool-Aid*, 224–25.

83. Wolfe, *Electric Kool-Aid*, 367.

84. Wolfe, *Electric Kool-Aid*, 387, 388.

85. Wolfe, *Electric Kool-Aid*, 388.

86. Michel Foucault, *Discipline and Punish: The Birth of the Prison* (New York: Random House, 1975), 195–228.

87. Michel Foucault, *History of Madness* (1961; reprint, New York: Routledge, 2006).

88. While it is certainly likely that Foucault and Kesey vaguely knew of each other through the popular press during the 1960s, I have not unearthed any evidence that they were in correspondence or read each other's work. But their strikingly similar concerns about institutional power and individual freedom are telling of the larger global engagement with citizenship during the late 1960s and into the 1970s.

89. Wolfe, *Electric Kool-Aid*, 402.

90. Carolyn "Mountain Girl" Adams Garcia, quoted in "Bonus Features: Panel Discussion," *The Trips Festival Movie*, DVD, dir. Eric Christensen (San Francisco: The Trips Festival LLC, 2007).

91. Allen Cohen and Michael Bowen, "Prophesy of a Declaration of Independence (1966)," quoted in Perry, *Haight-Ashbury*, 92–93. Sometimes the document is credited to the Psychedelic Rangers, a group of countercultural activists that included Bowen, mystic John Starr Cooke, and future Grateful Dead road manager Johnathan Riester; see, for instance, Brightman, *Sweet Chaos*, 155.

92. See Perry, *Haight-Ashbury*, 98, 116–23.

93. For more on the Diggers, see the works cited in Introduction, n. 40.

94. Wolfe, *Electric Kool-Aid*, 404.

95. *Be In*, short film, dir. Jerry Abrams (1967), http://vimeo.com/974954 [accessed October 20, 2010].

96. Foucault, "Of Other Spaces," 27.

CHAPTER 2

1. Wolfe, *Electric Kool-Aid Acid Test* (1969; reprint, New York: Picador, 2008), 231–32.

2. Handbill, Larry Miller, personal collection.

3. Michael Rossman, "KMPX on Strike," *San Francisco Express Times*, March 21, 1968, 3.

4. Larry Miller, email correspondence with author, June 26, 2010.

5. Jeff Jassen, "In Character: KMPX Walkout Beautiful," *Berkeley Barb*, March 22, 1968, 3.

6. See the works cited in Introduction, n. 38.

7. Michael Denning, *The Cultural Front: The Laboring of American Culture in the Twentieth Century* (New York: Verso, 1997).

8. Krieger, *Hip Capitalism*.

9. Most historians associate the counterculture and rock music with leisure and consumption. An important exception is Dominick Cavallo's "Rock and Work: Another Side of Sixties Music," in *A Fiction of the Past: The Sixties in American History* (New York: St. Martin's Press, 1999), 145–84. Among other historians, Peter Levy includes a chapter on the counterculture in *The New Left and Labor in the 1960s* (Urbana: University of Illinois Press, 1994), but mentions neither the KMPX strike, nor hippie workers in general. Michael Roberts begins to explore the connections between the labor movement and rock music in the 1960s, but positions the counterculture firmly in the sphere of leisure rather than labor. See Roberts, "A Working-Class Hero Is Something To Be: The American Musicians' Union's Attempt to Ban the Beatles, 1964," *Popular Music* 29, 1 (February 2010): 1–16; and Roberts, "You Say You Want a (Counter) Revolution? Attempts by the Musicians' Union to Jam Up Rock and Roll," *Labor: Studies in Working-Class History of the Americas* 4, 4 (Fall 2007): 33–54. Similarly, George Lipsitz and Alice Echols notice the attention to work among countercultural participants in the emerging rock music business but still keep the focus largely on the counterculture as a mode of consumption and leisure. See Lipsitz, "Who'll Stop the Rain?," 206–34; and Echols, "Hope and Hype in Sixties Haight-Ashbury," in *Shaky Ground*, 17–50. Recent histories that focus on countercultural efforts to rethink the place of small-scale production and looser habits of independent and self-driven work complicate the boundary between production and consumption, but these studies assert that the focus on labor within the counterculture marked a fundamental turn away from the antagonistic and oppositional traditions of radical labor activism. See Turner, *From Counterculture to Cyberculture*; and Sam Binkley, *Getting Loose*. Recently, art historians have begun to consider visual artists of the 1960s as workers. See Julia Bryan-Wilson, *Art Workers: Radical Practice in the Vietnam War Era* (Berkeley: University of California Press, 2009) and Helen Molesworth, ed., *Work Ethic* (University Park: Pennsylvania State University Press, 2003).

10. For more on Lordstown, see David F. Moberg, "Rattling the Golden Chains: Conflict and Consciousness of Workers" (Ph.D. diss., University of Chicago, 1978); and Richard Moser, "Autoworkers at Lordstown: Workplace Democracy and American Citizenship," in *The World the 60s Made: Politics and Culture in Recent America*, ed. Van Gosse and Richard Moser (Philadelphia, PA: Temple University Press, 2002), 289–315.

11. By and large, labor historians themselves have not studied hippie workers so much as the effects of countercultural values on traditional workers in the manufacturing industries: see Stanley Aronowitz, *False Promises: The Shaping of American Working-Class Consciousness* (New York: McGraw-Hill, 1973), 29–31; Jefferson Cowie, "'Vigorously Right, Left, and Center': The Crosscurrents of Working-Class America in the 1970s," in *America in the Seventies*, ed. Beth Bailey and David Farber (Lawrence: University Press of Kansas, 2004), 75–106; and Jefferson Cowie, *Stayin' Alive: The 1970s and the Last Days of the Working Class* (New York: New Press, 2010), 42–49.

12. See Carl Davidson, "The Multiversity: Crucible of the New Working Class (1967)," in *The University Crisis Reader*, vol. 1, ed. Immanuel Wallerstein and Paul Starr (New York: Vintage,

1971); Robert Gottlieb, Gerald Tenney, and David Gilbert, "The Port Authority Statement," *New Left Notes*, February 13, 1967; John and Margaret Rowntree, "Youth as a Class," *Our Generation* 1–2 (May–June–July, 1968); and Greg Calvert, "In White America: Radical Consciousness and Social Change," in *The New Left: A Documentary History*, ed. Massimo Teodori (Indianapolis: Bobbs-Merrill, 1969), 412–18. See also Norman Birnbaum, *The Crisis of Industrial Society* (New York: Oxford University Press, 1969); Alain Touraine, *Post-Industrial Society: Tomorrow's Social History—Classes, Conflicts, and Cultures in the Programmed Society* (New York: Random House, 1971); Christopher Lasch, "After the New Left," in *The World of Nations: Reflections on American History, Politics, and Culture* (New York: Alfred A. Knopf, 1973), 137; Serge Mallet, *Essays on the New Working Class*, ed. and trans. Dick Howard (St. Louis: Telos Press, 1975); Andre Gorz, *Strategy for Labor* (Boston: Beacon Press, 1967); Barbara and John Ehrenreich, "The Professional-Managerial Class (1977)," in *Between Labor and Capital*, ed. Pat Walker (Boston: South End Press, 1979), 5–48; Barbara Ehrenreich, "The Professional-Managerial Class Revisited," in *Intellectuals, Aesthetics, Politics, Academics*, ed. Bruce Robbins (Minneapolis: University of Minnesota Press, 1990), 173–88; and Carl Davidson, ed., *Revolutionary Youth and the New Working Class: The Praxis Papers, the Port Authority Statement, the RYM Documents, and Other Lost Writings of SDS* (Pittsburgh, PA: Changemaker Publications, 2011).

13. For more on the development of "Theory Y" management style, which emphasized creativity and flexibility in place of Taylorist efficiency and corporate hierarchy, see Frank, *Conquest of Cool*, 22–23. The most famous articulation of Theory Y was Douglas McGregor's *The Human Side of Enterprise* (New York: McGraw-Hill, 1960).

14. On this consolidation, see Chapple and Garofalo, *Rock 'n' Roll Is Here to Pay*; Goodman, *Mansion on the Hill*; and Sanjek, "Funkentelechy vs. the Stockholm Syndrome," 77–98.

15. Perhaps it is no surprise that "New Labor History" arose precisely during the era of the counterculture. It replaced stale Marxist categories of analysis with a broader investigation of working-class culture and was particularly sensitive to the porous line between independent artisans and small-scale craftsman and the new industrial wage class that accompanied the rise of industrialism. For a good survey of this historiographical turn, which I would argue was not unconnected to the participation of many of its practitioners in the contemporaneous ferment over work, class, and culture in the late 1960s and early 1970s counterculture and New Left, see Christopher Lasch, *The True and Only Heaven: Progress and Its Critics* (New York: W.W. Norton, 1991), 209–11.

16. Dick Meister, "1968: San Francisco's Year of the Strike," http://www.laborfest.net/2008/Meister68.htm [accessed January 15, 2011].

17. For more on the San Francisco State College student strikes, see San Francisco State University Leonard Library, "The San Francisco State Student Strike Collection," http://www.library.sfsu.edu/about/collections/strike [accessed July 31, 2010]. For more on People's Park, see W. J. Rorabaugh, *Berkeley At War*, 154–66 and Gitlin, *Sixties*, 353–61.

18. See Miller, *The 60s Communes*.

19. For more on the labor conflict at the Berkeley Barb, see *Barb on Strike*, 1, 1, July 11–17, 1969; Abe Peck, *Uncovering the Sixties: The Life and Times of the Underground Press* (New York: Pantheon, 1985), 188–89; and Arthur Seeger, *The Berkeley Barb: Social Control of an Underground Newsroom* (New York: Irvington Publishers, 1983).

20. Wolfe, *Electric Kool-Aid Acid Test*, 37.

21. Susan Douglas, "The FM Revolution," in *Listening In: Radio and the American Imagination* (Minneapolis: University of Minnesota Press, 2004), 256–83.

22. For more on the history of FM radio, see Michael C. Keith, *Voices in the Purple Haze: Underground Radio and the Sixties* (Westport, CT: Praeger, 1997); Michael C. Keith, ed., *Radio Cultures: The Sound Medium in American Life* (New York: Peter Lang, 2010); Jim Ladd, *Radio Waves: Life and Revolution on the FM Dial* (New York: St. Martin's Press, 1991); Richard Neer, *FM: The Rise and Fall of Rock Radio* (New York: Villard, 2001); Jesse Walker, *Rebels on the Air: An Alternative History of Radio in America* (New York: New York University Press, 2001); and Mark Fisher, *Something in the Air: Radio, Rock, and the Revolution That Shaped a Generation* (New York: Random House, 2007).

23. For an overview of KMPX's history, see Susan Krieger's *Hip Capitalism*. For a more detailed account, see Krieger's dissertation: Krieger, "Cooptation: A History of a Radio Station," parts 1 and 2 (Ph.D. diss., Stanford University, 1976).

24. Larry Miller, "Underground Radio: A Voice from the Purple Haze," in *Radio Cultures: The Sound Medium in American Life*, ed. Michael C. Keith (New York: Peter Lang, 2008), 115.

25. Larry Miller, email correspondence with author, June 28, 2010.

26. Rossman, "KMPX on Strike," 3.

27. Larry Miller Show, KMPX, October 11, 1967, http://www.jive95.com/kmpx.htm [accessed February 3, 2003].

28. Bromell, *Tomorrow Never Knows*, 1.

29. "Atmosphere of democracy" is Bruno Latour's phrase; see Latour, *Making Things Public*.

30. Rossman, "KMPX on Strike," 3.

31. Douglas, *Listening In*, 258–83.

32. Tom Donahue, "AM Radio Is Dead and Its Rotting Corpse, Stinking Up the Airways . . .," *Rolling Stone*, November 23, 1967. Krieger, *Hip Capitalism*, 31–70.

33. Tom Donahue, "AM Radio Is Dead"; Rossman, "KMPX on Strike," 3.

34. Darlington, "Creem at Winterland," in Marcus, *Rock and Roll Will Stand*, 76.

35. Rossman, "KMPX on Strike," 3. For more on the problem of universalist conceptualizations of citizenship and public life, see Rosalyn Deutsche, *Evictions: Art and Spatial Politics* (Cambridge, MA: MIT Press, 1998), xiii–xxiv. See, also, Lefort, *Democracy and Political Theory* and Robbins, ed., *Phantom Public Sphere*.

36. Krieger, *Hip Capitalism*, 64. Station gross income cited in Jassen, "KMPX Walkout Beautiful" and Jerrold Greenberg and Ben Fong-Torres, "KMPX-KPPC Shut Down: FM Workers Strike for Rights," 8.

37. Claude Hall, "KMPX-FM's Donahue Programs Music with a Wide Open View," *Billboard*, December 30, 1967, 18.

38. Eliot Tiegel, "KPPC-FM Makes Groovy Plans," *Billboard*, March 2, 1968, 22.

39. KMPX advertisement, http://www.jive95.com/kmpx.htm [accessed March 13, 2003].

40. See Echols, "We Gotta Get Out of This Place," in *Shaky Ground*, 61–74; Debra Michels, "From 'Consciousness Expansion' to 'Consciousness Raising': Feminism and the Countercultural Politics of the Self," in Braunstein and Doyle, *Imagine Nation*, 41–68; Fenn, "Daughters of the Revolution"; Rhodes, *Electric Ladyland*; Lemke-Santangelo, *Daughters of Aquarius*; and Stas, ed., *She's So Fine*.

41. Rhodes, *Electric Ladyland*, 164–65.

42. Dusty Street, "KMPX The Last Moments," audio file, http://www.jive95.com/kmpx.htm; also transcribed in Krieger, "Cooptation," 1:114. For more on Katie Johnson, see Krieger, "Cooptation," 1:52–53, 63–64, 79–85, 105–6, 110.

43. Sue Kagan, telephone interview with author, June 11, 2010.

44. Krieger, "Cooptation," 2:61–66. The rock radio stations that followed in KMPX's wake in the Bay Area also often became central places for feminist interventions by listeners; see Michael C. Keith, *Sounds In the Dark: All-Night Radio in American Life* (Ames: Iowa State University Press, 2001), 114.

45. Rossman, "KMPX on Strike," 3. Miller, "Underground Radio," in Keith, *Radio Cultures*, 117.

46. For the history of KPFA, see Matthew Lasar, *Pacifica Radio: The Rise of an Alternative Network* (Philadelphia, PA: Temple University Press, 1999).

47. Rossman, "KMPX on Strike," 3.

48. Krieger, "Cooptation," 1:17, 81–85.

49. Rossman, "KMPX on Strike," 3.

50. Rossman, "KMPX on Strike," 3.

51. Rossman, "KMPX on Strike," 3; Krieger, "Cooptation," 1:102–6.

52. Krieger, "Cooptation," 1:106.

53. See Bruce Nelson, *Workers on the Waterfront: Seamen, Longshoremen, and Unionism in the 1930s* (Urbana: University of Illinois Press, 1988).

54. Alice Echols, "Hope and Hype in Sixties Haight-Ashbury," in *Shaky Ground*, 27–28.

55. See Joshua B. Freeman, "Hardhats: Construction Workers, Manliness, and the 1970 Pro-War Demonstrations," *Journal of Social History* 26, 4 (Summer 1993), 725–44.

56. Perry, *The Haight-Ashbury*, 44.

57. Most musicians joined the musician's union out of necessity, since they might be banned from more conventional venues if they did not. Blair Jackson, *Garcia: An American Life* (New York: Penguin, 1999), 13; Dennis McNally, *A Long Strange Trip: The Inside History of the Grateful Dead* (New York: Broadway Books, 2002), 151, 234.

58. Sherri Cavan, *Hippies of the Haight* (St. Lous, MO: New Critics Press, 1972), 44.

59. Dusty Street, Email correspondence with author, January 18, 2009. Also mentioned in Krieger, "Cooptation," 2:122.

60. See Krieger, "Cooptation," 1:31.

61. Krieger, "Cooptation," 1:106, 117.

62. In Austin, Texas, a countercultural cooperative of publishers, the Armadillo Press, was also affiliated with the IWW, and then became an all-woman, feminist press, Red River Women's Press. See Rossinow, "Revolution," in Braunstein and Doyle, *Imagine Nation*, 99.

63. Card provided by Sue Kagan (*née* Henderson) from her personal archive.

64. Ed Bear and Bob McClay, "KMPX: The Last Moments," audio file, http://www.jive95.com/kmpx.htm [accessed February 2, 2008]; also transcribed in Susan Krieger, "Cooptation," 1:110, 113.

65. Jeff Jassen, "In Character," 3.

66. Unknown voice, "KMPX: The Last Moments."

67. Jassen, "In Character," 3.

68. Krieger, "Cooptation," 1:121–22, 135, 142–43; Jassen, "KMPX Walkout Beautiful"; Sandy Darlington, "KMPX on Mars," *San Francisco Express Times*, March 28, 1968, 13.

69. Letter from AFTRA to Bob McClay, April 4, 1968, Larry Miller Archive; "KMPX: The Last Moments," audio file, http://www.jive95.com/kmpx.htm; also transcribed in Krieger, "Cooptation," 1:113–15; Jassen, "KMPX Walkout Beautiful"; Krieger, "Cooptation," 1:124.

70. Rossman, "KMPX on Strike," 3.

71. Krieger, "Cooptation," 1:121, 135, 142–43; Greenberg and Fong-Torres, "KMPX-KPPC Shut Down," *Rolling Stone*, April 27, 1968, 22.

72. Krieger, "Cooptation," 1:141–42.

73. Krieger, "Cooptation," 1:122–23.

74. Demands reprinted in Rossman, "KMPX on Strike," 3.

75. Krieger, "Cooptation," 1:122–23.

76. Krieger, "Cooptation," 1:120–21. Whitney Harris, "KMPX—What It's All About," Letter to the Editor, *San Francisco Chronicle*, March 29, 1968.

77. Ralph Gleason, Jr., "On the Town: Scorpions, Destiny, and a 'Hippie' Strike," *San Francisco Chronicle*, March 20, 1968, 48; Krieger, "Cooptation," 1:135.

78. Harris, "KMPX—What It's All About"; Krieger, "Cooptation," 1:141–42; Greenberg and Fong-Torres, "KMPX-KPPC Shut Down," 22.

79. Krieger, "Cooptation," 1:135–36.

80. Jeff Jassen, "Larry Miller Throws Support to KMPX Strikers," *Berkeley Barb*, June 10, 1967.

81. Krieger, "Cooptation," 1:133–36.

82. Larry Miller, Letter, April 10, 1968, Larry Miller personal collection; reprinted as "And in His Exact Words," *Berkeley Barb*, April 12, 1968, 5.

83. Miller, Letter.

84. Miller, Resignation typed statement, Larry Miller personal collection.

85. Larry Miller, Correspondence with author, June 28, 2010.

86. Sandy Darlington, "KMPX on Mars," *San Francisco Express Times*, 13.

87. Sandy Darlington, ". . . And the Winner Gets the Radio Station"; Rossman, "KMPX on Strike," 3.

88. Ernie Barry, "Barry Challenges Jassen," *Berkeley Barb*, April 26, 1968, 4.

89. Barry, "Barry Challenges Jassen," 4.

90. Krieger, "Cooptation," 2:1–4.

91. Krieger, "Cooptation," 1:122–23.

92. Jeff Jassen, "Those Strikers: Let's See, They Say, Every Man Has His Price," *Berkeley Barb*, May 10, 1968, 7; McNally, *Long Strange Trip*, 252–66, 489–500; the bad business practices of Carousel manager Ron Rakow, one of rock's most notorious hustlers, did not help the ballroom either. The Carousel's anarchic character fits with Rebecca Klatch's portrayal of the libertarian links between right and left activists in the 1960s. See Klatch, "The Counterculture, the New Left, and the New Right"; and Klatch, *A Generation Divided*.

93. Krieger, "Cooptation," 2:174.

CHAPTER 3

1. Office of the Mayor Joseph L. Alioto, "Proclamation," Director Folder, Box 67, Berkeley Folk Music Festival Collection [hereafter BFMFC].

2. Barry Olivier, "Basic Notes from Breakfast Discussion of Music Festival," March 12, 1969, Council Folder, Box 66, BFMFC.

3. The producers of Woodstock had to move their festival a number of times due to intense opposition from local town governments and in the end took place not in the town of Woodstock, but rather on Max Yasgur's dairy farm forty miles away in Bethel. For more on Woodstock, see Robert Santelli, *Aquarius Rising: The Rock Festival Years* (New York: Dell, 1980), 121–53; Joel Makower, *Woodstock: The Oral History* (Washington, DC: Tilden Press, 1989); Andy Bennett, *Remembering Woodstock* (Burlington, VT: Ashgate, 2004); Michael Lang, *The Road to Woodstock* (New York: Ecco, 2009); Pete Fornatale, *Back to the Garden: The Story of Woodstock* (New York: Touchstone, 2009).

4. N.A., "Woodstock: The Wild East," *Berkeley Tribe*, August 22–29, 1969, 5, 24.

5. Joan Holden, "The Wild West Rock Show: Shooting Up a Rock Bananza," *Ramparts Magazine*, December 1969, 1.

6. For a useful critique of this narrative, see Michael Frisch, "Woodstock and Altamont," in *True Stories From the American Past, Volume II: Since 1865*, ed. William Graebner (New York: McGraw-Hill, 1997), 210–31. See also, Norma Coates, "If Anything, Blame Woodstock, The Rolling Stones: Altamont, December 6,1969," in *Performance and Popular Music: History, Place, and Time*, ed. Ian Inglis (Burlington, VT: Ashgate, 2006), 58–69.

7. For the history of folk music festivals, see Ronald D. Cohen, *A History of Folk Music Festivals in the United States* (Lanham, MD: Scarecrow Press, 2008); Cheryl Anne Brauner, "A Study of the Newport Folk Festival and the Newport Folk Foundation" (M.A. Thesis, Memorial University of Newfoundland, 1983); David E. Whisnant, *All That Is Native and Fine: The Politics of Culture in an American Region* (University of North Carolina Press, 1984); Millie Rahn, "Going Down to Newport or Staying Home: A Look Back at Club 47 and the Newport Folk Festivals," *New England Folk Almanac* (Summer 1997; Robert Cantwell, *Ethnomimesis: Folklore and the Representation of Culture* (Chapel Hill: University of North Carolina, 1993); Robert Cantwell, *When We Were Good: The Folk Revival* (Cambridge, MA: Harvard University Press, 1996), and Robert Cantwell, "Feasts of Unnaming: Folk Festivals and the Representation of Folk Life," in *If Beale Street Could Talk: Music, Community, Culture* (Urbana: University of Illinois Press, 2008), 71–110. For the history of jazz festivals, see John Gennari, "Hipsters, Bluebloods, Rebels, and Hooligans: The Cultural Politics of the Newport Jazz Festival, 1954–1960," in *Uptown Conversations: New Essays in Jazz Studies*, ed. Robert O'Meally, Brent Edwards, and Farah Jasmine Griffin (Columbia University Press, 2004), 126–49; Scott Saul, *Freedom Is, Freedom Ain't: Jazz and the Making of the Sixties* (Cambridge, MA: Harvard University Press, 2003), 99–143, 271–83. Also see Santelli, *Aquarius Rising*; and Richard A. Peterson, "The Unnatural History of Rock Festivals: An Instance of Media Facilitation," *Popular Music and Society* 2, 2 (1973): 97–123. Even the nonprofit Monterey International Pop Festival generated controversy about the funds it generated; see Michael Lydon, "The High Cost of Music and Love: Where's the Money from Monterey?," *Rolling Stone*, November 9, 1967, 1, 7.

8. For more on the San Francisco State College student strikes, see San Francisco State University Leonard Library, "The San Francisco State Student Strike Collection," http://www.library.sfsu.edu/about/collections/strike. For more on People's Park, see Rorabaugh, *Berkeley At War*, 154–66 and Gitlin, *The Sixties*, 353–61.

9. Grover Lewis, "Haight Street: Once It Was Love Street," *Village Voice*, April 17, 1969, Philosophy Folder, Box 64, BFMFC.

10. The distopian side of the Haight was widely reported, perhaps most famously by Joan Didion; see Joan Didion, "Slouching Toward Bethlehem," in *Slouching Toward Bethlehem* (New York: Farrar, Straus & Giroux, 1968), 84–130. See also Alice Echols, "Hope and Hype in Sixties Haight-Ashbury," in *Shaky Ground*, 17–50; Perry, *The Haight-Ashbury*.

11. Barry Olivier, "Basic Notes"; See also, Barry Olivier, "San Francisco Project Council list of members," Council Folder, Box 66, BFMFC.

12. Werber would later leave the Wild West planning committee due to a high-profile marijuana possession court case. Barry Olivier, "Phone notes from talk with Frank Werber," March 28, 1969; Barry Olivier, "Agenda for meeting wth Frank Werber," March 30, 1969; Barry Olivier, "Agenda for April 2, 1969, with Frank Werber," n.d.; Barry Olivier to Ron Polte, May 26, 1969; Barry Olivier to Frank Werber, June 2, 1969; Handwritten note, n.d.; "Frank Weber conversation," June 13, 1969; Barry Olivier to Frank Werber, February 27, 1970, Werber Folder, Box 67, BFMFC.

13. Ben Fong-Torres, "A Tidal Wave in the Wild West," *Rolling Stone*, August 9, 1969, SF / Xerox Masters, Box 65, BFMFC.

14. Olivier, "Sun. 3/16/69 Meeting at Donahue," March 16, 1969, SF / Records Folder, Box 67, BFMFC.

15. Olivier, "Basic Notes."

16. "Council Meeting, Fillmore West," May 1, 1969, SF / Records Folder, Box 67, BFMFC. Frank Werber owned the copyright for the song, which Dino Valenti had sold to him. Werber initially proposed the name, but others, such as Bill Graham, supported it as well.

17. Olivier, "Basic Notes." Olivier, "Breakfast Discussion of 1969 San Francisco Music Festival," SF / Records Folder, Box 67, BFMFC, 6.

18. Olivier, "Basic Notes." Olivier, "Breakfast Discussion of 1969 San Francisco Music Festival," SF / Records Folder, Box 67, BFMFC, 6. Underline in original; all formatting is in the original unless otherwise noted.

19. Tom Donahue, "Wild West Festival Press Conference," August 6, 1969, transcription in SF Xerox Masters Folder, Box 65, BFMFC, 2.

20. Tom Donahue, "Wild West Festival Press Conference," August 6, 1969, transcription in SF Xerox Masters Folder, Box 65, BFMFC, 2.

21. Olivier, "Breakfast Discussion," 1, 2.

22. Donahue, "Wild West Festival Press Conference," 2.

23. Olivier, "Breakfast Discussion," 12.

24. Olivier, "Breakfast Discussion," 9.

25. Olivier, "Breakfast Discussion," 18.

26. Olivier, "Sun. 3/16/69 Meeting," 1.

27. Olivier, "Breakfast Discussion," 12.

28. Olivier, "Breakfast Discussion," 10, 17.

29. Olivier, "Sun. 3/16/69 Meeting," 1.

30. The Jefferson Airplane performed at the Berkeley Folk Music Festival in 1966. Program, "9th Annual Berkeley Folk Music Festival," Box 49, Folder 9, BFMFC. Olivier organized programs around the discussion of rock as a form of folk music at subsequent Berkeley festivals. Program, "11th Annual Berkeley Folk Music Festival," Folder 11, Box 49, BFMFC.

31. Barry Olivier, "RJG 3/13/69," Philosophy Folder, Box 67, BFMFC.

32. Olivier, "Breakfast Discussion," 2.

33. "Sample Organizational Outline: For Proposed San Francisco Music & Arts Festival" Prepared by Barry Olivier, March 19, 1969, Council Folder, Box 66, BFMFC.

34. Barry Olivier, "Second Breakfast Discussion of 1969 San Francisco Music Festival," March 19, 1969, Records Folder, Box 67, BFMFC.

35. Barry Olivier, "FW," n.d., Philosophy Folder, Box 67, BFMFC and "Breakfast Discussion," 17.

36. Olivier, "Second Breakfast Discussion," 4.

37. Barry Olivier, "Evaluation of What's Happened To Date (3/28/69) With San Francisco Project," Director Folder, Box 67, BFMFC.

38. Olivier, "Evaluation." Barry Olivier, "'The Wild West' Festival—Report On Funds Acquire, Expended & Projected," Income Folder, Box 65, BFMFC, 1. Barry Olivier, "Staff Meeting notes 7/8/69," Staff Meetings Folder, Box 64, 2.

39. Olivier, "3/31/69 Meeting w/ Council," SF / Records Folder, Box 67, BFMFC, 3.

40. For more on the Diggers, see the works cited in Introduction, n. 40.

41. Barry Oliver, phone conversation with author, March 25, 2011.

42. Barry Olivier, "5/9/69—Meeting of Council—Trident Rest., Saulsalito," SF / Records Folder, Box 67, BFMFC, 1, 2.

43. Barry Olivier, "Council 9:30 actual start 5/1/69," SF / Records Folder, Box 67, BFMFC, 3.

44. San Francisco Music Council, May 2, 1969, Artists Meetings Folder, Box 67, BFMFC.

45. Barry Olivier to Darrow L. Sutton, May 5, 1969, Budget Planning Folder, Box 67, BFMFC.

46. Olivier, "Basic Notes."

47. Bruce Grimes, "Notes—Band Meeting—Stern Grove Clubhouse SF," SF Music Folder, Box 66, BFMFC, May 27, 1969, 1, 3, 4.

48. Barry Olivier, "Band Mting #2—3044 Pine Office—6/5/69," Artists Meetings Folder, Box 67, BFMFC, 2.

49. "Wild West Circus Jump For Joy We've Caught Fire Colored Cloud Meeting." SF Music Folder, Box 66, BFMFC.

50. Stanley W. Blackfield to Barry Olivier, June 7, 1969, Legal Matters Folder, Box 66, BFMFC.

51. Judi Freeman, "Staff Meeting—June 10, 1969—Tuesday," SF / Records Folder, Box 67, BFMFC.

52. "Press & Television Conference 2:00 p.m. Monday, June 16, 1969" Press Release, Box 67, BFMFC. N.A., "Coming Meetings . . .," SF / Records Folder, Box 67, BFMFC. N.A., "Eclectic 'Wild West': S.F. Festival for All Life-Styles," *San Francisco Chronicle*, June 17, 1969, 4.

53. Joel Selvin, *Any Day Now!* Newsletter Mockup, N.D., Newsletter Folder, Box 66, BFMFC.

54. Joel Selvin, *Any Day Now!* Mockup; Joel Selvin, *Any Day Now!*, July 18, 1969, 2, Box 66, BFMFC.

55. Joel Selvin, *Any Day Now!*, July 18, 1969, 2, Box 66, BFMFC.

56. Joel Selvin, *Any Day Now!*, July 18, 1969, 2, Box 66, BFMFC.

57. For more on women in the counterculture, see Lempke-Santagelo, *Daughters of Aquarius*.

58. "The Wild West!" KSAN Press Release, July 10, 1969, Press Matters Folder, Box 68.

59. Philip Elwood, "Ambitious Festival Plans," *San Francisco Examiner*, July 14, 1969, 20. Barry Olivier, photograph, Wild West Festival Billboard designed by Robert Fried, n.d., Barry Olivier, personal collection.

60. "Environmental Planning Meeting For Wild West," July 16, 1969, Records Folder, Box 67, BFMFC.

61. KSAN Press Release, July 10, 1969. Shela Xoregos to Barry Olivier, July 11, 1969, Correspondence Folder, Box 66, BFMFC.

62. Olivier, "Basic Notes From Council Meeting," June 28, 1969, Council Folder, Box 66, BFMFC.

63. "Film for Wild West, Meeting: 7/23/69."

64. Many early countercultural events such as the Invisible Circus took place at Glide Church. See "The Invisible Circus," http://www.diggers.org/diggers/incircus.html [accessed November 12, 2010].

65. "Staff Meeting," July 28, 1969, SF / Xerox Folder, Box 65, BFMFC.

66. "Staff Meeting," July 28, 1969.

67. S.F. Mime Troupe, "Wild West?," July 28, 1969, Wild West Festival, Box 67, BFMFC.

68. "General Staff Meeting," July 29, 1969, Staff Meetings, Box 66, BFMFC, 1.

69. Max Goldcrab, "Showdown at Wild West," *San Francisco Good Times (San Francisco Express Times)*, 31 July 1969, Clippings Forms Folder, BFMFC.

70. "General Staff Meeting," July 29, 1969, 1, 2.

71. "General Staff Meeting," July 29, 1969, 1, 2.

72. "General Staff Meeting," July 29, 1969, 2.

73. Goldcrab, "Showdown at Wild West."

74. Selvin, "Selvin/Meet [Draft for Newsletter]," 1, Newsletter Folder, Box 66, BFMFC.

75. "General Staff Meeting," July 29, 1969, 2.

76. The Haight Commune, "Strike Bulletin #1," July 31, 1969, Wild West Festival Folder, Box 67, BFMFC.

77. The Haight Commune, "Strike Bulletin #1."

78. The death of a small-time drug dealer, Eddy Baker, at the hands of the police had first sparked the creation of the Haight Commune; see Nixon, "Telling Like It Was," *Berkeley Tribe*, August 15, 1969 [August 8–14, 1969], 16.

79. Nixon, "Telling Like It Was," *Berkeley Tribe*, 16, Wild West Festival Folder, Box 67, BFMFC. The Haight Commune, "Stick 'Em Up, Wild West, Anti-Official Statement," August 11, 1969, Wild West Folder, Box 67, BFMFC.

80. The Haight Commune, "Stick 'Em Up, Wild West." Johnny Sundstrom, telephone interview with author, June 4, 2010. N.A., "Westward Whoa," *Good Times*, August 7, 1969, Clippings Folder, Box 65, BFMFC. It was not Sundstrom's first brush with rock music promoters. He had been involved in protests against Bill Graham at the Fillmore East ballroom in New York, where the Motherfuckers had violently demanded one free night a week for Lower East Side hippies and street kids; see Graham and Greenfield, *Bill Graham Presents*, 253–57; Neumann, *Up Against the Wall Motherf**ker*, 104–11; Patrick Burke, "Up Against the Wall: Sixties Rock, Radical Politics, and the Battle for the Fillmore East," presentation, Births, Stages, Declines, Revivals: International Association for the Study of Popular Music, United States Branch, Loyola University, New Orleans, April 8–11, 2010; and Burke, "Tear Down the Walls," 61–79.

81. The Haight Commune, "Stick 'Em Up, Wild West."

82. The Haight Commune, "Long Hair Is Not Enough! Is Your Soul Shaggy Too?," Wild West Festival Folder, Box 67, BFMFC.

83. N.A., "West Fest Struck," *Berkeley Tribe*, August 8–14, 1969, 4.

84. Sundstrom recalled that he was worried that Wild West would turn into a crackdown against the most vulnerable street kids in San Francisco, the very populations that in his view were at the cutting edge of the counterculture aesthetically and politically; Johnny Sundstrom, telephone interview with author, June 4, 2010.

85. The Haight Commune, "Stick 'Em Up, Wild West."

86. *The Good, The Bad, and the Ugly*, DVD, dir. Sergio Leone (1966, U.S. release, 1967; Los Angeles: MGM Home Video Entertainment, 2004).

87. The outlaw was a popular figure among counterculturalists, particularly those influenced by the Diggers. See Cavallo, "'It's Free Because It's Yours'," in *Fiction of the Past*, 97–144.

88. The Haight Commune, "Stick 'Em Up, Wild West."

89. The Haight Commune, "Stick 'Em Up, Wild West."

90. San Francisco Mime Troupe, "The Natives Were Restless," August 14, 1969, Wild West Festival Folder, Box 67, BFMFC.

91. The Haight Commune, "Long Hair Is Not Enough!"

92. The Haight Commune, "Long Hair Is Not Enough!"; N.A., "STRIKE against 'WILD WEST'."

93. The Haight Commune, "Long Hair Is Not Enough!"

94. Tom Donahue, "Wild West Festival Press Conference," August 6, 1969, transcription in SF Xerox Masters Folder, Box 65, BFMFC, 6.

95. Donahue, "Wild West Festival Press Conference," 6.

96. Donahue, "Wild West Festival Press Conference," 10.

97. Donahue, "Wild West Festival Press Conference," 10.

98. Donahue, "Wild West Festival Press Conference," 10, 12.

99. Donahue, "Wild West Festival Press Conference," 13–15.

100. Donahue, "Wild West Festival Press Conference," 29, 15.

101. N.A., "Rock Rip Off," *Dock of the Bay*, August 11–17, 1969, Clipping Forms Folder, Box 65, BFMFC.

102. Barry Olivier to Ron Polte, "Re: Council Reorganization & Meeting tonight at Fellowship Church," August 11, 1969, Council Folder, Box 66, BFMFC.

103. Barry Olivier, "Expanded Council Committee Meeting," August 11, 1969, Council Folder, Box 66, BFMFC, 4.

104. Bart [Queary], "Memo to All Staffers," August 12, 1969, Recreation Department Folder, Box 65, BFMFC. Ron Polte, "Dear Brothers," August 12, 1969, Wild West Festival Folder, Box 67, BFMFC.

105. Ron Polte, telephone interview with author, July 6, 2009.

106. Barry Olivier, "Statement by Barry Olivier, 'Wild West' Festival Director, Wednesday, August 13, 1969—At the Press Conference Called to Announce Cancellation of the Festival," Wild West Festival Folder, Box 67, BFMFC, 1.

107. Olivier, "Statement by Barry Olivier," 3.

108. Joe Russin, "Russin on Wild West," KQED, August 13, 1969 (transcription dated September 12, 1969), 3, Wild West Festival Folder, Box 67, BFMFC.

109. Dorena Wong to Wild West People, August 13, 1969, SF / Records Folder, Box 67, BFMFC.

110. V. I. Lemming, "Wild West Falls in Class Struggle," *Berkeley Barb*, August 22–28, 1969, 10.

111. N.A., "'Wild West' Festival Called Off," *San Francisco Chronicle*, August 14, 1969, 1.

112. San Francisco Mime Troupe, "Natives Were Restless."

113. *Good Times*, August 14, 1969, cover.

114. Judy Baston, "Comment: How Artists Relate to the Community—Issue of Cancellation in Music Festival," *People's World*, August 30, 1969, 11, Labor Archives and Research Center, San Francisco State University.

115. San Francisco Mime Troupe, "Natives Were Restless."

116. Wieder, "Public Works: How the West Was Lost," *Daily Californian*, August 19, 1969, Wild West Festival Folder, Box 67, BFMFC.

117. N.A., "The Wild West—Nobody Wins," *Daily Californian*, August 19, 1969, Wild West Festival Folder, Box 67, BFMFC, 4.

118. Allan Katzman, "Wild West Roped, Tied, and Cancelled," *Los Angeles Free Press*, SF Xerox Masters Folder, Box 65, BFMFC.

119. Allan Katzman, "Poor Paranoid's Almanac," *East Village Other*, August 27, 1969, in SF Xerox Masters Folder, Box 65, BFMFC.

120. Ralph J. Gleason, "On the Town: Why Bill Graham Is Leaving the City," *San Francisco Chronicle*, August 8, 1969, 46. Ralph J. Gleason, "Perspectives: Festival Paranoia," *Rolling Stone*, September 6, 1969, 24.

121. Marjorie Heins, "Gleason," *Dock of the Bay*, August 12, 1969, Clippings Folder, Box 65, BFMFC.

122. Peter Wiley, "Conversation," *Dock of the Bay*, September 29, 1969, Wild West Festival Folder, Box 67, BFMFC, 2.

123. Joan Holden, "The Wild West Rock Show: Shooting Up a Rock Bananza," *Ramparts Magazine*, December 1969, 1, 71, 74.

124. As John McMillian argues, print culture was a crucial aspect of the public sphere generated by the counterculture and New Left during the 1960s; see John McMillian, *Smoking Typewriters, the Sixties Underground Press and the Rise of Alternative Media in America* (New York: Oxford University Press, 2011).

125. Baston, "Comment," 11.

126. Sam Silver, "Wild West Ambush," *Good Times*, August 14, 1969, 4.

127. Lemming, "Wild West Falls in Class Struggle," 10.

128. Selvin, *Summer of Love*, 38–39.

129. Geoffrey Link, "Chet & Bill," *San Francisco Magazine*, March 1970, 26–30, 47–49. Helms and Graham were never quite the polar opposites many made them out to be; for the more complex interactions between them, see Graham and Greenfield, *Bill Graham Presents*, 146–49.

130. Art Johnson, "Rock Scene: Out on the Edge," *Berkeley Tribe*, August 8–14, 1969, 3.

131. Tari, "Lights Out at S.F. Ballrooms," *Berkeley Tribe*, 1–7 August 1969, 4.

132. Johnson, "Rock Scene," 3; Verne/Bill, "Personality Power," *Good Times*, August 7, 1969, 3.

133. Nixon, "Rock Shucks for Bucks," *Berkeley Tribe*, August 1–7, 1969, 4.

134. Johnson, "Rock Scene," 3.

135. Chet Helms, quoted in Graham and Greenfield, *Bill Graham Presents*, 277.

136. Graham and Greenfield, *Bill Graham Presents*, 253–57.

137. Verne, "Common Sense," *Good Times*, August 14, 1969, 4.

138. Verne, "Common Sense," 4.

139. Verne, "Common Sense," 3.

140. Helms, quoted in Graham and Greenfield, *Bill Graham Presents*, 280.

141. Muhammad Khan 1, "Rock Ripples Move Outside," *Berkeley Barb*, September 5–11, 1969, 10.

142. Perry, *Haight-Ashbury*, 276.

143. Frisch, "Woodstock and Altamont."

144. Hunter S. Thompson, *Fear and Loathing in Las Vegas: A Savage Journey to the Heart of the American Dream* (1971; reprint, New York: Vintage Books, 1998), 66, 68.

145. Fong-Torres, "Tidal Wave in the Wild West."

CHAPTER 4

1. Michael Herr, *Dispatches* (New York: Knopf, 1977), 176–77.

2. Herr, *Dispatches*, 57.

3. Herr, *Dispatches*, 123.

4. Herr, *Dispatches*, 6.

5. Reg E. Williams, an organizer of the Straight Theater and active participant in the Bay Area counterculture, recalls a friend in the Armed Forces whose job it was to accompany GI coffins from San Francisco area military installations to the cemeteries south of the city. See Reg E. Williams, "Fillmore Nights," in *The Straight on the Haight: A True Life Saga from the Psychedelic Era of Love, Drugs, and Rock and Roll*, excerpted on http://www.thestraight.com [accessed February 3, 2002].

6. Roger Steffens, "Nine Meditations on Jimi and Nam," in *Jimi Hendrix: The Ultimate Experience*, ed. Adrian Boot and Chris Salewicz (London: Boxtree Limited, 1995), 116.

7. Herr, *Dispatches*, 9.

8. Judith Johnson, "Bob Hope's Vietnam Christmas Tours," *Vietnam Magazine*, February 2010, http://www.historynet.com/bob-hopes-vietnam-christmas-tours.htm [accessed December 1, 2010]; Bob Hope, *Bob Hope's Vietnam Story: Five Women I Love* (New York: Doubleday, 1966); *Bob Hope: The Vietnam Years, 1964–1972* (DVD, Portland, OR: R2 Entertainment, 2004).

9. While many scholars have studied the presence of the Vietnam War in rock music, far fewer have documented the role of the music in the war. On Vietnam and rock, see Storey, "Rockin' Hegemony," in Louvre and Walsh, *Tell Me Lies About Vietnam*, 181–97; Ray Pratt, "'There Must Be Some Way Outta Here!': The Vietnam War in American Popular Music," in *The Vietnam War: Its History, Literature, and Music*, ed. Kenton J. Clymer (El Paso: Texas Western Press, 1998), 168–89; Douglas W. Reitinger, "Paint It Black: Rock Music and Vietnam War Film," *Journal of American Culture* 15, 3 (Fall 1992): 53–60; Kenneth Bindes and Craig Houston, "Takin' Care of Business: Rock Music, Vietnam, and the Protest Myth," *The Historian* 52 (November 1989): 1–23; Terry Anderson, "American Popular Music and the War in Vietnam," *Peace and Change* 11 (July 1986): 51–65; and Mary Ellison, "Black Music and the Vietnam War," in *Vietnam Images: War and Representation*, ed. Jeffrey Walsh and James Aulich (New York: St. Martin's Press, 1989), 226–54. For works on rock music in the Vietnam War itself, see Charlie Clark, "The Tracks of My Tears—When Rock Went to War: Looking Back on Vietnam and Its Music," *VVA Veteran*, February 1986, 10–23; Lee Andreson, *Battle Notes: Music from the Vietnam War* (Superior, WI: Savage Press, 2000); Chris Sabis, "Through the Soldiers' Ears: What Americans Fighting in Vietnam Heard and Its Effects, A Study of Former AFVN Members and Rochester, New York Veterans," Senior Thesis, University of Rochester, 2000), available at http://www.geocities.com/afvn/afvnhistory.html [accessed March 10, 2002]; and Craig Werner and Doug Bradley's work-in-progress, "We Gotta Get Out of This Place: Music and the Experience of Vietnam Veterans."

10. For more on morale in Vietnam, see Christian G. Appy, *Working-Class War: American Combat Soldiers and Vietnam* (Chapel Hill: University of North Carolina Press, 1993), 234–49.

11. "Historical Resume, Entertainment Activities," in "Organization and Functions Manual: United States Army in Vietnam Special Services Agency (Provisional)," March 1970, History Files 1970–1972, Entertainment Branch, USARV Special Services Agency, United States Forces in Southeast Asia 1950–1975, RG 472, NARA; also quoted in Meredith Lair, *Armed with Abundance: Consumerism and Soldiering in the Vietnam War* (Chapel Hill: University of North Carolina Press, 2011), 228.

12. Lair, *Armed with Abundance*, 228; Lair's source is *The USARV Command Historian and the USARV Deputy Chief of Staff for Personnel and Administration*.

13. The manpower and promotion system was of a piece with the technocratic administration of the Vietnam War by the American Armed Forces. See Ronald H. Spector, *After Tet: The Bloodiest Year in Vietnam* (New York: Free Press, 1993), 27. See also James William Gibson, *The Perfect War: Technowar in Vietnam* (Boston: The Atlantic Monthly Press, 1986).

14. For a brief overview of the growth of a GI counterculture, see Terry H. Anderson, "The GI Movement and the Response from the Brass," in *Give Peace A Chance: Exploring the Vietnam Antiwar Movement*, ed. Melvin Small and William D. Hoover (Syracuse, NY: Syracuse University Press, 1992), 91–115. On the GI antiwar movement in general, see Moser, *New Winter Soldiers*; Helmer, *Bringing the War Home*; Cortright, *Soldiers in Revolt*; Boyle, *GI Revolts*; Waterhouse and Wizard, *Turning the Guns Around*; Andrew E. Hunt, *The Turning: A History of Vietnam Veterans*

Against the War (New York: New York University Press, 1999); and the documentary film, *Sir! No Sir!*, DVD, dir. David Zeiger (Los Angeles: Displaced Films, 2005).

15. See David L. Anderson, *The Columbia Guide to the Vietnam War* (New York: Columbia University Press, 2002), 113–14. On class and GIs, see Appy, *Working-Class War*.

16. On the move toward decentralization and "participatory management," which was encouraged by Nixon's secretary of defense, Melvin Laird, see Dale Van Atta, *With Honor: Melvin Laird in War, Peace, and Politics* (Madison: University of Wisconsin Press, 2008), 314–15; and Cortright, *Soldiers in Revolt*, 171–200. Nixon's efforts were partially caused by the decision to abandon the draft and create an all-volunteer military; see Beth Bailey, *America's Army: Making the All-Volunteer Force* (Cambridge, MA: Harvard University Press, 2009), 1–65.

17. David E. James, "The Vietnam War and American Music," in *The Vietnam War and American Culture*, ed. John Carlos Rowe and Rick Berg (New York: Columbia University Press, 1991), 243.

18. The war left some 58,000 American GIs and possibly up to 2 million Vietnamese dead.

19. Even Jeremy Kuzmarov, who argues that there was far less drug use by American GIs in Vietnam than many at the time claimed, grants that it was still widespread; see Jeremy Kuzmarov, *The Myth of the Addicted Army: Vietnam and the Modern War on Drugs* (Amherst: University of Massachusetts Press, 2009), 5–6. See also: John Steinbeck IV, "The Importance of Being Stoned in Vietnam," *Washingtonian Magazine*, January 1968, 33–38; U.S. Congress, Senate Committee on Armed Services, *Staff Report on Drug Abuse in the Military*, Report of the Subcommittee on Drug Abuse, 92nd Congress, 1st Session, July 1971; and U.S. Congress, Senate Committee on Armed Services, *Drug Use in the Military*, Hearings Before the Subcommittee on Drug Abuse in the Military, 92nd Congress, 2nd Session, February 29 to April 6, 1972.

20. Much has been made of the impact on domestic culture of Vietnam as the first "television war," but less has been made of the ways in which mass communications technologies also brought domestic culture to Vietnam in unprecedented ways. See Michael J. Arlen, *Living Room War* (New York: Viking, 1969). For a theoretical overview of the collapse of home front and war zone, see Chris Hables Gray, "Postmodernism with a Vengeance: The Vietnam War," in *The Vietnam War and Postmodernity*, ed. Michael Bibby (Amherst: University of Massachusetts Press, 1999), 173–98.

21. Douglas Bradley and Craig Werner, "We Gotta Get Outta This Place: Music, Memory, and the Vietnam War," in Liner Notes to . . . *Next Stop Is Vietnam—The War on Record: 1961–2008*, by Hugo Keesing, ed. Bill Geerhart (Hambergen, Germany: Bear Family Records, 2010), 40.

22. Michael Herr saw lyrics such as "time is on my side," a popular Rolling Stones cover of Irma Thomas's soul song whose title took on an additional meaning for GIs hoping to survive their year-long tour of duty in Vietnam; Herr, *Dispatches*, 21.

23. Gunbunny, photograph, U.S. Militaria Forum: Collectors Preserving History, http://www.usmilitariaforum.com/forums/index.php?showtopic=46108&st=20 [accessed January 3, 2012].

24. The awareness of presenting opinions in public via helmet graffiti and of being seen wearing these messages suggests a strange kind of counterpublic in Vietnam, one in which, as Michael Warner argues, strangers exchange texts in the spirit of collective discussion and deliberation. See Warner, *Publics and Counterpublics*, especially 67–75.

25. Photographer unknown, image of Marine Corporal Michael Wynn in Da Nang, Republic of Vietnam, September 21, 1967, Bettmann/Corbis).

26. Photographer unknown, "Image of a soldier of the 1st. Cavarly Division, 12th Cavalry, 2nd Battalion, relaxes June 24, 1970, before pulling out of Fire Support Base Speer, six

miles inside the Cambodian border," AP Photos. Photograph by Tim Page, US soldier from 8th Regiment, riding atop a 9th Division armored personnel carrier, http://www.vietnampix.com/hippie3.htm [accessed January 13, 2003].

27. Quoted in James, "Vietnam War and American Music," in Rowe and Berg, *Vietnam War and American Culture*, 243. Originally in *Rock and Roll Confidential*, February 1985, reprinted in *The First Rock & Roll Confidential Report*, ed. Dave Marsh, Lee Ballinger, Sandra Choron, Wendy Smith, and Daniel Wolff (New York: Pantheon, 1984), 209. Intriguingly, Ballinger's critique of the position that rock was ideologically antiwar in any stable political way registers an awareness of civics as a crucial category of analysis. The music, Ballinger argues, "let civilians forget about the war, just as it allowed those who were in Vietnam or had somebody there to make it through just one more day without doing anything about the situation." Even when rock inspired political passivity or quietism, it did so by framing identity around citizenship: civilian as compared to soldier.

28. Billy Williams, "Armed Forces Vietnam Network (AFVN)," Broadcasting in Vietnam During the War, http://home.earthlink.net/~bfwillia/ [accessed March 24, 2006].

29. Lee W. Hauser, "A History of the American Forces Vietnam Network, 1962–1972," (M.A. thesis, University of North Carolina, 1972), 2.

30. The full history of AFRTS during the Vietnam War era remains to be written; the service itself maintains a "heritage" section of its Internet website, http://afrts.dodmedia.osd.mil/heritage/page.asp?pg=heritage [accessed November 1, 2011].

31. Hauser, "History of the American Forces Vietnam Network," 75.

32. *Good Morning, Vietnam*, dir. Barry Levinson (1987; Los Angeles: Buena Vista Entertainment/Touchstone, 2006).

33. James P. Sterba, "Radio and TV Accompany G.I.'s Into the Battle Area in Vietnam," *New York Times*, August 11, 1970, 12.

34. James Wentz, *Armed Forces Vietnam Network Audience Opinion Research & Analysis* (1968), 17; Steve Wiltsie, *Audience Opinion Research & Analysis* (1970), 13; and Gunar Grubaums, *Armed Forces Vietnam Network Audience Opinion Research & Analysis* (1971), 11, http://webspace.webring.com/people/rr/rmorecook/surveys.html [accessed March 24, 2004]. Stephen F. Kroft, "AFVN Answers GIs Requests," *Pacific Stars & Stripes*, December 14, 1970, Org. History File, AFVN, Folder II, 1969–1972, RG 472, Records of the United States Forces in Southeast Asia, Headquarters, Military Assistance Command Vietnam (MACV), Information Office (MACIO), American Forces Vietnam Network (AFVN), Organizational History, 1962 thru 1973, Box 1, NARA.

35. AFVN CDs #85, 86, 95, Chuck Kenney Collection, Boonville, NC. http://vietnam_war_sounds.tripod.com [accessed January 10, 2006].

36. Hauser, "History of the American Forces Vietnam Network," 100–1.

37. Pop Chronicles 41, Radio Round-Up, Issue 1522, Radio Transcription Unit, RU 16-1, 21 October 1970, Armed Forces Radio and Television Services Collection (hereafter AFRTSC), Division of Recorded Sound, Library of Congress, Washington, D.C.

38. Pop Chronicles 42, Radio Round-Up, Issue 1523, Radio Transcription Unit, RU 17-1, October 28, 1970, AFRTS.

39. Love, 77–79 LPA 63028–63045 and Radio Round-Up, Radio Transcription Unit, RU 3-1, July 22, 1970, AFRTSC. *Woodstock: Music from the Original Soundtrack and More*, LP (New York: Cotillion/Atlantic Records, 1970).

40. See, for instance, Storey, "Rockin' Hegemony."

41. "Stateside Top Thirty Countdown—October 1968," AFVN, www.geocities.com/afvn [accessed March 20, 2000].

42. Hendrix had been a member of the 101st Airborne Division before being discharged from the Army in 1962; see Charles Cross, *Room Full of Mirrors: A Biography of Jimi Hendrix* (New York: Hyperion, 2005), 84–95.

43. Steffens, "Nine Meditations," in Boot and Salewicz, *Jimi Hendrix*, 118.

44. Medic Buddy Roche, quoted in Steffens, "Nine Meditations," in Boot and Salewicz, *Jimi Hendrix*, 113.

45. Steffens says the pilot's name was "Johnny Pissoff," quoted in Roger Steffens, "Nine Meditations," in Boot and Salewicz, *Jimi Hendrix*, 112.

46. Jimi Hendrix, "All Along the Watchtower," *Are You Experienced?* (Reprise Records, 1968).

47. Werner, *Change Is Gonna Come*, 110.

48. Bob Dylan, "All Along the Watchtower," *John Wesley Harding* (Columbia Records, 1967).

49. Jon Landau, "John Wesley Harding," *Crawdaddy*, May 1968, reprinted in *It's Too Late to Stop Now: A Rock and Roll Journal* (San Francisco: Straight Arrow, 1972), 52. Christopher Ricks, *Dylan's Visions of Sin* (New York: Penguin/Viking, 2003), 359.

50. In this respect, the song resembles another hit song from 1967, Jefferson Airplane's "White Rabbit"; see Zimmerman, *Counterculture Kaleidoscope*, 52–90.

51. Eddie Kramer, *Hendrix: Setting the Record Straight* (New York: Warner Books, 1992), 136.

52. Jimi Hendrix, "Machine Gun," *Band of Gypsys* (Los Angeles: Capitol, 1970).

53. Paul Gilroy, "Bold As Love? Jami's Afrocyberdelia and the Challenge of the Not-Yet," in *Rip It Up: The Black Experience in Rock 'n' Roll*, ed. Kandia Crazy Horse (New York: Palgrave Macmillan, 2003), 28.

54. See also Katherine Kinney, *Friendly Fire: American Images of the Vietnam War* (New York: Oxford University Press, 2000), 119; Mike Daley, "Land of the Free, Jimi Hendrix: Woodstock Festival, August 18, 1969," in *Performance and Popular Music: History, Place, and Time*, ed. Ian Inglis (Burlington, VT: Ashgate, 2006), 52–57; and Charles Shaar Murray, *Crosstown Traffic: Jimi Hendrix and the Post-War Rock 'n' Roll Revolution* (New York: St. Martin's Press, 1989), 24.

55. Jimi Hendrix, "Machine Gun," *Live in Berkeley, May 30, 1970* (New York: MCA, 2003).

56. Gilroy, "Bold As Love?," 29.

57. Oliver Stone, "Born on the Fourth of July," in Boot and Salewicz, *Jimi Hendrix*, 125.

58. Steffens, "Nine Meditations," in Boot and Salewicz, *Jimi Hendrix*, 118.

59. N.A., "Fans Protest Soul Singer's Anthem Version," *New York Times*, October 8, 1968, 54.

60. Lauren Onkey, "Jimi Hendrix and the Politics of Race in the Sixties," in Braunstein and Doyle, *Imagine Nation*, 189–214. See also Steve Waksman, "Black Sound, Black Body: Jimi Hendrix, the Electric Guitar, and the Meanings of Blackness," in *Instruments of Desire*, 167–206.

61. See n. 42 above.

62. Herr, *Dispatches*, 181.

63. James E. Westheider, *Fighting on Two Fronts: African Americans and the Vietnam War* (New York: New York University Press, 1997), 76–77. Herr does not recall hearing Hendrix on AFVN, but his memories differ from evidence on preserved broadcasts. See also Ellison, "Black Music and the Vietnam War," in Walsh and Aulich, *Vietnam Images*, 57–68.

64. Martin quoted in Steffens, "Nine Meditations," in Boot and Salewicz, *Jimi Hendrix*, 120.

65. Stone, "Born on the Fourth of July," in Boot and Salewicz, *Jimi Hendrix*, 125.

66. Martin quoted in Steffens, "Nine Meditations," in Boot and Salewicz, *Jimi Hendrix*, 120.

67. R. Guy Slater, email correspondence, December 10, 2003, AFVN Stories Listserv, http://www.geocities.com/afvn/afvnfreefire.html [accessed December 10, 2003].

68. Cline quoted in Moser, *New Winter Soldiers*, 62–63.

69. Cline quoted in Moser, *New Winter Soldiers*, 62–63. Cline went on to be active in Vietnam Veterans Against the War as well as later antiwar movements.

70. Reminiscences of Jim Peachin, interviewed for Vietnam Veterans Oral History Project, 1973–1975 (hereafter VVOHP), Columbia University Center for Oral History (formerly Oral History Research Office), New York, 37–39.

71. Lydia Fish, "Informal Communication Systems in the Vietnam War: A Case Study in Folklore, Technology and Popular Culture" (unpublished manuscript, 2003). See also "Vietnam: Radio First Termer, An Audio Documentary Exploring the Role of Radio within Vietnam During the War," Interlock Media Associates Proposal, 1987, *Vietnam Research*, http://vietnamresearch.com/media/termer [accessed November 6, 2003] and NPR's *Vietnam Radio First Termer*, http://www.youtube.com/watch?v=sfcAZ-_SMsA and http://www.youtube.com/watch?v=WdCj6LBD0SE [accessed January 20, 2009].

72. Reminiscences of Jay Peterson, interviewed for VVOHP, 50.

73. Reminiscences of John Imsdahl, interviewed for VVOHP, 25.

74. Jefferson Airplane, "White Rabbit," *Surrealistic Pillow* (Los Angeles: RCA Victor, 1967), single released June 24, 1967. The song went to number eight on the Billboard Top 100.

75. Reminiscences of Peterson, interviewed for VVOHP, 69.

76. W. D. Ehrhart, *Vietnam-Perkasie: A Combat Marine Memoir* (Jefferson, NC: McFarland Press, 1983), 214.

77. Ehrhart, *Vietnam-Perkasie*, 214–17.

78. Jon Seikula and Paul Helbach, quoted in Andreson, *Battle Notes*, 117.

79. My argument here is almost a Brechtian one: rather than emphasize the immersive, sensorial overload that rock could produce, recreating certain experiences of battle, I focus on the distancing effect of rock. On the bullshit band, rock pulled listeners back from their experiences; from there, they were able to see their situations more clearly. See Bertolt Brecht, "On the Use of Music in an Epic Theatre" and "A Short Organum for the Theatre," in *Brecht on Theatre: The Development of an Aesthetic*, ed. and trans. John Willett (New York: Hill & Wang, 1964), 84–90, 179–205.

80. Radio First Termer (hereafter RFT), original restored show, January 1971, Radio First Termer Website, http://www.ibiblio.org/jwsnyder/rft/rft.html [accessed October 12, 2006]. Corey Deitz, "Vietnam War Pirate DJ Dave Rabbit Has Finally Come Forward: His Story in His Own Words," *About.com Radio*, http://radio.about.com/od/pirateradio/a/aa021506a.htm [accessed September 25, 2006].

81. Joe Simnacher, "David DeLay, Pirate-Radio DJ Who Entertained Vietnam Troops, Dies," *Dallas Morning News*, January 24, 2012, http://www.dallasnews.com/obituary-headlines/20120124-david-delay-pirate-radio-dj-who-entertained-vietnam-troops-dies.ece [accessed July 20, 2012].

82. RFT, January 1971.

83. Moser, *New Winter Soldiers*, 44–52.

84. Jim Scheukler quoted in Fish, "Informal Communication Systems," 2.

85. Reminiscences of Peterson, interviewed for VVOHP, 50.

86. Don North, "The Search for Hanoi Hannah," *Vietnam Generation*, 1991, http://www.psywarrior.com/hannah.html [accessed October 10, 2006]. North Vietnamese Radio Propaganda, http://www.youtube.com/watch?v=tXXoqhXdnvM [accessed December 1, 2010].

87. Peter McCabe, "Radio Hanoi Goes Progressive Rock," *Rolling Stone*, March 18, 1971, 8.

88. In this way, Radio First Termer provides evidence for the point made by Susan Jeffords that the Vietnam War and its aftermath were dominated by concerns about masculinity. Jeffords, *Remasculinization of America*.

89. RFT, January 1971.

90. RFT, January 1971.

91. RFT, January 1971.

92. RFT, January 1971.

93. RFT, January 1971.

94. Bloodrock, "Double Cross," *Bloodrock* (Los Angeles: Capitol Records, 1970). Rabbit incorrectly claims the track was on the following album, *Bloodrock 2*.

95. RFT, January 1971.

96. McBride, "Death City Radicals," in McMillian and Buhle, *New Left Revisited*, 117–18.

97. RFT, January 1971.

98. Sadler's use of "right on" was a classic example of what Eric Lott has described as the "love and theft" of African-American cultural forms by whites, especially white men; see Eric Lott, *Love and Theft*.

99. On race relations in Vietnam, see Westheider, *Fighting on Two Fronts* and Herman Graham III, *The Brothers' Vietnam War: Black Power, Manhood, and the Military Experience* (Gainesville: University Press of Florida, 2003).

100. Robbins quoted in Fish, "Informal Communication Systems," 3.

101. "Vietnam: Radio First Termer," special program, *All Things Considered*, prod. Alexis Muellner (Interlock Media Associates), National Public Radio, November 11, 1987. See also Interlock Media Associates, "Vietnam: Radio First Termer—An Audio Documentary Exploring the Role of Radio Within Vietnam During the War," http://vietnamresearch.com/media/termer/ [accessed October 15, 2006].

102. Michael Thomas Ford, *Full Circle: A Novel* (New York: Kensington Books, 2005), 205.

103. Fish, "Informal Communication Systems," 11.

104. Christian Parenti, "Good Morning, Baghdad!," *Salon*, September 23, 2006, http://www.salon.com/news/feature/2006/09/23/rabbit [accessed September 24, 2006]; Deitz, "Vietnam War Pirate DJ Dave Rabbit Has Finally Come Forward."

105. Wentz, *Audience Opinion Research & Analysis*, 52.

106. The use of a survey by the Armed Forces to measure the happiness of citizen-soldiers serving in Vietnam confirms Sarah Igo's argument that a kind of "statistical citizenship" emerged in the United States during the twentieth century. See Sarah E. Igo, *The Averaged American: Surveys, Citizens, and the Making of a Mass Public* (Cambridge, MA: Harvard University Press, 2007).

107. Grubaums, *Audience Opinion Research & Analysis*, 30.

108. Wentz, *Audience Opinion Research & Analysis*, 22–23; Wiltsie, *Audience Opinion Research & Analysis*, 18; Grubaums, *Opinion Research & Analysis*, 18.

CHAPTER 5

1. "Entertainment Vietnam" Vol. 2, Tours 1967–68 Folder, Records of the United States Army in Vietnam (USARV), Special Services Agency (Provisional), Entertainment Branch [hereafter USARV/SSA-Ent], History Files, General Historical Records, 1970–1972 through

"Entertainment Vietnam" V.2 (March–April 1969) (RG 472), National Archives—College Park, Maryland [hereafter NARA].

2. See Lair, *Armed with Abundance*, 107–44.

3. N.A., "Historical Background," Organization and Functions Manual Headquarters US-ARV General Orders Number 496, February 22, 1970, General Historical Records Relating to the Entertainment Branch, 1970–1972 Folder, NARA.

4. Frank Coffey, *Always Home: 50 Years of the USO—The Official Photographic History* (Dulles, VA: Brassy's Inc., 1991).

5. Johnson, "Bob Hope's Vietnam Christmas Tours"; *Bob Hope's Vietnam Story*; *Bob Hope: The Vietnam Years, 1964–1972* (DVD, Portland, OR: R2 Entertainment, 2004); and James Maycock, "Death or Glory: James Brown in Vietnam," *Mojo* 116 (July 2003): 66–75.

6. Historical Resume, Entertainment Activities, Albert B. Myers, DAC, GS-12, Staff Entertainment Director, RG 472, Records of USARV/SSA-Ent, History Files, General Historical Records, 1970–1972 through "Entertainment Vietnam" V.2 (March–April 1969), NARA.

7. Historical Resume, November 29, 1971, NARA.

8. "Something for Everyone," *Hi-Lite Magazine*, Spring 1969, 26, quoted in Lair, *Armed with Abundance*, 260.

9. See Atta, *With Honor*, 314–15; Cortright, *Soldiers in Revolt*, 171–200; and Bailey, *America's Army*, 1–65.

10. Frank, *Conquest of Cool*.

11. Untitled document, Correspondence and Memoranda Pertaining to Command Military Touring Shows, January 4, 1970–January 12, 1972 Folder. RG 472, USARV/SSA-Ent, General Administrative Records, April 1966–April 1972, NARA.

12. "Part III: Area Roundups," "Entertainment Vietnam," Vol 1. [Folder 2], RG 472, USARV/SSA-Ent, History Files, General Historical Records, 1970–1972 through "Entertainment Vietnam" V.2 (March–April 1969), NARA.

13. "Entertainment as a Tool of Public Relations," *Fourth U.S. Army Special Services News and Views* 15, 4 (December 1969): 23, Records Relating to Army Entertainment Program Aids Folder, RG 472, USARV/SSA-Ent, General Administrative Records, Entertainment Program AIDS, 01 April 1966–06 April 1972, Box Number 3, NARA.

14. "Draft, Special Services Conference, November 4–5, 1970, Entertainment Branch," Records Relating to Entertainment Conferences Within Vietnam, 1970 Folder, RG 472, USARV/SSA-Ent, General Administrative Records, April 1966–April 1972, NARA.

15. Entertainment Evaluation, Venable Service Club, Sp Svces Entertainment Director, May 1, 1971 and Entertainment Evaluation, FSB Mace, FSB Evelyn, 3rd Base, 1 Cav Div (Am) Special Services, May 7, 71, The Symbols, April 25, 1971 Folder, RG 472, USARV/SSA-Ent, After Action Reports Re: USO Tours in Vietnam, April–May 1971, NARA.

16. "Historical Background," Correspondence and Memoranda Pertaining to Command Military Touring Shows, January 4, 1970–January 12, 1972 Folder, RG 472, USARV/SSA-Ent, General Administrative Records, April 1966–April 1972, NARA.

17. "Draft, Special Services Conference, November 4–5, 1970, Entertainment Branch," NARA.

18. Zumwalt quoted in "'New Navy' Providing Hard Rock in Clubs and Beer in Barracks," *New York Times*, November 29, 1970, 79.

19. Lieutenant General George I. Forsythe quoted in Dana Adams Schmidt, "Army, Taking a Cue From the Navy, May Eliminate 'Mickey Mouse' Chores," *New York Times*, November 26, 1970, 11.

20. Zumwalt quoted in "Zumwalt Answers Critics," *New York Times*, June 10, 1971, 28.

21. For this history of *Grunt Free Press*, see publisher Ken Sams's essay, "Grunt Free Press," in *Nam: The Vietnam Experience, 1965–1975*, ed. Tim Page and John Pimlott (New York: Barnes & Noble Press, 1995), 412–16.

22. *Grunt Free Press*, August 1971, cover, http://www.craigsams.com/pages/grunt/grunt_august_1971.pdf [accessed July 13, 2010].

23. "Buzz Master Itinerary" and publicity poster, CMTS TOURS—Buzz (111)—December 2, 1971 Folder, USARV/SSA-Ent, After Action Reports re: CMTS Tours In Vietnam April–December 1971, Box 10 (RG 472), NARA.

24. "Peace-Pac Master Itinerary," CMTS Tours—Peace-Pac (79)—September 3, 1970 Folder, RG 472, USARV/SSA-Ent, After Action Reports re: CMTS Tours In Vietnam, June 1970–November 1970, Box 7, NARA.

25. "Subject: Command Military Touring Show, July 12, 1971, June 14, 1971," CMTS Tours—Fresh Air (99)—May 27, 1971 Folder, RG 472, USARV/SSA-Ent, After Action Reports re: CMTS Tours In Vietnam April–August 1971, Box 9, NARA.

26. Itinerary, Fixed Water, August 23, 1969, CMTS Tours—Fixed Water (52)—August 29, 1969 Folder, USARV/SSA-Ent, After Action Reports re: CMTS Tours In Vietnam March–August 1969, Box 4 (RG 472), NARA.

27. "Itinerary" and publicity poster, Fixed Water, November 26, 1969, CMTS Tours—Fixed Water No. II (62)—November 26, 1969 Folder, RG 472, USARV/SSA-Ent, After Action Reports re: CMTS Tours In Vietnam September 1969–November 1969, Box 5, NARA.

28. SP4 WM Smith Jr., "Entertainment Evaluation Form," Chu Lai, September 27, 1969, CMTS Tours—Fixed Water (52)—August 29, 1969 Folder, USARV/SSA-Ent, After Action Reports re: CMTS Tours In Vietnam March–August 1969, Box 4 (RG 472), NARA.

29. Eben EP Trevor, "Entertainment Evaluation Form," Ben Tre NCO/EM Open Mess, November 28, 1969, CMTS Tours—Fixed Water No. II (62)—November 26, 1969 Folder, RG 472, USARV/SSA-Ent, After Action Reports re: CMTS Tours In Vietnam September 1969–November 1969, Box 5, NARA.

30. William D. Founds, "Area After Action Report," October 3, 1969, CMTS Tours—Fixed Water (52)—August 29, 1969, RG 472, USARV/SSA-Ent, After Action Reports re: CMTS Tours In Vietnam March–August 1969, Box 4, NARA.

31. "'Fresh Air' After Action Report." June 24, 1971, CMTS Tours—Fresh Air (99)—May 27, 1971 Folder, RG 472, USARV/SSA-Ent, After Action Reports re: CMTS Tours In Vietnam April–August 1971, Box 9, NARA.

32. Donna D. Douglass, GS-9, Entertainment Director, MR2, to Mr. Brad Arrington, Entertainment Division, USARV Special Services Agency, "Subject: Fresh Aire [sic] CMTS," CMTS Tours—Fresh Air (99)—May 27, 1971 Folder, RG 472, USARV/SSA-Ent, After Action Reports re: CMTS Tours In Vietnam April–August 1971, Box 9, NARA.

33. Name illegible, "Evaluation Form," Tours in MR1—Ace Trucking Company (CMTS)—March 21–April 1, 1971 Folder, RG 472, USARV/SSA-Ent, Administrative Records Re: USO/CMTS Tours in MR 1, Record Group 472, Stack Area 270, Row 28, Compartment 5, Boxes 2, NARA.

34. "Itinerary," April 24, 1969, CMTS Tours—The Electric Grunts (71)—April 30, 1970 Folder, RG 472, USARV/SSA-Ent, After Action Reports re: CMTS Tours In Vietnam January 1970–June 1970, Box 6, NARA.

35. Buffalo Springfield, "For What It's Worth," *Buffalo Springfield* (Atco, 1967). The Beatles, "A Day in the Life," *Sgt. Pepper's Lonely Hearts Club Band* (EMI, 1967). Eric Burdon and the Animals, "Sky Pilot," *The Twain Shall Meet* (MGM, 1968).

36. "After Action Report," CMTS—The Electric Grunts (71)—April 30, 1970 Folder, RG 472, USARV/SSA-Ent, After Action Reports re: CMTS Tours In Vietnam January 1970–June 1970, Box 6, NARA.

37. "After Action Report," CMTS—The Electric Grunts (71)—April 30, 1970 Folder, RG 472, USARV/SSA-Ent, After Action Reports re: CMTS Tours In Vietnam January 1970–June 1970, Box 6, NARA.

38. "After Action Report," CMTS—The Electric Grunts (71)—April 30, 1970 Folder, RG 472, USARV/SSA-Ent, After Action Reports re: CMTS Tours In Vietnam January 1970–June 1970, Box 6, NARA.

39. Spector, *After Tet*, 273. "Report of Inquiry Concerning a Petition of Redress of Grievances by a Group of Soldiers of the 71st Tranportation Battalion One," May 23, 1968, Copy in IG Files, USARV, NARA.

40. Publicity poster, CMTS Tours—Jimmy and the Everyday People (104)—August 23, 1971 Folder, USARV/SSA-Ent, After Action Reports re: CMTS Tours In Vietnam April–August 1971, Box 9 (RG 472), NARA.

41. See Greil Marcus, "Sly Stone: The Myth of Staggerlee," in *Mystery Train: Images of America in Rock 'n' Roll Music* (1975; reprint, New York: Plume, 1997), 65–95.

42. A. E. Rowe, Jr., "MR4 Military Touring Shows Evaluation Report," CMTS Tours—Jimmy and the Everyday People (104)—August 23, 1971 Folder, RG 472, USARV/SSA-Ent, After Action Reports re: CMTS Tours In Vietnam April–August 1971, Box 9, NARA.

43. Johnson quoted in "Delta GIs Get 'High' On Group's Music," *Delta Dragon* 1, 5 (August 25, 1971), CMTS Tours—Jimmy and the Everyday People (104)—August 23, 1971 Folder, USARV/SSA-Ent, After Action Reports re: CMTS Tours In Vietnam April–August 1971, Box 9 (RG 472), NARA.

44. SP5 John D. Gallaspy, "Evaluation Form," MR2 Sp Svs, Rainbow Club, Cp McDermott, September 7, 1971, CMTS Tours—Jimmy and the Everyday People (104)—August 23, 1971 Folder, USARV/SSA-Ent, After Action Reports re: CMTS Tours In Vietnam April–August 1971, Box 9 (RG 472), NARA.

45. R. L. Brotzman, Letter, August 27, 1971, CMTS Tours—Jimmy and the Everyday People (104)—August 23, 1971 Folder, RG 472, USARV/SSA-Ent, After Action Reports re: CMTS Tours In Vietnam April–August 1971, Box 9, NARA.

46. "Delta GIs Get 'High' On Group's Music."

47. *Woodstock: Music from the Original Soundtrack and More*, LP (New York: Cotillion/Atlantic Records, 1970). *Woodstock*, dir. Michael Wadleigh (Burbank, CA: Warner Brothers, 1970).

48. Hoffman, *Woodstock Nation*.

49. "Delta GIs Get 'High' On Group's Music."

50. M. D. Magette, Asst Director, USO, Cam Ranh Bay, USO Showmobile, "Entertainment Evaluation," CMTS Tours—Jimmy and the Everyday People (104)—August 23, 1971 Folder, RG 472, USARV/SSA-Ent, After Action Reports re: CMTS Tours In Vietnam April–August 1971, Box 9, NARA.

51. Publicity poster, Ent Viet V. 3 Tours, January–March 1970 Folder, RG 472, USARV/SSA-Ent, History Files, "Entertainment Vietnam," V. 3, May 1969–December 1970, NARA.

52. Lair, *Armed with Abundance*.

53. Don Chandler, Area Entertainment Director, Cam Ranh Bay Army Post, "Entertainment Evaluation," CMTS TOURS—The Local Board—1st Cav Touring Show (61)—November 21, 1969 Folder, RG 472, USARV/SSA-Ent, After Action Reports re: CMTS Tours In Vietnam September 1969–November 1969, Box 5, NARA.

54. Johnnie M. Calitri, Entertainment Specialist, Pacesetter Services Club, Long Binh Post, "Entertainment Evaluation," CMTS TOURS—The Local Board—1st Cav Touring Show (61)—November 21, 1969 Folder, RG 472, USARV/SSA-Ent, After Action Reports re: CMTS Tours In Vietnam September 1969–November 1969, Box 5, NARA.

55. Notes for After-Action Report, CMTS Tours—Peace-Pac (79)—September 3, 1970 Folder, RG 472, USARV/SSA-Ent, After Action Reports re: CMTS Tours In Vietnam, June 1970–November 1970, Box 7, NARA. Donna D. Douglass, GS-9, Entertainment Director, MR2, to Mr. Brad Arrington, Entertainment Division, USARV Special Services Agency, "Subject: Fresh Aire [sic] CMTS."

56. Paul Englestad, "Disposition Form" with photographs of Johnny Flynn, Criminal Investigations Reports—July 1971 (CMTS Tours) Folder, RG 472, USARV/SSA-Ent, Criminal Investigation Reports December 1969–December 1971, Box 1, NARA. Johnny Flynn's CMTS audition card includes a photograph of the soldier with long hair and a hippie-ish bead necklace, CMTS Tours—Fresh Air (99)—May 27, 1971 Folder, RG 472, USARV/SSA-Ent, After Action Reports re: CMTS Tours In Vietnam April–August 1971, Box 9, NARA. The card has handwritten comments from an Entertainment Branch staff member: "He is a good lead guitarist. He is quick but sloppy. He has not acted well at his unit and so I'm skeptical about his attitude working for us. He says he's willing to conform to military standards for US."

57. Paul Englestad, "Disposition Form."

58. Reminiscences of John Imsdahl, interviewed for VVOHP, 28.

59. Reminiscences of Steve Hassna, interviewed for VVOHP, 99.

60. Reminiscences of Betty Wilkinson, interviewed for VVOHP, 92–93.

61. Charles Perry, "Is This Any Way to Run the Army?," *Rolling Stone*, November 9, 1968, 5.

62. Richard Moser, *New Winter Soldiers*, 54.

63. Michael Rodriquez, "Vietnam and Rock 'n' Roll," http://www.vietvet.org/rockroll.htm [accessed March 10, 2002].

64. Reminiscences of Jim Heiden, interviewed for VVOHP, 61.

65. Ken Sams, "Grunt Free Press," 416.

CHAPTER 6

1. N.A., "Happiness Is Acid Rock on Plantation Road," *Grunt Free Press*, September–October 1970, 3–4.

2. For more on the history and practice of cover songs, see George Plasketes, ed., *Play It Again: Cover Songs in Popular Music* (Burlington, VT: Ashgate, 2010); and Kevin Homan, ed., *Access All Ears: Tribute Bands and Global Pop Culture* (New York: Open University Press, 2006).

3. See, for instance, Manthia Diawara, "The 1960s in Bamako: Malick Sidibé and James Brown," in *Everything But the Burden: What White People Are Taking from Black Culture*, ed. Greg Tate (New York: Harlem Moon, 2003), 164–90. See also: Lloyd and Lowe, eds., *Politics of Culture in the Shadow of Capital*; Appadurai, *Modernity at Large*; Peter Burke, *Cultural Hybridity* (New York: Polity, 2009); May Joseph and Jennifer Natalya Fink, eds., *Performing Hybridity* (Minneapolis: University of Minnesota Press, 1999); Nestor Garcia Canclini, *Hybrid Cultures: Strategies for Entering and Leaving Modernity* (Minneapolis: University of Minnesota Press, 1995); and, for the particular issue of music, Bruno Nettl, *The Western Impact on World Music: Change, Adaptation, and Survival* (New York: Schirmer Books, 1985).

4. For more on Vietnamese cultural ideals of the family, see Alexander B. Woodside, *Community and Revolution in Modern Vietnam* (Boston: Houghton Mifflin, 1976), 95–102; Neil Jamieson, "The Traditional Family in Vietnam," *Vietnam Forum* 8 (1986): 91–150; Neil Jamieson,

Understanding Vietnam (Berkeley: University of California Press, 1993); Hue-Tam Ho Tai, ed., *The Country of Memory: Remaking the Past in Late Socialist Vietnam* (Berkeley: University of California Press, 2001); and George F. Dutton, Jayne S. Werner, and John K. Whitmore, *Sources of Vietnamese Tradition* (New York: Columbia University Press, 2012).

5. The term "Woodstock Nation" was coined by the "yippie" political activist Abbie Hoffman after attending the Woodstock Festival in upstate New York in August of 1969; see Hoffman, *Woodstock Nation*. For more on the concept of transnationalism, see Khamgram and Levitt, eds., *Transnational Studies Reader*; and Vertovec, *Transnationalism*.

6. See Davidson, *Vietnam at War*, 749–51.

7. For more on Vietnamization, see Prados, *Vietnam*, 256–550.

8. Gloria Emerson, "Saigon 'Cowboys' Race the Draft," *New York Times*, March 25, 1971, 6.

9. For more on the history of "nhac tre," see Jason Gibbs, "How Does Hanoi Rock? The Way to Rock and Roll in Vietnam," *Asian Music* (Winter/Spring 2008): 5–25.

10. David Butler, "Saigon: The Vietnamization of Rock & Roll," *Rolling Stone*, April 10, 1975, 20.

11. Nguyen Khac Vien and Phong Hien, "American Neocolonialism in South Vietnam, 1954–1975," *Vietnamese Studies* 69 (1982): 122–23; quoted in Philip Taylor, *Fragments of the Present: Searching for Modernity in Vietnam's South* (Honolulu: University of Hawaii Press, 2001), 42, 49.

12. Nyugen Giang Cao, phone interview by author, January 18, 2011.

13. "Happiness Is Acid Rock," 3.

14. "Happiness Is Acid Rock," 3, 4.

15. David Theis, "Ballad of Con Ba Cu," *Texas Monthly* (December 1988), 187.

16. Frank Ford, email correspondence with author, June 2, 2010. Phan Loan, Phan Linh, Phan Van, Phan Marie Louise, Phan Lan, Phan Lien, Frank Ford, Quang Minh, interview with author, Houston, TX, April 10, 2011.

17. See David Hunt, *Vietnam's Southern Revolution: From Peasant Insurrection to Total War* (Amherst: University of Massachusetts Press, 2008), 8–28; David Hunt, "Taking Notice of the Everyday," in *Making Sense of the Vietnam Wars: Local, National, and Transnational Perspectives*, ed. Mark Philip Bradley and Marilyn B. Young (New York: Oxford University Press, 2008), 171–98; and David Elliott, *The Vietnamese War: Revolution and Social Change in the Mekong Delta, 1930–1975* (New York: Sharpe, 2003).

18. Frank Ford, email correspondence. Phan Loan, et al., interview with author.

19. "Wipe Out" was originally recorded by The Safaris and released as a single on Dot Records in 1963. It reached number 2 on the Billboard Charts in the autumn of 1963. Tom Marlow, "Yea, We're the CBC Band . . .," *Rolling Stone*, November 24, 1970, 29.

20. CBC Band, untitled tape, recorded in Vietnam during the early 1970s (1972?), CD version in author's personal collection.

21. Phan Loan, et al., interview with author.

22. Frank Ford, email correspondence. Phan Loan, et al., interview with author.

23. "Subject: Approved Commercial Entertainment, February 12, 1972," General Correspondence and Memoranda of Entertainment Branch, January 1, 1972–April 4, 1972 Folder, RG 472, Records of the United States Army in Vietnam (USARV), Special Services Agency (Provisional), Entertainment Branch, General Administrative Records, April 1966–April 1972, NARA.

24. Don Morrison, *My Rock 'n' Roll War* (Bracken Ridge, Australia: Dog-Tag Books, 2001).

25. Rick Springfield, *Late, Late At Night: A Memoir* (New York: Touchstone, 2010), 83–97.

26. *Entertaining Vietnam*, DVD, dir. Mara Wallis (CustomFlix, 2003); Robert M. Smith, "Booking Agent Describes Army Club 'Kickbacks,'" *New York Times*, October 10, 1969, 1.

27. Reminiscences of Peter Cameron, interviewed for VVOHP, 33–34.

28. CBC Band, "People, Let's Stop The War," recorded at The Sherwood Forest Club, Saigon, Republic of Vietnam, May 9, 1973, http://www.youtube.com/watch?v=oph4q63QRRU [accessed October 10, 2008]. Grand Funk Railroad, "People, Let's Stop the War," *E Pluribus Funk* (Los Angeles: Capitol Records, 1971).

29. Sams, "Grunt Free Press," 416.

30. "Happiness Is Acid Rock," 3.

31. "Happiness Is Acid Rock," 3–4.

32. Marlow, "Yea, We're the CBC Band," 29. Frank Ford informs me that Tom Marlow probably took "creative license" with the exact quotation, though in Ford's estimation it reflected the essence of Loan's opinion; Frank Ford, email to author, April 13, 2012.

33. Marlow, "Yea, We're the CBC Band," 29.

34. "Happiness Is Acid Rock," 3.

35. "Happiness Is Acid Rock," 3.

36. CBC Band, untitled tape.

37. Grand Funk Railroad, "Sin's a Good Man's Brother," "Nothing is the Same," *Closer to Home* (Los Angeles: Capitol Records, 1970).

38. James Gang, "Walk Away," *Thirds* (Los Angeles: ABC, 1971); Carole King's "It's Too Late" and "You've Got a Friend," *Tapestry* (Los Angeles: A&M, 1971); Santana's "Soul Sacrifice," *Santana* (Los Angeles: Columbia, 1969), also performed at Woodstock; Janis Joplin's "Mercedes Benz," *Pearl* (Los Angeles: Columbia, 1971); Jimi Hendrix, "Star Spangled Banner," *Woodstock: Music from the Original Soundtrack and More*, LP (New York: Cotillion/Atlantic Records, 1970); Jimi Hendrix, "Purple Haze," *Are You Experienced?* (Los Angeles: Reprise, 1967); Black Sabbath, "Paranoid" (London: Vertigo, 1970; released in the United States, 1971); John Lennon, "Imagine," *Imagine* (London: Apple/EMI, 1971).

39. CBC Band, untitled tape.

40. Phan Loan, et al., interview with author.

41. "Happiness Is Acid Rock," 4.

42. Marlow, "Yea, We're the CBC Band," 28.

43. Marlow, "Yea, We're the CBC Band," 29.

44. Anderson argues that culture has always played a crucial role in state building by offering experiences of simultaneity across time and place; see Anderson, *Imagined Communities*, 145.

45. See Appadurai, *Modernity at Large*, 171–72. See also Montserrat Guibernau, *Nations Without States: Political Communities in a Global Age* (Cambridge: Polity Press, 1999). It is also similar to Fredric Jameson's notion of a "Third Worldism" that appeared on the left during the 1960s, though it was not explicitly linked to state power in the same manner; see Fredric Jameson, "Periodizing the Sixties," in Sayres et al., *The 60s Without Apology*, 179–209; and Fredric Jameson, "Third-World Literature in the Era of Multinational Capitalism," *Social Text* 15 (Fall 1986): 65–88.

46. Hoffman, *Woodstock Nation*.

47. Hoffman, *Woodstock Nation*, 77.

48. Hoffman, *Woodstock Nation*, 15, 63.

49. Hoffman, *Woodstock Nation*, 63, 93.

50. Sinclair, *Guitar Army*.

51. John Durham and Larry McQuillan, "Bomb Kills GI in Saigon Bar," *Stars and Stripes*, April 9, 1971, Frank Ford, personal collection. On April 8, 2011, the band performed

for an audience of Vietnam veterans who were present when the bar exploded. See Allan Turner, "Song Lifts Haze from Vietnam Tragedy," *Houston Chronicle*, April 9, 2011, http://www.chron.com/news/houston-texas/article/40-years-after-bomb-band-plays-again-for-Vietnam-1691080.php [accessed April 10, 2011].

52. Ford, email correspondence.

53. Phan Loan, et al., interview with author.

54. "Happiness Is Acid Rock," 4.

55. Gibbs, "How Does Hanoi Rock?"; Phan Loan, et al., interview with author.

56. Gloria Emerson, "G.I.'s and Vietnamese Youth: Sharing at Rock Festival," *New York Times*, May 30, 1971, 3.

57. Emerson, "G.I.'s and Vietnamese Youth," 3.

58. "Liberation Radio Scores South Viet-Nam's First International Rock Music Festival Held to Benefit Families of Killed Soldiers," Broadcast on Liberation Radio in Vietnamese, May 29, 1971, Item 2321830006, Virtual Vietnam Archive, Texas Tech University, http://www.vietnam.ttu.edu/virtualarchive/ [accessed January 10, 2011], 9.

59. CBC Band: Live at the Saigon Zoo television footage, May 29, 1971, http://www.youtube.com/watch?v=4iAB0YnzcA4 [accessed March 13, 2010].

60. For a deeper history of Vietnam, colonialism, and the emergence of modernity, see David G. Marr, *Vietnamese Tradition on Trial, 1920–1945* (Berkeley: University of California Press, 1981); and James Carter, *Inventing Vietnam: The United States and State Building, 1954–1968* (New York: Cambridge University Press, 2008).

61. Emerson, "G.I.'s and Vietnamese Youth," 3.

62. Emerson, "G.I.'s and Vietnamese Youth," 3.

63. The members of CBC were not wrong to fear persecution. Rock music was vehemently denounced by the communist regime in postwar Vietnam. See Philip Taylor, "Music as a 'Neocolonial Poison' in Postwar Southern Vietnam," *Crossroads: An Interdisciplinary Journal of Southeast Asian Studies* 14, 1 (2000): 99–131.

64. Frank Ford, email correspondence. Phan Loan, et al., interview with author.

65. "CBC Band: A Band on the Run," ABC news footage, July 15, 1975, http://www.youtube.com/watch?v=E_dgtEHKvxI [accessed October 10, 2008].

66. Dell Ford, "Viet Band Ends 19-Month Odyssey Here," *Fort Wayne Journal Gazette*, October 25, 1975, C1, in personal collection of Phan Linh and Marie Louise.

67. Frank Ford, email correspondence. Phan Loan, et al., interview with author. See also, David Theis, "Ballad of Con Ba Cu."

68. Allen Quinn, Photograph of CBC Band, Fort Wayne, 1975.

69. For more on the history of Vietnamese refugees to the United States in relation to music, see James Lull and Roger Wallis, "The Beat of West Vietnam," in *Popular Music and Communication*, 2nd ed., ed. James Lull (Newbury Park, CA: Sage, 1992), 207–36; Adelaida Reyes, *Songs of the Caged, Songs of the Free: Music and the Vietnamese Refugee Experience* (Philadelphia, PA: Temple University Press, 1999); and Caroline Kieu Linh Valverde, "Making Transnational Vietnamese Music: Sounds of Home and Resistance," in *East Main Street: Asian American Popular Culture*, ed. Shilpa Dave, Leilani Nishime, and Tasha G. Oren (New York: New York University Press, 2005), 32–54. See also Nhi T. Lieu, *The American Dream in Vietnamese* (Minneapolis: University of Minnesota Press, 2011); Phuong Tran Nguyen, "The People of the Fall: Refugee Nationalism in Little Saigon, 1975–2005" (Ph.D. diss., Los Angeles: University of Southern California, 2009); Le Ly Hayslip, *Child of War, Woman of Peace* (New York: Doubleday, 1993); James Paul Rutledge, *The Vietnamese Experience in America* (Bloomington: Indiana University Press,

1992); Nathan Caplan, Marcella H. Choy, and John K. Whitmore, eds., *Children of the Boat People: A Study of Educational Success* (Ann Arbor: University of Michigan Press, 1991); David W. Haines, *Refugees as Immigrants: Cambodians, Laotians, and Vietnamese in America* (Totowa, NJ: Rowman & Littlefield, 1989); Nathan Caplan, John K. Whitmore, and Marcella H. Choy, *The Boat People and Achievement in America: A Study of Family Life, Hard Work, and Cultural Values* (Ann Arbor: University of Michigan Press, 1989); Joanna C. Scott, *Indochina's Refugees: Oral Histories from Laos, Cambodia, and Vietnam* (Jefferson, NC: McFarland, 1989); James Freeman, *Hearts of Sorrow: Vietnamese-American Lives* (Palo Alto, CA: Stanford University Press, 1989); Paul Strand and Woodrow Jones, Jr., *Indochinese Refugees in America: Problems of Adaptation and Assimilation* (Durham, NC: Duke University Press, 1985); Barry Wain, *The Refused: The Agony of the Indochinese Refugees* (New York: Simon & Schuster, 1981); Darrel Montero, *Vietnamese Americans: Patterns of Resettlement and Socioeconomic Adaptation in the United States* (Boulder, CO: Westview Press, 1979); Walter Liu, *Transition to Nowhere: Vietnamese Refugees in America* (Nashville: Charter House, 1979); Gail Paradise Kelly, *From Vietnam to America: A Chronicle of the Vietnamese Immigration to the United States* (Boulder, CO: Westview Press, 1977). For an important work on citizenship and Asian-American immigrant experiences, see Lisa Lowe, *Immigrant Acts: On Asian American Cultural Politics* (Durham, NC: Duke University Press, 1996).

70. The CBC & Trung Nghia, video footage, http://www.youtube.com/watch?v=pZINE9yYZC4 [accessed September 6, 2009].

EPILOGUE

1. Havel, "Power of the Powerless," in Keane, *Power of the Powerless*, 47. The band was arrested and tried in 1976.

2. Havel, "Power of the Powerless," in Keane, *Power of the Powerless*, 47.

3. Havel, "Power of the Powerless," in Keane, *Power of the Powerless*, 46–47.

4. For more on the Plastic People of the Universe, see Tomás Pospisil, "Making Music as a Political Act: Or How the Velvet Underground Influenced the Velvet Revolution," http://angam.ang.univie.ac.at/EAASworkshop/pospisil.htm [accessed February 3, 2006].

5. See Gosse, *Where the Boys Are*; Farrell, *Spirit of the Sixties*; Rossinow, *Politics of Authenticity*; and Suri, "Rise and Fall of an International Counterculture," 45–68.

6. On rock in Brazil, see Caetano Veloso, *Tropical Truth: A Story of Music and Revolution in Brazil* (1997; English trans., New York: Da Capo Press, 2002), 187. Portions of Veloso's description also appear in Christopher Dunn, *Brutality Garden: Tropicália and the Emergence of a Brazilian Counterculture* (Chapel Hill: University of North Carolina Press, 2001), 135–36; see also Charles Perrone and Christopher Dunn, eds., *Brazilian Popular Music and Globalization* (Gainesville: University Press of Florida, 2001). On Mexico, see Eric Zolov, *Refried Elvis: The Rise of the Mexican Counterculture* (Berkeley: University of California Press, 1999). On Mali, see Manthia Diawara, "The 1960s in Bamako: Malick Sidibé and James Brown," in Tate, *Everything But the Burden*, 164–90.

7. Timothy W. Ryback, *Rock Around the Bloc: A History of Rock Music in Eastern Europe and the Soviet Union* (New York: Oxford University Press, 1990), 111–13. See also Sabrina Petra Ramet, "Rock: The Music of Revolution (and Political Conformity)," in *Rocking the State, Rock Music and Politics in Eastern Europe and Russia*, ed. Sabrina Petra Ramet (Boulder: Westview Press, 1994), 1–14.

8. Ryback, *Rock Around the Bloc*, 111–13.

9. Ryback, *Rock Around the Bloc*, 113.

10. Andrea Lee, *Russian Journal* (New York: Random House, 1981), 96.

11. Bromell, *Tomorrow Never Knows*, 92–95; Stephen Spender, *The Year of the Young Rebels* (New York: Random House, 1968), 137–38.

12. Jefferson Airplane, "White Rabbit," *Surrealistic Pillow* (Los Angeles: RCA Victor, 1967).

13. See the works cited in Introduction, n. 38.

14. Frank, *Conquest of Cool*, 1. Frank's work is an update in many respects of the Frankfurt School's analysis of capitalism's pseudo-freedom; the classic text that takes this position is Theodor Adorno and Max Horkheimer, "The Culture Industry: Enlightenment as Mass Deception," in *Dialectic of Enlightenment* (1947; reprint, New York: Continuum, 1997), 120–67.

15. Joseph Heath and Andrew Potter, *A Nation of Rebels: Why Counterculture Became Consumer Culture* (New York: HarperCollins, 2004), in its Canadian edition titled, *The Rebel Sell: Why Culture Can't Be Jammed* (Toronto: HarperCollins Canada, 2005).

16. Ryback, *Rock Around the Bloc*, 113.

17. Havel, "Power of the Powerless," in Keane, *Power of the Powerless*, 46–47.

18. Ellen Willis, *Beginning to See the Light: Sex, Hope, and Rock and Roll* (1981; reprint, Hanover, NH: University Press of New England / Wesleyan University Press, 1992), xvi.

19. CBC Band Live at Sherwood Forest Club, Saigon, Republic of Vietnam, 1973, http://www.youtube.com/watch?v=oph4q63QRRU [accessed July 10, 2010]. The band sings a version of "People, Let's Stop the War" by Grand Funk Railroad, released on the album *E Pluribus Funk* (Los Angeles: Capitol Records, 1971).

Index